During the twentieth century, American corporatio
can material productivity and American values sucl   ....,... ana
competitiveness around the globe. People in other nations have accepted
some aspects of American corporate culture while vehemently rejecting
others. *The Revolutionary Mission* explores this complex process as it unfolded in Latin America in the decades before World War II. Professor
O'Brien examines Latin American responses to that culture, which conveyed the promises of material betterment and individual freedom while
also emphasizing the cult of the individual, unquestioning acceptance of
disparities created by unremitting competition, and values legitimized by
functionality rather than historical precedent.

The influence of American corporate culture on Latin American societies prompted responses which ranged from crowds that flocked to Cecil
B. DeMille movies and rushed to acquire the latest American consumer
product to the mass mobilizations of middle- and working-class people
that seized American companies and demanded an end to American imperialism. American business, by promoting new values, transforming existing systems of social relations and introducing technology-intensive investments, contributed to political instability, labor unrest, political
radicalism and nationalist sentiment in Latin America. This volume argues that this complex interaction between Latin Americans and American corporate culture had far-reaching effects on the development of Latin
American societies and their relations with the United States.

THE REVOLUTIONARY MISSION

CAMBRIDGE LATIN AMERICAN STUDIES

GENERAL EDITOR
SIMON COLLIER

ADVISORY COMMITTEE
MALCOLM DEAS, STUART SCHWARTZ, ARTURO VALENZUELA

81

THE REVOLUTIONARY MISSION: AMERICAN ENTERPRISE
IN LATIN AMERICA, 1900–1945

*Publication of this book was supported by a grant
from the University of Houston.*

THE REVOLUTIONARY MISSION

AMERICAN ENTERPRISE IN LATIN AMERICA, 1900–1945

THOMAS F. O'BRIEN
University of Houston

CAMBRIDGE
UNIVERSITY PRESS

PUBLISHED BY THE PRESS SYNDICATE OF THE UNIVERSITY OF CAMBRIDGE
The Pitt Building, Trumpington Street, Cambridge, United Kingdom

CAMBRIDGE UNIVERSITY PRESS
The Edinburgh Building, Cambridge CB2 2RU, UK   http://www.cup.cam.ac.uk
40 West 20th Street, New York, NY 10011-4211, USA   http://www.cup.org
10 Stamford Road, Oakleigh, Melbourne 3166, Australia
Ruiz de Alarcón 13, 28014 Madrid, Spain

First published 1996
Reprinted 1998
First paperback edition 1999

Printed in the United States of America

Typeset in Garamond

A catalog record for this book is available from the British Library

Library of Congress Cataloging in Publication data is available

ISBN 0 521 55015 7 hardback
ISBN 0 521 66344 X paperback

To Diane
Who let me count the ways

Contents

Contents

Maps

Acknowledgments

For me, writing this book has been, like life itself, a long, often challenging, but always exciting journey. Along that road, family, friends and acquaintances have given of themselves to light my way and lift my spirits. I want to thank as many of them as I can.

Diane O'Brien's gentle and loving spirit is the soul of this work. Without her there simply would be no book. Matthew, Daniel and Sarah O'Brien forgave their father, and their gift of forgiveness reawakened his heart and his mind. Tom and Peg O'Brien shared their strength and wonderful humor with their youngest child. Those gifts guided him through life's dark passages. My good friend and colleague John Hart has been the best of traveling companions. He is a relentless and demanding critic who made this book far better than it otherwise would have been. Steve Mintz and Sue Kellogg are friends and colleagues who gently guided me back on course when my ignorance led me astray. Hugh Hamill shared his exceptional intellectual gifts with me, and gave me the confidence and the freedom to begin the journey. Joseph Criscenti taught me to love Latin American history and to believe I could be a historian. My friend Luis Ortega offered insightful criticisms of the chapter on Chile. But more importantly Luis has given me the example of an intellectual who has dared to live by his convictions. Harold Blakemore lived life with quiet courage and good humor. As one of the many recipients of his kindness and generosity, I have sorely missed his friendship and guidance. Bob Miller's wonderfully cynical wit kept a sometimes wayward pilgrim from losing touch with reality. Allen and Myra Woll shared the excitement and sorrow of Chile with me and have remained my friends ever since.

On this long journey I have met many strangers who have unselfishly offered their help, and their friendship. Over the years and the miles, Latin Americans like the González family, Juan Carlos González and Sonia Burbano have made me feel a part of their world and offered insights into their cultures which I could never have learned from books. Simon Collier as the editor of the Latin American series gave the needed support to this work that saw it through to publication. Mary Yeager provided a detailed critique of the manuscript and developed an invaluable set of suggestions that broadened its scope and strengthened its arguments. Archivists and other specialists at the National Archives, the Library of Congress, Tulane

University, the J. P. Morgan Library, the Baker Library, the Public Record Office, the Guildhall Library, the Phelps Dodge Corporation and the Boise Cascade Corporation gave generously of their time and their knowledge. I need to take special note of two of those people, Carleen Gage and Mike Swenson of the Boise Cascade Corporation, who shared their special knowledge with me while making me feel like a most welcome guest. Finally, the University of Houston through its Limited-Grants-in-Aid and the President's Research and Scholarship Fund provided the most basic but most essential travelers' aid, the coins to pay the tolls.

Abbreviations

BOLSA	Bank of London and South America Papers, The Library, University College, London
CNP	Chilean Nitrate Producers, Limited, London
EBASCO	Electric Bond and Share Company Archive, Boise Cascade Corporation, Boise, Idaho
EMJ	*Engineering and Mining Journal*
FO	Foreign Office Files, Public Record Office, Kew, Surrey
Gibbs Papers	Papers of Antony Gibbs and Sons, Guildhall Library, London
Grace Papers	Grace Papers, Rare Book and Manuscript Library, Butler Library, Columbia University, New York
HAHR	*Hispanic American Historical Review*
JLAS	*Journal of Latin American Studies*
Knox Papers	Philander C. Knox Papers, Library of Congress
Lamont Papers	Thomas W. Lamont Collection, Baker Library, Harvard Business School
M	Microfilm Series of State Department Records, U.S. National Archives, Washington, D.C.
Morgan Papers	J. P. Morgan Papers, Pierpont Morgan Library, New York
N&MF	Numerical and Minor Files of the Department of State, 1906–1910
NH	*Nueva Historia, Revista de Historia de Chile*

Phelps Dodge Papers	Papers of the Phelps Dodge Corporation, Phelps Dodge Corporation, Phoenix, Arizona
PP	Great Britain, Parliament, *Parliamentary Papers*
RG 59	Record Group 59, General Records of the Department of State
RG 84	Record Group 84, Records of the Foreign Service Posts of the Department of State
RG 151	Record Group 151, Records of the Bureau of Foreign and Domestic Commerce; Records Relating to Commercial Attachés' Reports
Root Papers	Elihu Root Papers, Library of Congress
Scudder Collection	Marvyn Scudder Financial Record Collection, Graduate School of Business, Columbia University, New York
Squier Papers	Ephraim George Squier Papers, Howard–Tilton Memorial Library, Tulane University, New Orleans, Louisiana
Standard Fruit Papers	Papers of the Standard Fruit and Steamship Company, Howard–Tilton Memorial Library, Tulane University, New Orleans, Louisiana
Taft Papers	William Howard Taft Papers, Library of Congress
Taylor Papers	Moses Taylor Papers, New York Public Library
UPAMC	University Press of America Microfilm Collection, U.S. Diplomatic Post Records, Honduras, 1930–1945
USNA	United States National Archives, Washington, D.C.
Vanderlip Papers	Frank A. Vanderlip Papers, Rare Book and Manuscript Library, Butler Library, Columbia University, New York

Introduction

Perhaps revolutions are the reaching of humanity traveling in this train for the emergency brake. (Walter Benjamin)

Frank Vanderlip, president of National City Bank, wrote to a colleague in 1918 that, given time, "we would revolutionize the world." Vanderlip's comment was no idle boast. Corporate reformers like Vanderlip were transforming the United States into the first modern corporate society. And American business leaders shared a bold vision of a world remade in the image and likeness of the United States. American companies carried their technologies, social relations and ideas of unbounded material wealth and individual freedom to the far corners of the earth – giving birth to the American century. At the beginning of that process Latin Americans underwent an intense experience of American corporate culture as their region became the leading recipient of direct U.S. foreign investment. American corporations devoted hundreds of millions of dollars to revamping mining and agriculture, developing the petroleum industry and modernizing electrical and telecommunications systems. These investments spurred Latin America's export economies to unprecedented new levels of growth, initially encouraged the expansion of small businesses, provided higher wages and benefits to workers and brought modern products and services to millions. At the same time American corporate culture's powerful vision of a society grounded in material prosperity and individual freedom had a compelling attraction for Latin Americans. But that experience did not generate the wave of popular gratitude that Vanderlip and his associates might have expected.

In 1933 a puzzled American observer in Peru noted that "our excessive loans and the introduction of American capital for legitimate development have had the peculiar result of provoking ill will and resentment."[1] In 1934 a relieved American diplomat in Santiago, Chile, reported that "we are no longer conscious of Chilean mobs howling for the blood of Ameri-

---

1 Fred Morris Dearing to secretary of state, Lima, April 7, 1933, 823.00/960, General Records of the Department of State Relating to the Internal Affairs of Peru, 1930–39, RG 59, USNA.

can industrialists."[2] The wave of demonstrations against American compa-
nies in Peru and Chile were but two examples of militant popular protests
against American corporations that erupted across Latin America in the
1930s. Workers, small planters and merchants struck against the United
Fruit Company in Central America. In Cuba, sugar workers occupied
American refineries and formed soviets, while the employees of General
Electric seized its plants and drove their American bosses from the island.
The Mexican government, in response to workers' demands, nationalized
American oil companies, while mining and electrical workers denounced
"American imperialism" and demanded control of their industries.

The turbulent events of the 1930s gave overt expression to a complex
interaction between American multinationals and Latin American societies. Workers and segments of the middle class selectively incorporated
elements of American corporate culture into their own value system.
While drawn to the American promise of material abundance and American values of freedom and individual initiative, these groups resisted corporate culture's harsher aspects. They frequently defined their resistance
in nationalist symbols sanctioned by their own elites, and in terms of justice and democracy that were so much a part of the American ideal.

This study of American enterprise in Latin America addresses some of
the basic issues surrounding the effects of globalizing American corporations. It explores the salient features of the culture these companies carried with them, and the responses of Latin Americans to enterprises that
epitomized American corporate culture. In the process it examines how
this interaction influenced Latin American societies and shaped their relationship with the United States – a relationship that prefigured the global
response to American culture during the remainder of the twentieth century.

The culture which American business leaders carried overseas bore features common to capitalist development in other nations of the North Atlantic. Central to that process was rationalization – the effort to systematically organize economic life, individual human beings and nature itself to
achieve maximum efficiency in production. Rationalization promoted
previously unimagined levels of material output in the second industrial
revolution. Entrepreneurs applied scientific knowledge directly to the
production process, especially in new industries such as chemicals and
electronics, and developed machines and work methods which replaced
skilled workers, dramatically increased output and intensified the control
which businessmen exercised over the work place. But these developments took on special significance as they interacted with certain features
of American society to create American corporate culture. The second in-

---

2 Hal Sevier to secretary of state, Santiago, Chile, 1934, 825.6374/1229, General Records of the Department of State Relating to the Internal Affairs of Chile, RG 59, USNA.

dustrial revolution operated in a particularly receptive atmosphere in the United States, with its perennial shortage of skilled labor and its huge internal market for mass produced goods of uniform quality. American individualism, the ideal of the self-made man, a fascination with newness, and a state which had promoted private initiative provided additional fuel for the new industrialism. But these forces also unleashed dramatic changes in America. American values of self-denial began to give way to the ideals of a consumer society with its beliefs in immediate gratification and the curative effects of material goods. At the same time strict work disciplines replaced the casual work environment as timeliness became a means of regulating the lives of Americans. As workers lost control over the work place and the middle class surrendered small farms and businesses for professional careers in big business or big government, they were freed to desire and strive for consumer goods. In this consumer society individuals were free to work hard to acquire goods that would supposedly meet both their physical and psychological needs.[3] Ultimately proponents of the new corporate culture would equate material and moral progress, branding such disparate groups as Indians and unemployed workers as savages for their failure to internalize the new ethic of hard work and acquisitiveness. Such explanations of inequality often went to extremes, giving vent to darker emotions. Scientific racism explained the subordinate position of blacks and Indians in a seemingly open competitive society as the failures of inherently inferior human beings.[4] This complex web of material accomplishments and the blending of new and old values gave American corporate culture its distinctiveness. It was also a source of considerable opposition to the modern corporate society it was creating.

The changes unleashed by American corporate culture had highly disruptive effects on American society, uprooting both workers and the middle class from positions and relations in which they had long functioned. Perhaps most importantly the new order offered a vision of humans preoccupied with competition and consumption and ever willing to cast aside the old to make way for the new. That view was considerably at odds with values which rejected materialism and emphasized cooperation, community and tradition. As a result, small business people and community leaders initially joined workers in struggles which in effect gave expression to community resistance to an alien culture. They were struggles which American corporate culture would once again trigger as it carried its mixed messages about the human condition beyond its own shores.

At the beginning of the twentieth century American culture had achieved a unique integration of the second industrial revolution's new scientific technology and rationalization of work relations with values that

3 William Leach, *Land of Desire: Merchants, Power and the Rise of a New American Culture* (New York: Pantheon, 1993), p. 3.
4 Alan Trachtenberg, *The Incorporation of America: Culture and Society in the Gilded Age* (New York: Hill and Wang, 1982), pp. 34, 71–74, 97–98.

promoted individual achievement, a consumer society, an openness to perpetual change and a vision of unremitting improvement in the human condition. American business leaders now set themselves the task of spreading this culture overseas. Latin America became the principal target of these early efforts, given the region's proximity and longstanding commercial linkages to the United States. Furthermore, Latin American elites had encountered considerable internal obstacles to their own efforts to achieve economic expansion and were anxiously seeking outside assistance. For U.S. business leaders, Latin America represented a familiar and seemingly friendly environment for their efforts. But popular forces in Latin America did not greet the introduction of American corporate culture with uncritical enthusiasm.

The five centuries of Latin American history that followed Columbus' first voyage were marked by ongoing struggles over the region's future. Spanish colonizers, and after independence their creole descendents, doggedly pursued policies designed to effectively exploit Latin America's human and material resources for their benefit. Such determination was essential in an environment which proved far less conducive to the development of capitalism than the one in North America. Rural villages and urban guilds opposed market forces that threatened to undermine their interests, and the state played a highly interventionist role in the economy, often promoting the creation and preservation of monopolistic institutions. Particularly determined resistance developed from diverse rural communities, some dating back to the preconquest, others emerging as recently as the twentieth century. Beyond the struggle for the land which underpinned these communities, such groups fought to reaffirm idealized, and at times romanticized, community values of mutuality and cooperation. Nor were these communities grounded only in the large rural population. They also found expression in the gradually expanding urban population, particularly in the mutualism of artisans.

While these struggles over the future of Latin America sometimes found expression in violent rebellion, more often conflict took on a more subdued form as communities turned to the legislation, institutions and ceremonies of the state and the church to defend their interests and project their own vision of the future. While popular resistance and cultural expressions often took the more subdued forms of lawsuits and popularized religious festivals, the effects were unmistakable to the Latin American elite by the end of the nineteenth century.

The internal crisis for which Latin American leaders sought external solutions centered on the material productivity of their societies. Despite considerable growth in the last quarter of the nineteenth century, it was clear that their economies were reaching the limits of their efficiency. Out of the conflicts between elite development models and popular resistance there had developed a reliance on labor-repressive systems which depended heavily on coercive techniques. Such techniques led to production systems which utilized labor-intensive methods, employing a large, poorly remunerated and poorly disciplined workforce. State efforts to push development often resulted in an expansion of monopolistic privileges such as the continued growth of the great landed estates. Furthermore, the region's political and judicial systems still did not encourage an individualistic competitive environment. As Latin America's economic growth model reached its limits at the beginning of the twentieth century, the limits of the elite's national vision were also exposed.

Although Latin American elites carried out their wars of independence against the Spanish Crown in the name of the nation, their nationalist vision was an exclusionary one. Like their North American counterparts, they had a highly disparaging view of those who resisted their version of modernization. However, for Latin American oligarchies that view encompassed nearly their entire national populations, composed as they were of Indians, blacks and mestizos. The elite did not envision most of their own people as fully equal fellow citizens, or as full partners and beneficiaries of a national development scheme. That philosophy affirmed the debased state of most of the population and thereby justified the use of force to carry out harsh economic policies. As Latin America's economies faced their productive crises, an ever increasing portion of their national populations called into question the elite's highly restrictive view of nationalism, and began to promote a more inclusive one which emphasized social and economic justice over order and progress. As American corporations entered Latin America to help resolve the crisis of productivity, they would be drawn into the intensifying domestic struggle and become a defining symbol for the new popular nationalism.

American corporate culture appeared to offer the solution to the dilemma of Latin American societies. From the perspective of the elite, American enterprise represented minimum costs, with a potential for maximum benefits, particularly in sectors such as electricity and petroleum with high entry costs and minimal local commitment. Even when they intruded on local interests in mining and agriculture, U.S. companies reinvigorated industries which could no longer compete internationally, offered higher wages than those available in the local economy, and at least initially provided an important stimulus to small businesses. Furthermore, American corporate culture's promises of unprecedented improvements in material wealth and the general human condition, coupled with its stress on individual achievement, had a powerful allure for most Latin Americans. Yet that culture would also prompt an ever more overt and violent reaction from many in Latin America. Part of that reaction stemmed from the sheer enormity of the American economic presence, which appeared to threaten national sovereignty. At times U.S. enterprises infringed on specific elite economic interests. They threatened to overwhelm substantial portions of the small business class, and they caused significant dislocation and disruption for peasants and workers. Part of that reaction stemmed inevitably from the racist perspective that often shaped American attitudes and actions toward Latin Americans. But beyond that contradictory aspect of American culture lay an even more fundamental challenge.

As a part of its promise of material progress and improvement in human welfare, American culture imposed stringent requirements for individualism, competition and an openness to change in virtually every aspect of human life. As they had in nineteenth-century America, such ideas represented a direct challenge to concepts of community, cooperation and stability in Latin America. The cult of the individual, a near obsession with the new, unquestioning acceptance of disparities created by unremitting competition, and values legitimized by functionality rather than historical precedent often posed fundamental threats to Latin Americans.

In the early decades of the twentieth century, communities of peasants, workers and small business people frequently countered American corporate culture with idealized concepts of mutuality and cooperation drawn from their own experiences. Not unlike the popular protests during America's Gilded Age, these movements rejected the intrusion of an alien culture. But unlike their American counterparts, these protesters could turn to the symbolism and rhetoric of nationalism as a central organizing theme and a powerful force to bind often disparate social elements together. Anti-Americanism offered a powerful weapon with which to assail the elite's model of national development, which depended heavily on foreign investment. Under the protective umbrella of anti-American nationalism, protesters could press an agenda protecting their own interests with a version of national development stressing social and economic justice. As the Great Depression eroded the American promise of perpetual material progress, American corporate culture became a central issue in struggles over definitions of the nation and conflicting programs for national development. Those struggles soon erupted in the radical actions of the 1930s which stunned and bewildered American corporate reformers.

The upheavals of the 1930s were only the most overt aspect of a process of encounter in which Latin Americans and American corporate reformers interacted, clashed and adapted to each other. That process was rich with complexities on both the American and the Latin American side. American companies invested in a variety of areas, from mineral extraction to agriculture to utilities. So too their levels of technology and labor intensity also varied significantly. They encountered Latin Americans not only in the work place but in the marketplace. In the latter environment those encounters ranged from the sale of canned goods to the provision of electrical services and appliances. Those factors influenced how Americans perceived and treated their hosts and how Latin Americans reacted to them. Latin Americans varied significantly in their reactions. Elites adopted an ambivalent attitude toward U.S. companies that could spur national growth but also threaten specific domestic economic interests.

And while communities of peasants, workers and small business people often joined together to oppose American corporate culture, the component groups of these communities often had distinct agendas. It is this complex process which forms the central subject of this study. Part I examines the broad contours of the historical evolution and increasing linkages between the United States and Latin America in the century after the American Revolution. The following five parts explore the interactions between American corporations and local societies in Central America, Peru, Chile, Cuba and Mexico in the first third of the twentieth century. Those five areas accounted for 80 percent of direct U.S. investment in Latin America at the time of the Great Depression and thus provide the richest material on direct encounters between American businesses and Latin American societies.

Despite its chronological and geographical scope, this work addresses only part of the complex interaction between American and Latin American cultures. At the beginning of this century, U.S. corporations were the primary but by no means the sole purveyors of American culture to Latin America. The U.S. departments of State and Commerce, the American Federation of Labor and Protestant missions are just a few of the numerous institutions that conveyed American culture to Latin American societies. This study deals with these points of interaction to only a limited degree. So too its treatment of American corporations is confined to some of the largest enterprises in fields such as mining and electrical generation. These companies led the promotion of the new corporate culture and had the most intense and pervasive encounters with Latin American societies. Again the magnitude of the subject compelled limited treatment of smaller corporations and such important fields of endeavor as telecommunications and the film industry. Hopefully this work will encourage others to explore many of the points of cultural intersection which are only touched upon here and further test some of its theoretical themes.

Structuralist analysis has had a pervasive influence on the study of modern history. While historians differed considerably in their conclusions, they tended to frame their analysis and their debates in terms of political institutions, economic systems and social relations. This study owes much to the achievements of that structuralist approach. Yet that perspective also introduced considerable rigidity into our efforts to understand our own century. Such limitations were particularly apparent in studies of the history of Latin America and of the region's relations with the United States.

The structuralist perspective has viewed Latin America's development problems as products of institutional impediments to modernization such as large inefficient landholdings and flawed credit markets, or as the result of a dependent relationship with the North Atlantic economies solidified by an alliance of foreign investors and the domestic ruling class. So too political and social history has been defined in terms of class struggle and intervention by foreign states and foreign capital. Despite its considerable accomplishments, the limits of this approach have become increasingly apparent. It is clear that Latin America is not characterized by a simple dichotomy between modern and traditional and that explanations focused on external forces underestimated the importance of internal developments. Most importantly, these theories that emphasize abstract forces minimize the role which Latin American people have played in making their own history. This problem is particularly obvious in the study of phenomena such as populism and nationalism which do not readily fall into structuralist analytical categories. As a result, earlier explanations have downplayed the role of popular forces in shaping these movements. Populism has been variously viewed as a product of popular naiveté played upon by charismatic leaders or a historical dead end, a mistaken initiative by the masses, who were then betrayed by their middle-class allies. Increasingly over the years, social historians like Herbert Gutman and anthropologists such as James Scott have demonstrated the very direct role subordinate classes have played in shaping history, and the often diverse alignments popular groups create in order to achieve their goals. This study builds on those approaches, arguing that the contemporary societies of the United States and Latin America are not merely the products of abstract forces or elites. Intense struggles among a broad spectrum of people with sharply differing views of the common good and distinct visions of the future created those societies. At the same time this work draws insight from structuralist analysis, particularly the dependency school's emphasis on externalities. It argues that while Latin American elites had already initiated a program of modernization and popular forces had begun formulating their own vision of nationalism, it was the presence of American corporate culture with its special blend of advanced technologies and values stressing perpetual change and individualism which gave added impetus and a unifying theme to Latin America's nationalist populist movements in the 1930s. In examining the interplay of domestic popular initiatives and external influences, this study offers a new approach to international relations.

In focusing on American corporate culture, this work seeks to move beyond our traditional understanding of international relations as interactions of nation states and intersections of economic systems. While it validates the importance of government policy and economics, it offers a larger vision of international relations as the intersection of societies which conflict with and adapt to one another on a number of levels. These political, economic and social interchanges are imbued with meaning by the human beings who undertake them. Through these actions people convey personal values and social norms, their perceptions of the past and their visions of the future. These complex interchanges of material conditions, values and visions lie at the heart of international relations. In attempting to understand them we can begin to understand the roots of our contemporary global society.

This work sheds new light on an aspect of international history long considered the preserve of economic historians and international relations experts. It seeks to broaden the perspectives which these specialists have offered, to reveal a process far more complex and far more human than trade and investment statistics or theories of international politics would suggest. This work also has much to tell about the notable figures who shaped giant American corporations and some of the powerful individuals who dominated Latin American societies. But that is only a small part of the story. In both North and South America, the people who farmed the land, worked the factories and tended shops played the central role in shaping their own societies and defining the terms of engagement under which two distinct cultures encountered each other. In a very real sense it is the story of how the people of the Americas made their own history.

PART I

Merchant republic to corporate empire

1

Merchant republic to corporate empire

. . . we must analyze the human mind and body carefully and see in what way it {sic} can be brought up to the highest state of productive ability. (Arthur Lovett Garford, Ohio Progressive party)

. . . in Chili, as in practically every Spanish speaking country, man in the eyes of the governing classes, possesses no commercial value, not even at all in comparison with the economic value of a jackass. (U. S. consular official)

A half century of violent anticolonial convulsions spawned distinctly different societies in the northern and southern halves of the Western Hemisphere. Despite a shared heritage of European colonialism, fundamental differences separated the United States and Latin America at the beginning of the nineteenth century. Those distinctive cultures and their internal transformations shaped relations between the new republics of North and South as their points of contact and interaction multiplied during the next half century.

The newly emergent republic in North America had evolved as a colonial appendage of Britain's mercantile empire. On the sparsely populated northern continent, British settlers had driven off or destroyed the indigenous population and shaped a society of freeholder agriculturists, artisan producers and a vibrant domestic merchant class. To the south, the Spanish had conquered a chain of densely populated, highly developed Indian civilizations strung out along a north–south axis from central Mexico to central Chile. After decapitating the political and religious hierarchies of these societies, the Spanish had forged a hegemonic order. Within that order, indigenous belief systems, values, institutions and social relations continued to play a significant role. Overseeing that process was an imperial bureaucracy patterned after the Iberian patrimonial order, which alternately warred upon and then protected the Indian village, the basic source of labor power and the fundamental obstacle to complete exploitation. Latin America, with its agrarian society dominated by the great estate and peasant villages, its social relations defined by the interaction of European and indigenous cultures, and its international commerce based on bullion exports, stood in stark contrast to the agrarian freeholder society of the British colonies.

The thirteen British colonies on the eve of the Revolution closely approximated the Jeffersonian ideal of a free small-farmer society, and that
reality would not be significantly altered in the early decades of independence. The vast majority of the population found its economic base in the
family farm.[1] By the early nineteenth century, signs of change pointed toward the commercialization of a subsistence agricultural system, particularly among farmers in eastern regions, whose locations gave them access
to urban and overseas markets. But at least until the 1830s, limited access
to markets and "a web of social relationships and cultural expectations
that inhibited the free play of market forces" ensured the predominance of
subsistence farming in the American countryside.[2] Yet while social values
constrained market forces, they certainly did not curtail their development, and commercial growth, particularly in international trade, was already forging close ties between the British and Spanish colonies in the
Western Hemisphere. Exports to the Caribbean and South America aver-
aged over 31 percent of U.S. exports between 1790 and 1812. Spain's
colonies, particularly Cuba, played an increasingly important role in this
interregional trade. Accounting for less than 10 percent of American exports to the region in 1794, the Spanish colonies increased their share to
40 percent by 1807. This connection played a critical role in creating opportunities for aspiring young merchants such as Moses Taylor, then a
clerk in the firm of G. C. and S. S. Howland, the leading New York merchant house in the Latin American trade.[3] But despite the increasing
commercial links, the British and Spanish colonies were already launched
on dramatically different courses.

European colonization brought elements of capitalism to both Latin
America and the United States, but conditions in the United States
proved far more favorable for its flourishing and maturation in the nineteenth century. While in Latin America rural villages and urban guilds
with their communal regulations continued to characterize the economic
landscape after independence, America's white population was comprised
of independent smallholders and free workers. Government institutions

---

1 Edwin Perkins, *The Economy of Colonial America* (New York: Columbia University Press, 1988), pp.
  2, 10, 71.

2 James Henretta, "Families and Farms: Mentalité in Pre-Industrial America," *William and Mary
  Quarterly* 3d ser., 35 (1978), p. 19; Bruce Laurie, *Artisans into Workers: Labor in Nineteenth-Century
  America* (New York: Noonday Press, 1989), p. 223.

3 Perkins, *Colonial America,* pp. 25–28; John H. Coatsworth, "American Trade with European
  Colonies in the Caribbean and South America, 1790–1812," *William and Mary Quarterly* 3d ser., 24
  (1969), p. 243; Javier Cuenca Esteban, "The United States Balance of Payments with Spanish
  America and the Philippine Islands, 1790–1819: Estimates and Analysis of Principal Components," in Jacques A. Barbier and Allan J. Kuethe, eds., *The North American Role in the Spanish Imperial Economy, 1760–1819* (Manchester: Manchester University Press, 1984), pp. 46–47; Douglass
  C. North, *The Economic Growth of the United States, 1790–1860* (New York: Norton, 1961), pp.
  34–45; Daniel Hodas, *The Business Career of Moses Taylor: Merchant, Finance Capitalist and Industrialist* (New York: New York University Press, 1976), pp. 3–4.

also functioned very differently in the two regions. In Latin America the state had long served a pivotal role in controlling the economy, regulating prices and granting monopolies, while the national government of the United States played a non-interventionist role in the economy. In the United States the ideals of social equality and open economic opportunity contrasted with Latin American emphasis on social hierarchy and economic privilege. Those contrasting value systems to some degree reflected reality. While the classic American tale of rags to riches proved the exception rather than the rule, certainly those of humble origins faced fewer obstacles to social and economic advancement in the United States than in Latin America. These differences would intensify and multiply during the first half of the nineteenth century.[4]

In the afterglow of independence, the threat of anarchy cast a lengthening shadow across Latin American societies. Interregional conflict, intra-elite struggles, turmoil in the central government and fiscal bankruptcy shattered the tranquility of the immediate post-independence period. The region's intellectuals perceived in these conditions the beginnings of a precipitous slide from civilization into barbarism. The region's oligarchies believed that they might well have won the battle of independence only to lose the war for social order. While destroying the structures of imperial rule and expelling the Spaniards, the creole elite had managed to keep in check the masses of Indian peasants, mixed-blood mestizos and black slaves, who constituted the vast majority of their national populations. Now with independence achieved, the forces of popular resistance besieged the creole oligarchy. During the early nineteenth century rural populations fought to preserve their own interests against the intrusions of a modernizing elite.

Latin American ruling groups differed sharply over policies of modernization, contributing to the internecine conflicts that marked this era. Traditionalists, while accepting the need for economic growth, feared that the secularism and individualism that characterized Western modernization would plunge their patriarchal social orders into chaos. As the century progressed, Latin American ruling classes gradually coalesced around a national agenda promoting a process of modernization based on the model of North Atlantic capitalist societies. That agenda included the adoption of the forms, if not the substance, of liberal political and cultural concepts and the commercialization of agriculture. But while ruling groups in Latin America eventually reached some degree of consensus about nation building, they faced a considerably more formidable task than did their counterparts in the United States. While Latin America possessed an abundant workforce, many rural workers were tied by debt peonage or other arrangements which limited the emergence of a free la-

---

4 Louis M. Hacker, *The Triumph of American Capitalism: The Development of Forces in American History to the End of the Nineteenth Century* (New York: Simon and Schuster, 1940), pp. 5–11.

bor market. At the same time the church and peasant villages still dominated the landholding patterns of the agrarian economy, and guilds continued to play a central role in the urban sector. Peasants and urban artisans remained reliant on village institutions and craft organizations to
defend their interests in societies where the political and legal systems
placed little emphasis on the individual's rights to equal economic and
political opportunities. These institutions and associations would defend
their interests against free market policies with considerable vigor. Peasants, for example, faced with an increasingly aggressive assault on the
communal land structures and subsistence agriculture that underpinned
their communities, responded with popular rebellions and more subtle
forms of resistance that tore at the fabric of Latin American societies.[5]
While large commercial interests were eventually won over to free trade,
many urban merchants did not initially support these policies, fearful of
being overwhelmed by European commercial houses. Like the urban
craftsmen, they too used surviving colonial trade associations to combat
liberalization policies that threatened their interests.

These distinct groups that opposed aspects of liberal modernization
also rallied around distinct sets of ideas. Peasants often coalesced around a
shared Indian identity and communal village values that prioritized common interests and cooperation over individual ambition and competition.
Urban artisans utilized age-old concepts of the just wage and the fair price
to defend their interests. Merchants such as those in Peru touted nationalism as the justification for protecting their interests. With their often divergent goals and strategies, these groups battered the liberal development agenda.[6]

When state liberalization policies did make headway, in agriculture
they usually contributed to the further expansion of large rural estates. In
seeking to promote business development in capital-poor societies with
minimal infrastructure development, the state most often relied on Spanish strategies of granting foreign or domestic monopolies. Latin American governments also remained sensitive to the protests of urban dwellers
against upward spirals in the cost of living and imposed price controls
and other regulations to ease urban unrest. And while the story of foreign
direct investment in Latin America in these early decades of independence was most often one of rapid failure, Europeans, and particularly the
British, became the most significant force in the region's international
trade.[7]

5 Bradford Burns, *The Poverty of Progress: Latin America in the Nineteenth Century* (Berkeley and Los Angeles: University of California Press, 1980), p. 17; Steve J. Stern, *Resistance, Rebellion, and Consciousness in the Andean Peasant World, 18th to 20th Centuries* (Madison: University of Wisconsin Press,
   1987), p. 74.
6 Stern, *Resistance, Rebellion*, pp. 16–115; Paul Gootenberg, *Between Silver and Guano: Commercial Policy and the State in Postindependence Peru* (Princeton: Princeton University Press, 1989), pp. 46–63.
7 Gootenberg, *Silver and Guano*, pp. 34–67; David Bushnell and Neill Macaulay, *The Emergence of
   Latin America in the Nineteenth Century* (New York: Oxford University Press, 1988), pp. 26–32.

Liberal modernization schemes in the first half of the century managed to sunder the social contract of the early colonial era without creating the conditions necessary for autonomous capitalist development. Even when urban merchants were won over to the side of free market policies, peasant resistance and popular protests in the cities still blocked fulfillment of liberal development schemes. That resistance only confirmed the worst views which the elite held about the popular classes. The Argentine intellectual and politician Domingo Sarmiento forcefully stated the elite's position – it was a struggle between civilization and barbarism. Sarmiento's statement also testified to the failure of liberals as well as conservatives to envision national development as a common national project incorporating the entire population. To the north, developments were taking a course far more favorable to capitalist development and to a wave of expansionism that swept across the merchant republic and into Latin America.

In the decades after independence the self-help themes of Benjamin Franklin echoed through American society, feeding into what can safely be termed the cult of the self-made man. Proponents of this ideal argued that the individual was master of his fate and that success depended simply on determination. In turn, success, including upward social mobility, was measured by the accumulation of wealth. Such ideas, often reinforced by families and the Protestant clergy, encouraged an intense work ethic in antebellum America. While the national government remained relatively unintrusive in economic affairs, aside from its commitment to private property rights, nevertheless federal, state and local governments did offer spurs to private enterprise. Government at all levels provided land grants, loans, stock subscriptions and other inducements to encourage private development of roads, canals and railroads. At the same time the American legal system tended to favor opportunity over the preservation of existing privileges or monopolies. And while European and particularly British capital continued to play a key role in the American economy, it did not hold a dominant role in U.S. development after the panic and depression of 1837 to 1843. Indeed, early American industrialists would describe their own campaign for protectionism as a moral crusade against the contaminating influence of European manufactures. That sense of moral mission also emerged in the work place, where owners tried to persuade their workers of the moral correctness of sobriety and hard work. Yet a society in which popular ideology, political institutions, religious values and the judicial system all seemed to conspire in favor of individualism and private enterprise was not without its darker side.[8]

By the mid nineteenth century, racialist interpretations of the human condition had gained widespread acceptance in the United States. Based on European ideas of race and the subordination of Indians and Africans on the North American continent, many Americans came to view them-

8 Hacker, *American Capitalism,* pp. 12–14; Stuart Bruchey, *Enterprise: The Dynamic Economy of a Free People* (Cambridge: Harvard University Press, 1990), pp. 197, 212.

selves as a branch of the dynamic Anglo-Saxon people in a world comprised of superior and inferior races. As market forces accentuated social differentiation, intensified economic uncertainties and concentrated wealth, Americans could find comfort in their presumed racial superiority. Those same market forces fed a process of territorial expansion partly justified by racialist views which eventually affected U.S. relations with Latin America.[9]

The expanding opportunities for private business in the United States proved especially fortuitous for America's international merchants. The end of the prolonged period of European wars in 1815 sounded the death knell for key segments of America's international trade position. The reenactment of European navigation laws, declining freight rates and foreign competition had dealt fatal blows to re-export and carrying trades. By 1850 they ceased to be expansive forces in America's international trade.[10] Northern merchants had already launched a search for alternative sources of profit in the 1820s. Many merchants initially confronted the new challenges by abandoning general commerce to specialize in particular products such as sugar and, especially, cotton. By the 1830s local mercantile houses had made New York City the commercial center of the cotton trade, accounting for over half of national exports. Phelps Dodge and Company, for example, built its business on the importation of tinplate from Great Britain. But the firm found its second most important source of business in the cotton trade. The company purchased cotton from factors in southern ports and brokers in New York for shipment to Liverpool. Such northern mercantile interests did not restrict themselves to trading relations with the slave states. In the early 1830s federal policy initiated the sale of millions of acres of Indian lands in Alabama and Mississippi to feed the growing demands of cotton planters for new and more fertile soil. Land speculators from the Northeast rushed to take advantage of this bonanza. These ventures symbolized the growing financial power of northern merchants that had also launched them into similar ventures in the American West.[11]

Despite the generally anemic performance of U.S.–Latin American trade, Moses Taylor had prospered after leaving the Howland brothers in 1832 by founding his own merchant house specializing in the Cuban sugar trade. Taylor built a fortune on the sugar trade, but by 1842 he had invested at least $202,000 outside his mercantile ventures, including

9 Reginald Horsman, *Race and Manifest Destiny: The Origins of American Racial Anglo-Saxonism* (Cambridge: Harvard University Press, 1981), pp. 1–97.

10 Douglass C. North, *Growth and Welfare in the American Past: A New Economic History* (New York: Norton, 1966), pp. 25, 61.

11 Richard Lowitt, *A Merchant Prince of the Nineteenth Century, William E. Dodge* (New York: Columbia University Press, 1954), pp. 22–27, 41; Mary Elizabeth Young, *Redskins, Ruffleshirts and Rednecks: Indian Allotments in Alabama and Mississippi* (Norman: University of Oklahoma Press, 1961), pp. 138–45.

$11,000 in the shares of City Bank. It was a small beginning for a major career in banking. Taylor became a director of the bank in 1837 and served as its president from 1856 until his death in 1882. Taylor used the bank as a private financial institution to fund a diversified business empire, built in partnership with other merchants such as William Earl Dodge of Phelps Dodge and Company. Their evolution from merchants to financiers by midcentury reflected a common pattern among northern mercantile interests. Taylor's investments also reflected the growing interest of these merchants in the American West. Moses Taylor's numerous directorships included a seat on the board of the New York Life Insurance and Trust Company, formed in 1830 with a $6 million investment fund, 70 percent of which was tied up in land mortgages, part of the frenzied activity of eastern land speculators in the American West.[12]

The decline of the re-export and carrying trades had forced the mercantile community to look south and west for new opportunities. The financing of the cotton trade, merchandise shipments to the South, land speculation and infrastructure development in the West and the South had bound the three regions of the country together through the networks of an expanding market economy. To understand the impetus which such developments gave to the forces of expansion it is essential to examine the response of southern and northern societies to this process.

Within the limits of slave labor, planters in the American South had introduced new technology in the 1820s with animal-powered plows. Yet such innovation proved episodic, and output improvement came to depend on closer supervision of slave gang labor and acquisition of new, more fertile lands. Simply put, slaveowners achieved production increases by adding more land and slaves and intensifying the labor of slaves.[13] The impulse of merchant investments transmitted through the South's slave labor system gave a special impetus to the forces of territorial expansion, for it was largely through such expansion and the intensification of labor that slavery could achieve higher levels of output. In the North, that impulse accelerated changes in the social productive process itself, with a similar intensification of pressures for expansion.

Even before merchants turned their attention to an expansion of the internal market economy, fundamental change had begun to affect society in the North. By the 1820s harsher, more impersonal work conditions began to alter the casual environment of workshops. As family-

12 Hodas, *Moses Taylor*, pp. 5–7, 57–61; Harold van B. Cleveland and Thomas F. Huertas, *Citibank, 1812–1970* (Cambridge: Harvard University Press, 1985), pp. 15–17; Paul W. Gates, *Landlords and Tenants on the Prairie Frontier: Studies in American Land Policy* (Ithaca: Cornell University Press, 1973), pp. 2–3.

13 Charles Post, "Primitive Accumulation, Class Struggle and the Capitalist State: Political Crisis and the Origins of the U.S. Civil War, 1844–1861" (Ph.D. dissertation, SUNY Binghamton, 1983), pp. 43–76; Gavin Wright, *The Political Economy of the Cotton South: Households, Markets, and Wealth in the Nineteenth Century* (New York: Norton, 1978), pp. 15–24.

centered work relations shifted toward impersonal wage labor, many entrepreneurs found solace in evangelicalism, with its temperance campaigns and promises of a new moral order. Deeply religious entrepreneurs such as William Earl Dodge saw in evangelicalism and temperance campaigns both personal salvation and the practical benefit of a more disciplined labor force. Only a minority of working people willingly accepted this new order. Increasingly impersonal and harsher working conditions, social differentiation and wealth concentration prompted a profound restlessness in many Americans. Much of America's newly emergent working class adopted a migratory pattern of life in order to barter their skills for better wages. Others migrated west hoping to find in the land an alternative to the harsher realities of nascent industrialism. But as commercialization penetrated rural America, the cost of farm making (buying land and equipment) rose dramatically. In turn, farmers and those who aspired to freeholder status clamored for territorial expansion as one means of lowering the cost of at least one capital input essential to farm making – the land itself. As a growing number of subsistence freeholders in the West became small commercial producers, they joined eastern merchants who sought a firm land base for their Asian trade and southern slave interests in demanding new lands to build their market economy. By then American society had also developed the racialist perspective which could justify an expansionary process against foreign nations.[14]

As American contact with Mexico intensified in the 1830s and 40s, American views of Mexican society came to reflect the racialist perspectives winning acceptance in the United States. That perspective presented Mexicans as a deplorable mix of Indian and Spanish blood which had created an immoral race lacking in intelligence and initiative, a race incapable of developing its own national resources. The war against Mexico became the project of an American society unified by the efforts of merchants who had turned their energies inward in the face of uncertainties in the world economy. The forces of the market economy, interacting with the slave society of the South, the freeholders of the West and the emerging industrial order of the North, had created a national coalition for expansion. That coalition acted with the assurance that it represented the best of an Anglo-Saxon race destined to displace the inferior Latin race to its south. Meanwhile in Mexico some of the forces which had doomed

14 Paul E. Johnson, *A Shopkeeper's Millennium: Society and Revivals in Rochester, New York, 1815–1837* (New York: Hill and Wang, 1978), pp. 58–106; Jonathan Prude, *The Coming of the Industrial Order: Town and Factory Life in Rural Massachusetts, 1810–1860* (Cambridge: Cambridge University Press, 1983), pp. 100–157, 217–37; John J. Rumbarger, *Power, Profits, and Prohibition: Alcohol Reform and the Industrializing of America, 1800–1930* (Albany: State University of New York Press, 1989), pp. 43–47; Burton J. Bledstein, *The Culture of Professionalism: The Middle Class and the Development of Higher Education in America* (New York: Norton, 1976), p. 15.

America's dreams of mercantile empire in Latin America ensured the success of its plans for a land-based empire.[15]

Mexican society typified the forces that tore at the social fabric of Latin America in the post-independence period. Intra-elite disputes, interregional conflict, peasant revolt and government instability reached epic proportions in Mexico during this era. As a result, Mexico could not present either a united military front that would ward off American expansionism or conduct a consistent and effective diplomacy to deter the merchant republic. But the war which signaled the triumph of the expansionist coalition also marked its demise. The rising social tensions that derailed American territorial expansion and eventually shattered the merchant republic focused on the expansion of slavery. Even many of the confirmed expansionists of the old Northwest (i.e. Ohio, Indiana, Illinois and Michigan) opposed the addition of new slave territories at the time of the Mexican War. For the western freeholders, exclusion from new territorial acquisitions threatened the promise of cheap lands with which to compete in the market economy. For slaveowners, exclusion would rob them of a basic solution to slavery's productivity problems. A compromise which envisioned a sharing of the soil could be temporary at best, for ultimately the state would have to pursue policies favorable to freeholders or guarantee the rights of slaveowners. At the same time the commercialization of western agriculture had strengthened the ties between the eastern and western sections of the country. The market represented by small farmers loomed large in the process of industrialization, with farm implements and machinery representing the largest specialized branch of machine making by 1860. Furthermore, free farmers produced the grains and meats that fed the burgeoning food processing industry.[16]

In the decade and a half after the war with Mexico, the growing conflict between the slave society of the South and the free farmer/industrialist alliance of the North had shattered the coalition and paralyzed the central government. It now fell to private interests to exploit expansionist opportunities created by Latin American upheavals. Mercenary filibustering expeditions into Caribbean Basin countries, such as William Walker's forays into Nicaragua, marked the years after the war with Mexico. These expeditions represented the last-gasp efforts of slaveowners and elements of the merchant community to fulfill their dreams of territorial acquisi-

15 Horsman, *Race and Manifest Destiny*, p. 210; Clarence H. Danhof, *Change in Agriculture: The Northern States, 1820–1870* (Cambridge: Harvard University Press, 1969), pp. 2, 78, 98, 189–222.

16 Norman A. Graebner, *Foundations of American Foreign Policy: A Realist Appraisal from Franklin to McKinley* (Wilmington, Del.: Scholarly Resources, 1985), pp. 223–41; Horsman, *Race and Manifest Destiny*, pp. 245–47; Barry Hindess and Paul Q. Hirst, *Pre-Capitalist Modes of Production* (London: Routledge and Kegan Paul, 1975), pp. 170–77; Barrington Moore Jr., *Social Origins of Dictatorship and Democracy: Lord and Peasant in the Making of the Modern World* (Boston: Beacon, 1967), p. 136.

tion. In the years after the Civil War, American interests in the nations to the south would focus on the creation of a commercial empire.

In the half century after the Civil War a number of factors coalesced to spur America's industrial development, not the least of which was the federal government's firm commitment to protectionist policies. At the same time the national government made an expanded commitment to railroad development, with additional land grants and concessions to spur the creation of a national rail network. The creation of federal agencies such as the Department of Commerce and the Federal Reserve Board was designed to facilitate the development of increasingly large and complex business organizations. The emergence of big business rekindled Jeffersonian and Jacksonian concerns about privilege and the dangers of bigness. Those renewed concerns found expression through the Populist and Progressive movements. In turn the federal government did address these issues with national railroad regulation and antitrust legislation. On balance, however, the federal government favored large corporations, but sought to keep them sufficiently in check to avoid the total suppression of competition in the national economy. The emergence of large modern corporations, however, was not the product of government action or inaction.

The relative scarcity of labor in North America had prompted a long-term drive to substitute machinery for labor wherever possible. In the second half of the nineteenth century that process began to pay substantial dividends, with the adoption of new technologies in steel and other industries, as well as the exploitation of new energy sources such as coal and oil. This period also saw the emergence of new industries such as chemicals and electricity which were based on the direct application of scientific discoveries. At the same time the completion of a national rail network sped the movement of products and helped create a truly national market. These developments gave several different impulses to the creation of large modern corporations.

Vastly increased production of standardized products which could be marketed on a nationwide basis gave rise to intense price competition which drove prices below production costs. In response, corporations in such industries as oil and sugar combined to control prices. The new consumer product lines and heavy industries such as steel and mining companies vertically integrated their operations to achieve economies of scale, expand marketing opportunities and fully exploit new technologies. In science-based industries such as electricity, large corporations like General Electric emerged from these same imperatives and a drive to monopolize the technologies that were the basis of their existence.

The adoption of new technologies, efforts to integrate them into continuous process production flows, vast expansion of markets and the rapidly increasing size of companies led to modifications in corporate structures as well. In large enterprises, family-run management systems with informal organizational structures gave way to modern corporations. Managers reorganized the internal management hierarchies of American companies into a series of distinct, but integrated, functional departments managed by individuals selected on the basis of objective criteria.[17] These dramatic changes in the means of producing goods and volumes of production, along with the reshaping of the enterprises that produced them, had dramatic effects on American society as well.

That the avenues of economic advancement remained open in America in the second half of the nineteenth century is evidenced by the humble origins of many of its leading industrialists. Some of America's new entrepreneurs emerged from among its master craftsmen, who converted the casual workshop manned by journeymen into modest factories. These incipient industrial enterprises employed skilled workers who increasingly carried out distinct tasks in what was once a wholistic craft production process. In brewing, the Best family, immigrant German brewers, founded a brewery in the 1840s which became the Pabst Company. The descendents of William and Frederick Havemeyer, European sugar masters, created the American Sugar Refining Company that dominated the refining business at the turn of the century.[18] In other cases aspiring industrialists sprang from even humbler origins.

In late March 1855 Edward McIvans, a foundry mechanic from Pottsville, Pennsylvania, arrived in New York for an interview with Moses Taylor. The meeting between a humble craftsman and the prominent Wall Street merchant and banker was made possible by a letter which McIvans carried from Joseph Scranton, one of the founders of the Lackawanna Iron and Coal Company. As Scranton explained in his note to Taylor, McIvans' hands and head were "about his only present available means." But McIvans also had ambitions. He wanted to open a machine shop, and Scranton suggested that Taylor might put him in touch with someone with capital to back the venture. Scranton concluded his note to Taylor by noting that "if you do it strikes me this is a *rare* chance."[19] If Taylor himself did not have the time to involve himself in McIvans' venture, it was because he and other leading American merchants were already heavily committed to the process of industrialization.

While cotton had underpinned the merchant republic's economy, cotton textiles assumed that role in America's emerging industrial society.

---

17 Alfred Chandler, *The Visible Hand: The Managerial Revolution in American Business* (Cambridge: Harvard University Press, 1974).

18 David M. Gordon, Richard Edwards and Michael Reich, *Segmented Work, Divided Workers: The Historical Transformation of Labor in the United States* (Cambridge: Cambridge University Press, 1982), p. 65; Alfred S. Eichner, *The Emergence of Oligopoly: Sugar Refining as a Case Study* (Baltimore: Johns Hopkins University Press, 1969), p. 28.

19 Joseph Scranton to Moses Taylor, Scranton, Pa., March 19, 1855, Box 288, Taylor Papers.

The textile mills of Moses Brown and those of the Boston Associates represented early ventures of merchant capital into the realm of manufacturing. By 1860 the value of cotton goods production in the United States had reached $107 million and ranked it as the number one manufacturing sector in terms of value added.[20] But most mercantile families that sought alternatives to commercial investments did not follow this early lead into manufacturing.

Moses Taylor's activities proved more typical of the pattern of mercantile fortunes in transition. Through his financial power, embodied in the City Bank, Taylor invested in railroads, coal mines and iron production. His holdings in railroads included controlling interests in the Delaware, Lackawanna and Western railroads. Taylor's efforts formed a part of the surge of merchant capital into the railroad sector that converted a 1,000-mile rail system in 1840 into a 100,000-mile national network by 1880.[21]

In 1858 Taylor became a director of the Lackawanna Iron and Coal Company and shaped it into one of the largest iron producers in the country. He also initiated the company's introduction of the Bessemer steel process, pushing the firm into the forefront of the steel industry. Once again Taylor's efforts mirrored larger developments in the American economy. Iron production soared from less than 1 million tons in 1860 to over 9 million in 1895. By 1880 steel production had already reached 1.2 million tons, marking the beginning of an upsurge that would increase output eightfold in the next two decades.[22] Taylor's dual role as a merchant banker who also took a very direct role in managing the enterprises in which he invested represented two distinct courses which merchant entrepreneurs pursued after midcentury.

After 1891, under the presidency of Taylor's protégé James Stillman, City Bank, now known as National City Bank, assumed the role of an investment bank underwriting securities issued to finance the reorganization of American railroads. The bank pursued this course into the underwriting of industrial securities as the process of corporate consolidation swept the economy at the turn of the century. As a result, the bank's industrial clients came to include such corporate giants as American Sugar Refining, International Harvester, Armour and Company, and Standard Oil.[23]

The course of the Taylor–Stillman interests from merchant banking to investment banking had already been chartered by Junius and J. Pierpont Morgan. Junius Morgan converted his prosperous Hartford, Connecticut, merchant operations into a merchant banking house which served as a

---

20 Gary M. Walton and Ross M. Robertson, *History of the American Economy*, 5th ed. (New York: Harcourt Brace Jovanovich, 1983), p. 253.

21 Hodas, *Moses Taylor*, pp. 80–101, 200–264; North, *Growth and Welfare*, p. 112.

22 Van B. Cleveland and Huertas, *Citibank*, p. 21; Louis M. Hacker, *The World of Andrew Carnegie: 1865–1901* (Philadelphia: Lippincott, 1968), p. 342.

23 Van B. Cleveland and Huertas, *Citibank*, pp. 32–41.

conduit for European capital that financed the building of much of the American railway system. Under his son, the house led the way in financing railroad consolidations and then underwrote some of the most important corporate mergers, such as General Electric and United States Steel.[24]

The flotation of bonds by railroads and state governments offered expanding opportunities for merchant houses like Brown Brothers and Company of New York which were moving from specialized trade to financing as their principal business. The firm traced its origins to Alexander Brown and Sons of Baltimore, which had specialized in the linen trade and then shifted into cotton. By the turn of the century the firm became one of the nation's leading international investment houses, with a growing commitment in Latin America.[25] While merchants like Taylor, Morgan and the Browns laid the foundations of America's modern financial institutions, others like William Earl Dodge and Meyer Guggenheim plunged into the development of natural resources.

William Earl Dodge and Moses Taylor had shared a number of railroad and mining investments, and Dodge's firm became heavily involved in lumbering and in brass manufacture. Two years before Dodge's death in 1883, his firm began to invest in copper mines in Bisbee and Morenci, Arizona. By the turn of the century Phelps Dodge and Company would become one of the leading mining corporations in the United States. The Dodge investments paralleled those of the Philadelphia merchant house of M. Guggenheim's Sons. Meyer Guggenheim, the founder and senior partner of the firm, had built his fortune in the wholesale goods and lace trades. But in 1879 Guggenheim purchased a part interest in a silver mine in Leadville, Colorado. Over the next three decades, he and his sons built that initial investment into a worldwide mining empire. Yet even as the accelerating industrial revolution created new opportunities for enrichment by merchants, craftsmen and humble workmen, it also created a permanent working class in America.[26]

American workers had countered the gradual replacement of the casual work environment by more impersonal working conditions in the first half of the century with their migratory habits. Yet even as they came to accept the permanency of their wage-earner status, they retained considerable influence over their work environment. The industrial revolution had reshaped most of America's physical plant by the 1870s. But the process of change proved far less consistent and pervasive in the social relations

24 Vincent P. Carosso, *The Morgans: Private International Bankers, 1854–1913* (Cambridge: Harvard University Press, 1987).

25 Vincent P. Carosso, *Investment Banking in America: A History* (Cambridge: Harvard University Press, 1970), p. 8.

26 Hodas, *Moses Taylor,* pp. 86–87, 99–101, 105–6, 148–49; van B. Cleveland and Huertas, *Citibank,* pp. 36–44, 97–101; Edwin Palmer Hoyt Jr., *The Guggenheims and the American Dream* (New York: Funk and Wagnalls, 1967), pp. 27–47.

which governed the work place. Although craft production fell into general disarray by the 1850s, in areas such as hat making and other finishing trades the roles and functions of craftsmen and journeymen survived within the confines of the craft shop.[27]

Even in those industries where the division of labor accelerated most rapidly and the introduction of power machinery seemed most pervasive, control of much of the work process remained in the hands of skilled workers. In sugar refining, the last stage of recrystallization could produce a purified product or a brown, tasteless mess. The proper handling of the process depended on the skill and knowledge of sugar masters. After the discovery of the Comstock Lode in 1859, mines became large-scale enterprises requiring heavy capital outlays and utilizing new techniques and technologies. Yet the individual miner remained the most critical factor in the success of the industry. The miner with his simple hand tools had to extract and sort the ore with the maximum mineral content. The knowledge and dexterity of iron molders, glass blowers, machine tenders and boiler makers proved equally critical to the success of a whole range of industries. As a result, control of much of the production process in the American industrial work place remained in the hands of those who labored there.[28]

By the time of the Civil War, unions had already emerged and fought to enforce work rules and demand higher wages. At the Lackawanna Iron and Coal Company, Joseph Scranton reported that miners had committed the "monstrous outrage" of demanding higher pay and insisting that the few non-union miners be fired. And he later lamented, "I would about as soon be in Purgatory as in control of the Miners, Puddlers, Blast Furnace Men, Laborers etc. just now."[29]

A further barrier to the entrepreneurs' control of the work place came from the communities in which they operated. Even in its incipient stages, industrialization had considerably altered social relations within communities. The patriarchal order in which wage earners and masters related to each other within family-centered enterprises had given way to a set of relations based solely on wage labor. Class divisions became apparent not only on the shop floor but in urban residential patterns and social mores.[30] Despite the physical and social distances which developed between classes, a strong sense of community still survived outside the great urban centers.

27 Laurie, *Artisans,* pp. 44–45; Gordon, Edwards and Reich, *Segmented Work,* p. 64.

28 Eichner, *Sugar,* p. 28; Harold Barger and Sam H. Schurr, *The Mining Industries, 1899–1939: A Study of Output, Employment and Productivity* (1944) (New York: National Bureau of Economic Research, 1975), pp. 101–6.

29 Joseph Scranton to Moses Taylor, Scranton, Pa., April 13, 1863, July 12, 1864, Box 288, Taylor Papers. Also see Gordon, Edwards and Reich, *Segmented Work,* pp. 96–97.

30 Johnson, *Shopkeeper's Millennium,* pp. 37–61.

Initially, workers who chose to take militant action against industrialists could frequently count on the support of local politicians and elements of the business community. As the 1877 railroad strike spread across the country, strikers gained the support of local merchants, farmers and clergymen who opposed the policies of the railway companies. In 1887 western miners seized A. J. Seligman, son of one of the senior partners of the New York–based Seligman financial house, and held him until the company paid their back wages. The mayor and merchants of Lynn, Massachusetts, supported striking leather workers in 1890. In the same period, the shopkeepers of Silver City, Idaho, came out in support of local miners' demands for the eight-hour day. This coalescence of community resistance to corporate penetration, which would later be replicated in Latin America, stemmed from several factors. Tradesmen, shopkeepers and many professionals had risen from a lower social station and could empathize with the plight of laborers. In addition, workers represented a substantial constituency and market for local politicians and businessmen. Furthermore, smaller communities often viewed the arrival of large corporations as an invasion by "foreign capitalists."[31]

Resistance to the transformation of the work place accelerated as increased mechanization in the latter decades of the century threatened workers with deskilling or displacement. In the steel industry, for example, mill owners introduced technology that reduced their dependence on skilled workers such as puddlers, mechanics and rollers. International Harvester offered a compelling example of this same process, installing new machinery to replace its skilled molders after a successful strike in 1885. When the workers struck again in 1886, the company broke the union by replacing its members with unskilled laborers.[32] Yet revolutionizing the social relations of the work place, breaking the grip of labor on the production process, proved a costly imperative.

Increasing efforts by management in the United States to control the work place prompted widespread resistance by American workers, particularly in the period 1912 to 1922. The seriousness of the challenge from

31 Trachtenberg, *Incorporation of America,* p. 40; John T. Cumbler, "Labor, Capital, and Community: The Struggle for Power," in Milton Cantor, ed., *American Workingclass Culture: Explorations in American Labor and Social History* (Westport, Conn.: Greenwood Press, 1979), pp. 149–66; Herbert G. Gutman, "The Workers Search for Power: Labor in the Gilded Age," in H. Wayne Morgan, ed., *The Gilded Age* (Syracuse, N.Y.: Syracuse University Press, 1963), pp. 38–68; Herbert G. Gutman, *Power and Culture: Essays on the American Working Class* (New York: Pantheon, 1987), pp. 76–77; Melvyn Dubofsky, *We Shall Be All: A History of the Industrial Workers of the World* (1969), 2d ed. (Urbana: University of Illinois Press, 1988), pp. 26, 37, 56; Richard E. Lingerfelter, *The Hard Rock Miners: A History of the Mining Labor Movement in the American West, 1863–1893* (Berkeley and Los Angeles: University of California Press, 1974), p. 105; Mark Wyman, *Hard Rock Epic: Western Miners and the Industrial Revolution, 1860–1910* (Berkeley and Los Angeles: University of California Press, 1979), pp. 61–62.

32 Gordon, Edwards and Reich, *Segmented Work,* pp. 115–16.

labor was clearly recognized by Frank Vanderlip, who succeeded James Stillman as president of the National City Bank. Commenting on the growing unrest among American workers in 1919, Vanderlip observed:

Here with full employment, high wages, constantly bettered conditions, and I believe, a really marked tendency toward greater fairness and sympathy by employers, there has developed the most general unrest and dissatisfaction. The dissatisfaction is deeper than any mere claim to higher wages. It is a challenge of some of the fundamentals of some of our present social and capitalistic order.[33]

In the face of such conflict, promoters of capitalist development fought to redefine the terms of debate over the future of American society. They succeeded in presenting rationalization, the process of constantly increasing the efficiency of economic activity, individual human beings and nature itself, as a civilizing mission that would bring perpetual progress and improvement in the human condition. Much like their counterparts in Latin America, the American economic elite came to portray their continent's indigenous inhabitants who resisted the new economic system as barbaric opponents of civilization. It did not take a very great leap of reason to extend that definition to a much larger category of propertyless people who did not work – the unemployed.[34] In 1885 the economist David Wells went a step further, describing all those who talked of socialism and demanded the eight-hour day as new "barbarians" who were attacking civilization from within. Henry George warned of "carnivals of destruction" from "whence shall come the new barbarians . . ."[35] Such descriptions seemed particularly appropriate for the growing number of recent immigrants among the American workforce, who brought with them their own customs and languages and proved at least as resistant as their locally born comrades to changes in the work environment. In place of workers' denunciations of exploitation and speedup, corporate reformers defined the struggle as one over efficiency and productivity. Business leaders had in fact redefined the meaning of labor: "In business rhetoric, the term *labor* increasingly signified merely a large unwashed class of dependent, selfish wage earners, rather than the broader antebellum definition of a public-spirited citizenry of small freeholders, shopkeepers, laborers and artisans."[36] A critical group involved in these struggles over the work place and debates over defining America was the American middle class.

Professional engineers emerged as the driving force in the design of machinery and rules to capture greater control of the work process for man-

33 Frank Vanderlip to Henry Bell, New York City, September 22, 1919, File B-1-8, Vanderlip Papers.
34 Trachtenberg, *Incorporation of America*, pp. 34, 74.
35 Ibid., p. 48.
36 Sarah Lyons Watts, *Order Against Chaos: Business Culture and Labor Ideology in America, 1880–1915* (Westport, Conn.: Greenwood Press, 1991), p. 4.

agement and to heighten efficiency. Their work soon spread beyond the work place as they applied their techniques of scientific research and analysis to corporate structures themselves, designing systems of scientific management that affected every aspect of corporate function from the board room to the shop floor. Working in tandem with the engineers in shaping the modern American corporation came cadres of accountants, whose new accounting methods and controls gave managers effective new mechanisms for shaping virtually every aspect of corporate operations.[37] These new professionals, precursors of the "confidential employees" so essential to the management of American corporations in Latin America, had emerged from the old middle class.

During the last quarter of the nineteenth century, the American middle class of independent professionals, small business people, farmers and white collar employees began to undergo a significant transformation. Many of these people, like James Hawley, a Democratic lawyer and politician from Idaho, had been allies of workers. But they began to perceive threats to their own survival in the intensifying struggle between labor and capital. Hawley, for example, abandoned his role as a defender of mine workers to become a prosecutor of labor organizers and a law and order activist. This shift in allegiance changed the balance of power in communities, and "whereas in the 1870s industrialists had often been ostracized and opposed as 'alien' influences, by the 1890s it was workers who began to find themselves isolated from previous sources of community support."[38] This transformation of the middle class and its impact intensified in succeeding decades.

A culture of professionalism came to permeate the descendents of the old middle class. Challenges to the survival of small business and the loosening of community strictures and ties gave rise to professions and professional associations which defined the ground rules for individual ambition. Beyond glorifying and routinizing the paths of individual achievement, the new professionals became the models of the modern organization man.[39] The United Fruit Company captured the essence of the new professional in its eulogy to accountant Norman L. Haring, who died

---

37 Harry Braverman, *Labor and Monopoly Capital: The Degradation of Work in the Twentieth Century* (New York: Monthly Review Press, 1974), pp. 100–131; David Montgomery, *Workers' Control in America: Studies in the History of Work, Technology, and Labor Studies* (Cambridge: Cambridge University Press, 1979), pp. 33–37; David Noble, *America by Design: Science, Technology and the Rise of Corporate Capitalism* (New York: Knopf, 1977); Chandler, *Visible Hand*, pp. 94–208; Dan Clawson, *Bureaucracy and the Work Process: The Transformation of U.S. Industry, 1860–1920* (New York: Monthly Review Press, 1980), pp. 182–253.

38 Melvyn Dubofsky, *Industrialism and the American Worker, 1865–1920* (New York: Crowell, 1975), p. 49; Dubofsky, *We Shall Be All*, p. 38.

39 Bledstein, *Culture of Professionalism*, p. 105; Barbara Ehrenreich and John Ehrenreich, "The Professional Managerial Class," in Pat Walker, ed., *Between Labor and Capital* (Boston: South End Press, 1979), p. 19.

while trying to rescue company records from a warehouse fire. As the firm noted:

> An inspection made of the accounts of Mr. Haring developed that every transaction up to . . . the time the fire broke out, was in excellent shape and it was possible to resume work on the books as soon as the fire was extinguished. The condition of the books was highly commendable and a tribute to the manner in which the accounting work of the Company was carried on by Mr. Haring.[40]

Beyond dedication to the corporation and its rationalized procedures, the new professionals saw their central role as harmonizing the conflicting interests of capital and labor. Such a momentous task meant rationalizing not only corporations but the entire social order. That effort found myriad expressions, including the revamping of the work place and management structures by engineers and accountants, schemes for social engineering promoted by groups such as the YMCA, and the broader appeals for reformed public policy from the Progressive political movement.[41] While the attempts of the new professionals to modify the harsher aspects of the new industrial order occasionally brought them into conflict with businessmen, on the whole the middle class through the process of professionalization legitimized the discourse of the business elite, which "joined morality to utility and technocracy and in doing so reintegrated political, economic and intellectual authority for the twentieth century."[42] The professional middle class and corporate leaders came to share a set of principles that centered on rationalization of the work place and society with the goal of perfecting individual humans as instruments of production. As the Progressive politician and businessman Arthur Lovett Garford explained, ". . . we must analyze the human mind and body carefully and see in what way it [*sic*] can be brought up to the highest state of productive ability."[43] Those ideas represented a shift in emphasis in the way many corporate leaders approached the problem of the working class.

Unlike their Latin American counterparts, U.S. business leaders did not view the national working class as utterly irredeemable. Unlike the largely Indian and mestizo popular classes of Latin America, the majority of American workers were of European origin and therefore could be viewed as "racially sound." As an alternative to the conflicts that racked American industry, and anticipating their strategies in Latin America, businessmen offered a new order that accommodated workers within the corporate environment. Firms such as General Electric instituted pro-

---

40 *UNIFRUTCO*, July 1931.

41 Ehrenreich and Ehrenreich, "Managerial Class," pp. 19–24; Emily Rosenberg, *Spreading the American Dream: American Economic and Cultural Expansion, 1890–1945* (New York: Hill and Wang, 1982), p. 109.

42 Watts, *Order Against Chaos*, p. 14.

43 Rumbarger, *Prohibition*, p. 171.

grams that combined social welfare benefits, recognition of organized labor, pay incentives and "joint control" policies in an effort to transform workers into "an efficient adjusted part of the corporate mechanism." Eventually the reformers would even penetrate the homes of their employees in an effort to encourage such conformity.[44]

The anti-saloon and prohibition movements represented one effort by businessmen to reshape American society and especially the American working person into a more efficient factor of production. In 1893 the Committee of Fifty for the Investigation of the Liquor Problem was formed. Its membership included Jacob Schiff, of the Kuhn Loeb financial house, and William E. Dodge, who had come to share his father's concern with temperance. When two decades of anti-saloon campaigns failed to rid American workers of their fondness for drink, corporate reformers such as Frank Vanderlip, along with Protestant activists, social reformers and the Progressive political movement, launched what became a successful campaign for prohibition.[45] But by the end of the nineteenth century corporate leaders offered more than moral platitudes about sobriety and responsibility to workers, and ideals of efficiency and professionalism to the middle class.

In the 1890s the emphasis in American corporate culture began to shift from themes of self-denial and hard work as morally justified to the material rewards of such behavior. As William Leach has described it, "The cardinal features of this culture were acquisition and consumption as the means of achieving happiness; the cult of the new; the democratization of desire; and money value as the predominant measure of all value in society."[46]

Some of these ideas had deep roots in American history. Since colonial times Americans had accustomed themselves to thinking of their nation as the New World; to the religiously devout, the New Jerusalem. So too the accumulation of wealth had long served as the principal determinant of success and social status. But these concepts now took on a new intensity and were placed in the service of corporate culture. There they blended with the idea that the acquisition of material goods in itself constituted the achievement of personal fulfillment, a good life suffused by an aura of contentment. And while real disparities in wealth could not be banished, Americans would all enjoy the right to long for and strive for the acquisition of consumer products.

The new aspects of American corporate culture served a number of practical purposes. They offered a partial solution to the overabundance of products generated by American industry. Access to a growing array of goods and services also offered some compensation to workers and members of

---

44 Montgomery, *Workers' Control*, pp. 10–44; Noble, *America by Design*, pp. 286–87.
45 Rumbarger, *Prohibition*, pp. 89–181.
46 Leach, *Land of Desire*, p. 3.

the middle class who had lost economic independence as employees of large corporations. At the same time the opportunity to purchase consumer products offered a secular incentive to both groups to work hard and save in order to acquire these elements of the good life. Indeed, by the 1920s labor unions gave high wages which allowed increased consumption priority over earlier demands for a shorter work week.[47] This new consumer culture served as a powerful symbol of American corporate success, which won the admiration of people around the globe. Yet there remained a dark side to the American dream.

At the end of the century American leaders still held a low opinion of people alien to their own corporate culture. Anglo-Saxon racialism, which permeated American society and justified the war against Mexico in the middle of the nineteenth century, took on a new intensity and meaning in subsequent decades. Social Darwinism and "scientific" racism provided new evidence to support a new mission. The Anglo-Saxon republic would no longer seek territorial acquisitions. Instead it would subordinate and transform inferior races through the force of American corporate culture. The instruments of mass culture such as Buffalo Bill's Wild West Show and the movies of D. W. Griffith popularized this view, disseminating images of a civilized white race in mortal combat against the barbarism of inferior races.[48] It was a message that became part of the American mission to the world.

At the turn of the century American corporate culture entered upon a global mission. It carried to the world its unique blend of the most advanced technologies and work methods of the second industrial revolution with longstanding American values of individualism and competitiveness as well as an intensified concern with the new and the acquisitive values of a consumer society. That culture also contained the powerful vision of a society grounded in individual freedom, opportunity and achievement. At the same time it imposed rigorous requirements for corporate control of the work place, the intensified disciplining of workers and the promotion of individual ambition and consumerism in place of community relations and values. Together these requirements imposed on individuals and communities the need for perpetual change and adaptation in response to the corporate demands for ever greater efficiency in the productive process. Embedded within the ideology of this mission lay the contradictory tenet that American corporate culture would better societies composed of inherently inferior human beings. Whatever its flaws and contradictions, American corporate culture would have a profound effect on Latin America as the United States rapidly emerged as the dominant foreign economic power in the region.

47 Ibid., pp. 5–16; Gary Cross, *Time and Money: The Making of Consumer Culture* (London: Routledge, 1993), p. 79.

48 Rosenberg, *American Dream,* pp. 14–37.

The changes that transformed the American work place and American society by the turn of the century provided tremendous competitive advantages to U.S. corporations in the world market. American companies now challenged their international competitors with new scientifically designed management techniques that improved administrative efficiency, and new production technologies and work processes that could produce massive quantities of goods of consistent quality. New marketing and merchandising techniques that encouraged mass consumption complemented this large-scale production process. Those advantages became manifest in the growth of American trade with Latin America.[49]

U.S. exports to Latin America grew from $64 million in 1880 to $348 million in 1913. By the latter date petroleum, chemicals, metals manufactures and machinery accounted for nearly 50 percent of all U.S. manufactured exports to South America. Not surprisingly, these product groups that led the American export surge came from industries that ranked high both in terms of degree of mechanization and levels of corporate concentration.[50] These same forces that expanded American trade contributed to the creation of an American investment empire. Technological advances, new forms of corporate organization and advanced marketing techniques which encouraged American corporations to compete in world trade also provided powerful advantages for U.S. foreign investment. While U.S. trade with Latin America grew by 750 percent between 1900 and 1929, direct investments in approximately the same period shot up by 1,200 percent, from $320 million to $5.2 billion.[51]

As of 1929, electric, sugar, mining and petroleum companies accounted for 70 percent of American direct investment in Latin America. The predominance of some of these sectors is partly understandable in

49 John H. Dunning, "Changes in the Level and Structure of International Production: The Last One Hundred Years," in Mark Casson, ed., *The Growth of International Business* (London: Allen and Unwin, 1983), p. 86; Mira Wilkins, *The Maturing of Multinational Enterprise: American Business Abroad from 1914 to 1970* (Cambridge: Harvard University Press, 1974), pp. 3–4; Rosenberg, *American Dream*, pp. 15–23.

50 U.S. Department of Commerce, Bureau of the Census, *The Statistical History of the United States: Colonial Times to 1957* (Stamford, Conn.: Fairfield Publishers, 1965), pp. 904, 906; William H. Becker, *The Dynamics of Business–Government Relations: Industry and Exports, 1893–1921* (Chicago: University of Chicago Press, 1982), p. 13; Harry Jerome, *Mechanization in Industry* (New York: National Bureau of Economic Research, 1934), p. 269. U.S. trade statistics for Mexico and Cuba, America's leading trading partners in the region, reveal a similar pattern. In 1912 machinery, metals manufactures and chemicals accounted for nearly 40 percent of all imports from the United States and over two-thirds of all manufactured imports. In Cuba these same products accounted for about 30 percent of all U.S. imports. Mary Locke Eysenbach, *American Manufactured Exports, 1879–1914: A Study of Growth and Comparative Advantage* (New York: Arno, 1976), pp. 211–13; U.S. House of Representatives, Doc. 1452, 62d Conf., 3d sess., vol. 1, *Commercial Relations of the United States with Foreign Countries During the Year 1912* (Washington, D.C.: Government Printing Office, 1914), pp. 17, 108–9, 138.

51 J. Fred Rippy, *Globe and Hemisphere: Latin America's Place in the Postwar Foreign Relations of the United States* (1958) (Westport, Conn.: Greenwood Press, 1972), pp. 39–40.

light of the effects of changes in the American economy. Sugar production responded to the burgeoning consumer market in the United States. In addition, the growing domestic demand for mineral products transformed the United States from a net exporter to a net importer of minerals by 1920.[52] Beyond meeting the needs of the national economy, corporations also responded to firm-specific factors. Four of the most compelling forces that prompted corporations to invest overseas were access to sources of supply, efforts to maintain or expand market share, the drive to protect technologies and efforts to reduce risk through geographical diversification. While the significance of any single factor depended on the type of company involved, most corporations found themselves driven by more than one of these forces for overseas investment.[53]

The United Fruit Company appeared to be a classic example of a firm driven by concerns of market share. United and its one serious competitor, Standard Fruit, developed from the increasingly specialized commodity trade with the Caribbean Basin. Initially they relied on purchases of fruit from local growers and successful marketing in the United States to build their business. However, by the 1920s the American fruit companies, or *fruteras,* had taken direct control of most of the banana plantations of Central America in an effort to gain more effective control over quality and supply of the product. The fruteras' ability to achieve quality control of a highly perishable commodity led them to integrate backward into the production process. The United Fruit Company, which controlled the lion's share of banana production and marketing in the Caribbean Basin, reported assets of $242 million in 1930. The company's 295 square miles dedicated to banana cultivation represented a small portion of nearly 3.5 million acres which it leased or owned in the region.[54] In a somewhat similar fashion, Standard Oil of New Jersey initially headed overseas as a result of market considerations.

Standard Oil built its position in the United States prior to World War I by controlling transportation, refining and marketing outlets. Given the surplus of oil on the domestic market, Standard opened operations in foreign locations such as Mexico in order to expand its sales. Increasing world demand, however, placed a new emphasis on access to new sources of oil. As a result Standard turned to investments in overseas oil fields and

---

52 Ibid., p. 40; Neal Potter and Francis T. Christy Jr., *Trends in Natural Resource Commodities: Statistics of Prices, Output, Consumption, Foreign Trade and Employment in the United States, 1870–1957* (Baltimore: Johns Hopkins University Press, 1962), pp. 19, 112.

53 Wilkins, *Maturing of Multinational Enterprise,* pp. 60–128; Rosenberg, *American Dream,* 23–28.

54 Charles David Kepner Jr., *Social Aspects of the Banana Industry* (New York: Columbia University Press, 1936), pp. 17, 21; Robert Read, "The Growth and Structure of Multinationals in the Banana Export Trade," in Mark Casson, ed., *The Growth of International Business* (London: Allen and Unwin, 1983), pp. 180–213; Mark Casson, "Transaction Costs and the Theory of the Multinational Enterprise," in Alan M. Rugman, ed., *New Theories of the Multinational Enterprise* (New York: St. Martin's, 1982), pp. 34–43.

production facilities, including some in Mexico and Peru, during World War I.[55]

In contrast to the market-led strategies of the fruit and oil companies, mining and sugar corporations were driven primarily by supply considerations. After the turn of the century, American investors with financing from J. P. Morgan formed the Cerro de Pasco Corporation to develop Peru's mining wealth. The American Smelting and Refining Company and the Vanadium Corporation soon joined Cerro de Pasco in the Peruvian mining sector, accounting for 97 percent of Peru's mineral exports by 1929. In Chile, the Guggenheims led the way in penetrating the mining sector. In addition to the Braden Copper Company, which the brothers capitalized at $23 million, they formed the Chile Copper Company with $95 million in stock to develop Chuquicamata, a mountain with hundreds of millions of tons of copper ore. Yet more than simple issues of supplying the domestic market drove these enterprises overseas. The opportunity to exploit new technologies in low-cost labor markets also played a central role. The development of the Braden and Chuquicamata mines revolutionized the technology of the antiquated Chilean mining industry. El Teniente, the principal Braden mine, was the first in the world to apply the flotation process in concentrating low-grade ores. Further north, huge mechanical shovels carved Chuquicamata into the largest open-pit mine in the world, while the brothers' engineers developed a new refining technique to treat its ore.[56]

In Cuba, American investments reached $1.3 billion by 1925, with over half committed to the sugar industry. Large American-controlled corporations such as the Punta Alegre Sugar Company dominated the industry and the island's economy. Part of that effort was a massive renovation of the production process, with fifty-three new *centrales,* or refineries, built between 1924 and 1927. Cuba also became a focus of investment for one of America's leading technology-driven corporations, General Electric.

By 1919 G. E. had established a significant presence in the international economy with plants on four continents and holdings in a number of overseas affiliates. During the 1920s the company pursued a policy of buying into every major foreign electric corporation. G. E.'s efforts served

55 George Philip, *Oil and Politics in Latin America: Nationalist Movements and State Companies* (Cambridge: Cambridge University Press, 1982), pp. 7–11.

56 On U.S. investment in Peruvian mining in this period, see Adrian De Wind Jr., "Peasants Become Miners: The Evolution of Industrial Mining Systems in Peru" (Ph.D. dissertation, Columbia University, 1977); Alberto Flores Galindo, *Los mineros de la Cerro de Pasco, 1900–1930* (Lima: Pontífica Universidad Católica del Perú, 1974); Florencia Mallon, *The Defense of Community in Peru's Central Highlands: Peasant Struggle and Capitalist Transition, 1860–1940* (Princeton: Princeton University Press, 1983); Elizabeth Dore, *The Peruvian Mining Industry: Growth, Stagnation, and Crisis* (Boulder, Colo.: Westview Press, 1988). On Chile, see Thomas F. O'Brien, " 'Rich Beyond the Dreams of Avarice': The Guggenheims in Chile," *Business History Review* 63 (Spring 1989), pp. 129–31.

to protect its technology by using subsidiaries to defend its patent rights in foreign countries. But its overseas investments served other purposes as well. They allowed the company to stabilize markets and concentrate on research, as well as reduce its risks through international diversification.[57] Where large corporate partners were not available to facilitate this strategy, such as in Latin America, G. E. simply invested directly in power systems. In 1923 the overseas expansion of G. E.'s subsidiary EBASCO prompted the creation of the American and Foreign Power Company, or AFP, which took control of all EBASCO's foreign investments. In turn, AFP could safely exploit G. E.'s technical advantages in overseas markets. Between 1922 and 1933 the company invested over $100 million in Cuba and transferred to the island the latest scientific technology in electrical generation and the new scientific management methods. By 1930 G. E.'s AFP subsidiary had invested approximately $500 million in eleven Latin American countries.[58]

The factors which propelled these companies overseas also helped shape their relations with their host societies. While the fruit companies would largely be concerned with recruiting unskilled workers and disciplining them to the demands of the early industrial work place, General Electric had far more concern with skilled workers and trained managers. Mining and sugar companies sought a workforce that spanned the spectrum from unskilled laborer to professional manager. Thus while many Latin Americans shared a common experience of being recruited by American companies, they often encountered distinct work environments. At the same time, while most Latin Americans were not directly affected by work in the American corporate environment, the enormous impact which mining and fruit companies had on local economies made them important issues in debates over national development. Conversely, utilities like G. E. might not play as dominant a role in the national economy, but much of the national population became familiar with them as symbols of American corporate culture because of their consumer services. Nor were large direct investors the only purveyors of American corporate culture. Latin Americans also encountered it in consumer products from canned food to cars, were enthralled by its mass entertainment device, the motion picture, and at times inspired by its institutions of reform such as the YMCA. Whatever the eventual popular reactions to these encounters, it is clear that American companies arrived in Latin America driven not only by their own self-interest but attracted by elite pleadings for their investment.

57 Mira Wilkins, *The Emergence of Multinational Enterprise: American Business Abroad from the Colonial Era to 1914* (Cambridge: Harvard University Press, 1970), pp. 93–96, and *Maturing of Multinational Enterprise*, pp. 65–68, 131–33.

58 "American & Foreign Power Company Inc.: History of the Company," pp. 1–36, Box 145445, EBASCO; Oscar Pino Santos, *El asalto a Cuba por la oligarquía financiera yanqui* (Mexico City: Editorial Nuestro Tiempo, 1975), pp. 44–76; Louis Banigan to William Phillips, New York, December 6, 1933, 837.6463 EB&S Co./11, RG 59, USNA.

After midcentury the forces of popular resistance in Latin America began to retreat before the advances of a more coherent and determined oligarchy. The 1850s witnessed a series of victories for those forces promoting development based on free market economics. In 1855 the Mexican Liberals seized power and after fifteen years of internal strife and foreign invasion consolidated their authority under Porfirio Díaz. Justo José de Urquiza's overthrow of Juan Manuel de Rosas in 1852 shifted Argentina in the direction of strong central government and liberal economics. In Guatemala the presidency of Justo Rufino Barrios (1871–1885) marked the definitive triumph of liberalism.

The liberals who came to power in this period set about the task of nation building from a perspective shaped by post-independence struggles which they viewed as conflicts between a civilized elite and popular forces of barbarism. They interpreted these internal struggles over the future of their societies within the context of contemporary Social Darwinism. Domingo Sarmiento, the Argentine intellectual who had been the first to define his country's internal turmoil as a struggle between civilization and barbarism, assumed his nation's presidency in 1868. The nationalist ideologies which he and other liberal state builders constructed justified the encouragement of market forces and the suppression of indigenous protest in the name of order and progress. While these new leaders recognized the common historical and religious threads which ran through their societies, they tended to emphasize linguistic and cultural differences which divided them. Convinced of the innate inferiority of their own national populations, these architects of the new order in Latin America instituted a series of draconian measures to strip rural villages of their land and compel the population to work in commercial enterprises. Such policies pursued in the name of progress brought considerable change to Latin American societies.

These regimes quickly implemented or accelerated policies designed to privatize and commercialize the agrarian sector as part of a larger plan to create vibrant primary product export economies. Laws which broke peasant villages' control of the land served as the legal instruments for that policy in Mexico. By the 1870s Argentina's semi-nomadic gauchos had been reduced to wage laborers, while in Guatemala the state sanctioned and encouraged debt servitude and the gradual disintegration of communal villages.

The effects of commercialization rapidly manifested themselves as Latin America's foreign commerce grew by 43 percent between 1870 and 1884. The region's booming export economies needed markets, sources of imports, and rail and port development, as well as financing for their impoverished capital markets. British trade, banking and transportation systems dominated the international sector of most Latin American economies. Railways and public works projects which the British financed ensured lower-cost delivery of Latin American exports to the world market. But

British development of Latin America's infrastructure proved an insufficient answer to looming economic problems.

The great price depression which had driven down prices of manufactured goods and raw materials for a quarter of a century ended in 1897. But the end of the price depression did not necessarily reinvigorate prices for primary goods. This proved especially true for some of the leading commodities on which Latin American countries had built their export prosperity. The world price of sugar dropped steadily between the mid 1870s and the outbreak of World War I. The current price for sugar in 1922 was 25 percent lower than it had been in 1875. Copper had experienced an even more dramatic slump by 1925. So too coffee prices in the first two decades of the twentieth century fell well below levels recorded in the 1890s.[59] The impact of these losses in value were tempered in Latin America by increased output and declining exchange rates for national currencies. But it was clear that producers faced intensifying competition in what was fast becoming a global market place. It was a competitive struggle for which Latin American societies proved generally ill equipped.

During Latin America's prewar export boom the region's "productive structures were changed but slowly. With certain exceptions, they tended to remain characterized by low levels of productivity."[60] While low labor costs and natural advantages may account in part for the feeble efforts at renovation, the most pervasive factor was the strength and intractability of lord–peasant relations. Efforts to promote economic expansion faced a serious obstacle in the constricted supply of labor. Most Latin American peasants in the last quarter of the nineteenth century retained some access to the land, usually in the form of village property or squatter settlements. Large landowners and other entrepreneurial groups resorted to labor-repressive control mechanisms such as debt.

In Peru's Cerro de Pasco mining region the central government employed labor drafts and enforcement of *enganche* contracts (a form of debt peonage) to counter the labor scarcity resulting from the vibrance of the peasant economy. But "consistently, tenaciously and militantly, the peasantry resisted government and elite efforts to expand the market for labor . . ."[61] That resistance created bottlenecks in production and transportation that by 1900 seriously impeded efforts by local entrepreneurs to develop the area's mines. A similar labor scarcity affected the sugar- and cotton-producing estates of the coast. Peasant resistance

---

59 Orris C. Herfindahl, *Copper Costs and Prices: 1870–1957* (Baltimore: Johns Hopkins University Press, 1960), p. 203; Christopher J. Schmitz, *World Non-Ferrous Metal Production and Prices, 1700–1976* (London: Cass, 1979), pp. 290–91.

60 Bill Albert, *South America and the First World War: The Impact of the War on Brazil, Argentina, Peru and Chile* (Cambridge: Cambridge University Press, 1988), p. 11.

61 Mallon, *Defense of Community*, pp. 164–65.

stymied efforts by wool growers in the southern sierra to launch an enclosure movement.[62]

In Chile the traditional relations in the countryside took a different form but bore equally serious consequences for the generation of national wealth. The Chilean oligarchy dismantled the country's independent campesino economy in the first half of the nineteenth century, but the migratory lifestyle adopted by Chile's rural population became one means of resisting the disciplines of permanent wage labor. Unable to implement a meaningful wage labor system, hacendados and mine owners settled for a low-paid, ill-disciplined labor force. That compromise produced enterprises in both mining and agriculture characterized by labor intensity, low capital investment and minimal technical innovation.[63]

Mexican peasants went far beyond the more subtle forms of protest that marked Chile's rural society. Despite the imposition of the Porfirian dictatorship, peasant rebellions swept the Mexican countryside. As in Chile, the labor-repressive order of the rural sector carried over into mining, where traditional labor-intensive methods of production prevailed.[64]

The persistence of labor-intensive production systems in Latin American rural societies contributed to a web of interrelated problems for the region's economies even as export levels soared to new heights. As illustrated in the Chilean case, a labor-intensive rural order created problems of labor scarcity and control which carried over into mining. Labor-repressive mechanisms which obtained and controlled a scarce labor force were enormously expensive to run. The execution and enforcement of debt peonage and enganche labor systems drained off large amounts of private and public capital. That process contributed to a general problem of capital scarcity and poorly developed credit markets in Latin American countries which deterred efforts to upgrade national infrastructures and reinvest in production. Liberal reforms had swept away many elements of the old colonial order, fracturing the tie between church and state, privatizing church lands as well as many communal properties, and dissolving Spain's closed trading system. But many aspects of a privileged society remained.

62 Rosemary Thorp and Geoffrey Bertram, *Peru, 1890–1977: Growth and Policy in an Open Economy* (London: Macmillan, 1978), pp. 63–64; Peter Klarén, *Modernization, Dislocation, and Aprismo: Origins of the Peruvian Aprista Party, 1870–1932* (Austin: University of Texas Press, 1973), p. 25; Mallon, *Defense of Community*, pp. 165–66.

63 Arnold J. Bauer, *Chilean Rural Society from the Spanish Conquest to 1930* (Cambridge: Cambridge University Press, 1975), pp. 101–5, 159–61; Charles Bergquist, *Labor in Latin America: Comparative Essays on Chile, Argentina, Venezuela and Colombia* (Stanford: Stanford University Press, 1986), pp. 37–47.

64 John Mason Hart, *Revolutionary Mexico: The Coming and Process of the Mexican Revolution* (Berkeley and Los Angeles: University of California Press, 1987), pp. 41–51; Marvin D. Bernstein, *The Mexican Mining Industry, 1890–1950: A Study of the Interaction of Politics, Economics and Technology* (Albany: State University of New York Press, 1965), pp. 38–43, 49–60; American Institute of Mining and Metallurgical Engineers, *Transactions* 32 (1902), p. 58.

Liberal efforts to free up lands such as those in Mexico often contributed
to the further growth of large landed estates. State-devised schemes for
economic development often translated into the granting of monopolistic
privileges to foreign or domestic business interests. In a more intangible
way, Latin American countries had not yet fully developed political or legal systems which encouraged individualistic, competitive social and economic environments. Family connections and substantial economic resources remained essential ingredients to success. The persistence of these
barriers to development in the face of intensifying international economic
competition cast doubt on the viability of the entire liberal project of national development.

After the turn of the century a variety of social groups began to call
into question the efficacy of the elite's liberal program. Peasant communities still defended village lands and the peasant communal societies which
they underpinned. As had occurred in an earlier epoch in the United
States, an incipient working class as well as elements of the petite bourgeoisie began to challenge the headlong plunge into a market economy. In
Latin America those critiques evolved from a number of perspectives, including Marxism, Anarchosyndicalism, Populism and those that claimed
indigenous roots. These movements' often idealized versions of the past
and the future offered popular alternatives to the project of liberal modernization. Like a specter from the post-independence era, popular mobilization came to haunt the dreams of the elite at the turn of the century.

The diverse groups that comprised the sources of popular protest interacted in varying combinations and alliances at the beginning of the twentieth century to disrupt the apparent social calm of Latin America. An alliance of peasants, workers and petite bourgeoisie destroyed the Díaz
regime in Mexico. Cuban workers and elements of the middle class jointly
protested discrimination and exploitation in the work place. Small shopkeepers, planters and workers struck out at the established order in Central America. Operating independently of one another, nitrate workers in
Chile's North and urban workers and middle-class elements in the capital
staged massive protests against harsh working conditions and inflation.
At least initially, the elite could denounce most of the protest ideologies
as alien dogmas and deal with the most recalcitrant protesters with force.
But popular nationalism, with its more inclusive vision of the nation and
its emphasis on social and economic justice, had begun to challenge the
elite's grip on national political discourse. The oligarchy's ability to reject
or suppress challenges to the existing order now depended on its ability to
continue generating economic growth. Latin America's liberal regimes
found themselves caught between popular social mobilization that challenged them politically and social productive systems that threatened to
undermine economic growth and with it the legitimacy of the regimes.
Breaking down the obstacles to improved efficiency became critical to the
survival of the existing order.

The transformation of the production process provided the basis for the unprecedented success of American corporations in Latin America at this time. With their enormous increases in output and efficiency, American companies held out the promise of seemingly endless improvements in material well-being. American companies resuscitated the mining industries of Chile and Peru, they made Mexico a raw materials giant producing everything from copper to henequen to petroleum, and assured Cuba and Central America of leading roles in the world commodities market. They provided Latin American countries with modern electric power and telephone networks while offering high wages, housing and medical assistance to their workers. Many of these accomplishments were grounded in new, more efficient technologies and, at least as important, a vision of humans in the work place that differed radically from the one then prevailing in Latin America. An American consular official graphically described that distinction:

... in Chili, as in practically every Spanish speaking country, man in the eyes of the governing classes, possesses no commercial value, not even at all in comparison with the economic value of a jackass. In these countries the ruling classes cannot and will not appreciate that man, in the economy of the nation, is an automated machine representing a capital value ... [65]

The influence of American corporations also spread beyond the work place as they offered their workers and the Latin American people as a whole new commodities, new forms of entertainment and, perhaps most importantly, a new vision of the future. They projected a vision of societies in which individuals with their skills honed to a fine edge would create an era of unprecedented material abundance within a social environment marked by individual freedom and achievement. Given its accomplishments and its promises, it is little wonder that American corporate culture proved intensely attractive for millions of Latin Americans. Yet the changes wrought by American corporate culture also became a source of serious challenges and threats to the new American empire.

As American multinationals conveyed the broad array of factors that constituted American corporate culture to Latin America, they would encounter resistance from sources that spanned the social spectrum. For much of the workforce in Latin America, which was in transition from peasant to proletarian status, American corporations represented their first experience with the rigors and regimen of industrial labor. Many of these same workers found themselves totally dependent on market forces for their incomes and the products which they now relied on for subsistence. They frequently struck out directly at these institutions of modern capitalism while attempting to define their relationship to the new reality.

65 J. Perkins Shanks, "Labour Situation in Northern Chile," Antofagasta, September 3, 1921, RG 84, USNA.

For workers with more experience in the modern work place, efforts to break down cooperative work practices and speed up work rhythms became points of contention, just as they had for American workers. Furthermore, for a variety of reasons, American companies usually made minimalist efforts to implement industrial welfare programs. Agricultural enterprises required relatively few skilled workers whom companies felt compelled to accommodate with strong support services, and for extractive industries in general their workforce did not represent a potential consumer market to be created with higher wages. Finally, most corporate managers remained convinced that their Latin American workers' racial inferiority constrained the beneficial impact of these programs. And, as had occurred in American society, corporate commitment to unremitting change and challenges to concepts of community and closely held norms triggered opposition from multiclass alliances.

American multinationals created an array of challenges to small business people in Latin America. Local merchants from Central America to Peru faced economic extinction as American corporations internalized local commodity markets. Petty commodity producers in Central America and Cuba found themselves reduced to little more than contract employees for American agribusiness giants. Rationalization and professionalization challenged the patriarchal environment in which Latin American managers had operated. And these middle-class groups, like the workers, faced the new realities and vagaries of consumerism. The fact that foreign corporations inserted this new order gave the petite bourgeoisie and workers a common nationalist rallying point.

U.S. companies became important symbols for popular forces seeking to press forward with a new nationalism focused on social and economic justice. The elite found itself hard pressed to define popular nationalism directed against American companies as an alien dogma. Furthermore, Latin American oligarchies discovered that American investment was a mixed blessing. The ability of American corporations to renovate selected economic sectors exacerbated existing disparities within national economies. American control often excluded local elites from direct participation in these prosperous sectors. Elements of the elite would at times second popular protests against American companies out of a real sense of grievance or out of political opportunism. But even more fundamental in stirring those responses were American ideas of what constituted the most important human values.

For American business leaders the ideal human was one who had an unrelenting commitment to change to the new, dispensing with the old and the outmoded in order to absorb more goods, services and experiences. For Latin Americans this seeming obsession with change and consumption ran counter to the importance they placed on long-held values and relationships, which often revolved around family and community and a sense of connection with a past which helped define them and their societies.

These differences took on critical importance as Latin Americans became involved in long and protracted struggles which would determine the degree to which they would absorb, modify and reject American corporate culture. During the first decades of the twentieth century that complex process often took on dramatic, sometimes violent, forms which heavily influenced the history of Latin American nations.

American culture had a compelling appeal for Latin Americans, while it also presented challenges to groups that spanned the Latin American social spectrum from workers and peasants to elites. When the Great Depression sharply curtailed the ability of American multinationals to generate material wealth, they became the focal point of protests by workers, peasants and small business people. These groups forged their own communities which challenged the harsher aspects of American corporate culture and the order and progress dictums of the elite with nationalist ideologies calling for the empowerment of the entire population and a national agenda emphasizing social welfare. These interactions between popular forces and American corporate culture played a central role in defining inter-American relations and contemporary Latin American societies.

PART II

Marines and cultural revolution in Central America

Map 2.1. Central America.

2

Liberal revolutions and corporate culture

Central America and the islands of the Caribbean with their enormous resources must be brought into use at least as effectively as the Mississippi Valley. The United Fruit seems to be the agent in subduing disease, developing many of the resources, and ultimately leading the way to political and social order. (Judge G. W. Anderson)

For some time now, most of the inhabitants of this north coast of Honduras have been feeling asfixiated; this asfixiation has been caused by the extortion of the United Fruit Company, *a ruthless banana company that day after day absorbs the energies of these young people who are striving for greater progress and well being. (Romulo López, independent banana grower)*

A confidential report to Secretary of State Frank B. Kellogg in 1928 painted a grim picture of two decades of U.S. intervention in Nicaragua. After repeated attempts to create a rationalized state – and social stability – American policymakers found themselves grappling with a national administration at least as corrupt as its predecessors. Meanwhile, U.S. marines trudged across the rugged Nicaraguan countryside in a frustrating effort to crush the rebellion led by Augusto Sandino. The report's author, William Cumberland, the international economist for the State Department, concluded:

In its contact with backward peoples the United States stands for roads, schools, public health facilities and those other material improvements which are reflected in security, wealth, literacy, health and progress. Our record in Nicaragua is not up to the mark. . . . It is . . . humiliating to see such countries as Salvador and Costa Rica, in which American political control does not exist, surpass in real achievement, Nicaragua, in which we have intervened for many years.[1]

Honduras, Nicaragua's northern neighbor, represented the other extreme in American relations with Central America.

---

1 William W. Cumberland to secretary of state, Managua, March 10, 1928, 817.51/1921, General Records of the Department of State Relating to the Internal Affairs of Nicaragua, 1910–29, rl. 89, M-632, RG 59, USNA.

47

While less materially developed than some of its neighbors, Honduras had emerged as the world's leading producer of bananas. And if its political stability left something to be desired, it did not require the presence of thousands of U.S. marines. In Honduras it was not the State Department, but American corporations, which held sway. As the American chargé in Honduras concluded, "The United [Fruit Company] controls the Honduran Government to an unprecedented and incredible extent."[2] In the extremes of Nicaragua and Honduras could be discerned the complex series of relationships between the American state, American corporations and Central American societies that shaped events in the region during the early twentieth century. At the turn of the century, American corporations led United States penetration of Central America.

Although tax revenues from the banana industry remained negligible, American multinationals did bring infrastructure development to the Caribbean coastlines of Central American nations, increased their exports and helped finance their governments. By 1913 bananas accounted for over half of coffee-rich Costa Rica's exports. During the 1920s Guatemala, Honduras and Nicaragua tripled their exports of the fruit. The American *fruteras* also accounted for 800 of the 1,200 miles of national railways built in Central America, in addition to the hundreds of miles of track which they laid for their exclusive use. The companies also provided millions of dollars in loans to the frequently insolvent regimes of the region. From the perspective of Central American elites these benefits had been purchased at relatively low cost. Central American governments had made generous grants of land and rights of way along their forbidding tropical coasts that bordered the Caribbean Sea. Opportunity costs of land in those regions were near zero, meaning any benefits from the American investments fell on the plus side of the ledger.[3] But this favorable cost–benefit analysis left out other unforeseen consequences of American investment. The interaction between American multinationals and Central American republics had a destabilizing effect on local political processes, and the insertion of American corporate culture sparked social upheaval in these rural societies. That turmoil resulted from both the actions of the *fruteras* and the conditions which prevailed in individual Central American countries at the time of their arrival. Nicaragua represented one such case.

Nicaragua's conservative governments during the second half of the nineteenth century had, like their liberal neighbors, sought to commercialize the agrarian sector. This included the use of violence to discipline rural labor for regularized work on commercial estates. Nevertheless, the lack of sufficient labor to man the coffee *fincas* remained largely unre-

---

2 Lawrence Higgins to secretary of state, Tegucigalpa, November, 20, 1933, 815.00/4592, General Records of the Department of State Relating to the Internal Affairs of Honduras, 1930–39, RG 59, USNA.

3 Victor Bulmer-Thomas, *The Political Economy of Central America Since 1920* (Cambridge: Cambridge University Press, 1987), pp. 6–8, 16, 33.

solved and brought the liberals to power under José Santos Zelaya. The doubling of coffee exports during the liberal era demonstrated the success of Zelaya's efforts to reorganize rural society through the commercialization of agriculture. However, the rural population successfully resisted some of the more determined efforts of the liberals to discipline the workforce, setting the stage for Zelaya's downfall and U.S. military intervention. The intervention would only serve to exacerbate the conflict over implementing the liberal agenda, assuring continued domestic instability and long-term American involvement. Honduras may have been spared a similar level of violence and dislocation by the manner in which it resolved its own struggle over the agrarian question.[4]

For most of the nineteenth century, smallholder subsistence agriculture and a livestock industry that produced largely for export characterized the Honduran countryside. As late as the 1890s, the bulk of cultivated land in Honduras consisted of *ejidal,* or communal properties, worked by subsistence producers. Low population density and a rugged terrain aided the rural population in its successful resistance to liberal programs of modernization.[5] Not surprisingly, the enfeebled elite came to depend heavily on American business to overcome their own failure to insert agrarian capitalism into Honduras.

The divergent paths of liberal revolutions in Central America created distinct environments in which local social forces would interact with the energies of corporate America. The continuing struggle over the liberal agenda in Nicaragua led to conditions hostile to the rapid growth of American investment. In Honduras the failure of the liberal experiment left an enfeebled elite that would depend heavily on American corporations for its growth. It was into these distinct settings that the dynamism of American corporate culture would pour in the late nineteenth century.

In 1870 the Honduran consul in New York, Ephraim George Squier, complained to the U.S. State Department, "The Government of Honduras sees with regret the decline of American interests in its own and adjacent territories . . ."[6] Squier's comment reflected the fact that protected American industries had found an ever expanding internal market to occupy their energies after the Civil War. What Squier could not foresee were the momentous changes that were about to alter that state of affairs.

---

4 Benjamin I. Teplitz, "The Political and Economic Foundations of Modernization in Nicaragua: The Administration of José Santos Zelaya, 1893–1909" (Ph.D. dissertation, Howard University, 1973), pp. 182–233.

5 José Guevara-Escudero, "Nineteenth-Century Honduras: A Regional Approach to the Economic History of Central America, 1839–1914" (Ph.D. dissertation, New York University, 1983), pp. 38–54, 57, 228.

6 Ephraim Squier to Department of State, n.p., n.d., File 48, Box 1b, Squier Papers. Internal evidence suggests the letter was written in 1870.

Americans had turned their attention to the Central American isthmus time and again because of its potential as a transit route. From William Aspinwall's Panama railroad to Cornelius Vanderbilt's Nicaraguan transit concession, the region's narrow configuration held the promise of more efficient connections between America's East and West coasts and easier access to world markets. Despite the focus of American manufacturers on the domestic market in the postwar period, transportation and communication interests soon turned toward Central America once again.

By the end of the 1880s, the American-owned Central and South American Telegraph Company had extended its cable network to the region, and the Maritime Canal Company had obtained a concession for a Nicaraguan canal. Following close on their heels came American shipping and merchant interests. The American firm of W. R. Grace and Company established shipping and mercantile links with such countries as Guatemala and Costa Rica. The activities of the Grace firm reflected the increasing vibrance of the region's coffee export economies. Sam Weil and Company and Brown and Harris were just two of a dozen or more New Orleans merchant houses which had set up operations at Nicaragua's Atlantic port of Bluefields by 1890. Their interests represented a link with the region's economies which was being forged by the increasing specialization of American merchants.

In America's antebellum economy, William Earl Dodge's focus on tin imports and cotton exports and Moses Taylor's preoccupation with the sugar trade typified a shift by merchants from diversified commercial transactions toward product specialization. That trend had affected the traditional West Indian carrying trade by the 1870s. In 1876 Lorenzo D. Baker, a Boston sea captain, helped form the Standard Steam Navigation Company, a pioneering step in the creation of companies specializing in the banana trade. By that time American sailing vessels were already making spot purchases of the tropical fruit on the Central American coast.[7] This further acceleration of trade with the area, combined with the desire of liberal regimes to encourage foreign investment, led to a growing number of direct U.S. investments in Central America.

In Nicaragua, Sam Weil had obtained several lucrative mining concessions by the end of the century. The Valentines, a New York merchant family, received a mining concession from the Honduran government and established the New York and Rosario Mining Company in 1880. The firm became the largest mining operation in Honduras. In addition, the Valentines secured control of the wharf and railway at Puerto Cortés on Honduras' Atlantic coast.[8] In 1870 the Costa Rican government, anxious

---

7 Read, "Banana Export Trade," pp. 183–84.
8 Kenneth Finney, "Precious Metal Mining and the Modernization of Honduras: In Quest of El Dorado (1880–1900)" (Ph.D. dissertation, Tulane University, 1973), p. 13; Thomas L. Karnes, *Tropical Enterprise: The Standard Fruit and Steamship Company in Latin America* (Baton Rouge: Louisiana State University Press, 1978), p. 15; Charles A. Brand, "The Background of Capitalistic Underdevelopment: Honduras to 1913" (Ph.D. dissertation, University of Pittsburgh, 1972), p. 55.

to export coffee from its tropical Caribbean coast, turned to the American railroad entrepreneur Henry Meiggs.

The task of building a railroad from the Costa Rican capital of San José to Puerto Limón fell to Meiggs' nephew, Minor C. Keith. To help finance the venture, Keith began planting bananas on lands granted as part of the railway concession. By the 1890s Keith had become the world's leading banana producer, and his interests had spread from Costa Rica to Panama, Colombia and Nicaragua. In 1899 Keith merged his interests with those of the Boston Fruit Company, the successor to Lorenzo Baker's earlier enterprise, to form the United Fruit Company.[9] After the turn of the century, United Fruit extended its operations into Honduras and Guatemala. In Honduras, United Fruit would compete with two New Orleans–based enterprises, the Vaccaro Brothers, a produce firm that had entered the banana trade in 1899, and Samuel Zemurray's Cuyamel Fruit Company. By 1910 total direct American investments in Honduras and Nicaragua had reached at least $20 million.[10] This large influx of American capital had been anxiously encouraged by Central American elites.

Liberal schemes for modernization included foreign capital as a fundamental part of their programs. Concessions to American entrepreneurs expanded transportation facilities, developed capital-intensive sectors such as mining, exploited the resources of inhospitable tropical coastlands and generally compensated for the capital impoverishment of Central American governments. Furthermore, these foreign companies could be left to grapple with the large segment of the rural population which still spurned employment on coffee estates and clung to local villages and their subsistence forms of agriculture.

At first the fruteras bore a greater resemblance to the British merchant houses that preceded them in Latin America than the technology-based American multinationals which followed them. Their initial relations with Central America rested on commercial exchange, some limited infrastructure improvements and a relatively undifferentiated management

9 Read, "Banana Export Trade," pp. 186–93; Ernest Dale Owen to secretary of state, New York, February 10, 1911, 317.115B62/99, RG 59, USNA.

10 Cleona Lewis, *America's Stake in International Investments* (Washington, D.C.: Brookings Institution, 1938), pp. 575–606; Brand, "Capitalistic Underdevelopment," pp. 104–5, 163; Gene Sheldon Yeager, "Honduras, Transportation and Communication Development: The Rise of Tegucigalpa, 1876–1900" (Master's thesis, Tulane University, 1972), pp. 74–75; Karnes, *Tropical Enterprise,* p. 32; Ernest Dale Owen to secretary of state, New York, February 10, 1911, 317.115B62/99, RG 59, USNA; "Cuyamel Fruit Company," Scudder Collection; Otto Schoenrich to Secretary of State William J. Bryan, Managua, January 4, 1915, 417.00/220, RG 59, USNA; Emery Claim, Case 146/43, 125, rl. 26, M-862, N&MF, USNA; Philander C. Knox to Elliott Northcott, Washington, D.C., June 2, 1911, 817.504, rl. 70, M-632, RG 59, USNA; Case 19475/45–50, rl. 1066, M-862, N&MF, USNA; Ernest Dale Owen to secretary of state, New York, February 10, 1911, 317.115B62/99, RG 59, USNA; William Rees to Philander C. Knox, Pittsburgh, July 17, 1911, 817.51/203, rl. 71, M-632, RG 59, USNA; Elliott Northcott to secretary of state, Managua, May 4, 1911, 817.504, rl. 70, M-632, RG 59, USNA; report by S. H. Baker, Manager, Bluefields Fruit and Steamship Company, to Head Office, New Orleans, Bluefields, August 24, 1912, RG 84, USNA; Teplitz, "Modernization in Nicaragua," p. 358.

structure. The fruteras' presence provided an important stimulus to small business. Their shipping facilities, improvement of land transportation, regularity of operations and efforts to expand the U.S. market opened new opportunities for local subsistence farmers, who switched to commercial fruit growing. While the companies' shift from spot purchases to contracts denied growers some of the fast profits to be made in a volatile market, it also provided them with insulation from the catastrophic risks in that same market. In turn, the planters' success translated into prosperity for an expanding contingent of small merchants in coastal towns such as La Ceiba and Bluefields. Those merchants also benefited from increasing sales to the workers who flocked to the coast.

Peasants from the interior of Central America joined the expanding community of small growers and merchants on the coast, drawn by the promise of easy money and a consumers' El Dorado. They found wage levels far in excess of anything they encountered in the domestic labor market, and a dazzling array of consumer goods from canned foods to machine-made clothes to electric lights. But by the turn of the century the structure of the fruteras and their relationships with Central American societies changed dramatically as the companies responded to problems they encountered.

The early banana trade had been fraught with risks, since plantings were subject to storm damage and the fruit could easily be ruined during handling and shipping. Perishability of the product added to the problem of volatility in terms of supplies and prices. The use of purchase contracts had marked an initial step in a dual process of vertical and horizontal integration in which the companies sought to reduce their risks and ensure quality control.

The joining of the Boston Fruit Company with the Keith interests to form United Fruit represented a critical step in the solution of these problems. The merger gave the new company control over 78 percent of the U.S. market. More importantly, Keith's landholdings in Costa Rica, Panama and Colombia meant that the company could now exercise direct control over a significant portion of its production. In 1911 the firm accelerated this process with a campaign to purchase huge tracts of land. Its holdings, which totaled under 300,000 acres in 1904, had risen to over a million acres by 1915. While the company had supplied 35 percent of its own bananas in 1911, that figure had risen to nearly 50 percent by 1929.[11]

The increasing entry of United Fruit and other large companies into banana production served a number of purposes. First, it gave them greater quality control at the point of production. Second, producing such a large portion of the product allowed them greater control in price negotiations with local growers. Finally, the control of vast tracts of geographi-

---

11 Kepner, *Social Aspects*, p. 66.

cally dispersed land provided insurance against the effects of disease, created a formidable barrier to potential competitors and forced local peasants into positions as wage laborers on the companies' plantations. These developments represented a process of monopolization and cultural modification pursued by the fruteras.[12] The United Fruit Company justified its virtual monopoly of the banana trade in terms of the small size of the banana market in relation to the high risks and need for economies of scale of production. But in Central America the process of monopolization extended beyond the production system to the political system as well. Since the fruteras accounted for over half of the $250 million of U.S. investment in Central America by 1929, they possessed the potential to significantly influence local political processes. Control over political institutions could provide the fruteras generous land concessions, minimal levels of taxation, acceptance of administered banana prices for local planters and government action to ward off potential competitors. As their land policies demonstrated, such control did not have to achieve total monopolization of political power. Influence over a substantial portion of the political actors in Central American countries would permit the banana enterprises to blunt efforts by local governments to raise their costs. These transformational processes extended beyond the political realm to the larger cultures of the Central American countries where the companies had concentrated their operations.

Although the fruit companies proved a stimulus to small business and attracted large numbers of peasants to work for them, their relationships with these groups became increasingly contentious. Their contracts with growers did protect planters from some of the wilder market fluctuations but did not insulate them from rising costs or the danger of crop failure. Furthermore, when market prices for bananas rose in the 1920s small planters did not see this reflected in their contracts. But when prices fell at the end of the decade their contract prices were revised downward. Those developments reflected the increased control over the market which the fruteras enjoyed thanks to their direct production of the fruit. In turn, the declining fortunes of the growers harmed merchants, who also lost their market among workers to the fruteras' company stores.[13] Those stores symbolized the increased control which the fruit companies sought over their workers in exchange for high wages.

In return for higher wages and increased access to consumer goods, workers had to surrender their previous lifestyle, which often mixed subsistence farming and occasional wage labor. In its place they accepted full-time paid labor and complete dependence on corporate policies and market forces, which determined wages as well as the supply and prices of subsistence goods. The fruteras also enforced strict work regimens requir-

12 Read, "Banana Export Trade," pp. 189–200.
13 Bulmer-Thomas, *Political Economy of Central America*, p. 36.

ing timeliness and intensified work rhythms. They created a new social hierarchy based on functional positions within the corporate production process, as opposed to familial or other "non-rational" determinants of status. The fruit companies promoted the concept of individualism and competition with individualized work contracts and task-based pay schemes.

Despite the fruteras' concern with disciplining workers and their creation of company towns as a part of that process, the American companies had little interest in policies of industrial welfare that were gradually being adopted in the United States. They required large numbers of unskilled workers for planting, harvesting, digging ditches and other menial tasks. As a result they had little interest in welfare programs that would improve job satisfaction or educate workers for skilled positions. Those conditions ensured the recruitment of gang bosses and managers who viewed their task as one of extracting the maximum amount of manual labor from an undifferentiated mass of workers. Furthermore, company managers saw little purpose in trying to improve conditions for workers whom they considered to be racially inferior. These developments turned the relationship between the fruteras and the coastal communities into a highly conflictual one during the early decades of the twentieth century.

By the time of the Great Depression, former peasants who had become rural workers would challenge the fruteras in an effort to define their relationship to a permanent wage labor system. Their demands reflected their efforts to cope with principles of individualism, their vulnerability to market forces and the rigors of the modern work place. They would frequently be joined in their protests by small planters and merchants who found themselves affected by these forces of American corporate culture. Together, banana workers and small business interests forged resistance communities that formulated challenges to the fruteras' power. A decade before such challenges appeared, the increasing penetration of American business into Central America's transitional societies would draw in the United States government as an ally of the fruteras and Central American elites in the process of renovation.

By the turn of the century, the United States government, at the behest of American companies, had adopted an increasingly interventionist policy in the Caribbean Basin. Policymakers couched their analyses in terms of corrupt governments and nefarious schemes, perspectives that reflected their racialist views about the inherent inferiority of Latin Americans. But U.S. officials clearly understood that the increasing insertion of American business and its efforts to influence local political processes had a destabilizing effect on the Central American societies. The unstable conditions which threatened American corporations necessitated U.S. government involvement.

As the cost of direct interventions in Central America rose to over $1 million per year, Secretary of State Philander C. Knox turned to promoting loans by U.S. banks to Central American governments as a means of stabilizing these regimes. Yet the ultimate objective remained the same. Stable finances and stable governments would protect American corporations and "save the United States the constant expense of sending war vessels . . . and otherwise intervening to protect American interests endangered by revolutionists."[14] But the goals of American policymakers ranged well beyond the stabilization of political institutions.

If American enterprise failed to do so, U.S. government leaders were quite prepared to impose the features of a corporate society on their neighbors to the south. Their goals were to create an environment more conducive to U.S. investment and to extend the benefits of American corporate culture to the region. Such a project included the rationalization of state functions, a free market system, upgrading of educational institutions, a Protestant missionary effort, protection of private property and the creation of an electoral system which, if not democratic, at least provided for the regularized transfer of power.[15] By 1912 the United States government and American private interests had launched such a project in Nicaragua.

---

14 "Notes for Argument in Favor of Honduras and Nicaragua Loan Conventions," n.p. n.d., vol. 9, Knox Papers.
15 See for example Boaz Long to Robert Lansing, memorandum, February 15, 1918, 711.13/55, and Lansing's memorandum, June 11, 1914, 710.11/185 1/2, RG 59, USNA.

3

Nicaragua

Formerly United States Marines were considered by the Nicaraguans as invincible. That reputation has for the moment been superseded by open contempt for the inability of American forces, with all modern equipment, to capture the bandits adhering to Sandino, though the latter are greatly outnumbered. (William Cumberland)

American visitors to Nicaragua's Atlantic port of Bluefields in 1894 could be forgiven if they at first mistook it for a New England seacoast village. Two-story wood frame houses topped with shingles and boarded in white trim hugged the shore. American steamships churned the harbor's waters. Along the town's main street grocers peddled the products of American consumer industries. A local bottling plant added ginger ale and sarsaparilla to the array of consumer perishables. Residents enjoyed the benefits of English-language schools and newspapers as well as Protestant churches.[1]

Less apparent to the casual observer was the fact that this entry point for American material culture now stood at center stage in a momentous historical drama. Political revolution in western Nicaragua and the increasing pace of American economic activity on the nation's Atlantic coast would eventually lead to U.S. military intervention and the outbreak of a war for national liberation. By 1894 sudden political changes in Managua, the nation's capital, were reverberating on Nicaragua's Atlantic coast with profound and destabilizing effects. A leadership crisis within Nicaragua's long-ruling Conservative party in 1893 allowed José Santos Zelaya to seize power and launch a program of liberal modernization. Zelaya's program focused on three areas: the commercialization of agriculture, policies to promote domestic industries and encourage foreign investment, and the full incorporation of the Atlantic coast into the national economic and political system.

Zelaya's agrarian program did not represent a radical departure from that of his Conservative predecessors. By the late 1870s the Conservatives were offering foreigners free public land, selling the properties of peasant

---

1 Craig L. Dozier, *Nicaragua's Mosquito Shore: Years of British and American Presence* (Tuscaloosa: University of Alabama Press, 1985), pp. 141–46.

Figure 1. Bluefields, Nicaragua. The white picket fences and offices of U.S. companies gave Bluefields a distinctly American appearance. (United Fruit Company Collection, Baker Library, Harvard Business School)

villages and Indian communities, and instituting a system of agricultural judges to control laborers, who refused to abide by their contracts with landowners. They also offered crop subsidies as a further stimulus to export production.[2] But the Conservatives provided a less than vigorous enforcement of these policies. The Conservatives drew much of their support from the provinces of Granada, Rivas and Chontales, which lay to the south and southeast of Managua. Cattle raising and cacao production in these provinces had long been the mainstays of the national economy. The

---

2 David Radell, *Historical Geography of Western Nicaragua: The Spheres of Influence of León, Granada and Managua, 1519–1965* (Berkeley and Los Angeles: University of California Press, 1969), pp. 202–3; Teplitz, "Modernization in Nicaragua," p. 182; Jaime Wheelock, *Nicaragua: imperialismo y dictadura: crisis de una formación social* (Havana: La Habana Editorial de Ciencias Sociales, 1980), p. 77.

Figure 2. Pearl Lagoon, a small town on Nicaragua's Miskito coast, in 1891 was typical
of settlements on Central America's banana coast before the coming of the American
fruteras. (United Fruit Company Collection, Baker Library, Harvard Business School)

Conservatives therefore had little incentive to promote the coffee fincas
that had sprouted on the southern rim of Managua and spread northeast
into the provinces of Matagalpa, Jinotega, Esteli and Nueva Segovia by
the 1870s. The emergence of the city of León, the home base of their Liberal opponents, as the commercial center for the coffee trade offered a further disincentive for aggressive action by the Conservatives. Zelaya's Liberal regime would breathe new life into programs to transform the
agrarian sector.

In 1894 the Liberals promulgated a labor law which in effect instituted
a national labor draft. They also increased the number of rural judges, employed the military to hunt down fugitive laborers, accelerated the sale of
public lands, renewed the assault on Indian communal property and
seized church lands. To cope with problems of undercapitalization, the
government increased subsidies for coffee and expanded the national
money supply. These efforts produced a doubling of coffee exports during
the sixteen years (1893–1909) of the Zelaya regime.[3] The Liberals also
turned their attention to promoting other segments of the national economy.

As the development of Bluefields clearly indicated, Nicaragua's Atlantic, or Miskito, coast contained a treasure chest of exploitable natural
resources. But when Zelaya assumed power, the Nicaraguan government
exercised only a tenuous sovereignty over the region. In 1860 Great Britain

3 Teplitz, "Modernization in Nicaragua," pp. 190–233.

surrendered the formal protectorate which it had long exercised over the area's Miskito Indians. In its place the British created the Mosquito Reserve, an autonomous Miskito government which technically fell within the sovereign territory of the Nicaraguan government. Real political power in the Reserve was exercised by the creoles, English-speaking blacks who had migrated to Mosquitia from the British West Indies. By the early 1890s American merchants and planters had also gained considerable political influence, symbolized by Sam Weil's position as mayor of Bluefields. In 1894 Zelaya acted to end the ambiguous status of the Atlantic coast, displacing the nominal Miskito government with Spanish-speaking bureaucrats from western Nicaragua. Creoles and Americans, who had enjoyed considerable latitude in their economic activities under the Miskito government, resented the installation of direct rule from Managua. But many Americans soon profited from the generous concessions which Zelaya granted for the exploitation of the coast's resources.[4]

To encourage domestic industry, the Zelaya government granted a series of monopolies for a range of products including *aguardiente* (rum), beer, bricks and coal. The monopolies, combined with protective tariffs, offered strong incentives for industrial development within a limited domestic market. And much like his liberal counterparts elsewhere in Central America, Zelaya made monopolistic concessions to attract foreign capital to his country's forbidding Caribbean coast. The concessions created the possibility of developing the coast's largely untapped wealth at little or no cost to domestic interests while leaving foreign concession holders to assume all of the risks. American investors plunged into mining, lumbering and the banana business with the promise of creating a vibrant export economy in Nicaragua's underdeveloped eastern territories. The Liberals had set their three-part development program in motion, and their political future seemed assured.[5] Conservative challenges to Zelaya's rule appeared to be the dying gasps of a doomed political movement. Liberalism had long since triumphed in other Central American countries, and domestic economic power was already shifting toward León and the coffee-growing regions. Yet serious fissures soon appeared in the Liberal front.

Aggressive policies to discipline the rural population to regularized labor on commercial estates, along with the growth of coffee exports, masked formidable problems in the Liberals' agrarian reform. Transportation facilities in the coffee-growing Northeast remained woefully inade-

4 Peter Sollis, "The Atlantic Coast of Nicaragua: Development and Autonomy," *JLAS* 21 (October 1989), pp. 484–86; Karl Bermann, *Under the Big Stick: Nicaragua and the United States Since 1848* (Boston: South End Press, 1986), pp. 125–28.

5 Teplitz, "Modernization in Nicaragua," pp. 241–42; Charles Stansifer, "José Santos Zelaya: A New Look at Nicaragua's Liberal Dictator," *Revista Interamericana* 7 (Fall 1977), pp. 468–85; Jeffrey L. Gould, *To Lead as Equals: Rural Protest and Political Consciousness in Chinandega, Nicaragua, 1912–1979* (Chapel Hill: University of North Carolina Press, 1990), pp. 23–25.

quate. Planters had to rely on the expensive option of mules to move most of their harvest. Nicaragua's coffee boom also coincided with a sharp decline in international coffee prices, which continued throughout Zelaya's administration. In the face of falling prices, coffee growers expanded production, but as an American observer noted in 1903, "for several years past coffee planting has not been profitable in this country, and many of the principal planters have been forced into bankruptcy . . ."[6] Resistance by the rural populace to the Liberal reforms added to the woes of the coffee growers.

As late as 1908, Zelaya conceded that Indian villages, which controlled some of the best coffee land in the country, were still stubbornly resisting government efforts to dismantle their communal holdings. Of greater immediate concern was the failure to effectively discipline the rural workforce. Nicaragua's low population density and the availability of virgin lands on the northeast coffee frontier made flight a viable alternative for those who rejected work on the coffee fincas. Thousands of rural laborers continued to confound planters by signing work contracts with several growers, collecting their advances and then fleeing to the frontier. Troops conscripted from the countryside proved less than diligent in arresting fugitive workers. The resulting shortage of laborers endangered the 1901 coffee harvest. With the coffee industry falling short of the economic boom envisioned by the Liberals, the government's concession policy emerged as an issue of contention.[7]

Zelaya politicized the granting of domestic monopolies, an important avenue of economic opportunity, as concessions became the almost exclusive domain of his friends and family. Monopolies of domestic products and protective tariffs, which raised consumer prices, alienated the country's artisans, who had been staunch Liberal supporters. By 1904 domestic competitors for concessions began to covet the generous grants made to American investors.[8]

Sam Weil, the New Orleans merchant and one-time mayor of Bluefields, became a close associate of José Zelaya. When El Salvador and Honduras threatened military action against Nicaragua, Weil had loaned Zelaya $30,000 to purchase a gunboat. In return, Weil secured a contract in 1903 to collect the duties on liquor imported on the Miskito coast. Weil also received several mining concessions of dubious validity. However, Zelaya's political family became increasingly jealous of Weil's influence and profits. The Aguardiente Syndicate, which held the monopoly on the local alcoholic beverage, and in which Zelaya had a personal inter-

6 U.S. House of Representatives, 57th Cong., 2d sess., Doc. 438, part 3, vol. 72, *Consular Reports, July 1903: Nicaragua* (Washington, D.C.: Government Printing Office, 1903). On falling coffee prices, see Marco Palacios, *Coffee in Colombia, 1850–1970: An Economic, Social, and Political History* (Cambridge: Cambridge University Press, 1980), p. 130.

7 Teplitz, "Modernization in Nicaragua," pp. 124–28, 177–232.

8 Ibid., pp. 246–51.

est, approached Weil shortly after he obtained the liquor concession. The representatives of the Syndicate advised Weil to begin distributing the Syndicate's product on the Atlantic coast if he wished to avoid problems. Weil heeded their advice, but he failed to salvage his relationship with Zelaya.[9]

In 1906 Zelaya canceled Weil's contract to collect the liquor duty. Weil also found his gold mines being exploited by Nicaraguans with links to the president. Weil's appeals to Washington brought U.S. diplomatic intervention. By 1908 the suspect nature of Weil's agreements with Zelaya led the State Department to drop the protest. But with the Weil claim, American representatives had sensed a new "avaricious" policy toward U.S. concessionaires. They became convinced that Zelaya could not be relied on to protect American economic interests.[10]

The pressure on Zelaya to tap the wealth generated by foreign monopolies led him into a series of confrontations with American concessionaires. In 1906 the government violated an exclusive purchasing agreement with the American-owned Central American Commercial Company by placing orders with other merchant houses. Two years later the Zelaya administration instituted legal proceedings to cancel the concessions of the La Luz and Los Angeles Mining Company and the Siempre Viva Mining Company. In 1906 Zelaya had canceled an 1894 concession to the George D. Emery Company for logging millions of acres of mahogany on the Atlantic coast. The president managed to extract an additional $65,000 out of essentially the same concession by granting logging rights to another U.S. company on part of the Emery holdings. State Department officials became increasingly incensed as the Nicaraguan government stalled efforts at arbitration for two years.[11]

Even after strong diplomatic pressure brought a settlement favorable to the Emery Company in 1909, U.S. officials remained convinced of Zelaya's unreliability. William Lawrence Merry, the U.S. minister to Central America, who had interceded on behalf of both Weil and Emery, was nearly apoplectic in his denunciation of Zelaya, accusing him of torturing his domestic enemies with enemas concocted of hot chili peppers and alcohol. Merry had developed a deep personal animosity toward Zelaya, partly out of frustration over his failed attempts to resolve the Weil claim. Merry also had a close personal link to another American business interest that had fallen out with Zelaya. Merry's son-in-law, Harry F. Meiggs, was a nephew of Minor C. Keith. Keith had been highly solicitous of his nephew's interests, loaning him $10,000 for an orange plantation in Costa Rica. Merry, in return, strongly supported United Fruit, providing the

9 Case 146/43 1/2, 145, rl. 26; Case 19475/61–74, rl. 1066, M-862, N&MF, USNA.

10 Frederick M. Ryder to James Bacon, New Haven, September 5, 1906, Case 146/43 1/2, rl. 26, M-862, N&MF, USNA.

11 Otto Schoenrich to Secretary of State William J. Bryan, Washington, D.C., January 4, 1915, 417.00/220, RG 59, USNA; Case 17608/2–3, rl. 1066, M-862, N&MF, USNA.

company with official State Department files to assist in a lawsuit against an American competitor. By the time Merry denounced Zelaya, once cordial relations between United Fruit and the Nicaraguan president had disintegrated into an acrimonious dispute.[12]

United's Nicaraguan investments developed from the activities of Charles and Jacob Weinberger, New Orleans merchants who had entered the Central American banana trade in 1888. They consolidated their interests in 1897 with those of two competing firms to form the Bluefields Steamship Company. The United Fruit Company purchased a controlling interest in the Bluefields Company two years later. Charles Weinberger, who had become manager of United's Fruit Despatch Company in New Orleans, negotiated a concession for exclusive navigation rights on the Escondido River from the Zelaya government in 1904. The concession gave United Fruit an iron grip on the banana industry in the Bluefields area, since the river represented the only practical means of shipping produce to Bluefields. The six hundred small American and creole planters who worked lands along the river's edge were now dependent on United Fruit.[13]

Charles Weinberger defended the concession and spoke of "harmonious cooperation between planter and shipper" as "the consummation devoutly to be wished."[14] But control of the Escondido, combined with the fact that United Fruit already produced a quarter of the bananas exported from Bluefields, clearly indicated that the company held the upper hand in the local banana economy. The small growers in the Bluefields area resisted United's policy of monopolization. In 1901 and again in 1905 the planters attempted to boycott United and destroyed the bananas of growers who defied the boycott. In 1903 they had purchased tugboats and loading facilities in an effort to compete with the American company. But government troops destroyed the bananas they had prepared for shipment. Organized as the Planters Association, they sued the Bluefields Company in 1905 over losses suffered as a result of the government seizure of their product.[15]

The conflict between the planters and the Bluefields Company presented a serious dilemma for Zelaya and his dreams of national development. Bluefields was providing immediate resources to the state. The concession called for annual payments of $15,000 to the government, and United had arranged a $1 million loan for the regime through the Na-

12 William Lawrence Merry to Philander C. Knox, San José, December 9, 1909, Box 39, Knox Papers. On Merry's ties to United Fruit, see James G. Bailey, secretary of American Legation, Costa Rica, to Robert Bacon, acting secretary of state, Washington, D.C., June 23, 1907, Case 1723/14, rl. 184, M-862, N&MF, USNA.

13 Otto Schoenrich to William J. Bryan, Washington, D.C., January 4, 1915, 417.00/220, RG 59, USNA. Also see correspondence contained in 317.115B62/97–99, RG 59, USNA.

14 *The American* (Bluefields), July 27, 1905.

15 Ibid., August 1, 1905.

Figure 3. A local banana grower's home and farm on the Escondido River, Nicaragua, in 1891. (United Fruit Company Collection, Baker Library, Harvard Business School)

tional State Bank of New Orleans. Over the long term, the company's riverboats, freighters and telegraph connections promised to expand and solidify the Nicaraguan banana trade. At the same time, Zelaya's reincorporation of the Miskito coast had stirred deep resentment in the area's creole population. Their political power had been quashed by public servants from western Nicaragua and their English-language culture threatened by Zelaya's determination to Hispanicize the region. The Escondido concession became the latest in a series of grants to American investors, which further circumscribed economic opportunities for the black population.

In an effort to assuage the planters' growing resentment, Zelaya arranged a modification of the Escondido monopoly in 1906 which set minimum requirements for the shipping of the independent growers' bananas by the Bluefields Company. Zelaya also allowed local courts and eventually even his own Supreme Court to find in favor of the Planters Association in their suit against United. But as soon as the Supreme Court ruled in favor of the Association in 1907, Zelaya began looking for ways to undo the decision. No matter what modifications were made in the Escondido concession or what decisions the Supreme Court reached, Zelaya kept the United monopoly intact. Smoldering discontent along the Escondido River finally reached the flashpoint.[16]

Early in 1909, as local growers struggled to recover from severe storm damage, the Nicaraguan government increased tariffs on bananas and im-

16 Ibid., April 2, September 3, 1906; September 30, 1907.

ported products. The planters' protests prompted Zelaya to temporarily reduce the import tariff on a few essential items. But the growers found that, combined with a declining exchange rate, the tariff wiped out their profit margins. They turned to United Fruit, requesting an increase in the price it paid for bananas, but the company rejected their plea. The Bluefields planters once again turned to President Zelaya. After an interview with the president, in which he assured them of his support, the growers' representatives called for a strike.[17] The planters along the Escondido now refused to sell their crop to United and destroyed the bananas of growers who continued to cooperate with the company.

United wasted no time in appealing to Zelaya, who threatened to shoot the strikers and ordered troops from the river town of Rama to protect the company's growers. The soldiers, however, failed to provide the promised protection. Convinced of Zelaya's double dealing, United appealed to the U.S. government, which quickly dispatched a warship to Bluefields. The local governor now sent troops out from Bluefields and under Zelaya's orders began arresting hundreds of planters. Zelaya insisted the action was taken because of the threat of American intervention, which he claimed was designed to secure a canal route through his country.

Supporters of the planters had a different view of events. They viewed the growers' movement as a struggle against United's attempt to control them as part of its production process, and they argued that the planters were victims of racist policies. According to one supporter, the growers acted to "prove beyond a doubt that when the Bluefields Steamship Company bought the river they have not been sold along with it, and therefore do not form part of the goods and chattle of the B.S.S. Co." And he argued, "Had the planters been white men, they probably would have been given a better treatment, but what right has a Nicaraguan, and especially so a nigger – as some of the Bluefields S.S. Co's people said – to rebel and find fault with the treatment meted out to them?"[18] The wives of the imprisoned planters swore to continue the strike. Three of them, armed with pistols, commandeered a barge loaded with bananas for the Bluefields Company and destroyed the cargo. But the power of the Nicaraguan military proved effective in quelling the uprising.[19]

As the planters' movement disintegrated, so did Zelaya's control over the region. Zelaya now had the worst of all possible situations. Both the creole population and the United Fruit Company were convinced of his duplicity. Meanwhile American officials sent to investigate the affair agreed that the growers had justifiable complaints against United Fruit, but concluded that it was Zelaya's granting of the concession and his failure to maintain order which had caused the incident. As early as May,

17 Henry Gregory to secretary of state, Bluefields, April 30, 1909, Case 19475/8, rl. 1066, M-862; Case 19475/61–74, rl. 1066, M-862, N&MF, USNA.
18 *The American* (Bluefields), May 31, 1909.
19 Ibid., May 17, 1909; Case 19475/61–74, rl. 1066, M-862, N&MF, USNA.

Bluefields was rife with rumors of rebellion, which centered on the local governor, Juan Estrada, a long-time critic of Zelaya. Estrada's uprising would enjoy the backing of American interests, the creole population and the U.S. State Department.

On October 11 Estrada declared himself in rebellion and established a provisional government at Bluefields, where he was soon joined by the Conservative leaders Emiliano Chamorro and Adolfo Díaz. Convinced of the rebellion's viability, Secretary of State Philander C. Knox broke off relations with Nicaragua in December, effectively throwing official support to the Conservatives.[20] Faced with this array of opponents, Zelaya resigned and appointed the Liberal José Madriz as president. By May of 1910 the Liberals had blockaded Bluefields, but U.S. warships intervened to break the blockade. The presence of American forces in Bluefields prevented a Liberal assault on the town and allowed the Conservatives to remain in control of the port and its customs revenues, which financed the Conservative rebels. By August the Madriz government collapsed, and the triumphant Conservative forces entered Managua. The resuscitation of the Conservative cause owed a great deal to American economic interests.

The rapid acceleration of American corporate activity in a society still in the throes of its liberal revolution had had a highly destabilizing effect on the whole country. Part of the problem stemmed from Zelaya's reliance on monopolistic concessions and tariffs to spur development. Domestic monopolies and tariffs had already cost him support among the nation's artisans, and a foreign concession and tariffs soon antagonized the small planters on the Miskito coast. As the Liberal agrarian reform encountered problems of worker resistance and falling coffee prices, foreign concessions became a source of contention among Zelaya's followers. By 1906 those internal pressures had led the president to infringe on almost every important concession granted to U.S. companies. As the president's actions narrowed his domestic base of political support and antagonized U.S. businesses, the rising tensions between domestic interests and foreign concessionaires on the Escondido River reached their combustion point.

The United Fruit Company's effort at monopolization, with its absorption of the Bluefields Steamship Company, was greatly facilitated by the Escondido concession. In 1909 that concession trapped Zelaya in the middle of the clash between the creole planters and United. Zelaya managed to antagonize both sides and assured their support of Estrada's rebellion. As the U.S. minister to Nicaragua noted in 1911, "The Department is aware of the fact that this [Escondido] concession created great bitterness during the last regime, and was one of the principal causes of the past revolution."[21] Infuriated by Zelaya's infringement on their concessions,

---

20 Doyle memorandum to Knox, n.p., November 19, 1909, vol. 9, Knox Papers.
21 Franklin Gunther to secretary of state, Managua, October 22, 1911, 817.602/13, rl. 95, M-632, RG 59, USNA.

American interests provided important support for the Conservative rebellion.

The American corporate enemies of Zelaya became the foreign backers of the rebellion. The Emery Company reportedly shipped arms to the rebels from New Orleans. Direct financial backing included $80,000 from Sam Weil and his partner J. M. Cohn, $100,000 from United Fruit, and another $210,000 from other American companies at Bluefields.[22] American corporate interests also provided the impetus for the actions of the U.S. government. Officially, the State Department's support for the rebellion stemmed from Zelaya's meddling in the affairs of other Central American countries. Zelaya had certainly engaged in such intrigues, as did Manuel Estrada Cabrera, his counterpart in Guatemala. What distinguished Zelaya from other Central American executives were his repeated violations of American business interests. That motivation for U.S. actions became fully apparent as Washington intervened directly in Nicaraguan domestic affairs.

Central to U.S. support for the new Nicaraguan government was Estrada's acquiescence to a loan from American banks to be secured by customs receipts. The State Department explained the purpose of this exercise in dollar diplomacy and the reason the U.S. backed the Estrada rebellion in a telegram to Ernest H. Wands, a monetary expert sent to reform Nicaraguan finances:

With New Orleans filibustering, the machinations of the United Fruit Company, and the schemes of different Americans in collusion with corrupt Central American politicians have been the greatest external contributors to the situation the United States seeks to end. All these American interests in Central America, including those founded on reprehensible schemes, must be reckoned with because of the political pressure they are able to bring to bear, but with . . . the present understanding of Nicaragua, the Department is in a position to say to all comers that all proper measures have been taken to protect every legitimate American interest or equity.[23]

The State Department's belief that it could quickly institute reforms which would create a stable environment for U.S. investment proved totally erroneous. It was, in fact, the beginning of two decades of direct American intervention.

U.S. attempts to rationalize the Nicaraguan state and develop the country's economic infrastructure constantly ran up against the harsh realities that its Conservative allies represented a distinct political minority and were as anxious as Zelaya had been to profit from control of the state. The Liberals, the natural allies of American corporate interests elsewhere

---

22 Huntington Wilson to George T. Weitzel, Washington, D.C., February 29, 1912, 417.00/120, RG 59, USNA.
23 Department of State to Ernest H. Wands, Washington, D.C., July 10, 1911, 817.51/168, rl. 71, M-632, RG 59, USNA.

in Central America, constituted a majority opposition with a powerful appeal to Nicaraguan nationalism, violated by American intervention. These facts, along with American attempts to reform the Nicaraguan state, drew the United States ever more deeply into Nicaraguan affairs in a futile attempt to create an environment conducive to the expansion of American corporate culture.

American intervenors soon learned just how formidable a task they faced. Internal wrangling among the rebels quickly led to the ousting of Estrada from the presidency by Conservative Luis Mena. Adolfo Díaz, a former employee of the La Luz and Los Angeles Mining Company, replaced Estrada. Despite Díaz's promise to U.S. chargé Franklin Gunther that he would leave the settlement of war reparations to a claims commission, the new president proceeded to dispense $1.75 million to U.S. companies and Conservative leaders such as Mena and Emiliano Chamorro. As Díaz explained to Gunther, since Chamorro had already received $500,000, he could hardly deny Mena and his followers their payments. Since the national treasury was now empty, Gunther accepted Díaz's promise to halt further disbursements. Meanwhile Mena used part of his payment to buy a majority in the National Assembly.[24]

When his Conservative rivals refused to accept his presidential aspirations, Mena rose in rebellion in 1912 and was joined by the Liberals. The rebellion posed a serious threat to American interests. The rebellion endangered the Nicaraguan Pacific Railway, now controlled by J. W. Seligman and Company and Brown Brothers as a partial guarantee of $2.1 million in loans to the Díaz regime. The partners of J. W. Seligman and Company had once ransomed one of their offspring from outraged American miners. Now they found their investments held hostage by rebellious Nicaraguans who, like the American miners, treated the Seligmans as alien intruders. The Liberals also threatened the American coffee growers in Matagalpa. In response, the U.S. government committed 3,000 troops and eight warships to crush the rebellion.[25]

The failed Mena uprising became the first in a series of fiascos that marked U.S. plans for rationalization of the Nicaraguan state. The Mena rebellion itself provided the excuse for $1 million in claims from Conservatives and U.S. companies. Meanwhile the expenditure of state revenues was marked by "graft, extravagance, carelessness, extortion, and in some cases direct fraud." This confirmed the U.S. intervenors' belief that the Nicaraguans operated on "a different standard of ethics or honesty as compared with the Anglo Saxon's."[26]

24 Gunther to secretary of state, Managua, January 11, 1912, 417.00/120, RG 59, USNA.
25 The size of the military contingent sent to Nicaragua was designed not simply to subdue the rebels but to impress other Latin American nations with U.S. determination to deal effectively with disorders that threatened its interests.
26 A. L. Lindberg to B. L. Jefferson, Managua, August 5, 1916, 817.51/828, rl. 76, M-632, RG 59, USNA.

Despite American controls over customs receipts and eventually the national budget, Conservative creativity consistently triumphed over American rationalization. Graft and corruption siphoned off millions of dollars in state revenues during the era of Conservative control. Furthermore, with the Conservatives firmly under the thumb of the Chamorro faction with its base in the cattle-ranching and cacao-producing regions south of Managua, the party showed little interest in promoting the infrastructure development needed to encourage coffee growing. The cost of coffee delivered at the port rose nearly 80 percent between the end of the Liberal era and 1925. Nicaragua ranked fourth in output among five coffee-producing Central American countries, and only the doubling of coffee prices in the same period salvaged the growers' profit margin. The failure to rationalize state functions also affected the rate of foreign investment.[27]

Given their virtual exclusion from Zelaya's concessionary program, the Conservatives insisted on canceling all concessions granted by Zelaya. But they proved quite willing to grant new foreign concessions as part of an effort to create a positive environment for U.S. investment. Their policy was rewarded in 1919 when Samuel Zemurray's Cuyamel Fruit Company invested $2.5 million in banana production in the Bluefields area. By 1924 the Vaccaro brothers, operating as the Bragmans Bluff Lumber Company, had begun logging and banana growing around Puerto Cabezas in the northeastern part of the Miskito coast. Their investment in these operations reached $12 million in 1929.[28] But these large new American investments proved to be the exception rather than the rule.

Between the fall of Zelaya and the Great Depression, U.S. investment in Nicaragua doubled to approximately $20 million. That rate paled in comparison to the fivefold and fortyfold increases in Guatemala and Honduras, leaving Nicaragua with the smallest amount of U.S. investment in Central America. A number of factors accounted for this poor performance. Nicaraguan banana lands proved less productive than those elsewhere in Central America and were soon affected by the Panama disease that had already blighted banana fields in Panama and Costa Rica. Low levels of investment also stemmed from internal political conditions.[29]

27 Dana G. Munro, memorandum, Department of State, Division of Latin American Affairs, November 18, 1922, 817.51/1382, rl. 84, M-632; Clifford Ham to secretary of state, Managua, October 22, 1917, 817.51/1034, rl. 79, M-632; Jeremiah W. Jenks to Secretary of State Charles Evans Hughes, New York, June 20, 1922, 817.51/1328, rl. 83, M-632; Lindberg to secretary of state, Managua, June 18, 1920, 817.51/1225, rl. 81, M-632; Harold Playter, "The Coffee Industry in Nicaragua," Corinto, May 26, 1926, rl. 96, 817.6133/1, rl. 96, M-632, RG 59, USNA; Bulmer-Thomas, *Political Economy of Central America*, p. 24.

28 Samuel Fletcher, "Foreign Investments in Latin America," Bluefields, March 24, 1930, 811.503110 Statistics/9, RG 59, USNA; "Cuyamel Fruit Company," Scudder Collection.

29 H. D. Scott, progress report, Bragmans Bluff, January 23, 1926, File 5, Box 10, Standard Fruit Papers.

American investors resented the high taxes imposed on the Atlantic coast in order to service loans from U.S. banks. Conservative officeholders in the region raised the art of corruption to new heights, interfering with American logging claims and causing a general breakdown in public services. American firms also found their efforts to influence local political processes stymied by the presence of American bankers and intervenors and by the deep divisions in the Nicaraguan political elite.[30]

In 1926 the Vaccaro brothers' Bragmans Bluff Company guaranteed $50,000 in loans from a New Orleans bank to President Emiliano Chamorro. In return, Chamorro canceled a new export duty on bananas. When Bragmans attempted to collect, Chamorro and his successors explained that budget restrictions imposed by American banks and intervenors prevented them from repaying the loan. The company finally agreed to cancel the debt in 1930.[31] By then Nicaraguan political instability posed a far larger threat than just the nonpayment of loans.

While officially American bureaucrats claimed to be creating a political democracy in Nicaragua, what they actually implemented was a system for a regularized transfer of power among members of the elite. Privately American officials made no pretense that the Nicaraguan electoral system, where voters were routinely bought off or intimidated, was a democracy.[32] But what truly frustrated the intervenors was the failure of this system to meet their minimal criterion – regularized transfers of political power.

For most of the period between 1913 and 1924, martial law remained in effect, backed up by a 100-man marine legation guard in Managua. Despite these measures, dissidents made ten attempts to overthrow the government. The failure to create a stable political environment owed much to the American intervention. Direct U.S. involvement in Nicaragua's internal affairs had resuscitated the minority Conservative party and provided a prime target for Liberal nationalism. Over the years, hostile demonstrations against American troops and brawls between marines and Nicaraguans, including the local police, became commonplace. Such incidents fed the flames of Liberal anti-Americanism, particularly among the artisan-based *obrerista* movement, which had resumed its staunch support of the Liberal cause after the fall of Zelaya. In 1924 the *obreristas* called for the overthrow of the national government "propped up by U.S. bayonets and the influence of Wall Street bankers." In fact neither the marines nor the bankers proved very successful at stabilizing Nicaragua. While marines antagonized the populace, U.S. financial controls failed to stem internal political corruption, and American collection of tariffs helped preclude their

30 Cornelius Ferris to Benjamin Jefferson, Bluefields, November 16, 1914; William C. Teichmann, American consul, report, Bluefields, 1917, RG 84, USNA; Dozier, *Mosquito Shore*, pp. 189–90.
31 Files 20, 32–44, 48, 50, Box 10, Standard Fruit Papers.
32 Dana Munro to secretary of state, Managua, September 22, 1927, 817.51/1841, rl. 88, M-632, RG 59, USNA.

use by the Conservatives to placate their less vociferous Liberal opponents.[33] The political system once again teetered on the brink of collapse in 1926, opening the way for a revolutionary challenge to the political order and posing a direct and immediate threat to U.S. investment.

By the early 1920s, the coffee industry finally offered a basis for a possible political compromise. President Bartolomé Martínez, a Conservative coffee grower elected in 1923, fashioned a coalition known as the Transacción, which included moderate Conservatives willing to promote coffee exports and Liberals willing to accept American dominance. The Transacción elected Carlos Solórzano as president in 1926, only to see him ousted by the old Conservative warhorse Emiliano Chamorro. The Liberals quickly rose in revolt. Fighting between the Liberal and Conservative armies caused extensive damage to American corporate operations on the Atlantic coast.[34] With American investments and the entire U.S. reform program at risk, the State Department dispatched Colonel Henry Stimson to Nicaragua. Stimson arranged a compromise between the Liberals and Conservatives in May 1927, but one Liberal commander, Augusto Sandino, rejected both the deal and continued American intervention. Sandino launched a guerrilla war against the old political order and American domination, forcing the United States to commit 6,000 marines to a long and costly war to crush the Sandinista movement.

Sandino's ability to mount his challenge can be explained in part by U.S. intervention. American intervention had revived the increasingly anachronistic Chamorro faction of Nicaraguan conservatism, delaying the coalescence of interests around commercial agriculture which provided a basis for elite political harmony in other Central American countries. Disarray among the elite allowed Sandino to harness the discontent of Nicaraguans staunchly opposed to American political domination and, more importantly, those most intensely exposed to American corporate culture. Sandino, the son of a moderately well-to-do Liberal landowner, had at various times worked for the Vaccaro brothers in Honduras and an American oil company in Mexico. In 1926 he returned to Nicaragua and took a position as a timekeeper with the American-owned San Albino Mining Company. It was there, among the Nicaraguans who labored for an American corporation, that Sandino found the social base for revolution.[35]

33 For the quotation on marines and bankers, see Gould, *To Lead as Equals*, p. 33. On incidents between the marines and Nicaraguans, see Bermann, *Big Stick*, pp. 162, 176. On the Conservatives' problems with U.S. financial controls, see William C. Teichmann, American consul, report, Bluefields, 1917, RG 84, USNA.

34 Theodore Sykes to secretary of state, Long Island City, September 8, 1926; memorandum, Division of Latin American Affairs, September 20, 1926, 317.115As8/1/6, RG 59, USNA; Karnes, *Tropical Enterprise*, pp. 124–26.

35 On Sandino's life and ideas, see Gregorio Selser, *Sandino*, trans. Cedric Belfrage (New York: Monthly Review Press, 1981); Donald C. Hodges, *Intellectual Foundations of the Nicaraguan Revolution* (Austin: University of Texas Press, 1986); Neill Macaulay, *The Sandino Affair* (Chicago: Quadrangle, 1967).

At the time of Sandino's return, the Nicaraguan labor movement remained in its incipient stages, consisting largely of the pro-Liberal *obrerista* movement. Labor challenges to American corporations, such as a strike against the Cuyamel Fruit Company in 1921, had been few and short-lived. The labor peace which American companies enjoyed until the 1920s resulted from the organization and work relations which characterized American enterprises, and from conditions in the Miskito coast. The fruteras remained largely removed from the work process in the production of bananas. More than half of their product was produced by small planters, whose continued attempts to challenge the fruit companies collapsed in the face of the fruit companies' control over transportation and shipping facilities. Whether working for small planters or the fruteras themselves, laborers were secured by independent contractors, who supervised their work. As a result, cooperative work relations were largely limited to dockworkers, who operated in gangs of two to three hundred and who struck in 1906 and 1909.[36] In this early period the most significant impact of the companies on workers came in the form of consumer products.

The Miskito Indians along Nicaragua's Caribbean coast had been trading foodstuffs for manufactured goods with the British for several centuries before the Americans arrived in force. That trade had been integrated into the Miskito activities of hunting, fishing and subsistence agriculture. The arrival of the American fruit companies expanded the range of goods, which came to include manufactured cloth, tools, processed food and even sewing machines – items on which the Miskitos became increasingly dependent. The companies offered opportunities to obtain such goods not only by barter for foodstuffs but also through occasional wage labor. For the Miskitos the Americans offered expanded participation in a consumer economy, a far more inviting prospect than the political displacement and taxation which Nicaraguan rule had brought.[37] Such ethnic distinctions would remain relevant even when the nature of the fruteras' relationship to the local society changed dramatically.

Under the Bluefields Company, which concentrated on transportation facilities and the purchase of bananas from local growers, the banks of the Escondido remained dominated by the palm-leaf huts of small banana planters, who worked their holdings with family members and occasional laborers from the immediate countryside. The operations of the Vaccaro brothers' Bragmans Bluff Company represented a significant change in the relationship of American corporations to the local society and environment.

36 File 4, Box 11, Standard Fruit Papers; report by S. H. Baker, manager, Bluefields Fruit & Steamship Co., Bluefields, August 24, 1912, RG 84, USNA; *The American* (Bluefields), June 18–25, 1906; April 26, 1909.

37 Mary W. Helms, *Asang: Adaptations to Culture Contact in a Miskito Community* (Gainesville: University of Florida Press, 1971), pp. 4–7, 110–13, 220–25.

Bragmans Bluff directly penetrated the countryside in Mosquitia. The company's investments included not only port facilities but one hundred miles of railroads, bridges, an electrical plant, a creosote plant, an ice factory, a company store and housing for managers and workers, as well as segregated mess halls. The company entered the production process more directly, with individual farm managers supervising work on the company's plantations.

Bragmans Bluff offered a wide array of enticements to its workers. They received higher wages than in the domestic economy, housing and a diverse range of consumer goods, and could avail themselves of medical care. Yet with those benefits came dramatic new requirements as to how they lived and worked. The company made it clear that its 2,000 workers were now strictly wage earners, whom the firm paid directly in the form of company scrip. They were no longer occasional day laborers who might engage in subsistence agriculture. When a black carpenter built a home along a creek bed and began clearing land for a few crops, the firm's manager, H. D. Scott, ordered him to stop, for, as he noted, "Why have a man on a salary working against the company's interests?"[38] In addition to the end of their lifestyle of occasional labor to supplement subsistence agriculture, workers soon discovered that the corporate edifices represented a new regimentation which strictly divided the once common rural environment of work place and home. When workers' families began using the mess hall as a community center, it brought a quick reproach from the company. The role of women was changing dramatically. Their direct role in producing material goods for the family via food preparation, work in the fields etc. would be shifting to that of the principal buyer of consumer products.[39]

Much like the experience of early industrial workers in Western Europe, bewilderment and disorganization characterized workers' initial attempts to come to grips with the new reality of the large-scale enterprises that now directly entered their environment. The disorientation and disorganization of the local populace in the face of these rapid changes in work relations and material conditions were suggested by H. D. Scott, who commented "that there are a lot of good men here that are capable of giving the company good service, but there seems to be a lack of cooperation and team work."[40] Divisions within coastal society further complicated efforts at united action.

Reflecting the ethnic diversity of the coastal region, the workforce at the Bragmans Bluff Company included creoles, Indians and Hispanic Nicaraguans. Strong ethnic tensions had long existed among these

38 Scott to John Miceli, Bragmans Bluff, August 5, 1925, File 3, Box 10, Standard Fruit Papers.
39 Files 3–5, Box 10, Standard Fruit Papers.
40 Susan Buck-Morss, *The Dialectics of Seeing: Walter Benjamin and the Arcades Project* (Cambridge: MIT Press, 1989), p. 70; Scott to Miceli, Bragmans Bluff, July 13, 1925, File 3, Box 10, Standard Fruit Papers.

groups, reflecting the shifts in political and economic power which had occurred in the region over the past half century.[41] The company found cultural differences compatible with its own division of labor. Indians, who were not inclined to drink alcoholic beverages, were preferred as employees on the farms, where the bootlegging traffic proved difficult to control. Their mestizo counterparts, who enjoyed alcohol, worked in railway construction, where they could be more closely supervised. Even distinct Indian groups related to the company in different ways. Many Miskito Indians supplemented their subsistence activities by selling foodstuffs to the company. Sumu Indians vehemently protested against government concessions which turned over their lands to the firm.[42]

Despite the signs of disorientation that marked the company's early workforce, Bragmans manager H. D. Scott confidently predicted that with assurances of long-term employment "in a short time these men will be pulling together and quit being at cross purposes which seems to be the popular pastime at present."[43] Longer exposure to Bragmans Bluff would in fact bring increased cooperation in work and in resistance. If the social and material culture of American enterprises, along with ethnic differences, initially divided and disoriented workers, it also gave them common ground for dissent. Nicaraguan workers were not entirely unprepared for their new environment. Workers from the small banana plantations of the Atlantic coast, and those from the coffee estates of western Nicaragua, as well as independent growers, had previously operated within a market economy where wages played a role. They also possessed a set of values that they would posit in opposition to American corporate culture's emphasis on individual accumulation and ambition.

The country people of western Nicaragua sprang from the mutualist culture of rural subsistence settlements that attributed the accumulation of wealth to pacts with the devil, and interpreted wage labor as a form of bestiality. This rural mythology embodied a set of normative values that challenged capitalism's disintegrative impact on rural social relations and institutions that provided a degree of social and economic equality. Emerging from these experiences, Nicaraguans would attempt to fashion a set of relationships with the American corporations that were redefining the social and economic order.[44] Those responses were also shaped by the type of American enterprise with which they were dealing.

The company town in the United States, with its housing, stores and medical facilities, had become a common symbol of industrial welfare designed to appease workers, and it provided the indirect benefit of expand-

41 H. D. Scott, progress report, Bragmans Bluff, January 23, 1926, File 5, Box 10, Standard Fruit Papers; Ferris to Jefferson, Bluefields, November 6, 1914, RG 84, USNA.

42 Helms, *Asang,* pp. 112–13; Dozier, *Mosquito Shore,* p. 201.

43 Scott to Miceli, Bragmans Bluff, July 13, 1925, File 3, Box 10, Standard Fruit Papers.

44 Milagros Palma, *Por los senderos míticos de Nicaragua* (Bogotá: Editorial Nueva América, 1987), pp. 160–62; Gould, *To Lead as Equals,* pp. 29–31.

ing internal markets. In Central America, U.S. corporations which focused on export industries had had little interest in wage policies designed to expand internal demand. Moreover, the banana companies relied on their supervisors to secure large numbers of unskilled workers and extract the maximum amount of physical exertion from them. Those conditions, combined with American racial attitudes, gave a low priority to industrial welfare programs. The failure to actively pursue such programs, combined with the disruptions and demands of the new environment, prompted overt protests by workers.

In seeking to shape their relationship to the new enterprises that now comprised the principal social and physical elements of their environment, Nicaraguans focused on the issues of the wage system, their vulnerability within a commodity economy and the work discipline now imposed on them. Responses to those conditions emerged first among workers in large-group, cooperative situations. In October of 1921, the dockworkers at Bluefields struck against the Cuyamel Company until it agreed to rescind a wage cut. Such direct challenges to the companies ran the risk of overt repression. In September 1925 a group of fifty Cuyamel farm workers intent on demanding a pay increase headed down the San Gregorio River toward the firm's regional headquarters. Troops from the local military detachment aborted the labor protest by ambushing and killing a number of the workers.[45] Discontent soon stirred among mine workers as well and provided the support base for Augusto Sandino.

When Sandino joined the Liberal cause in 1926, he recruited his first group of followers from among the miners at the San Albino mine in northern Nueva Segovia province. His small band had centered its attention on attacking Conservative strongholds. But the willingness of the mine workers to join him reflected their long experience with cooperative work environments and a growing discontent with conditions at the mine. That discontent would eventually focus on the American enterprise itself.[46]

Charles Butters, an American mining engineer with long experience in South Africa and Mexico, had invested some $750,000 in the San Albino mine. Butters created a patriarchal environment, responding to the individual needs and personal emergencies of his workers. However, in August 1926 he installed a system of company scrip, or *vales*. As his funding ran low, Butters arranged for a local merchant to honor the scrip in return for an exclusive company store concession. The mine workers soon found themselves facing extortionist prices for basic necessities. In December 1926 they engaged in a four-day strike, demanding higher wages and payment in cash. By June 1927, with conditions at the mines reaching the breaking point, Sandino announced that if full cash payment were not

45 Thomas W. Waters to secretary of state, Bluefields, October 13, 1921, 817.5045/5, rl. 70, M-632, RG 59, USNA; Rafael de Nogales y Mendez, *The Looting of Nicaragua* (New York: R. M. McBride, 1928), p. 199.

46 Selser, *Sandino*, p. 65; Macaulay, *Sandino Affair*, pp. 54–55.

made to the workers by the fifteenth of the month, he would seize the company and pay the miners. True to his word, Sandino and his followers occupied the mine and operated it for several months, until U.S. marines threatened to invade the area. At that point, the Sandinistas demolished the mine and retreated.[47]

The events at San Albino captured in microcosm the social forces that fed Sandino's movement and the factors that motivated many of his followers. With their own set of mutualist values, Nicaraguans from U.S.-owned mines, banana plantations and logging operations had attempted to negotiate the new economic terrain of work in American enterprises, only to experience denial of newly found aspirations for material improvement. Those experiences helped sway these Nicaraguans to Sandino's cause. For them Sandino's movement, which challenged the repressive actions of both the Nicaraguan state and American military forces, represented an opportunity for direct action against the harsher aspects of American corporate culture that undermined its larger promise of improvement in the human condition. As William Cumberland reported in April 1928:

Formerly United States Marines were considered by the Nicaraguans as invincible. That reputation has for the moment been superseded by open contempt for the inability of American forces, with all modern equipment, to capture the bandits adhering to Sandino, though the latter are greatly outnumbered.[48]

The opportunity which Sandino's movement provided for workers to respond directly to the new social and economic environment in which they now lived became even clearer when Sandino attacked the La Luz and Los Angeles Mining Company in eastern Nicaragua.

The La Luz corporation represented an American tradition in Nicaragua. Its concession dated back to the late nineteenth century. The Fletchers, a prominent Pittsburgh business family who had enjoyed close ties to U.S. Secretary of State Philander C. Knox, owned the concession. Cancellation of the concession had prompted the Fletchers to help finance the Estrada rebellion, and their former employee Adolfo Díaz had served as president of Nicaragua. By 1928 the Fletchers' links to Nicaragua's Atlantic coast had multiplied, with one member of the family, Samuel Fletcher, serving as consul at Bluefields while his brother Martin became superintendent of the Bragmans Bluff commissary at Puerto Cabezas. On April 24 a Sandinista force seized the La Luz mine and demolished it with twenty-five cases of dynamite. They then headed off to attack another of the company's mines.

47 Munro to secretary of state, Managua, September 17, 1927; Charles Eberhardt to secretary of state, Managua, July 3, 1928, 317.115B98/5/12, RG 59, USNA.
48 William W. Cumberland to secretary of state, Managua, March 10, 1928, 817.51/1921, rl. 89, M-632, RG 59, USNA.

Sandino could hardly have chosen a more appropriate symbol for his campaign to drive out or redefine the nature of American investment in Nicaragua. Yet the attack arose from more than a nationalist campaign. Workers at the mine received $1.50 per day in wages, of which $1 was deducted for food and medical services, leaving the miners 50 cents to clothe and feed their families. The Fletchers paid strictly in scrip, and their company store charged exorbitant prices. Added to this were ten-hour workdays in the shafts. As an American engineer reported, "The miners in this and many other ways deprived of making even a modest living have had good reason for revolt and found in Sandino's movement a splendid opportunity to take revenge over their former superiors."[49] That dissent finally turned on the Bragmans Bluff Company as well.

By 1931 the Great Depression had struck the Moskito coast, leading the Bragmans Bluff Company to undertake major layoffs. Rising unemployment added to the growing discontent with the company. Between 1931 and 1932 the Sandinistas launched three major attacks on the company's facilities, the most important coming in April 1931. Despite the presence of a fifty-man detachment of the U.S.-trained and -commanded Nicaraguan National Guard, paid for by the company, the Sandinista forces laid waste the firm's facilities at Logtown and killed nine Americans, including a U.S. marine captain. The company's local network of paid informants failed to warn of the guerrillas' approach during any of the three attacks. The U.S. commander of the Guardia explained that the failure stemmed from the support which the rebels enjoyed in the region. Local residents aided the insurgents while refusing to supply information to the Guardia.[50] Before he was killed by an American air strike during the Logtown attack, the rebel leader Pedro Blandón explained the Sandinistas' mission. They had come to drive off the Americans, who exploited Nicaraguan farm workers and treated them as slaves. Despite Blandón's efforts to conduct a disciplined military operation, many of Bragmans' unemployed workers ignored his warnings and launched their own attacks on the company's property.[51] Yet the attacks on Bragmans Bluff marked a high-water mark for the Sandinista movement.

The experience of American corporate culture provided an important base of support for Sandino among the workers of U.S. mining, logging and banana companies in northern and eastern Nicaragua. The Sandinista movement also drew support from among peasants along the coffee frontier in Nueva Segovia. But even among these groups there were limits to Sandinismo's appeal. Many Miskito Indians with a strong reliance on American consumer goods and an antipathy toward Nicaragua's Spanish-

49 Fletcher to American minister, Managua, Bluefields, May 17, 1928, 317.115L15/6, RG 59, USNA.

50 317.115ST2/1–60, RG 59, USNA.

51 Statement of Austin Murphy, Bragmans Bluff, May 9, 1931, File 60, Box 10, Standard Fruit Papers.

speaking population would join Americans in defining the Sandino era as "the time of the bandits."[52] Furthermore, the bulk of the nation's rural population, located in western Nicaragua, shared an experience distinct from that of these wage workers and free peasants. Most still clung to village lands, squatted on small parcels of public or private land, or served as tenants or occasional laborers for the coffee fincas and other agrarian estates. Their relationships of tenancy and debt peonage provided a distinct experience from that of the free peasants and wage laborers of Nueva Segovia and the Moskito coast. For them Sandino's message of anti-Americanism had little immediate significance.[53] American intervention provided a further limitation to the spread of Sandinismo.

Despite the stunning successes of Sandinista raids in northern and eastern Nicaragua, the western half of the country remained securely under the control of U.S. marines and the National Guard during the insurgency. Although the Sandinistas could pose a threat to coffee growers as far south as Matagalpa province, most of the countryside remained under government control. Lacking viable alternatives, workers in western Nicaragua continued to throw their support to the traditional Liberal party. As the social and tactical limits of Sandinismo became apparent, the strength of the National Guard grew.[54] By the beginning of 1933, the American-trained and -equipped Guardia, now commanded by the Liberal politician Anastasio Somoza, had battled Sandino to a military standoff, and a truce was declared. With the truce in place, the Guardia choked off important sources of support for the movement such as the Bragmans Bluff workers.

A Nicaraguan officer assumed command of the 150-man Guardia unit at Puerto Cabezas in December 1932. However, the officer was not one of the new breed of U.S.-trained officers, but a civilian from Masaya. As a result he failed to show the special concern for American corporate interests that became a hallmark of Somoza's Guardia. When workers at Bragmans Bluff attempted to organize a union to press for higher wages and better working conditions, the company manager threw the labor organizers off the company's property. The local Guardia commander objected on the ground that workers had a right to organize in their own country. When the American vice consul visited the officer, the commander asserted that his duty was to protect Nicaraguans as well as foreigners. The company manager arranged for Somoza to remove the offending officer. The commander's departure prompted local residents to turn out to express both their support for him and their anti-American sentiments. By February 1933 the workers were once again organizing, pressing for higher wages

---

52 Helms, *Asang,* p. 112.

53 Wheelock, *Imperialismo y dictadura,* pp. 17–108.

54 Matthew Hanna to secretary of state, Managua, May 15, 1931, 317.115ST2/35, RG 59, USNA; Munro to secretary of state, Managua, January 12, 1928; Eberhardt to secretary of state, Managua, February 14, 1928, 817.5045/16, 17, rl. 70, M-632, RG 59, USNA; Gould, *To Lead as Equals,* pp. 35–37.

and better living and working conditions. But the company could now turn to the new American-trained commander of the Somocista Guardia detachment to counter those efforts.[55] Exactly one year later, Somoza arranged the assassination of Augusto Sandino and soon seized power in his own name. Despite Somoza's reputation as a creation and creature of the U.S. government, American corporations contributed to many of the historical forces that led to the emergence of Somoza as Nicaragua's dominant political force.[56]

American corporations had played a central role in the national development plans of both Liberals and Conservatives. And American companies had responded with an array of activities which expanded Nicaraguan exports of bananas, hardwoods and mining products and placed new revenues in the hands of the Nicaraguan government. That program of economic growth allowed Nicaragua's rulers to exploit the resources of a region over which they had previously held only tenuous political and economic control. Yet none of the principals could foresee the extent to which these activities would destabilize Nicaragua. Elite plans for foreign-assisted national development would eventually clash with the interests of small business people and workers. Under Zelaya, monopolistic concessions and tariffs designed to spur development alienated not only the *obreristas* but planters who found their interests subordinated to those of United Fruit. In attempting to appease both sides, Zelaya sowed the seeds of his own destruction. The American government's reformist intervention opened the way for Sandino by prolonging the crisis within the Nicaraguan elite and by giving Sandino the nationalist issue of anti-Americanism to distinguish himself from his former allies in the Liberal party and his old foes in the Conservative party. But again it was American corporate culture that generated much of the social base for rebellion inspired by Sandinismo and that determined the limits of that movement.

Despite their diverse backgrounds, the Nicaraguans who labored in the plantations and mines of American corporations drew on prior experiences with wage labor, patriarchal work conditions, subsistence agriculture and the relations and institutions of peasant society to cope with the new reality they encountered in the American work place. Pure wage labor, a rationalized social hierarchy based on productive functions and the commodity economy constituted an alien environment, prompting both adaptation and rebellion by Nicaraguan workers. Sandino's armed nationalist campaign provided these social forces with the opportunity to overtly express their reactions to American corporate culture. Yet Sandinismo's appeals for a crusade against American political domination and the opportunity it provided to vent opposition to American corporate culture

---

55 Eli Taylor to secretary of state, Puerto Cabezas, January 3, 18, 1933, 817.00/7691, 7722, RG 59, USNA.

56 On Somoza, see Gould, *To Lead as Equals,* pp. 65–112.

meant little to the majority of the population of western Nicaragua. Thus American penetration helped spur the emergence of Sandinismo at the same time as it defined some of its limits. Just to the north, in Honduras, American corporations would play an even larger role in shaping events in Central America.

4

Honduras

. . . we learned that everything that was said in the interior about the North Coast was false. We lived enveloped by a tempestuous, poor and terrible life. (Prisión verde)

In 1916 the American consul in Puerto Cortés, Honduras, observed, "An account of the independent banana industry, must necessarily be historical, for although the poverty stricken planters and their grass grown plantations are of the present, the industry is now of the past."[1] That observation captured one important aspect of the revolutionary changes which American fruteras brought to Honduras, making it Central America's leading banana exporter and the country most affected by American corporate culture in the first third of the twentieth century.

Because of exceptionally favorable soil and climatological conditions, Honduras became the primary theater of operations for a competitive war among three American corporate giants, the United, Standard, and Cuyamel fruit companies. The enfeebled condition of the Honduran elite allowed these corporations to operate with little interference from the central government. Nowhere else in Central America would the companies enjoy such complete freedom to introduce American corporate culture. And nowhere else in Central America would they have as dramatic an impact on local society. The fruteras would remake the northern coast of Honduras. They would dominate the area's economy and its political institutions. That control allowed the fruit companies to introduce the material products, work disciplines, social hierarchy and value systems of American corporate culture to an unprecedented degree.

The three American companies invested over $70 million in the region. They built hundreds of miles of railroads, dredged rivers and built port facilities and factories as well as telegraph and radio networks. Their expansion of the banana trade prompted the emergence of a vibrant group of small planters and merchants, while the wages they paid and the consumer goods they offered attracted thousands of Honduran peasants to the

---

1 Walter F. Boyle, consul, "Annual Report on Commerce and Industries, 1915," Puerto Cortés, July 7, 1916, RG 84, USNA.

coast. In the process they transformed the country into the world's leading banana producer. At the same time the fruteras' interactions with a local elite, stymied in its attempts at modernization, severely destabilized the nation's political process. Over time the companies' relationships with coastal residents would disintegrate. Merchants and planters would battle the fruteras' increasing control over the local economy. Peasants, while assimilating aspects of corporate culture such as consumer goods, reacted against the modern work discipline and the vagaries of wage labor and market forces. They eventually allied themselves with small planters and merchants to exploit cracks in the facade of elite power and redefine their relations with American corporations. The emergence of these resistance communities triggered the most protracted series of overt responses to American corporate culture in Central America. The roots of this complex process of assimilation and rejection can be found in the failure of Honduras' liberal revolution.

The effort at liberal modernization began in earnest during the last quarter of the nineteenth century. But the hoped-for economic miracle failed to materialize. Only the foreign mining concessions generated substantial results, and Honduras' export levels paled in comparison with those achieved by its neighbors. Down to the end of the nineteenth century, smallholder subsistence agriculture and a livestock industry that produced largely for export characterized the Honduran countryside. As late as the 1890s the bulk of cultivated land in Honduras consisted of *ejidal* properties worked by subsistence producers. The persistence of communal properties can in part be attributed to demographic and geographic factors. Low population density and a rugged terrain contributed to the survival of subsistence agriculture and facilitated popular resistance to state projects for modernization such as road building.[2]

In the absence of a strong, domestically controlled export sector, the state, despite its limited resources, remained the target of political squabbles among regional caudillos. At the same time the timidity of the elite's efforts to reshape peasant society spared Honduras the deeper social conflicts and political instability that afflicted its neighbors. Between 1841 and 1903 the country enjoyed an exceptional degree of political stability as fourteen presidents governed for fifty-eight of those sixty-two years.[3] And while domestic forces failed to transform the countryside, foreign corporations would soon undertake that task.

As early as the 1870s, New Orleans merchant vessels visited Honduras' tropical Atlantic coast to purchase bananas from a thriving community of small planters. By 1896 this trade accounted for nearly 23 percent of all national exports. But the business remained a high-risk one with severe price volatility and a product that was extremely perishable. The Ameri-

---

2 Guevara-Escudero, "Nineteenth-Century Honduras," pp. 38–57, 145, 228.
3 Brand, "Capitalistic Underdevelopment," p. 40.

can fruit companies secured a degree of price stability by arranging purchase contracts with local growers, but increased control over local transportation and land were essential to safeguard their enterprises and ensure their continued growth. The Honduran elite welcomed the American companies for two reasons. First, the inhospitable climate and lack of infrastructure on the Atlantic coast discouraged large-scale domestic development of the area. If the Americans would undertake the task, they would assume the risk of developing an area which had little immediate value to the elite. Furthermore, in light of Honduras' failed program for commercializing agriculture, the Americans offered the one immediate hope of creating a significant export economy. Honduran political leaders offered a range of generous concessions for railroads, land and ports, complemented by the free import of equipment and consumer goods. Banana taxes of 1.5 cents per stem were among the lowest in Central America. Those generous concessions accomplished their purpose of attracting large-scale American investments. When the Vaccaro brothers purchased their first banana plantations in 1899, they initiated three decades of frantic activity in Honduras by American fruteras.

The Vaccaros focused their initial activities on their own plantations, supplemented by purchase contracts with local growers. Operating out of the coastal village of La Ceiba, the Vaccaros extended their activities inland with a 1904 government concession to build a railroad and to dig channels in the sand-clogged Saldo and El Porvenir rivers. A second railway concession in 1910 gave the firm 250 hectares of public land for each kilometer of rail built. By 1927 the Vaccaro interests, now incorporated as the Standard Fruit and Steamship Company, had invested $27 million in banana lands, railroads, the wharf at La Ceiba, a sugar mill, a brewery and a bank.[4] At the same time, a second giant frutera emerged to the west of La Ceiba, near the Guatemalan border.

In 1911 Samuel Zemurray bought an American-owned concession for 5,000 hectares of land along the Cuyamel River and formed the Cuyamel Fruit Company. Exporting his fruit from Puerto Cortés, Zemurray also extended his holdings eastward toward the Ulúa and Chamelicón rivers. Less than a decade after its establishment, the company's holdings had a value of $16 million and included over 24,000 acres of cultivated banana lands, more than 100 miles of railroads, and a sugar mill, as well as electrical and water plants.[5] Zemurray had gone heavily into debt to finance his initial plunge into Honduras, and his repayment of that debt opened the way for United Fruit's investments there.

The United Fruit Company had extended its control in the banana industry by partially financing such competitors as the Vaccaros and Ze-

4 "Report on American Investments in Honduras, 1930," 811.503115/4, RG 59, USNA; Karnes, *Tropical Enterprise*, pp. 46–50, 71–73, 90–92.
5 Boyle, "Annual Report on Commerce and Industries, 1915," July 7, 1916, RG 84, USNA; "Report on American Investments in Honduras, 1930," 811.503115/4, RG 59, USNA; "Cuyamel Fruit Company," Scudder Collection.

murray and receiving stock in return. United owned 60 percent of the Hubbard–Zemurray Company, and Zemurray's debt grew with his investments in Honduras. By 1912 Zemurray had used his Honduran political connections to free himself of United's control. He obtained a railway concession with generous land provisions for the port of Tela, which lay to the east of the Vaccaro holdings. He then transferred this concession to United, which quickly obtained a second concession for the port of Truxillo, also known as Puerto Castilla. United soon emerged as the country's leading banana producer. The company's holdings, valued at $24 million, included over 450 miles of railways and 400,000 acres of land, 80,000 acres of it cultivated in bananas. The American multinationals had not only transformed the face of Honduras' Atlantic coast, they had also destabilized its political system.[6]

Along with purchase contracts and land concessions, American fruit enterprises saw in the enfeebled condition of the Honduran state an opportunity to safeguard their investments and ensure the growth of their ventures. Control of the state offered an array of potential benefits for the companies, including even lower taxation and more generous land grants, as well as policies to discourage competitors. But in the short term the three companies' efforts to monopolize the state turned it into an arena for competitive struggles among the fruteras.

The American banana companies totally dominated the national economy. The government collected over half its customs duties from the fruteras. In a country of only 650,000 people, they directly employed some 22,000. Their payroll disbursements alone exceeded the annual national budget. With the local elite lacking a strong domestic economic base, the fruteras' dominance of the local economy gave them a central role in the national political process. The companies' official payroll figures did not reflect the fact that virtually every state official on the Atlantic coast, from customs clerks to governors, received payments from the companies that exceeded their government salaries. Faced with a perpetually impoverished treasury, Honduran executives regularly turned to the fruteras for extensions of credit or guarantees of bank loans.[7]

Given the banana companies' importance, local caudillos periodically targeted the fruteras in their political struggles. The Atlantic coast became a logical launching pad for attempted coups, since challenges to the region's banana companies threatened the financial base of the national government. Regional caudillos regularly harassed the companies to se-

---

6 Mario Posas and Rafael del Cid, *La construcción del sector público y del estado nacional de Honduras, 1876–1979* (Ciudad Universitaria Rodrigo Facio, Costa Rica: Editorial Universitaria Centroamericana, 1981), p. 32; Karnes, *Tropical Enterprise*, chap. 4; "Report on American Investments in Honduras, 1930," 811.503115/4, RG 59, USNA.

7 Gaston Smith, "Expenditures Made in Honduras by the Various Corporations Controlled by the United Fruit Company of the U.S.A," Tegucigalpa, January 21, 1932, 815.6156/44, RG 59, USNA; Karnes, *Tropical Enterprise*, pp. 76–77; Lawrence Higgins to secretary of state, Tegucigalpa, November 20, 1933, 815.00/4592, RG 59, USNA.

cure bribes, enhance their local standing and grab the attention of the national government. Yet it was the fruteras themselves that incited much of the political turmoil.

In 1911 Samuel Zemurray stymied a U.S. government effort to put Honduran government finances under the control of J. P. Morgan. Zemurray financed a successful coup by former president Manuel Bonilla and then had himself appointed as the Honduran government's fiscal agent in the United States. The entrepreneur arranged a $500,000 loan through a New Orleans bank and received generous land and railway concessions in return. In the aftermath of that intervention, the government became the scene of a mounting power struggle between Zemurray and United Fruit.[8]

In 1923 United paid a $15,000 bribe to the Honduran minister of the interior for authorization to dig an irrigation canal. When Cuyamel protested that the canal would reduce water flow to its plantations in the Ulúa Valley, President Raphael López Gutierrez agreed to rescind the concession. However, the president's private secretary assured a United representative that a $25,000 payment would keep the concession in force. When United refused to pay, López Gutierrez rescinded the canal authorization and received a $100,000 loan from Cuyamel. While steering clear of the Cuyamel–United fray, Standard Fruit also secured government influence with over $1.5 million in loans and credits. The hand-to-mouth financing of the Honduran state assured pliable regimes. This strategy was backed up with the influence that the fruteras exercised over regional caudillos.[9]

Cuyamel kept a number of local power brokers, such as General Gregorio Ferrera, on its payroll. Cuyamel financed Ferrera's activities as an independent banana planter in the San Pedro Sula region near the Guatemalan border. It also paid him a retainer of $1,000 per month. Ferrera's importance stemmed from his private army of 2,000 Intibuca Indians. Individual power brokers like Ferrera could harass competing fruit companies and the central government, or they could ensure stability in the regions where the fruteras operated and grant important favors when they rose to positions in the national government.[10]

In the ongoing battle between Cuyamel and United Fruit, the companies tended to identify with specific political factions. Cuyamel enjoyed

8 Charles D. White to secretary of state, Tegucigalpa, February 4, 1912, 815.51/326, rl. 36, M-647, RG 59, USNA. Given the fruteras' subsequent strategy of keeping the Honduran government on a short leash by granting it only small loans, Zemurray's failure to secure a larger loan may have been deliberate.

9 Franklin E. Morales to secretary of state, Tegucigalpa, December 18, 1923, 315.1141C99; William Spencer to secretary of state, Tegucigalpa, August 31, 1921, 815.51/442, rl. 37, M-647, RG 59, USNA; Karnes, *Tropical Enterprise,* pp. 75–78.

10 Julius G. Lay to secretary of state, Tegucigalpa, August 6, September 6, 1930, rl. 1, UPAMC, RG 84, USNA; Posas and del Cid, *Sector público,* p. 50.

strong ties to the Liberals, but the company also had close relations with Manuel Bonilla, the founding father of the National party. Its opposition to the Nationals largely focused on the faction led by Tiburcio Carías Andino. Carías, an influential merchant and planter from the Atlantic coast, had became a close ally of United. His faction of the National party in the Honduran Congress repeatedly stymied the efforts of Cuyamel to resolve a dispute with the government over rail lines that Cuyamel had illegally constructed.[11] In 1924 Cuyamel and United attempted to reach a truce, with both companies agreeing "to stop advancing money to the Government of Honduras and rival political leaders and generally to stop interfering in politics . . ."[12] Yet the truce soon collapsed, and the banana wars continued.

As local elites vied to tap the new resources of the state and the fruteras, and the corporations competed to monopolize the national political process, Honduras entered into one of its most tumultuous political periods. Between 1901 and 1933 the government changed hands fourteen times, and the country experienced 159 rebellions.[13] As the U.S. minister to Honduras noted, the fruit companies rejected attempts by the U.S. State Department to stabilize Honduran finances because "their interests appear to be best served when the country is in a state of turmoil and the Government financially embarrassed – conditions which permit the companies to obtain valuable concessions, exemptions, privileges etc."[14] Banana workers, small planters and merchants took advantage of the turbulent relationships between the national state, the fruteras and regional caudillos, forming alliances which challenged the radical changes that American corporations had brought to the Atlantic coast.

In the last quarter of the nineteenth century a vibrant class of independent banana planters emerged on the coast. They had been attracted both by the opportunities of the fast-growing banana trade and by a national agrarian law that provided for the purchase or free leaseholding of public lands. The growth in their numbers and business derived in large measure from the activities of American fruit companies, which expanded the U.S. market for the fruit, introduced regular shipping schedules and eventually upgraded local transportation facilities. Even as the banana trade came under the control of firms such as the Vaccaros and United Fruit, and merchandising shifted from spot to contract purchases, their relations with the banana companies remained freewheeling and contentious. They frequently had a member of their extended family negotiate and sign

---

11 Mario Posas, *Luchas del movimiento obrero Hondureño* (Ciudad Universitaria Rodrigo Facio, Costa Rica: Editorial Universitaria Centroamericana, 1981), p. 69; Posas and del Cid, *Sector público*, p. 48.

12 Dana Munro to Francis White, Division of Latin American Affairs, memorandum, October 30, 1924, 123M793/45, RG 59, USNA.

13 Posas and del Cid, *Sector público*, p. 51.

14 Lawrence Dennis to secretary of state, Tegucigalpa, September 5, 1925, 815.51/607, rl. 38, M-647, RG 59, USNA.

fixed-price contracts with the companies, leaving them free to sell their produce on the open market should prices rise above the agreed-on figure. The companies responded in kind, allowing employees who did not possess power of attorney to sign the agreements. As the contract system took hold, local growers lost the advantage of price swings that could suddenly increase profits, but also gained some degree of protection from the volatility of the export market.[15]

The Vaccaro brothers established stable contractual relations with a number of local producers. The Cuyamel company relied strictly on its own production and therefore did not directly impact market conditions for growers. In fact, Samuel Zemurray, intent on building a local political base, took advantage of the duty-free import clauses of his concessions to provide equipment and other necessities to well-to-do planters in the regions which Cuyamel developed. But the fruteras' direct entry into the production process after the turn of the century shifted the balance of power sharply toward the companies.[16]

As the banana corporations developed the capability to produce at least half of all the fruit they shipped, their bargaining power with local planters increased dramatically. Their control of rail lines, channeled waterways and ocean steamers allowed them to dictate prices and choke off exports by independent growers when market conditions deteriorated. The local growers complained that even when they delivered bananas under contract, the companies often rejected a significant portion, leaving planters convinced that the rate of rejection depended on the price in the United States rather than the quality of the fruit.[17] While small planters retained control over their land, their operations were increasingly regulated by the fruit companies. The price for their product, their access to transportation, even the wages they paid their own workers had all become functions of the fruteras. For those whose enterprises failed completely, wage labor on corporate plantations became a final, desperate resort. These growers found themselves in a social and economic environment largely dictated by the fruit companies.[18] Local merchants discovered themselves in a similar position.

The coastal merchant class, like the planters, emerged from the commodity economy generated by the banana trade. And as with the planters, commercial interests divided into two distinct groups. Eight large trading firms handled over 60 percent of the coastal commerce that did not fall under the direct control of the fruit companies. A much larger group of small merchants, many of them of American and Middle Eastern origins, accounted for the remaining third of local trade. The growth of the

15 Bulmer-Thomas, *Political Economy of Central America*, p. 36.

16 Karnes, *Tropical Enterprise*, p. 28; Charles David Kepner Jr. and Jay Henry Soothill, *The Banana Empire: A Case Study in Economic Imperialism* (1935). (New York: Russell and Russell, 1967), pp. 115–16.

17 David Myers to secretary of state, Puerto Cortés, December 5, 1913, RG 84, USNA.

18 Kepner, *Social Aspects*, p. 105.

fruteras indirectly benefited small merchants. Growth in the banana trade increased the numbers and activity of small planters, who in turn provided the most direct stimulus to local business. The thousands of workers attracted by the fruit companies represented another expanding clientele for local shopkeepers. However, as the power of the fruteras increased, their impact on merchants became increasingly negative. The decline of local growers meant the disappearance of some of the merchants' best customers. The growth of the coupon and commissary system increasingly excluded small merchants from the frutera marketplace. The fruit companies, with concessions that granted them duty-free imports, could easily undersell local shopkeepers. By the time of the First World War, the Atlantic coast was torn by an increasingly bitter struggle which pitted the banana companies against the shopkeepers and small planters. It was a struggle in which workers would ally themselves with the coast's small business people.[19]

Until the end of the nineteenth century, Honduras' population had remained concentrated in the central highlands. As late as 1905, about 45,000 people, or less than 10 percent of the national population, lived in the rural communities which had grown up around Atlantic coast villages and towns such as La Ceiba and Tela.[20] In those settlements, Honduran peasants constructed their thatched shacks close by the small plots of beans and rice that provided them with sustenance. Bananas provided an occasional cash crop for the unscheduled visits of New Orleans merchant vessels. After the turn of the century, population increases in the highlands and more aggressive government efforts at commercializing agriculture brought on a slow but certain collapse of the campesino economy. Combined with the prospects of vacant lands to squat on and possible employment with the new fruteras, a growing number of Honduran peasants migrated to the coast. Between 1905 and 1927 the coastal population doubled, compared with a 40 percent increase in the national population.[21]

The promise of material prosperity which attracted Honduras' rural population to work for the fruit companies is eloquently described in Ramón Amaya-Amador's work *Prisión verde*. In that novel, a banana worker described how he and his family had migrated from the highlands, lured by the promise of the new El Dorado on the Atlantic coast:

The time came when just the name of the North Coast or of the Companies awakened ambitions, and the popular mind fashioned the most fantastic tales about the marvelous life that moved to the captivating rhythm of the Dance of the Dollars. . . .

19 Walter F. Boyle, "Annual Report of Commerce and Industries," Puerto Cortés, January 13, 1917, RG 84, USNA; Boyle, "Annual Report on Commerce and Industries, 1915," July 7, 1916, RG 84, USNA.

20 "República de Honduras, Censo de la Población, 1910," 815.5011/1, rl. 33, M-647, RG 59, USNA.

21 "República de Honduras, Censo de la Población, 1927," 815.5011/2, rl. 33, M-647, RG 59, USNA.

Figure 4. Workers' housing on a United Fruit banana plantation near Tela,
Honduras, 1925. While the barracks had a drab and monotonous appearance,
American managers believed that these manufactured dwellings were far more
suitable for human habitation than local thatched huts. (United Fruit Company
Collection, Baker Library, Harvard Business School)

My father could not escape that fever of adventure: the North Coast rang in his head until
he was delirious, and after selling what little he possessed for next to nothing we began
our journey across valleys and mountains, on foot![22]

These migrants did encounter a world of wonders created by the fruteras.
On the once-barren coast, the companies had built wharves and entire
towns while stretching their impact inland with steel rails and engines.
These facilities throbbed with activity long into the night under the arti-
ficial luminescence of electric lights. For workers the companies meant
higher wages than they could earn in the interior, access to housing and
medical treatment, and stores stocked with a cornucopia of consumer
goods. Yet the transition to this new life was not an easy one.

These migrants brought with them their own life experiences of independent rural villages, centered on communally held lands and subsistence economies. As a group, the rural population of the coast represented

22 Ramón Amaya Amador, *Prisión verde* (1950) (Tegucigalpa: Editorial Universitaria, 1987), pp.
32–33.

Figure 5. Superintendent's residence on a United Fruit farm near Tela, Honduras,
1925. The more elaborate housing provided for managers gave physical expression
to their power over local workers in the new corporate order. (United Fruit
Company Collection, Baker Library, Harvard Business School)

poor material for the wage labor force the fruit companies sought to create. As one American observer noted, "The Honduran laborer has never
known peonage or serfdom, the many political upheavals in the country
and the various dictatorships in years gone by have never developed a system of peonage . . ."[23] The Hondurans' experience of peasant villages and
economies stood in sharp contrast to the new reality that confronted them
in the world of the frutera.

The American banana companies in building their towns had replaced
leaf-covered huts with manufactured wooden buildings. The fruit companies carefully regimented and segregated these new communities. The
wood frame homes of the overseers and foremen with their white trimmed
porches and screened windows, carefully set off from the drab manufactured wood shacks of the workers, defined the new social hierarchy. The
facilities for Hondurans were further subdivided between shacks for families and barracks for single males.[24] Work itself became a highly regi-

23 Boyle, "Annual Report of Commerce and Industries," January 13, 1917, RG 84, USNA.
24 See photographic evidence in the United Fruit Company Collection, Baker Library, Harvard Business School, Cambridge, Mass.

mented function, largely conducted on the basis of the task system. Directing this process were an array of administrators, from the head of the agricultural division to district chiefs, individual farm overseers and timekeepers. They carefully subdivided the work process into a set of highly specific tasks that were to be evaluated in terms of quality. United Fruit's description of a timekeeper's functions conveys the precision now demanded in the field. A timekeeper must know "the different classes of work, how the work is assigned, the bases for fixing prices, the points to note," and his "office work should be taken up with the field work, stressing the importance of keeping all data posted up to date, accurately and legibly. The importance of the reports cannot be overemphasized since they are standardized and become permanent records."[25] Fruit companies, which depended on a large unskilled workforce to carry out physically demanding tasks, also created a managerial culture in which supervisors emphasized rigorous discipline to extract the maximum amount of labor with minimal concern for the welfare of workers. In this unforgiving, regimented, standardized world, the Honduran peasant would also find himself thrust into the wonders and vagaries of the consumer market.

Participation in this new world of commodities was not entirely a matter of choice. Workers often received their pay in *ordenes,* or coupons, exchangeable only at the company commissary. Furthermore, the companies rapidly reduced the options available outside the wage and commodity system. Production of foodstuffs in the coastal zone dropped precipitously during the first two decades of the twentieth century for several reasons. As the banana trade grew, local planters converted to banana production. The vast holdings of the fruteras reduced access to tillable lands within reach of principal population centers. These enormous holdings separated peasants from the land and converted them into wage laborers. This process, along with the other social and material aspects of American corporate culture, had a powerful attraction for the Honduran peasantry, but it also contributed to the disintegration of peasant society on the Atlantic coast.[26] In *Prisión verde* the banana worker eloquently describes some of these effects:

. . . we learned that everything that was said in the interior about the North Coast was false. We lived enveloped by a tempestuous, poor and terrible life. The banana camps were something incomprehensible for us simple country people. It was as if we were swept into a turbulent river with everyone else . . . the Company brought progress . . . But my friend this change provoked something terrible in people, like an internal convulsion. On the one hand men felt free from some unknown force while at the same time they felt the shackles of another. This produced chaos. Every day men committed suicide and diseases added to the toll. Liquor and gambling shackled the campesinos in cruel chains.[27]

As the existing physical and social order of the coastal plain disintegrated under the impact of the fruteras, ethnic tensions added to the chaos.

25 *UNIFRUTCO,* June 1927.   26 Kepner, *Social Aspects,* p. 40.
27 Amaya Amador, *Prisión verde,* pp. 32–33.

The collapse of the West Indian sugar industry in the last quarter of the nineteenth century had sent wave after wave of black workers into the economies of the Caribbean Basin. They labored in the sugar fields of Cuba, in the muck and grime of the Panama Canal and in United Fruit banana plantations throughout the region.[28] Experienced in the discipline of plantation work and the realities of wage labor, blacks represented an ideal labor force for the banana companies in Honduras, where the slow disintegration of highland peasant society was failing to provide an adequate labor supply. As one American official explained, black workers, "are traditionally steady dependable workers, while natives can not, as a rule, be depended on to stay at work. The turnover in their case is high and expensive." A second American official explained that Honduran campesinos suffered from "a false race pride . . . whereby few are content to be servants or subordinate workmen."[29]

As a result of the reluctance of Hondurans to submit completely to the new work discipline, the fruteras came to depend heavily on black laborers from Jamaica and British Honduras. By 1927 as many as 4,000 blacks resided on the coast, with their presence guaranteed by a treaty between Honduras and Great Britain. The cultural differences between English-speaking blacks and the local Hispanic population, divisions of labor that ran along ethnic lines, and the use of black workers as scab labor increased tensions between the two groups as the banana companies expanded their operations.[30]

Despite the disorientation of the new social and material environment and rising ethnic tensions, Honduran peasants rapidly came to grips with their changing environment. In less than two decades, rail lines, bridges, port facilities, manufactured housing and commissaries stocked with consumer goods had reshaped the coastal landscape and defined a new social order grounded in wage labor and a commodity economy. Honduran peasants were not entirely unprepared for the experience of a market economy. Those who came directly from the highlands had been exposed to the commercial activity surrounding muleteer activity in rural villages. Earlier arrivals had played a role in the banana trade as small-scale producers and occasional laborers for the larger growers. As a result, banana workers possessed an experiential base on which to draw in confronting their new environment. Their direct actions expressed efforts to retain past security and an effort to establish a viable relationship with the new reality. They would be joined in their protests by local planters and merchants.

On the eve of the Great War, independent growers complained bitterly that the United Fruit Company was deliberately refusing to purchase ba-

28 Philippe I. Bourgois, *Ethnicity at Work: Divided Labor on a Central American Banana Plantation* (Baltimore: Johns Hopkins University Press, 1989), pp. 50–51.

29 Willard L. Beaslian to secretary of state, Puerto Cortés, July 16, 1924, 815.5045/46, rl. 33, M-647, RG 59, USNA; E. M. Lawton, "Annual Report, 1915," Tegucigalpa/La Ceiba, November 8, 1916, RG 84, USNA.

30 Ernest Evans to secretary of state, La Ceiba, January 26, 1927, 815.00/4061, rl. 20, M-647, RG 59, USNA.

nanas shipped on the National Railway as a means of depressing the purchase price of the line, which United wished to acquire. Both planters and merchants believed that if United acquired the line it would use its transportation monopoly to destroy their enterprises. They won only a partial reprieve in 1917 when the Cuyamel Company agreed to purchase bananas shipped on the railway to complete its own cargoes. Cuyamel in return received a 50 percent reduction in rail freight charges for its own bananas. And in 1920 the company obtained full operating control of the railway in return for a $1 million loan to the government. With little direct influence at the national level, the growers and traders tried to exercise influence in regional institutions to checkmate the banana companies.[31]

At least until the 1920s, when ports like La Ceiba and Tela had been completely transformed into company towns, merchants and small growers could effectively voice their discontents through municipal governments. They also appealed to local caudillos, many of whom, like Tiburcio Carías, sprang from the merchant and planter class. In 1914 the shopkeepers of Tela protested bitterly over the fact that United Fruit's commissary was underselling them. Furthermore, United land concessions now completely surrounded the town, preventing its expansion without United's permission. The merchants secured the backing of a local military official, Colonel Mendieta, the brother-in-law of the Honduran minister of war, in an effort to break United's control of the port. Their attempts proved futile, and by the 1920s United had achieved effective control of Tela. Local financial institutions provided another focal point for the conflict.[32]

The fruteras dominated the banking system of the Atlantic coast. The Vaccaro brothers established the Banco Atlantida in 1913 with the assistance of the Guaranty Trust Company of New York, while the Banco de Comercio in Tegucigalpa included the United Fruit Company and the National City Bank as participants. Given the fact that the fruit companies earned most of the region's foreign exchange, the banks could easily manipulate exchange rates. When the banks forced down the exchange rate during the war, damaging the interests of small planters and merchants, these groups struck back. The Chamber of Commerce of La Ceiba launched a campaign calling for an increase in the exchange rate. Merchants in the region initiated a boycott of the banks' paper money. They also boycotted a large American wholesale establishment that refused to cooperate in the campaign. The Banco Atlantida responded, refusing to extend credit to merchants who participated in the boycott. On this occa-

31 "Record of a Conversation which took place in the Diplomatic Room between Messrs Gray and Sanders, Minister Mebreno and Mr. Long," Tegucigalpa, March 10, 1914, 815.77/–, rl. 45, M-647; David J. Myers to Charles D. White, Puerto Cortés, March 15, 1913, 815.77/171, rl. 46, M-647, RG 59, USNA; Boyle, "Annual Report of Commerce and Industries," January 13, 1917, RG 84, USNA.

32 Guevara-Escudero, "Nineteenth-Century Honduras," p. 178; Boyle to secretary of state, La Ceiba, November 28, 1914, RG 84, USNA; *UNIFRUTCO,* June 1927.

sion, local interests carried the day, and the banks began raising the exchange rate. The merchants and planters also allied themselves with banana workers in their struggle against the companies.[33]

By 1913 the fruit companies, particularly Cuyamel, faced the first period of serious unrest among their workers. The banana workers began demanding higher wages. Local municipalities, which at this incipient stage of the fruteras' development still served as independent supply and transportation centers, supported the strikers' cause. Samuel Zemurray's plantations were particularly vulnerable to such pressure, since he was trying to build a local base of political support to counterbalance the economic power of United Fruit. Under these conditions, the municipalities pressured Zemurray into granting a 33 percent wage increase and paying workers an additional subsistence allowance for transporting bananas to the coast. These events marked the beginning of two decades of militant actions by the banana workers. In their campaign, they would ally themselves with local merchants, regional caudillos and independent planters, forming effective communities of resistance.[34]

In their transition from subsistence peasants to wage laborers, banana workers defined their relationship to the new order in terms of wages and the spreading commodity economy. Fluctuations in Honduran exchange rates during the war, which affected workers' incomes, compelled them to action. After the merchants' boycott, the banks stabilized the gold exchange rate but allowed the rate for silver to rise rapidly. Since the banana companies continued to use the silver rate in their company stores while paying their workers on a gold-based rate, prices at the commissaries soared, and discontent spread throughout the Atlantic coast. By mid 1916 the widening differentials in exchange rates triggered a new strike for higher wages by 600 Cuyamel workers, in which they enjoyed the support of local civilian authorities. When Cuyamel's effort to use strikebreakers failed, the military stepped in and arrested 400 of the strikers.[35]

In the fall of 1917, workers at all three American banana companies struck for higher wages. Plantation workers at the Vaccaro facilities burned the farms, seized a train and headed for La Ceiba. A military detachment halted the train and opened fire, killing forty workers. Despite the violent suppression of the strike, the workers' movement proved successful, and all three fruit companies increased wages. The workers' success stemmed in part from the cooperation of a local military commander.[36]

---

33 Boyle, "Annual Report on Commerce and Industries, 1915," July 7, 1916; "Annual Report of Consul Francis J. Dyer, Ceiba Consular District," La Ceiba, June 10, 1916, RG 84, USNA.

34 David J. Myers to secretary of state, Puerto Cortés, December 5, 1913, RG 84, USNA.

35 Posas, *Movimiento obrero*, pp. 70–71; Víctor Meza, "Historia del movimiento obrero en Honduras," in Pablo González Casanova, ed., *Historia del movimiento obrero en América Latina* (Mexico City: Siglo Veintiuno, 1985), p. 137.

36 George A. Mackinson to secretary of state, Ampala, October 29, 1917, 815.50/2, rl. 33, M-647, RG 59, USNA; also see, on the same reel, 815.504/2–5.

Filberto Díaz Zelaya, a National party stalwart and a local military co-mandante, had been involved in an ongoing feud with the Cuyamel Fruit Company. Díaz Zelaya had been harassing Cuyamel for some time, refusing to issue government documents essential to the company's operation and using the drafting of banana workers for military service to disrupt the company's operations. During the strike, Díaz Zelaya threw his support to the workers, making it difficult for the banana companies to completely repress the strike. After the strike, Cuyamel successfully employed the influence of the State Department to request Díaz Zelaya's removal. But over the next fifteen years, Díaz Zelaya continued to use his influence among banana workers to harass the fruit companies. As for the workers, they had successfully exploited differences between a local power broker and the fruteras to press their demands for higher wages. Fissures in the structures of hegemony soon opened new opportunities for the workers.[37]

The war years proved difficult for both banana workers and independent planters. Price increases continued to eat away at the workers' buying power. Either because of wartime conditions or by deliberate policy, the fruit companies took an ever smaller portion of the bananas produced by local growers. A delegation of growers sent to the United States to plead with the fruteras' management failed in its mission. Animosity toward the American fruit companies continued to grow until conditions on the national political scene provided an opening for its expression.[38]

In his 1919 campaign for the presidency, Raphael López Gutierrez sought to garner support on the Atlantic coast. A Gutierrez supporter, Eduardo Guillén, made campaign trips to the region, promising an eight-hour day and a minimum wage of $2 per day. Once Gutierrez assumed the presidency, banana workers took him at his word and launched a series of strikes, beginning in May 1920. For the preceding two years, trouble had been brewing in the banana region as workers demanded better living conditions and higher wages to compensate for the increased cost of living. Workers at the Cuyamel and United Fruit operations struck first. Experienced dock and plantation workers at United, well aware of the company's vulnerability due to the perishability of bananas, waited until some 50,000 bunches had been cut to declare a strike. Facing a loss of $50,000, United agreed to the workers' demands, as did Cuyamel. On the Vaccaros' facilities, however, the strike soon led to violence.[39]

37 Wilbur J. Carr to Boyle, Washington, November 30, 1917; Department of State to Boyle, Washington, December 11, 1917; Boyle to secretary of state, Puerto Cortés, November 26, 1917, 815.504/3, 4, 5, rl. 33, M-647; George A. Mackinson to secretary of state, Ampala, October 29, 1917, 815.50/2, rl. 33, M-647, RG 59, USNA.

38 Boyle, "Annual Report on Commerce and Industries, 1915," July 7, 1916, RG 84, USNA.

39 Albert Gerberich to secretary of state, Puerto Cortés, June 15, 1920, 815.5045; Gerberich to secretary of state, Puerto Cortés, July 28, 1920, 815.504/1; William Garrity to secretary of state, La Ceiba, September 3, 1920, 815.5045/25; Garrity to secretary of state, La Ceiba, November 20, 1920, 815.504/29, rl. 33, M-647, RG 59, USNA.

On Sunday, August 15, a train crammed with 1,200 machete-wielding banana workers pulled into the port of La Ceiba. Jacobo Munguía, a local planter, led the workers in seizing the Vaccaro facilities. The action against the company had begun a month earlier among small planters in the region west of La Ceiba. They soon rallied the company's workers in a strike, which spread to the dockworkers at the port. After their arrival on the fifteenth, the laborers maintained control of the town and brought activities at the port to a halt. The national government, in which Guillén now served as minister of finance, urged local officials to negotiate with the workers and seek a peaceful solution, but the Vaccaros refused to bargain. The local comandante, Antonio Ramón Lagos, urged negotiations and ignored the Vaccaros' demands to use force. As he politely explained to the American consul, civilized countries did not shoot workers for going on strike. Lagos had good reason for caution. A brother of the Honduran minister of war, Lagos had been appointed to his position as a stepping stone to the presidency and could hardly afford to antagonize the local populace.[40]

After four days of failed attempts at negotiations, the strikers reboarded the train and headed out of the town. Over the next several weeks they established control over the area between La Ceiba and Tela, cut off land transportation between the towns and burned bridges, company commissaries and farms. Neither the arrival of an American warship nor a government mediation commission brought a resolution. Faced with increasing losses, the Vaccaros finally agreed to a fifty-cent wage increase. By the time Munguía returned to La Ceiba, Lagos had been transferred, and Mungía as well as other leaders of the uprising were arrested and jailed. In explaining the origins of the strike, Jacobo Munguía pointed to the plight of local growers. With credit, prices and wages dictated by the fruteras, the growers had become little more than tenant farmers. Unable to pay their own laborers a decent wage, their condition had become much like that of the banana companies' workers. While planters struggled to preserve their independence as petty commodity producers, the workers acted on an agenda that spanned past and present.[41]

In tracing the origins of the 1920 strike, the American consul in La Ceiba pointed to the population's transition from free peasants to wage workers. As he explained:

Formerly the native laborer depended entirely upon the products of the soil for his subsistence. He cultivated sufficient rice and beans supplementing these with native fruits, how-

40 Gerberich to secretary of state, Puerto Cortés, July 28, 1920, 815.504/1; Vaccaro Brothers to secretary of state, New Orleans, August 16, 1920, 815.5045/4; Garrity to secretary of state, La Ceiba, August 19, September 3, 1920, 815.5045/11, 25; Parker Buhrman to secretary of state, La Ceiba, November 23, 1920, 815.5045/29, rl. 33, M-647, RG 59, USNA.
41 See correspondence contained in 815.5045/11, 20–29, rl. 33, M-647; William Garrity to secretary of state, La Ceiba, November 20, 1920, 815.504/29, rl. 33, M-647, RG 59, USNA.

ever as banana cultivation becomes more centralized it precludes the possibility of relying on these native products other than fruit, and while there may be no preconceived policy on the part of the Fruit Company, it is undoubtedly true that the natural tendency of the industrial development of the banana and sugar cultivation is to force the native laborer to rely on the company's commissaries for his supplies.[42]

The fruit companies had made Honduran peasants totally dependent on the companies for subsistence. The workers' actions represented both a reaction to their lost independence and an attempt to come to grips with the new reality, in which wages determined subsistence and symbolized social relations. A new wave of discontent swept the coast four years later.

National political conflict shook Honduras between 1924 and 1925, opening the way for new labor protests. During an unsuccessful bid for the presidency in 1924, Tiburcio Carías denounced the growing immigration of West Indian laborers, who he claimed were stealing jobs from Hondurans. After Carías' failed election attempt, Gregorio Ferrera launched a rebellion against the national government, which dragged on into 1925. These events created new opportunities for planters and workers, who had already launched fresh initiatives against the fruteras.

In March 1923 United Fruit dockworkers struck. When local authorities refused to intervene, the national government ordered the arrest of Nicaraguan exiles, who had organized the movement, and broke the strike. United workers at Tela and Puerto Castilla struck in May 1924. The strike enjoyed the backing of the region's merchants, who were resentful of United's refusal to accept company scrip, which workers expended in local shops. Juan Angel Vallardes, the comandante at Puerto Castilla, who also supported the strike, was arrested for his efforts. At the same time, with the return of Jacobo Munguía to the La Ceiba area in May 1924, unrest once again stirred in the countryside as banana inspectors were driven out of the interior.[43]

The unrest on the coast also gave expression to rising ethnic tensions as demonstrations against Jamaican workers broke out in Puerto Castilla and La Ceiba. The anti-black campaign in Ceiba also gave vent to rising anti-American sentiments and revealed a culture of terror that came to characterize relations between Hondurans and Americans. During the La Ceiba protests, demonstrators threatened to destroy all foreign property and "clean out the gringos" before U.S. marines could arrive to stop them. When one of Standard Fruit's Italian workers was murdered, a local satiri-

---

42 Buhrman to secretary of state, La Ceiba, November 20, 1920, 815.5045/29, rl. 33, M-647, RG 59, USNA.

43 Morales to secretary of state, Tegucigalpa, March 14, 1923, 815.5045/32; Willard L. Beaulac to secretary of state, Puerto Castilla, May 26, 1924, 815.5045/35; George P. Waller to secretary of state, La Ceiba, June 15, 1924, 815.50/9, rl. 33, M-647, RG 59, USNA; "Staff Meeting," August 9, 1924, File 16, Box 7, Standard Fruit Papers; Meza, "Movimiento obrero," p. 138.

cal sheet urged: "Let us civilize the foreigners as we did the Italian in true Honduran style."[44]

As the protesters' threats suggested, the fruteras regularly called on the marines to protect their property and intimidate the local population. Standard Fruit had gone a step further by 1920, creating a spy network to ferret out troublemakers among their workers. Not to be outdone, United hired the notorious Honduran killer Gustavo Pinel to head its security network. Through threats, intimidation and murder, Pinel relieved small growers of their property and dealt with the company's critics. Despite such steps, the local populace fought back through the actions of caudillos like Jacobo Munguía, now known as the "Terror of the Coast," and the ever active Filberto Díaz Zelaya.[45]

In February of 1925, Díaz Zelaya backed a strike by United farm workers in the Truxillo district. The following year the caudillo switched his base of operations to La Ceiba, where he continued to challenge American interests. Standard Fruit also faced harassment from Joaquín Palma, a worker who had led a strike at the company's Monte Cristo Sugar Plantation in 1925. Palma had the backing of the Sociedad de Artesanos, a local labor syndicate composed of some three hundred skilled workers employed by the frutera. Rumors that the Sociedad was preparing a hit list of Standard employees gave pause to American officials, who wanted Díaz Zelaya and Palma removed from the area. The American consul in La Ceiba, George Waller, advised against arresting Palma on the grounds that Díaz Zelaya and the Sociedad would break him out of jail and massacre the Americans in the port.[46]

The role which terror had come to play in defining social relations on the Honduran coast was captured by two Americans, Henry F. Plummer and his son Allen. The senior Plummer, a stockholder in United Fruit, visited the region in 1924 and reported that "the feeling of the natives against the Americans on the north coast was exceedingly bitter, largely because of the conduct of the Americans and their attitudes."[47] Allen

---

44 Beaulac to secretary of state, Puerto Castilla, July 16, 1924, 815.5045/46; George P. Waller, "Political and Economic Conditions in La Ceiba," La Ceiba, March 1, 1925, 815.5045/58; Beaulac to secretary of state, Puerto Castilla, March 4, 1925, 815.5045/60; Waller to secretary of state, La Ceiba, October 8, 1924, 815.50/18, rl. 33, M-647; Waller to secretary of state, telegram, La Ceiba, August 7, 1924, 315.11/51, RG 59, USNA; Waller to secretary of state, telegram, La Ceiba, August 29, 1924, 815.00/3321, rl. 16, M-647, RG 59, USNA.

45 William P. Garrity to secretary of state, January 27, 1920, 315.11/21; T. Monroe Fisher to secretary of state, Tela, September 30, 1930, and enclosures (*El Chichicaste*, August 9, 16, 1930), 315.1127 Tela RR Co./34, RG 59, USNA.

46 Ernest Evans to secretary of state, La Ceiba, January 26, 1927, 815.00/4061, rl. 20, M-647; memorandum of conversation with Mr. C. Doufour of Vaccaro Brothers, State Department, April 15, 1926, 315.11/69, RG 59, USNA; Waller to secretary of state, La Ceiba, May 1, 1926, 315 orig, RG 59, USNA; Evans to secretary of state, La Ceiba, November 6, 1926, 815.11/4001, RG 59, USNA.

47 Memorandum, Munro to White, Latin American Division, October 2, 1924, 815.00/3057, rl. 15, M-647, RG 59, USNA.

Plummer, who worked as a manager for Standard Fruit, offered the view of Americans who actually lived and worked in the area. The younger Plummer feared for his life, for, as he explained, "You see we are here among Hondurians, and they are quite treacherous, and often kill one another, and quite frequently the Americans are threatened."[48] More serious challenges to the companies would shake the Atlantic coast as the fruteras' wage labor force matured and as the companies accelerated the processes of rationalization and internalization.

As worker and planter protests escalated during the war years, the fruteras brought basic changes to the industry to ensure greater control over production and raise productivity. Unlike his rivals, the Vaccaros and United, who often seemed caught in a transition between mercantile operations and direct production, Zemurray plunged completely into the production process. He relied almost exclusively on output from his own acreage, utilizing the most up-to-date techniques to produce the highest-quality, lowest-cost bananas in Honduras. In 1918 Cuyamel introduced electrically driven belt conveyors on its wharf at Puerto Cortés to replace manual loading. Cuyamel also introduced irrigation to banana planting, building cement-lined canals equipped with electric pumps to irrigate and drain its acreage. In view of Zemurray's competitive challenge, the Vaccaros and United quickly followed suit.[49]

As the banana companies increasingly penetrated the production process during the 1920s, they raised new challenges for banana workers as well as for local planters and merchants. For workers, increased efficiency threatened job security. For planters, the process meant further reduction in the companies' need to purchase their bananas. By 1929 United's Tela division produced 81 percent and the Truxillo division 91 percent of the bananas they shipped. The banana companies improved their competitive position with higher-quality fruit and access to virgin lands to escape the scourge of Panama disease. Increased reliance by the fruit companies on irrigation also launched battles with local growers over water rights. For merchants, the continued decline of local planters spelled disaster for some of their most important clients. In this increasingly tense environment, the work of the Honduran Communist party and the onset of the Great Depression served as catalysts for action.[50]

As the effects of the depression began to impact Honduras' Atlantic coast, the Communist party took a more serious interest in the banana

---

48 Allen Plummer to Senator W. B. Bankhead, La Ceiba, June 22, 1923, 315.11/25, RG 59, USNA.
49 Charles Morrow Wilson, *Empire in Green and Gold: The Story of the American Banana Trade* (1947) (Westport, Conn.: Greenwood Press, 1968), pp. 222–25; Boyle, "Annual Report on Commerce and Industries, 1915," July 7, 1916, RG 84, USNA; Files 7, 10, 16, Box 7, Standard Fruit Papers; *UNIFRUTCO*, April 1931; "Intensive Drainage Methods at Tela, Honduras," Engineering Department, United Fruit Company, Boston, Mass., December 1930; Wilson, *Empire in Green and Gold*, p. 233.
50 *UNIFRUTCO*, August and September 1948; Kepner, *Social Aspects*, p. 66.

workers. Organizers such as Juan Pablo Wainwright and Manuel Calix Herrera, working through the newly formed Federación Sindical Hondureña, began to agitate among banana workers. Coastal workers had already taken organizational steps of their own with the creation of the Sociedad de Artesanos and with rail and port workers forming mutualist societies as early as 1920. After the 1925 strikes, the Liga Sindical del Norte was formed with the specific purpose of confronting the fruteras. Yet if the workers had new allies and new organizational capabilities, they also faced a considerably more powerful opponent.[51]

After his failed attempt at a truce with United Fruit in 1924, Samuel Zemurray initiated a very different strategy. In 1926 he and his associates began buying up United Fruit stock. Then in 1929 Zemurray sold the Cuyamel company to his corporate rival for $30 million in United stock. This maneuver, plus a few additional stock purchases, gave Zemurray effective control of United by 1930. Beyond further consolidation of the fruteras' economic power, the merger had a substantial effect on the Honduran political process. With the Vaccaros largely avoiding confrontation with United, the process of corporate rivalry within the Honduran political system essentially ceased, leaving United as the dominant corporate interest in the national political order.[52] United's relations with the Honduran state improved even further when its old ally Tiburcio Carías assumed the presidency in 1933. As the U.S. minister reported, "The United Fruit Company probably never had a Honduran Congress more acquiescent in its desires. Indeed no Fruit Company, I believe, ever exercised a more powerful influence and control on a Honduran Government . . . than does the Company now on the Government of President Carías."[53] Even American consular officials fell under the control of United Fruit. As the American chargé reported in 1933, "the political work of a consular officer . . . usually is kept within channels dictated by the politics . . . of the Fruit Company upon which he himself is dependent for many things."[54] The increasing merger of corporate and state interests reduced the ability of local caudillos to challenge the central government and gave United a more cooperative ally in confronting challenges from popular forces on the Atlantic coast.

In February of 1927, the Vaccaro workers threatened to strike and attempted to recruit Jacobo Munguía as their leader. The workers demanded not only higher pay but the firing of two American farm overseers. The workers also indicated that the memory of subsistence farming, which

51 Longino Becerra, "The Early History of the Labor Movement," in Nancy Peckenham and Annie Street, eds., *Honduras: Portrait of a Captive Nation* (New York: Praeger, 1985), pp. 96–97; Posas, *Movimiento obrero,* pp. 83–88.

52 Lt. Col. Fred T. Crust, "United Fruit Company," San José, February 19, 1931, 813.615/4; Lay to secretary of state, Tegucigalpa, March 29, 1932, 815.77/443, RG 59, USNA.

53 Lay to secretary of state, Tegucigalpa, April 28, 1932, 815.032/129, RG 59, USNA.

54 Higgins to secretary of state, Tegucigalpa, November 20, 1933, 815.00/4592, RG 59, USNA.

Figure 6. Old Tela, Honduras. The paved street and curbs were the work of the United Fruit Company. (United Fruit Company Collection, Baker Library, Harvard Business School)

freed them from total dependence on the company, had not died. They insisted that the government provide them with parcels of land which it had promised them. The intervention of the local comandante, however, pre-empted further action by the laborers. As for Munguía, in a final futile gesture he and a hundred armed men seized a train and rode it into La Ceiba, only to retreat a day later. The pressures of the depression and Communist organizing efforts eventually prompted a new wave of strikes.[55]

In 1930 workers struck against both the Vaccaros and United Fruit. The United workers demanded not only higher wages but better living and working conditions. Assisting the workers was Juan Pablo Wainwright, who had been actively organizing banana laborers for the past year. This time, however, the Honduran state and United were prepared. United's private security guards harassed the organizers and developed intelligence files on the Communists, including their photos. When the

55 James B. Stewart to secretary of state, La Ceiba, February 10, 1927, 815.504/16, rl. 33, M-647, RG 59, USNA; Karnes, *Tropical Enterprise*, p. 173; Nelson R. Park to secretary of state, La Ceiba, September 1, 1929, 815.5045/47, rl. 33, M-647; Park to secretary of state, La Ceiba, August 31, 1929, 815.00B/13, rl. 22, M-647, RG 59, USNA.

government declared a state of siege, military forces moved in and arrested the organizers. Wainwright soon escaped to Guatemala, where he was executed in 1932. But increasing tensions on the coast quickly triggered a new series of strikes.[56]

Tensions along the coast reached new levels of intensity in United's company towns. In response to past resistance from the town of Tela, United had built its own company town of New Tela across the river from the old municipality. New Tela came complete with a forty-member force of company watchmen, who frequently intruded on the authority of officials in the old town, arresting citizens there and forcing them to work off their sentences in the employ of United Fruit. When the company promoted the sale of beer in New Tela, it issued only mess hall vales to workers so they could not patronize beer halls in Old Tela. Matamoros Lucha, who published a weekly paper critical of United, found himself forced out of his position as the schoolteacher in Old Tela. The growing resentment between the citizens of the old municipality and the frutera reached the flashpoint in 1930.[57]

On March 12, 1930, the New Tela police arrested five United employees, including three Hondurans, for their alleged role in a payroll theft. Bound hand and foot and with twine wrapped tightly around their testicles, the men were subjected to a night of unrelenting torture. An aggressive State Department investigation prompted United to dismiss Gustavo Pinel for his involvement in the affair. But the damage had already been done. The U.S. consul in Tela explained that as a result of the incident "practically all Latin American laborers in this district are anti-American, and strongly anti–Tela Railroad Company."[58] By the summer of 1930 the Tela newspaper *El Chichicaste* had formulated those sentiments in specific anti-imperialist and nationalist terms. Declaring, "The trumpet of patriotism has sounded, we must stoutly impede the way of Yankee imperialism which has arrived in the country by means of the United Fruit Company," the paper appealed for workers and peasants to join "the campaign that true nationalism demands . . ."[59] Those sentiments took on new significance for Honduras' coastal society as political control began to disintegrate.

The run-up to the 1932 presidential election exacerbated what was already a tense political situation. In the waning months of 1931 early returns pointed to Liberal losses in a series of municipal elections. Since control of local governments was essential to victory in the national race,

---

56 Posas, *Movimiento obrero,* pp. 76–77, 87; Thomas Wasson to secretary of state, Puerto Cortés, January 14, 1931, 815.00B/34, RG 59, USNA.

57 *El Chichicaste,* August 16, September 6, 20, 1930, 315.1127 Tela RR Co./37, RG 59, USNA.

58 State Department correspondence described the events at Tela and their aftermath in great detail; see in particular 317.1127 Tela RR Co./23, 34, 37, 110, 128, RG 59, USNA.

59 *El Chichicaste,* June 21, 1930, 315.1127 Tela RR Co./34, RG 59, USNA.

Liberal partisans began burning ballot boxes and demanding new elections. The ensuing struggle left many coastal municipalities with competing governments and Liberal politicos anxious to exploit any opportunity.[60] The United Fruit Company exacerbated these local tensions by cutting the wages of its farm workers by 20 percent. In addition, when the government slapped on United a $15,000 fine for an improper manifest document, the company struck back by cutting the price paid to independent growers from 40 to 30 cents per stem. The planters responded by destroying the bananas which contract growers deposited at rail sidings. Amidst these mounting animosities, three strikes erupted almost simultaneously on the coast.[61]

In January 3,000 Standard Fruit farm workers in the region bounded by the towns of Savo, Los Planes and Sonaguera struck, demanding a 15 percent pay hike. They also protested expensive medical supplies, high commissary prices, poor housing and high rents. They demanded an end to the system in which farm supervisors ran the mess halls and prohibited workers' wives from providing their meals for them.[62] The striking workers enjoyed the protection of the local military commandant and Liberal politico, General Rodas Alvarado. The general was motivated by a sense of comradeship and practical political considerations. Alvarado had commanded many of the strikers when they served in the military. The workers also provided a local constituency for Alvarado. Yet the workers did not simply rely on Alvarado as their advocate. They appealed to the Workmen's Club and the Chamber of Commerce of La Ceiba for support. The result of these appeals is unclear, but the strikers did receive material support from the communities of Savo, Los Planes and Sonaguera. Given the rather formidable coalition that the workers had fashioned, Standard quickly acceded to all their demands except wages.[63] Meanwhile, United faced strikes at two different locations.

During the first week of January, dockworkers at United's Tela facilities struck over a 5-cent-per-hour wage cut. The strikers enjoyed the support of the Federación Sindical, and railway workers walked out in sympathy with the stevedores. The strike movement also had the support of local planters and merchants. Their support resulted from United's increasing control over the local water supply and reductions in the price it paid for bananas. General José María Reina, the Liberal candidate for vice president, obstructed efforts to put down the strike, supporting local military officials, who refused to provide protection even when the central government declared martial law. The government's dispatch of troops from La

60 Myron H. Schraud, "Strike of Workers on Truxillo Railroad Banana Farms," Puerto Castilla, April 16, 1932, rl. 6, UPAMC, RG 84, USNA.
61 Higgins to secretary of state, Tegucigalpa, June 24, 1932, rl. 5, UPAMC; Wasson to secretary of state, telegram, Puerto Cortés, January 2, 1932, rl. 5, UPAMC, RG 84, USNA.
62 Warren C. Stewart to Lay, La Ceiba, January 20, 21, 1932, rl. 5, UPAMC, RG 84, USNA.
63 Stewart to Lay, La Ceiba, January 25, 29, 1932, rl. 5, UPAMC, RG 84, USNA.

Ceiba ended in frustration when the soldiers began to fraternize with the workers. After the walkout had paralyzed the port for ten days, Colonel Luis Alonso López arrived with 125 troops from San Pedro Sula and crushed the strike.[64] But the most serious threat to United lay ahead.

On February 7 fruit cutters at the company's Truxillo facilities struck, and by the twenty-second of the month the labor action had paralyzed every one of its farms in the district. As the strike dragged on into the month of March, Julius Lay, the U.S. minister in Tegucigalpa, concluded that the action was funded directly from Moscow – otherwise how could 3,000 workers survive for weeks without wages? While Communist labor organizers were certainly active in the strike movement, the most important sources of support were much closer to home. The strikers got large donations from independent growers and local merchants. Furthermore, many workers from the interior simply returned home to their villages to live with friends and relatives. The local military commander, General Arturo Matute, slowed efforts to break the strike. He took a lenient attitude toward the workers and complained of a lack of troops. When the government sent 100 troops from La Ceiba, Matute discharged them and patiently awaited a "fee" from United to underwrite recruitment expenses for a new detachment.

The ever present General Reina put in an appearance along with the Liberal presidential candidate, Zuniga Huete. In an ostensible show of support, Reina and Huete visited the strikers on March 7. The workers turned a cold shoulder when the politicians failed to directly address the question of the strike. Two weeks later the strikers ignored Reina and Huete when they called for an end to the labor action. But the strike action had already reached its zenith.

The strikes addressed the specific concerns of workers, planters and merchants and as a result enjoyed widespread support on the coast. But the coastal society still represented no more than 15 percent of Honduras' population. Furthermore, the larger population of the country had felt little direct effect from the presence of the fruteras. Appeals to nationalist sentiment based on anti-Americanism had limited significance in the interior and, given the relatively low level of communication and transportation development, would be hard to spread among that larger audience. As a result, joint actions by the company and the government would soon overwhelm the workers.[65]

When the plantation workers had first struck, United's security forces had quickly gone into action. United bribed the secretary of the strikers' organization into revealing details of the organizers' infrastructure. At the end

64 Posas, *Movimiento obrero*, pp. 78–80; Becerra, "Labor Movement," p. 97; Lay to secretary of state, Tegucigalpa, January 4, 1932, rl. 5, UPAMC; Stout to Lay, Tela, January 4, 6, 8, 11, 1932, rl. 5, UPAMC; Stout to Lay, telegram, Tela, January 15, 1932, rl. 6, UPAMC, RG 84, USNA.
65 Henry J. Hanes to Lay, Puerto Castilla, February 22, 25, March 14, 1932; Schraud, "Strike of Workers on Truxillo Railroad Banana Farms," April 16, 1932, rl. 6, UPAMC, RG 84, USNA.

of March the central government stepped in and dismissed the local military commanders, including General Matute. President Mejía Colindres sent his personal military aide, General Salvador Cisneros, to the region to aid United. He arrested 700 people involved in the strike and sent them into internal exile. United then provided facilities for the Honduran military to launch an assault on the labor organizations throughout its holdings on the Atlantic coast, including Tela and San Pedro Sula. The army seized facilities used by the strikers and sent laborer organizers into exile.[66]

With the labor movement on the Atlantic coast effectively smashed, United responded to adverse economic conditions with a general policy of retrenchment, cutting back operations, reducing its workforce and lowering wages. It could do so with the assurance that labor organizations had been crushed and that it now enjoyed the full cooperation of local military authorities such as Macos A. Collier, the commander of the Progreso garrison. As the American consul at Tela noted, "Colonel Collier is not brilliant but he is energetic, is moderate in his political activities, and is distinctly pro-American."[67] That confidence proved justified as labor peace prevailed during the retrenchment and for the next two decades.

By the early 1930s the peasants of the Atlantic coast had successfully adapted to their new condition as wage laborers. They demonstrated an increasing ability to organize and to focus their demands on wages and the working and living conditions that defined their new environment. With the continued support of local planters and merchants and the organizational efforts of the Communist party, they formed an effective community of interests which successfully pressed for many of their demands in early 1932, despite the impact of the depression. Yet the tide was already turning against them.

Much as in Nicaragua, the community of interests on the coast represented a small portion of the population, and their nationalist message of anti-Americanism had limited immediate relevance and would be difficult to spread in the interior. Furthermore, the merger of Cuyamel and United in 1929 ended the corporate feuding which had contributed to national political instability. As United increasingly internalized the local political process, coordination of corporate and state policies became more effective. That process also deterred the challenges by local caudillos, which had created repeated opportunities for labor militancy. When Tiburcio Carías assumed the presidency in 1933, he initiated sixteen years of authoritarian rule, which provided continued repression of the labor movement. As for the workers' planter allies, their position continued to deteriorate in the face of the fruteras' power and the impact of Panama disease.

66 Beccera, "Labor Movement," pp. 97–98; Kenneth S. Stout to secretary of state, Tela, February 23, 1932, rl. 4, UPAMC, RG 84, USNA; Meza, "Movimiento obrero," pp. 147–48.
67 Stout, "Economic Program of the United Fruit Company," Tela, June 18, 1932, 810.6156/l, RG 59, USNA.

In 1937 Romulo López, an independent planter from San Pedro Sula, wrote to Franklin Roosevelt pleading for his intervention against the United Fruit Company and its monopolistic practices. The Honduran planter was certainly familiar with the American dream and the potential support it could provide for his own cause. López began his letter by praising the United States as an exemplar and promoter of democracy, and President Roosevelt as an extraordinary man who had fought for the poor and to achieve equality within and among nations. As López explained, it was those very qualities which convinced him that the American president would respond favorably to his complaint.

The planter's defense of his region was both clear and impassioned. He pointed out how

for some time now the inhabitants of this north coast of Honduras have been feeling asfixiated; this asfixiation has been caused by the extortion of the *United Fruit Company,* a ruthless banana company that day after day is absorbing the energies of these young people who are striving for greater progress and well being.[68]

López closed by reaffirming his faith in a man known as a friend of just causes and by urging the president to complain to United Fruit and to provide Honduran growers with the names of other companies that would buy their fruit. The response to López's letter came in a terse note from a State Department bureaucrat explaining that the department knew of no companies competing with United Fruit. The local growers' subordination to the fruteras would continue. As for the merchants, they would survive and once again support the workers who launched a general strike in 1954.[69]

Through the early decades of the twentieth century, the encounter between the American fruteras and Honduran society moved from a symbiotic relationship to one of conflict. The fruteras had transformed Honduras into the world's leading banana producer, encouraged the growth of a small business class of growers and merchants, and provided jobs, housing and medical treatment to local peasants. But as much as local merchants and planters shared the basic entrepreneurial vision of American business, they found themselves being overwhelmed by the control the fruteras came to exercise in the banana trade. For peasants the encounter was even more traumatic. Although attracted by the promises of American material culture, they faced demands for work disciplines that disrupted existing family and work relations, while laboring for American enterprises that put little stock in industrial welfare. Despite differences

---

68 Romulo López to Franklin Roosevelt, San Pedro Sula, April 7, 1937, 615.117/3, RG 59, USNA.
69 G. Oury-Jackson, "Cooperation of American Fruit Company with Independent Banana Planters," Tela, May 18, 1938, 815.6156/73; John Erwin to secretary of state, Tegucigalpa, March 25, 1939, 815.6156/80, RG 59, USNA; Meza, "Movimiento obrero," p. 162.

in their experiences, small business people and workers shared a common antipathy toward the fruit companies which helped weld them into communities of resistance during the 1920s and 30s. But their campaigns of resistance were limited by the fact that the direct effects of the fruteras were confined to the population on the banana coast. Far to the south, Peruvian experiences with American corporate culture prompted more widespread demands for radical changes.

PART III

Peru

Map 5.1. Peru.

5

The alliance for modernization

In a country of over four million people {where} there are only about fifty thousand white people or people who can even read or write, the masses are much to be feared. They are mostly Indians or cholos (a mixture of negro, Indian, Chinese etc.) and are most dangerous when aroused. (U.S. diplomat)

. . . if I could have my way, Peru would be practically American within ten or fifteen years. (Augusto Leguía)

In August 1930 a coup d'etat by Major Luis Sánchez Cerro broke President Augusto B. Leguía's eleven-year grip on power. As the Leguía regime crumbled, nationalistic workers struck the American-owned Cerro de Pasco Mining Corporation in the central Andes. Aided by urban radicals and sympathetic elements in the military, the workers paralyzed the company's operations for four months. Less than two years later, sugar workers and petit bourgeois elements from Peru's northern coast attempted to topple the Sánchez Cerro regime. This period of upheaval continued until 1934, when a combination of state power and American technology crushed the politically potent dockworkers at Peru's principal port.

These events which the Great Depression triggered represented a culminating phase in Peru's development. Faced with a crisis in their program of modernization, the Peruvian elite had formed an alliance with American corporations at the turn of the century. Over the next three decades American companies doubled mining production, helped triple sugar output, increased oil production tenfold, contributed to industrialization and played a central role in improvements in communications and transportation. But the renewal and acceleration of Peru's transformation under the aegis of American corporate culture unleashed a highly uneven and unstable process of social change in Peru's central highlands, northern coast and the metroplex of Lima and Callao. Those changes culminated in the turbulent events of the early 1930s.

A seemingly disparate set of social groups challenged the forces of modernization. Middle-class and small-business contingents included white-collar employees, junior military officers, university students and small landowners and merchants. The labor movement proved equally diverse. Copper miners and sugar workers shared recent experiences of the transition from peasant to wage worker and repression under the Leguía dictatorship. But copper workers of the central highlands operated in an environment totally dominated by American corporations, while coastal sugar workers functioned in a sector where local capital still played a significant role. The port workers of Callao, in contrast, had over a half century of experience as wage laborers in a foreign-controlled enterprise and had enjoyed a position of relative privilege under Leguía.

These distinctive backgrounds and experiences gave rise to a complex series of alliances and competitive struggles as the collapse of Leguiismo created the opportunity for overt political expression and social protest. Although geographically confined to those areas most intensely exposed to American corporate culture, these groups emerged into a series of activist communities and came to share a common nationalist theme. As in Central America, ardent nationalist protests against foreign, particularly American, corporations provided a bond for the diverse social elements that comprised these communities. Rooted within that anti-Americanism were a varied set of protests against the country's transformation by American corporations and their Peruvian allies. The origins of those protests can be traced to earlier attempts by diverse groups to rally behind nationalist symbols to protect their interests from disruptive market forces of transformation.

In the first decades after independence, the powerful merchant guild, or *consulado,* of Lima had waged an anti-foreign campaign in the name of economic nationalism. Seeking to protect their own business from disruptions arising out of Peru's growing interaction in the world market, the merchants denounced increased trade with the British or Americans as a threat to the nation's incipient industrial base. They were joined in their campaign by shopkeepers and craftsmen anxious to protect their specialized trade with the elite from an influx of foreign goods. But the Lima merchants' nationalism lacked a democratic base, showing little concern for the acute social and economic inequities of Peruvian society, and the industrial base it supposedly sought to protect proved largely an illusion. Local perspectives on free trade soon shifted as Peru uncovered a viable product with which to engage in international commerce.

Between the 1840s and the 1870s Peru enjoyed a unique period of economic expansion based on the export of guano, or bird excrement. The Peruvian state, which initially managed the trade through European merchant houses, injected its new wealth into the local economy through expansion of the civil and military bureaucracies, overly generous payments on the internal debt and grandiose public works projects such as the national railway system. Peruvian merchant houses and banks which came to share in the bonanza invested funds in local undertakings, particularly the sugar estates along the northern coast.[1]

The stimulus to the economy solidified support for liberal policies of national development. The growing availability of capital spurred increased competition for land to produce export products and foodstuffs for the urban population. Inflationary pressures resulting from Peru's increasing integration into the world economy encouraged free trade policies, partly in response to popular protests over the cost of living. Those policies in turn undermined the power of artisans and shopkeepers, who were left to continue the anti-foreign nationalist campaign which Lima's great merchants had abandoned.[2] Yet the new liberal nationalism proved no more democratic or inclusive than its conservative predecessor. That reality became apparent as the accelerated penetration of Peruvian society by market forces exposed continuing problems with labor recruitment and triggered urban unrest.

From the time of the Spanish conquistadors to the era of American corporate penetration, access to and control of human labor in Peru has created a dilemma for those who have attempted to exploit the country's abundant natural resources. Peruvian peasant society in the Andean highlands rested on a complex pattern of communal and private landholdings. Mining operations during the colonial era had introduced market forces and social differentiation into some villages of the central highlands. Yet most of Peru's rural residents retained access to the land and felt little need to support themselves as permanent wage workers.[3]

Given the problem of local labor recruitment, sugar growers and mine owners turned to the labor recruitment system of *enganche* by the 1870s. Under this system, employers made money advances to peasants, who then had to work off the debt. Enganche proved a costly system that produced only marginal results.[4] Labor supply problems finally contributed to the end of Peru's guano prosperity.

By the mid 1870s Peru had entered a multidimensional crisis. The world price depression and the declining quality of the guano beds ate away at the nation's ability to service its foreign debt. The unresolved issue of labor recruitment inhibited growth in other economic sectors. Increased commercialization of agriculture and the use of enganche height-

1 Shane J. Hunt, "Growth and Guano in Nineteenth-Century Peru," in Roberto Cortés Conde and Shane J. Hunt, eds., *The Latin American Economies: Growth and the Export Sector, 1880–1930* (New York: Holmes and Meier, 1985), pp. 255–318; Gootenberg, *Silver and Guano*, pp. 100–137.

2 Paul Gootenberg, "Caneros y Chuno: Price Levels in Nineteenth-Century Peru," *HAHR* 70 (1990), pp. 37–40; and *Silver and Guano*, p. 115.

3 Norman Long and Bryan Roberts, *Miners, Peasants and Entrepreneurs: Regional Development in the Central Highlands of Peru* (Cambridge: Cambridge University Press, 1984), pp. 25–31.

4 Michael J. Gonzales, *Plantation Agriculture and Social Control in Northern Peru, 1875–1933* (Austin: University of Texas Press, 1985), pp. 90–91, 117, 118; Hunt, "Growth and Guano," pp. 266–67.

ened tensions in the countryside. In Lima craftsmen saw their positions
erode under free trade policies, while inflationary pressures stirred discontent among the general populace. In 1858 and again in 1872, urban artisans and workmen rioted against trade policies that threatened their
livelihoods, taking up the banner of anti-foreign nationalism which
Lima's great merchants had forsaken. And in 1851 and 1878 bread riots
swept the capital.[5] When war erupted with Chile, Peru's southern neighbor, the stresses building under the liberal program erupted. As the
Chilean army laid siege to Lima, pent-up urban animosities exploded.
Crowds looted and burned the establishments of Chinese merchants, symbols of "alien" exploitation. It was the opening skirmish in a domestic
struggle that would be waged in conjunction with resistance to the
Chilean occupation.

The Chilean invasion destroyed what remained of Peru's guano prosperity. The conquerors burned estates, stripped plantations, mines and railroads of machinery, and collected tribute from local businesses. Amidst
the economic devastation, social animosities threatened to flare out of
control in both the coastal regions and in the Andean highlands. When
the Chilean army occupied coastal plantations, Chinese workers mim-
icked the popular protests in Lima, joining the Chileans in looting and
burning. In the central highlands, small hacendados, merchants and peasants launched a three-year insurgency against the Chileans, and in fighting the foreigners developed a sense of being Peruvian.[6]

The Chilean occupation brought the Guano Age to a violent end and
provided an opening for the expression of the social antagonisms spawned
by Peru's liberal nationalist project. That effort had helped integrate Peru
into the world economy but had exacerbated internal social and economic
inequities. With the conclusion of the war in 1883, the animosities displayed by urban and rural popular forces would subside as Peru fell into a
decade of economic depression that paralyzed the elite's program for modernization. Once economic recovery began, resistance would once again
accelerate, threaten the process of transformation and force the elite to
seek an alliance with American corporations.

Between 1895 and 1900 Peru enjoyed a highly successful period of locally controlled economic reconstruction. The growth of the industrial-
ized economies of Western Europe and the United States increased demands for Peruvian products such as sugar, cotton and copper. Those

5 Vincent Peloso, "Succulence and Sustenance: Region, Class and Diet in Nineteenth Century Peru,"
   in John C. Super and Thomas C. Wright, eds., *Food, Politics and Society in Latin America* (Lincoln:
   University of Nebraska Press, 1985), p. 57.
6 Heraclio Bonilla, "The War of the Pacific and the National and Colonial Problem in Peru," *Past
   and Present* 81 (1978), pp. 92–118; Gonzales, *Plantation Agriculture*, pp. 32, 91; Mallon, *Defense of
   Community*, pp. 80–101. Whether or not the actions of Peruvian peasants constituted a form of incipient nationalism remains a subject of academic debate. On this issue, see the articles by Bonilla
   and Mallon in Stern, ed., *Resistance, Rebellion, and Consciousness*, pp. 213–79.

expanding markets, combined with a falling exchange rate that reduced local production costs, launched Peruvian business interests on a new investment surge. In the last decade of the nineteenth century, sugar production grew by 83 percent, while copper leaped into third place on the list of national exports. Local capital also poured into urban manufacturing and public utilities. But by the turn of the century a series of factors combined to threaten the nation's newfound prosperity.[7]

Peru's switch to the gold standard in 1897 slowed the process of currency depreciation and its advantageous effect on production costs. By 1902 world prices for sugar, coffee and copper had experienced a sharp decline, and despite government roadbuilding projects, transportation problems multiplied. The initial movement of export products such as sugar and copper still relied on a system of mule and llama trains. Renewed economic growth had stretched the carrying capacity of that primitive and expensive system to its limits.[8] Along with these difficulties, problems in labor recruitment and control had reemerged.

Given the rural population's continued access to the land, private initiatives in the mining and agricultural export sectors and even the state's central highway project relied on a reinvigorated and expanded system of enganche for labor recruitment. At best, enganche constituted an expensive and inefficient method of labor control. Highland merchants who served as labor recruiters, or *enganchadores,* required advance payment of the loans made to peasants. Peasant resistance contributed substantially to the expense and inefficiency of enganche. Workers who fled before completing their contracts or who challenged the agreements in the courts became a growing problem for the Peruvian elite by the end of the century. Government efforts to enforce enganche contracts proved only marginally effective. Furthermore, problems with enganche did not represent the only form of popular resistance to the elite's plans.[9]

Workers on the nation's railways and in the ports offered further challenges to the process of transformation. Those problems were particularly apparent along the docks of Callao. Those who labored in Peru's principal port comprised a complex community of workers who handled cargo,

7 Thorp and Bertram, *Peru, 1890–1977,* pp. 23–43; Rory Miller, "The Making of the Grace Contract: British Bondholders and the Peruvian Government," *JLAS* 8 (May 1976), pp. 73–100.

8 Mallon, *Defense of Community,* pp. 164–65.

9 J. C. Pickering, "Transportation Costs and Labor in Central Peru," *EMJ* 85 (March 1908). An extensive literature deals with the enganche system in Peru. Among the primary works are Ernesto Yepes del Castillo, *Perú, 1820–1920: un siglo de desarrollo capitalista* (Lima: Campodónico Ediciones, 1972); Heraclio Bonilla, *El minero de los Andes* (Lima: Instituto de Estudios Peruanos, 1974); Julian Laite, *Industrial Development and Migration Labour in Latin America* (Austin: University of Texas Press, 1981); Adrian De Wind Jr., "Peasants Become Miners: The Evolution of Industrial Mining Systems in Peru" (Ph.D. dissertation, Columbia University, 1977); Peter Blanchard, "The Recruitment of Workers in the Peruvian Sierra at the Turn of the Century: The Enganche System," *Inter-American Economic Affairs* 33 (1980), pp. 63–83; Mallon, *Defense of Community,* pp. 159–67; Gonzales, *Plantation Agriculture,* pp. 131–43.

owner-operators of launches and clerical workers such as tally clerks. This group held a strategic position in the national economy, with most of the country's international trade passing through the port. The stevedores led this militant community, striking repeatedly between 1894 and 1906, demanding higher wages and defending their control of work assignments and the pace of their labor.[10]

As an increasingly competitive world market demanded improved productive efficiency, Peru's elite faced an array of challenges to continued transformation of their society. Faced with problems which threatened to shackle their entrepreneurial activities, they turned to the capital and technology of American companies to overcome some of the most intractable obstacles to continued development. An American observer accurately described the intersection of interests which occurred at the point of American technology:

A greater supply of cheap labor is one of Peru's most crying needs, consequently, the advent of such modern [American] machinery . . . which can be operated by a few skilled employes, and a comparatively small number of the cheap laborers, is certain to be welcomed most gladly everywhere.[11]

The new alliance between American capital and local entrepreneurs found its most striking expression in the Cerro de Pasco Corporation. The American mining company began acquiring properties in the central highlands in 1902. By the early 1920s it accounted for over 80 percent of Peru's metal mining production. The company's entry into Peru responded to the nation's transformational crisis and to fundamental changes sweeping the American mining industry.

By the 1890s developments in the smelting industry (the separation of metals from the ore) tested the limits of the established techniques of systematic mining. The increasing capacity of reverberatory furnaces and the introduction of the converter method of smelting in the early 1880s demanded increased efficiency in mining. The response came with the mechanization of functions previously done by hand such as the use of power drills and the introduction of mechanized forms of hauling and lifting. As mining and smelting became technified and increasingly integrated into a single continuous manufacturing process, increased capital requirements shifted control from individual entrepreneurs to large corporations.[12] New York investment banks such as J. P. Morgan and Com-

10 Peter Blanchard, *The Origins of the Peruvian Labor Movement, 1883–1919* (Pittsburgh: University of Pittsburgh Press, 1982), pp. 26–27, 55–56, 69–72. On the earlier organization of stevedores in Peru, see Thomas F. O'Brien, *The Nitrate Industry and Chile's Crucial Transition: 1870–1891* (New York: New York University Press, 1982), p. 91 n. 59. Blanchard deals only with stevedores, but the reports cited below in Chapter 6, nn. 45 and 47, describe a complex port community ranging from tallymen to launch owners.
11 George Handley, "Excavating and Mining Machinery," Lima, January 13, 1914, RG 84, USNA.
12 Barger and Schurr, *The Mining Industries,* pp. 99–121; W. H. Dennis, *A Hundred Years of Metallurgy* (Chicago: Aldine, 1964), pp. 57–133.

pany and the National City Bank met the growing capital requirements of mining and smelting operations. In 1899 the National City Bank and the Morgan interests financed the Amalgamated Copper Company's purchase of James Ben Ali Haggin's Anaconda Copper Mining Company. That operation responded to the capital intensification under way in mining and to the growing demand for industrial metals in the United States.[13] In turn, new technical developments in smelting made it possible for these large corporations to undertake overseas ventures. Improved fuel-to-ore ratios in smelting by the end of the nineteenth century enabled mining companies to construct smelters in close proximity to mines. This development made the formation of vertically integrated international mining corporations possible. The new technologies, combined with expanded sources of corporate financing and a growing demand for industrial metals, led to a new marriage of interests between James Haggin and J. P. Morgan.

In early 1902 Haggin, with the backing of J. P. Morgan, formed a syndicate which eventually became known as the Cerro de Pasco Corporation. The company, capitalized at $10 million, acquired 730 claims in the Cerro de Pasco region, at a cost of $2.5 million, and the right to build a rail line that would link the claims to the central railway at Oroya. The company's rapid acquisition of mining properties from Peruvian owners reflected the dismal prospects for the industry at this time. Falling international copper prices, flooding in the mines, transportation bottlenecks and the increasing expense and inefficiency of enganche labor made Haggin's purchase offers extremely attractive. The American firm then closed the existing mines and began wholesale renovations.[14]

During the first ten years of operation, the Cerro de Pasco Corporation invested $25 million revamping mining in the central highlands. It constructed the largest smelter in Peru at nearby Tinyahuarco, built a 125-mile rail link south to Oroya, acquired 2,000 acres of coal properties, and erected two hydroelectric plants close to Oroya. The company also began the systematic exploitation of the mines. Where Peruvian miners had dug tunnels at an angle to follow the richest veins of ore and allow workers to carry ore out on their backs, the company's engineers installed a system of vertical shafts and horizontal adits and tunnels. Electric hoisting winches would now remove the ore which miners extracted with compressed air drills while electric pumps drained rising water and provided ventilation.[15]

13 Isaac F. Marcosson, *Anaconda* (New York: Dodd, Mead, 1957), pp. 93–96.

14 Syndicate Book #3, Morgan Papers; De Wind, "Peasants Become Miners," pp. 8–20; Mallon, *Defense of Community*, pp. 166–67; Thorp and Bertram, *Peru, 1890–1977*, pp. 79–81.

15 De Wind, "Peasants Become Miners," pp. 23–47; J. C. Pickering, "The Mining Districts of Central Peru," *EMJ* 85 (May 16, 1908), and "Recent Developments at Cerro de Pasco, Peru," *EMJ* 85 (April 11, 1908); Thorp and Bertram, *Peru, 1890–1977*, pp. 81–85; "Cerro de Pasco Corporation," Scudder Collection; Dirk Kruijt and Menno Vellinga, *Labor Relations and Multinational Corporations: The Cerro de Pasco Corporation in Peru (1902–1974)* (Assen: Van Gorcum, 1979), pp. 43–45.

While the Cerro de Pasco Corporation now introduced the manufacturing age in Peruvian mining, other American companies injected capital and technology into oil production, manufacturing, sugar estates and public utilities. In 1913 the Standard Oil Company, through its subsidiary the International Petroleum Corporation (IPC), purchased the most important oil fields in Peru from a British firm. Over the next decade the company would expend $30 million producing oil in Peru and would also gain control of the country's oil distribution system. American business also penetrated the sugar sector.[16] In 1867 Michael and William Grace founded the mercantile house W. R. Grace and Company in Peru. By the end of the nineteenth century the firm had turned increasing attention to direct investments in Peru. With Peruvian sugar planters reeling from the effects of the War of the Pacific, the Graces foreclosed on loans to local planters and acquired the Cartavio sugar hacienda in the Chicama Valley on Peru's northern coast. Nine years later W. R. Grace formed the Cartavio Sugar Company, capitalized at $1 million. With investments in improved agricultural techniques and mechanized plows for the estate, as well as more efficient milling equipment, Grace doubled output at both the plantation and the *ingenio,* or mill, between 1896 and 1908. Nor did the Graces limit their activities to the sugar industry.[17] By 1918 Grace controlled the Vitarte Cotton Mill Company, capitalized at $1 million and accounting for 45 percent of the country's textile production. W. R. Grace became the marketing agent for the General Electric Company in 1902. Over the next two years it sold $225,000 in electrical generation equipment to the Peruvian-controlled Empresas Eléctricas de Santa Rosa in Lima.[18] But unlike the fruteras in Central America, American companies in Peru did not simply invest in economic sectors in which the local elite had little interest. While Cerro de Pasco's purchase of mines offered handsome returns to their owners, and IPC's investments represented largely a change in the source of foreign control of oil, their activities represented the long-term exclusion of local interests from these profitable sectors. That displacement triggered a series of bitter disputes between American companies and Peru's rulers.

Under a government contract, the Empresa Socovanera de Cerro de Pasco constructed a tunnel to drain water from the district's mines and laid claim to 20 percent of the ore from the mines. The company's promoters included some of the leading business and political figures in

16 Thorp and Bertram, *Peru, 1890–1977,* pp. 100–105.
17 Klarén, *Modernization, Dislocation,* p. 9; Edward Eyre to M. P. Grace, New York, March 14, 1902, April 21, 1904; W. R. Grace to Lima House, New York, May 8, 1905, Box 74; Cartavio board meetings, London, April 2, 1891, December 27, 1899, May 6, 1909, Box 126; L. H. Sherman to M. P. Grace, Lima, January 23, 1909, Box 126a, Grace Papers; Lawrence A. Clayton, *Grace: W. R. Grace & Co.: The Formative Years, 1850–1930* (Ottawa, Ill.: Jameson, 1985), pp. 286–96.
18 Bertram and Thorp, *Peru, 1890–1977,* pp. 33–34; certificate of incorporation, Vitarte Cotton Company, n.p., January 29, 1917, Box 145, Grace Papers; Clayton, *Grace,* p. 297.

Peru, but the Cerro de Pasco company rejected the claim. In response, Peruvian troops prevented the shipment of ores. The American firm eventually granted the empresa $60 million in new shares in the American company. The company in effect had acknowledged "that rich Americans who have secured mining property worth many millions and upon which they have expended many millions, may be made to divide those millions with natives."[19]

Even W. R. Grace and Company, whose investments had made it a partner of many noted Peruvian families, found its sugar plantations under attack by the most prominent planter in the Chicama Valley. Some of Grace's American corporate allies also found themselves in direct confrontations with Peruvian interests. With William R. Grace serving as a director of the National City Bank, his firm emerged as the bank's agent in Peru. In 1912 the bank attempted to arrange a $5 million loan to the Peruvian government. But the American financial institution found itself outwitted by José Payan, the most prominent figure in Peruvian finance. His Banco de Londres y Perú snatched the loan away from the National City Bank, a reflection of its influence among Peruvian congressmen.[20]

Payan's success represented the elite's continuing assertion and protection of their rights in the face of increasing direct American penetration of the national economy. But the elite's conflicts with U.S. interests smacked of the autocratic nationalism of Lima's nineteenth-century merchants with all its attendant limitations. They would never consider making their antipathy toward U.S. investors a matter of popular protest, for they shared the American view that "the [Peruvian] masses are much to be feared. They are mostly Indians or cholos (a mixture of negro, Indian, Chinese etc.) and are most dangerous when aroused."[21] The moment was fast approaching, however, when social protest and nationalist protest would coalesce in a brief but violent eruption. American corporations contributed to the intensifying strains on Peru's social and political fabric which led to that violence.

As they had done in the American industrial revolution, American entrepreneurs in Peru first built upon existing social relations. The Cerro de

---

19 Details of the dispute are contained in Case 2842, rl. 227, M-862, N&MF, USNA. De Wind, "Peasants Become Miners," pp. 11–12; Thorp and Bertram, *Peru, 1890–1977*, pp. 82–83.

20 Thorp and Bertram, *Peru, 1890–1977*, pp. 108–9; memorandum, Asuntos de Cartavio, 1910, Box 126a, Grace Papers; C. L. Chester to Seth L. Pierpont, New York, July 13, 1912, 823.51/48; Samuel McRobert to Huntington Wilson, New York, July 29, 1912, 823.51/51, rl. 17, M-746; H. Clay Howard to secretary of state, Lima, February 21, 1913, 823.51/58, rl. 24, M-746, RG 59, USNA. The Diamond Match Company found itself fighting off an attempt by José Payan to arrange a government takeover of its El Sol enterprise: memorandum, Division of Latin American Affairs, June 19, 1924, 823.602C73/–; Holman to Mr. Cox, New York, June 20, 1924, 823.602C73/3; Miles Poindexter to secretary of state, Lima, June 29, 1925, 823.602C73/13, rl. 24, M-746, RG 59, USNA.

21 Albert W. Bryan, memorandum, Division of Latin American Affairs, February 5, 1914, rl. 2, M-746, RG 59, USNA.

Pasco company secured most of its workers from *enganchadores* or from *contratistas,* local contractors who furnished laborers and supervised their work in the mines. These methods of recruitment reduced the company's labor costs, since the growing number of mine workers remained a transitional labor force of temporary workers who still earned much of their subsistence from peasant agriculture. So too laborers on Peruvian sugar plantations retained the dual status of peasant/worker. The outbreak of World War I would lead to intensified efforts to meet growing labor requirements through contracted indebtedness.[22]

Europe's plunge into the abyss generated a seemingly insatiable demand for products such as copper and sugar. With demand as well as profits soaring, the Cerro de Pasco company and coastal planters scoured the Andean countryside for labor. In the central highlands wealthy peasants now competed with local merchants as enganchadores. In northern highland departments such as Cajamarca, hacendados required tenants to fulfill part of their obligations as workers on the coastal sugar estates. These developments converted traditional patron–client relations into an ever more onerous system of labor recruitment.[23] The wartime boom also exposed a growing number of Peruvians to at least partial dependence on wage labor and the vagaries of a market economy. Employment in plantation agriculture and mineral extraction grew at a rate of 4.2 percent between 1908 and 1920. In Lima, working-class employment rose from 21,000 to 27,000 between 1908 and 1920.[24] At the same time, wartime inflation caused real wages and salaries for the working and middle classes to stagnate or decline.

Peru's capital became home to an expanding petite bourgeoisie and an emergent middle class who struggled to make a place for themselves in a growing market economy. By the 1920s shopkeepers, vendors, bakers, tailors, shoemakers and other tradesmen totaled over 20,000, as did the number of white-collar employees and professionals. Throughout Peru this group faced an array of threats and obstacles. Educational opportunities remained limited, the salaries of government employees were declining, small-scale agriculturists on the coast faced absorption by expanding plantations, and merchants confronted withering competition from foreign commercial houses and large corporations which circumvented their local marketing networks. White-collar employees in the commercial sector endured low pay and long hours in the midst of wartime inflation. Shortly after the war, the stresses building at both the middle and lower levels of the Peruvian social system erupted and brought on the collapse of the national political order.[25]

22 De Wind, "Peasants Become Miners," pp. 152–64.

23 Mallon, *Defense of Community,* pp. 206–10; Gonzales, *Plantation Agriculture,* p. 126.

24 Thorp and Bertram, *Peru, 1890–1977,* p. 117; Steve Stein, *Populism in Peru: The Emergence of the Masses and the Politics of Social Control* (Madison: University of Wisconsin Press, 1980), p. 71.

25 Klarén, *Modernization, Dislocation,* pp. 50–83; Thorp and Bertram, *Peru, 1890–1977,* pp. 116–17; Stein, *Populism,* p. 74.

The petite bourgeoisie and middle and working classes gave vent to their growing discontents in a variety of ways. Small farmers in the Chicama Valley struck out violently against the large plantations which choked off their access to water. Bitter competition between enganchadores and the increased use of traditional relationships to extract labor from peasants triggered ever more violent clashes in the countryside. In contrast, Lima's Sociedad de Empleados de Comercio, formed in 1903, limited itself to accepted forms of political protest during the war years. The capital's expanding group of white-collar employees saw themselves as a class apart from workers, with inherently greater material needs. Many still treasured patriarchal relationships with their employers and eschewed the more militant actions of workers. But the middle class would eventually feel compelled to adopt working-class organization and tactics to achieve their goals. Sugar workers on plantations along the northern coast struck in 1917 and again in 1919. In January 1919 strikes broke out in the oil fields and at Cerro de Pasco's facilities. During that same month the working class in Lima and Callao, which had been relatively quiescent during the war, launched a general strike.[26]

The Peruvian elite proved itself ill equipped to respond to this challenge. A loose and often fractious coalition of groups tied to the export economy, the Peruvian oligarchy had dominated the nation's politics since 1895 through the Partido Civil. In response to the general strike, the Civilista regime hurriedly consented to the strikers' principal demand for the eight-hour day. It proved too little too late.

A firestorm of death and destruction swept the capital of Peru in the closing days of May 1919. For over a month, workers' committees in Lima and the nearby port city of Callao had been demanding reductions in the prices of food and other essentials. On May 25 saber-wielding mounted police attacked a public demonstration led by working-class women who denounced capitalists for pushing their families to the point of starvation. That same evening the authorities arrested the leaders of the Lima committee, prompting the call for a general strike on Tuesday. Lima's early morning tranquility on that Tuesday was soon broken by the sound of gunfire. Police and soldiers armed with machine guns fought running battles with demonstrators, who hurled rocks in response. Demonstrators in the urban areas, frustrated by unbridled market forces, directed their rage against foreign interests and their local allies. The crowds vented their anger on the most obvious symbols of their plight, stoning the offices of W. R. Grace and Company and sacking two hundred Chinese-owned grocery stores. By Friday an uneasy calm settled over the capital as

26 Baltazar Caravedo Molinari, *Clases, lucha política y gobierno en el Perú (1919–1930)* (Lima: Retama Editorial, 1977), p. 30. On the events of 1919, see Blanchard, *Peruvian Labor Movement,* pp. 148–72. See also Gary Richard Garrett, "The Oncenio of Augusto B. Leguía: Middle Sector Government and Leadership in Peru, 1919–1930" (Ph.D. dissertation, University of New Mexico, 1973), pp. 167–73.

a White Guard of local businessmen and foreign residents patrolled the streets. The tragic days of May had led to three hundred arrests and left five hundred dead. The Peruvian oligarchy had made a strategic retreat in January; now it rejected and suppressed all claims by the popular forces who had once again taken to the streets.[27]

On its surface, the upheaval in May 1919 appeared to be another episode in a long series of periodic protests by Limeños against a rising cost of living. Yet the May uprising signaled more than another round of urban protest. Amidst the tumult, an old social order was dying and a new one struggling to be born. In the quarter century preceding the tragic days of May, the national elite's new partnership with American corporations had overcome internal obstacles to the transformation of the Peruvian economy. That alliance triggered sweeping changes and rising tensions in Peruvian society that erupted in new popular protests against foreign influences and the elite's model of liberal development.

The tragic days in May, which exposed the bankruptcy of Civilista rule, erupted in a climate of political crisis. Shortly before the general strike, Augusto Leguía, a longtime political maverick, had won the recent presidential election. Fearful that the Civilista bureaucracy would rob him of his victory and anxious to break the party's grip on power, Leguía staged a coup on July 4. Leguía had learned important lessons from the Civilistas' rejection of popular demands and from their program of American-led modernization. Over the next eleven years (known as the *oncenio*) he neutralized the Civilistas politically, attempted to fashion a new social base of support for the state and pressed forward with a plan of American-led modernization.

In shaping his new political order in 1919, Leguía turned to individuals much like himself: minor but ambitious members of the economic elite. Cognizant of the new social forces that had undermined the Civilista state, he also forged an initial coalition with both the middle and working classes. In response to demands by white-collar employees, Leguía decreed Sunday a legal holiday and required all commercial enterprises to close by 7 p.m. In 1924 he solidified his support from the Sociedad de Empleados de Comercio with the *ley de empleados,* which provided white-collar employees with retirement funds and other social benefits. University students also threw their backing to Leguía and his promises of educational reform. Nor did Leguía neglect the working class. Three days after seizing power, he addressed the capital's disgruntled workers, promising them housing, cheaper food and educational opportunities. Leguía's honeymoon with labor was brief. Within a few months he imposed compulsory arbitration on labor disputes, and over the next four years his policies toward

---

27 *West Coast Leader* (Lima), May 27, 31, 1919; Ricardo Martínez de la Torre, *Apuntes para una interpretación marxista de la historia social del Perú,* 4 vols. (Lima: Confederación General de Trabajadores Peruanos, 1947), 1, p. 37; Handley to secretary of state, Lima, May 27, 30, 31, June 6, 1919, 823.5045/16, 20, 22, 26, rl. 14, M-746, RG 59, USNA.

labor would become increasingly harsh. The port workers of Callao managed to avoid the crackdown because they could cripple Peru's international commerce. Equally important to the survival of the Leguiista regime was the continued growth of American investment.[28]

During the oncenio, the Cerro de Pasco Corporation remained the single most important foreign enterprise in Peru. Between 1915 and 1919 the company completed its acquisition of mining properties in the central highlands and committed $10 million to building a new smelter to the south of Cerro de Pasco in Oroya. The firm's development policies increased its total investment to $58 million by 1922. The International Petroleum Corporation continued to dominate the petroleum sector and would expend $87 million on oil production during the oncenio. W. R. Grace added to its Cartavio sugar interests in 1926 with the purchase of the Paramonga sugar estate for $4.6 million. In addition, International Telephone and Telegraph took control of the national telephone system in 1930. Under the favorable conditions created by Leguía, U.S. investment in Peru climbed from under $45 million in 1914 to $95 million in 1929.[29]

These growing investments continued to have a variety of positive impacts on Peru's economic performance. Peruvian sugar production increased from 140,000 tons in 1900 to 400,000 tons in 1930. Under IPC, crude petroleum output increased tenfold by 1930. Cerro de Pasco not only played the central role in doubling metal production in the two decades after 1910, it also returned a considerable portion of its revenues to the domestic economy. Between 1916 and 1930 the company earned $310 million in Peru but returned 55 percent of those revenues in payments to labor, local suppliers and the Peruvian government. Many of the gains which came during the oncenio resulted from the revamping of production systems and social relations by American companies. Once again the Cerro de Pasco Corporation led the way.[30]

Cerro de Pasco's rationalization of production during the 1920s was driven by a number of factors. The increased output of copper in Chile and Mexico signaled ever more competitive world market conditions to which the company had to respond. Furthermore, the mineral content of the company's ores had fallen off sharply by 1920. The firm's continued acquisition of mining properties also required increased integration of its operations and expansion of its smelting capacity. The new smelter at

28 *West Coast Leader*, September 27, 1919; Garrett, "Middle Sector Government," pp. 97, 167–75, 64–65.

29 "Cerro de Pasco Corporation," Scudder Collection; Kruijt and Vellinga, *Labor Relations*, p. 37; Thorp and Bertram, *Peru, 1890–1977*, pp. 83–85, 155; *West Coast Leader*, October 16, 1926; William C. Burdett to secretary of state, Callao, October 15, 1931, 812.63/824 [*sic*], rl. 122, M-1370, RG 59, USNA.

30 Clayton, *Grace*, p. 323; *West Coast Leader*, March 18, 1920; July 28, 1925; Rippy, *Globe and Hemisphere*, pp. 38, 41; Thorp and Bertram, *Peru, 1890–1977*, pp. 80, 87, 340–41.

Oroya symbolized the company's response to these challenges. The Oroya smelter, which began operations in 1922, incorporated the latest in industrial technology. Its highly mechanized operations could generate 2,500 tons of copper a day, an output which equaled the combined capacity of the two smelters which the company was then operating. Nor was the Oroya facility the only technological advance introduced by the company. By the turn of the century, concentrators replaced hand sorting of ores. In this process huge mechanical grinders crushed the ore before it was shipped to concentrating plants, which used gravity methods to separate the ore from the waste material. As early as 1920 the Cerro de Pasco company had installed mechanical separators to treat ore before it was smelted at Tinyahuarco, and by 1920 the firm had acquired three concentrators. In 1924 the company installed a concentrator based on the new more efficient flotation process. At the same time that Cerro de Pasco mechanized its surface operations, it also pressed ahead with the rationalization of extraction.[31]

Because of the small ore bodies at Cerro de Pasco, the company had relied on selective mining techniques of square-set timbering in developing those mines. But during the 1920s it began using more efficient nonselective methods such as shrinkage stoping and glory holes at its newly acquired Casapalca mines. Although selective mining methods continued to dominate in the company's mines, those processes as well were subject to increased rationalization. The prevailing low price of copper made it essential that mining operations achieve the maximum efficiency possible. This required increased standardization of operations in the shaft and a division of the workforce into one of several job classifications. A worker was moved among the various job categories to determine the one to which he was best suited. The miner would then stay in that position so he could reduce the job to a simple and efficient routine. Such a process of course required that labor turnover be minimized in order to create a stable workforce. During the 1920s the Cerro de Pasco Corporation undertook such a project.[32]

As a part of its new policies, the company reduced its dependence on *contratistas*. Contractors, who directly supervised the workers they recruited, interfered with the corporation's efforts to directly manage underground operations. The firm also reduced its reliance on costly enganche labor. In addition to its high cost, enganche seriously impacted the efficiency of mine workers. Peasants recruited in this manner resisted the company's efforts to introduce shorter shifts. They insisted on working

31 De Wind, "Peasants Become Miners," pp. 49–51; *West Coast Leader*, November 22, 1922, April 15, 1920; also see issues of *Boletín de Minas y Petroleo* in rl. 25, M-746, RG 59, USNA; *West Coast Leader*, January 22, 1920; Barger and Schurr, *Mining Industries*, pp. 153–55.

32 W. C. Burdett, "Mining in Peru," Callao/Lima, November 25, 1930, RG 84, USNA; *Mining and Metallurgy*, November 1945; De Wind, "Peasants Become Miners," p. 46; *EMJ* 121 (April 24, 1926); 124 (September 10, 1927).

thirty-six-hour shifts followed by a twelve-hour rest period in order to complete their contracts as quickly as possible and return to their fields. As a result, much of their time underground was spent making up for lost sleep. During the 1920s the Cerro de Pasco company increasingly turned to direct-hire workers known as *maquipueros*. During the 1920s these direct hires came to constitute just under 50 percent of the company's labor force. As the corporation's workforce expanded to an all-time high of 12,000 in 1928, a growing number of peasants remained with the company a year or more, compared with the few months which had been typical in the past. As a whole, Cerro de Pasco exposed its workers to an ever more routinized and mechanized form of work.[33]

In assessing the impact of the changing technologies and work relations which Cerro de Pasco introduced into the central highlands in the 1920s, it is important to recognize that the degree of change varied among the distinct operations of the corporation, and that a series of equally distinct communities absorbed the impact of those changes. The company's smelters represented the most advanced case of technological innovation and transformed work relations.

Compared with work in the mineshafts, the continuous industrial production processes of the smelters represented a different experience and placed distinct requirements on the Peruvian peasants recruited to work there. The smelter at Oroya, with its highly mechanized operations, depended heavily on a resident body of workers who had mastered specific tasks in the plant. To secure that labor force, the company turned to direct hires and built a workers' village of corrugated metal shacks, and provided company stores and medical services. To socialize workers into the requirements of this new industrial environment, the company undertook welfare programs such as night classes. In recognition of the status of this new labor force, the company insisted that the workers' village be referred to as the "workmen's town" rather than by the derogatory expression "cholo town." Even before they finished the smelter, company officials noted with satisfaction that because of their socialization project, a growing number of the workers' wives were adopting Western-style clothing and shoes.[34]

Although the company made some efforts to create a more stable work force at Oroya, its policies hardly constituted a full-fledged program of social welfare. The workmen's town provided only a thousand rooms for a community that numbered five thousand, and had no educational facilities for the workers' children. A social club, the Club Peruano, built at the workers' expense, remained under the company's control. As for the firm's Peruvian *empleados,* or white-collar workers, they technically had access to the exclusive

33 Mallon, *Defense of Community,* pp. 223–24; Kruijt and Vellinga, *Labor Relations,* p. 67; Pickering, "Transportation Costs and Labor in Central Peru"; De Wind, "Peasants Become Miners," p. 165; Flores Galindo, *Los mineros de la Cerro de Pasco,* pp. 60–63.

34 *West Coast Leader,* April 15, 1920.

Club Inca, but only five of them gained membership. The managerial culture of the company was not far removed from that of the fruteras in Central America, which emphasized extracting the maximum amount of labor from mostly unskilled workers through rigorous discipline with limited attempts at industrial welfare. And much like the fruteras' administrators, Cerro de Pasco's managers viewed anything more than these minimal social welfare efforts as wasted on their "uncivilized" cholo laborers.[35]

In addition to the distinct industrial experience which workers at the Oroya smelter encountered, they themselves constituted a distinct group from the Mantaro Valley, which lay to the south of Cerro de Pasco. The smelter workers tended to be better educated because they came from the more prosperous villages that dotted the valley, as opposed to the poorer communities of the *puna,* or surrounding mountainsides. In turn, many of the smelter workers sought to increase their incomes by setting up small stores and shops in the town. As that stable and increasingly differentiated wage labor force emerged in the company town, the corporation also made a significant impact on the larger community of Oroya.

Before the central railway reached Oroya in 1893, the area consisted of haciendas and communal landholding groups engaged in pastoral activities. The commercial opportunities created by the railway accelerated a process of differentiation within the *comunidades* as much of their land became concentrated in a few hands. The Cerro de Pasco company's decision to build its smelter at Oroya further impacted the *comuneros* as the company began purchasing communal lands as a part of its development plans. But the most significant effect on the comuneros came after the smelter began operations in 1922.

The smoke which belched from the Oroya smelter was laced with lead, arsenic and other contaminants. The ash that rained down on the area from the smelter's smokestacks devastated livestock and crops. By 1924 the company had responded to mounting protests with agreements which offered alternative land sites outside Oroya or long-term payments to comuneros. Many of the comuneros who were also employed in the smelter accepted cash payments which allowed them to retain their residence in Oroya. Despite the destructive effects of the smoke, the resolution of the dispute had in effect drawn residents of the town and some of the smelter employees into a long-term relationship with the company. To the north in the municipality of Cerro de Pasco, conditions were significantly different.[36]

35 Martínez de la Torre, *Interpretación marxista,* 1, pp. 39–40, 131–32; Charles Cunningham, "Labor and Police Conditions in the Cerro de Pasco Mines," Lima, October 26, 1930 (cited hereafter as "Labor Conditions"), 323.114 Cerro de Pasco Corp./30, RG 59, USNA.

36 Julian Laite, "Processes of Industrial and Social Change in Highland Peru," in Norman Long and Bryan R. Roberts, eds., *Peasant Cooperation and Capitalist Expansion in Central Peru* (Austin: University of Texas Press, 1978), pp. 73–97; Pilar Campaña and Rigoberto Rivera, "Highland *Puna* Communities and the Impact of the Mining Economy," in Normal Long and Bryan Roberts, eds., *Miners, Peasants and Entrepreneurs: Regional Development in the Central Highlands of Peru* (Cambridge: Cambridge University Press, 1984), p. 93.

Cerro de Pasco's history as a mining town dated back to the colonial era. As a result, the company drew most of its labor force from Cerro de Pasco's pool of experienced miners, and maintained only a small camp for migratory workers. The generational experience in mine work and the workers' continued residence in the town created the most manageable labor force which the corporation encountered in the central highlands. The company's relations with the town as a whole, however, proved less than satisfactory.[37]

As the corporation drove its shafts and tunnels deeper into the hillsides of Cerro de Pasco, it undermined the land on which the town was built. The resulting subsidence caused $1 million in damages to homes and shops in the municipality. Prior to Augusto Leguía's seizure of power, the municipal government began demanding compensation from the corporation. Anxious to squelch potential challenges to his regime, Leguía had clamped down on provincial and regional councils. In Cerro de Pasco, Leguía replaced the municipal government with his appointees, who were more willing to protect the company's interests.[38] Throughout the oncenio, local resentment toward the company would continue to smolder beneath the surface. In other communities where the corporation operated, local conditions led to more overt signs of protest.

In sharp contrast to conditions at Cerro de Pasco, the company's operations at Morococha represented one of the most volatile labor situations with which the corporation had to cope. The camps in Morococha held some 2,500 laborers, almost all of them recruited from the puna, or hillside villages, of the Mantaro Valley. As with most of its mining operations, the company was dealing with a largely unskilled and transient labor force. As a result, managers saw little reason to extend even the limited elements of industrial welfare which they practiced in Oroya. At Morococha, the peasant miners endured the less than tender mercies of the Onofres, a nouveau riche family of labor contractors known for their labor speedups and the exorbitant prices they charged at the camp stores. The migrant workers offered continuing challenges to the corporation. In 1919 they struck for a 50 percent wage increase and dynamited the company's power transmission lines. Little more than a year later the miners struck again and tossed sticks of dynamite into the "gringo" managers' camp. The company responded by packing the entire workforce on trains and ordering them never to return.[39]

The Morococha labor force developed new grievances toward the corporation during the 1920s. Despite the company's installation of screening

---

37 *West Coast Leader,* April 20, 1920; "Labor Conditions," 323.114 Cerro de Pasco Corp./30, RG 59, USNA.

38 "Labor Conditions," 323.114 Cerro de Pasco Corp./30, RG 59, USNA; Carl F. Herbold Jr., "Developments in the Peruvian Administrative System, 1919–1930: Modern and Traditional Qualities of Government Under Authoritarian Regimes" (Ph.D. dissertation, Yale University, 1973), p. 112.

39 Handley to secretary of state, Lima, January 14, 21, 1919, 823.5045/7, 15, rl. 14, M-746, RG 59, USNA; *West Coast Leader,* April 8, 1920.

devices on its Oroya smokestacks, the smelter smoke continued to spread destruction southward throughout the Mantaro Valley. Damage to land and livestock compelled poorer peasants with a fragile grip on subsistence to seek permanent employment in mining. In 1928 a cave-in sent water flooding into the mine and killed twenty-eight workers. The miners' vehement protests again led to the dispatch of troops to the camp.[40]

Empleados, or white-collar employees, at Morococha often worked twelve-hour days, seven days a week. High prices at the company store siphoned off their meager salaries, leaving them at the level of subsistence. Promotions did not automatically bring salary increases, and senior administrative positions remained the exclusive preserve of Americans and other foreigners.[41] By 1929 the company had created yet another hotbed of dissent near Oroya.

To meet its growing needs for electrical power, the Cerro de Pasco Corporation constructed an enormous new hydroelectric plant at Malpaso. Given its expanding demands on the local labor supply and the temporary nature of the work, the company exercised less discrimination in its choice of employees. In addition to *contratista* labor, the firm allowed workers previously dismissed from other camps for insubordination to work at Malpaso. Living conditions were less than commodious, with workers sleeping five to a room. Even empleados found the company "hotel" held few beds, forcing many of them to sleep on the floor. As worker and empleado dissent grew in camps like Malpaso and Morococha, resentment of the company also spread among petit bourgeois elements in the region.[42]

During its development the Cerro de Pasco Corporation had forged strong bonds with enganchadores and created new opportunities for merchants and peasants with sufficient resources to benefit from the increased demand for local products. The decade of the 1920s, however, sharply altered those beneficial relationships for much of the valley's population. The company's shift toward a permanent wage labor force delivered a fatal blow to many enganchadores, while company stores began to limit the access of small merchants and itinerant peddlers to the large market represented by the corporation's laborers. Leguía, with his policy of replacing local elected officials with appointees of the central government, severely constrained political expression of these discontents.

By the end of the decade, many of the region's small merchants and farmers, artisans and teachers turned to the populist Alianza Popular Revolucionaria Peruana (APRA), which had developed on Peru's sugar-producing north coast, and to the Lima-based Communist party.[43] That

40 Flores Galindo, *Los mineros de la Cerro de Pasco,* pp. 77–78.
41 "Labor Conditions," 323.114 Cerro de Pasco Corp./30, RG 59, USNA; Martínez de la Torre, *Interpretación marxista,* 1, p. 132.
42 Ibid.
43 "Labor Conditions," 323.114 Cerro de Pasco Corp./30, RG 59, USNA; Mallon, *Defense of Community,* pp. 235–38.

political shift also marked an alliance with the valley's lower classes. For both small business interests and the peasant workers of the central highlands, the Cerro de Pasco Corporation, which had initially opened a new world of opportunities to them, came to represent a threat to their interests. The region's popular elements joined together in a common nationalist project that struck a sympathetic chord among many of their countrymen. As an American official later noted:

There is a feeling on the part of all Peruvians that the Company has enormous resources which have accrued to it during the recent years as a result of the exploitation of the natural resources of Peru and that, in spite of general unsatisfactory business conditions in the world. A large share of these resources, they feel, belong to the Peruvian nation and should be distributed to Peruvian workmen in the form of higher wages and better living conditions.[44]

How successfully that regional alliance could pursue its goals and link up with sympathetic elements at the national level would be determined during events triggered by the Great Depression. Meanwhile, on the northern coast, domestic and foreign entrepreneurs pursued their own process of capitalist rationalization that would forge another alliance between the petite bourgeoisie and peasant workers.

Between the 1890s and 1920s, the Peruvian sugar industry underwent a process of technical renovation which paralleled the changes in the mining sector. During the 1890s, World War I, and the early 1920s planters introduced modern mills, improved transportation systems and advanced agricultural techniques. Yet in the Chicama Valley, where those changes were most pronounced, foreign capital played a less dominant role than in mining. By the late 1920s the Gildemeister interests and W. R. Grace dominated the Chicama Valley's sugar industry. The Gildemeisters, a German family who made their fortune in Peru's nitrate industry, had shifted their investments to sugar in the 1890s. They merged with a German syndicate in 1910 to secure funds for the continued modernization of their plantations, but their long residence in the country gave some justification to their claims of being a Peruvian enterprise. This composite of foreign and domestic capital had brought sweeping changes to the society of the Chicama Valley.

In search of greater efficiency, planters on the north coast gradually abandoned enganche for a direct-hire system which would ensure a more stable labor force. Yet much like the fruteras of Central America, the sugar companies continued to rely on large numbers of unskilled workers for long hours of physically demanding work, ensuring the survival of a managerial system which used harsh measures to extract the maximum amount of effort from its workforce in the shortest possible time. Those conditions, combined with falling world sugar prices and rising food prices, triggered

---

44 "Labor Conditions," 323.114 Cerro de Pasco Corp./30, RG 59, USNA.

widespread labor uprisings in the valley in 1921. After failed attempts at mediation, the Leguía government sent troops to suppress the strikes. Workers continued to organize during the remainder of the decade and would eventually ally themselves with the region's small business interests.

The growth of the valley's large sugar enterprises gradually engulfed thousands of small landholders. The major growers gained control of water boards, which allowed them to undermine small farms and eventually absorb them. Local merchants and shopkeepers who had prospered from the revival of sugar production in the 1890s now faced ruin from the consolidation and vertical integration of the industry. In 1915 the Gildemeisters secured a government port concession at Malabrigo on the north coast. The Gildemeisters used the low-cost goods imported through Malabrigo to compete directly for the region's retail trade. The valley's displaced petite bourgeoisie and sugar workers formed a community of resistance to the transformation of the sugar industry and provided the popular political base for APRA.[45]

Founded in 1924 by Víctor Raul Haya de la Torre, APRA adopted a stance against Yankee imperialism as one of its principal tenets. Ironically, the region's largest sugar producer was in fact a Peruvian-German corporation, and many of the area's woes during the 1920s stemmed from adverse conditions in the world sugar market. The APRA position reflected the widespread recognition that American corporations represented the driving force behind the transformation of Peru and the disruption of social relations that gave birth to the Aprista movement. Opponents of that transformational process vented their dissatisfaction in terms of Peruvian nationalism. It was a theme whose legitimacy could not be denied even by the Peruvian oligarchy, who had relied on it in the 1820s to promote protectionist policies, appealed to it again in the case of the Empresa Sacovanera, and generally had their own mixed experiences with American enterprises. As new challenges to Leguía's alliance with American corporations emerged, the Lima–Callao region remained the one area where the president still held together the petit bourgeois and middle- and working-class elements of his political coalition.

Leguía's alliance with the middle class in the capital rested on an increase in middle-class employment in the Lima–Callao area from 52,000 to 72,000 during the 1920s. The renewal of economic growth during the oncenio prompted part of this improvement. A hectic program of public works generated new business opportunities in the form of state contracts. In addition, Leguiista policies for rationalization of the state created five thousand new civil service positions. Leguía also managed to maintain close ties to the community of interests at the Callao docks.[46]

Soon after his seizure of power, the Peruvian president replaced his efforts to coopt the labor movement with a policy of outright repression.

45 Klarén, *Modernization, Dislocation,* pp. 3–83.
46 Garrett, "Middle Sector Government," pp. 97, 162.

Figure 7. Callao's old port facilities. The two circular structures are the government wharves. In the background are the docks built by a French company in the nineteenth century and the causeway that connected the piers to Callao's main business district. (United States National Archives)

However, he continued to court the favor of the Callao port community. That policy reflected the strategic position of these groups in Peru's international commerce and their ability to provide effective political support to the regime. Thanks to the limited capacity of the dock and channel system, most seagoing vessels had to be unloaded by a fleet of lighters. On the docks a system of aging iron cranes handled cargoes. As a result, the process of loading and unloading ships remained labor-intensive. Despite the high labor requirements of the Callao dock system, it could provide work for no more than half of the one to two thousand laborers who sought employment there. A system which required shipping firms to give hiring preference to registered stevedores and to rotate work assignments distributed limited employment opportunities among the stevedore community. In a series of labor disputes between 1894 and 1913, the dockworkers won wage increases and the eight-hour day and effectively maintained their control over the work process.[47]

The port workers represented a problem distinct from that of the transitional labor force in the highlands. The community which grew up around the docks represented a diverse group ranging from stevedores to private lighter owners and white-collar port employees. That community demonstrated a clear perception of its own interests and a willingness to use its strategic position to protect those interests. These groups expressed their in-

---

47 *West Coast Leader*, October 30, 1925; Blanchard, *Peruvian Labor Movement,* pp. 69–72, 89–90.

terests through a series of *gremios* that operated in close cooperation to achieve their ends. These disparate groups all had a vested interest in maintaining the existing dock system, in essence representing a coalition against the rationalization of Callao's wharves. For stevedores, their interests centered on the length of the workday and levels of employment which would ensure subsistence for as many of their number as possible. And they did not hesitate to use their influence in the government to pursue those goals.[48]

Six months after Leguía seized power, the stevedores struck against Sunday and night work. Despite his policy of enforced arbitration of labor disputes, Leguía refused to intervene. The following year the president issued a decree banning work after midnight on the docks. In return, the dockworkers regularly supplied demonstrators for Leguiísta rallies in Lima. Finally, in February 1928 the regime issued a decree which required shipping companies to hire union members on a rotational basis. The companies now had to hire union members through the government-appointed captain of the port and could not fire these workers or attempt to make their own selection of union members. When Leguía won reelection in August 1929, he accepted the congratulations of a cheering throng of stevedores in Lima's Plaza de Armas. The celebrating workers could hardly have appreciated that Leguía had already set in motion a process that would eventually cripple their movement.[49]

By 1927 the ability of the Callao dockworkers to maintain labor-intensive work methods in the face of expanding international trade had led to congestion in the port. The Cerro de Pasco company, which had invested heavily in improving and expanding its operations in the central highlands, now faced new constraints from Peruvian workers at its principal link to the international market. Leguía finally bowed to the corporation's demands that he modernize the Callao docks.

In March 1928 the Frederick Snare Company of New York won a $5 million contract from the government for the Callao project. Caught between his reliance on the political support of the stevedores and Cerro de Pasco's effort to further rationalize its operations, Leguía decided that the situation could "cure itself through the substitution of modern mechanical facilities for the obsolete equipment of today."[50] The new dockworks represented one small part of a massive public works project which American financing made possible and which helped ensure Leguía's survival.

48 Arthur D. Jukes, "Supplement to Report on Opening of New Maritime Terminal at Callao, Peru," Callao, November 2, 1934, RG 84, USNA; William C. Burdett to secretary of state, Lima, August 18, 1932, 823.1561/54, RG 59, USNA.

49 Frederick Lathrop Mayer to secretary of state, Lima, August 6, 1929, 823.00/570, rl. 7, M-746, RG 59, USNA; Arthur D. Jukes, "Labor Problems in the Callao Waterfront," Callao, February 3, 1932; James Roth to secretary of state, Callao, December 16, 1920, 823.5045/34, rl. 14, M-746, RG 59, USNA.

50 Matthew E. Hanna to secretary of state, Lima, October 9, 1928, 823.00/553, rl. 7, M-746, RG 59, USNA; Hanna to secretary of state, Lima, March 6, 1928, 823.1561/13, rl. 10, M-746, RG 59, USNA.

In a 1918 visit with Frank Vanderlip, president of the National City Bank, Augusto Leguía had urged the banker to assist in financing a grandiose series of public works which he envisioned for Peru. In the early years of the oncenio, however, American banks showed little interest in Peru because of the postwar economic slump. But by the mid 1920s, changing conditions in Peru and the United States triggered a flood tide of U.S. credit. As the Peruvian economy surged upward in the latter half of the oncenio, American banks entered a fierce competitive struggle in the Peruvian market. While Peru's ability to repay loans was improving, conditions in the U.S. domestic market had taken a downturn. A shift in U.S. income distribution toward the upper income brackets created a condition of "oversavings." At the same time the rate of growth of the gross national product was slowing. These factors created a situation in which banks found themselves with increasing capital resources but a declining number of high-return investments where those resources could be placed. In an intensely competitive environment, banks turned to the development of a middle-class consumer market for bond issues. Many of those issues proved to be Latin American government bonds as American financial institutions also responded to competition by seeking out overseas lending opportunities.[51]

Under Frank Vanderlip, National City Bank opened a series of offices in Latin America, responding to the requests of corporate customers in the region and to an increasingly competitive domestic banking environment. National City also joined with J. P. Morgan; Kuhn, Loeb; and other leading New York financial institutions in a South American Group which shared large financing opportunities such as government loans. Two members of that group, the Guaranty Trust Company and J. W. Seligman, joined National City Bank to loan Leguía $130 million between 1924 and 1928. Over half of that total was devoted to a massive program of public works. Those projects included some 18,000 kilometers of roadways, irrigation projects, sanitation works and urban renewal in Lima. While Leguía could readily claim that foreign loans and the public works they helped to finance were part of a larger modernization scheme, in fact they served short-term economic and political needs.[52]

The increasing role of foreign investment in Peru diverted a large part of the nation's export earnings and its overall economic surplus to American corporations. Borrowing from U.S. banks served to redress at least part of that imbalance. Public works projects created numerous opportunities for profit. By the time government funds filtered down through the

51 L. C. Bennett to Miles Poindexter, Lima, April 24, 1923, 823.51/304, rl. 19, M-746; William E. Gonzales to secretary of state, Lima, July 26, 1921, 823.6363/48, rl. 25, M-746, RG 59, USNA; Barbara Stallings, *Banker to the Third World: U.S. Portfolio Investment in Latin America, 1900–1986* (Berkeley and Los Angeles: University of California Press, 1987), pp. 150–64, 244–46.

52 Materials on these developments can be found scattered through the Vanderlip, Morgan and Lamont papers.

informal bureaucracy, only 50 cents of every public works dollar was actually spent on construction. In the headlong rush to grant international
loans, the financial houses ignored their own managers' warnings that low
consumption of manufactured goods; foreign control of natural resources,
which siphoned off wealth overseas; and a president surrounded by "ras-
cals" created poor prospects for debt repayment. The members of the
South American Group proved reluctant to rein in government corruption
because competitors always stood ready to step in with more lenient loan
terms. And as the bankers well knew, "public works contracts were essential to the maintenance of his [Leguía's] political power . . ."[53]

In Peru, unlike Central America, U.S. financial institutions played a
central role in the local encounter with American corporations. J. P. Morgan and Company played a major part in the creation of Cerro de Pasco,
and Joseph Grace served as a director of National City Bank, which in turn
helped finance the national government. From the U.S. perspective it
might appear that a phalanx of American corporations and banks were aggressively and successfully pressing forward with Peru's modernization.
From the Peruvian perspective it could well appear to be a cabal of American interests which threatened to totally control the national economy and
society. The latter view would find particular resonance if Leguía's economic miracle should falter. But in the short term the renovation of the nation's capital seemed to capture the essence of the renewed alliance with
American corporate culture that was shaping Peru's brave new world.

Lima at the turn of the century bore the physical trappings of its lumi-
nous past. Its baroque architecture, narrow streets and cathedral spires testified to its history as a vital urban outpost in the Spanish colonial empire.
Augusto Leguía set out to transform the physical appearance of the capital
to reflect its role as the critical link between Peru's resurgent export economy and the world's developed nations. The Foundation Company of New
York City, serving as the principal contractor to the central government, installed a new water and sewage system, paved streets with asphalt and refurbished public buildings. Avenida Leguía typified these changes. The broad
boulevard ran south from the city toward new residential areas such as Mi-
raflores and the coastal resort of Chorillos. The avenue provided four paved
lanes for traffic divided by a broad center strip adorned with trees, flowers
and electric lighting. With the central government providing basic utilities
for undeveloped land along the avenue, the Peruvian aristocracy and par-

53 Mayer to secretary of state, Lima, January 30, 1929, 823.51/433, rl. 20, M-746, RG 59, USNA;
   Garrett, "Middle Sector Government," p. 108; Rosemary Thorp and Carlos Londoño, "The Effect
   of the Great Depression on the Economies of Peru and Colombia," in Rosemary Thorp, ed., *Latin
   America in the 1930s: The Role of the Periphery in World Crisis* (New York: St. Martin's, 1984), pp.
   82–86; *New York Herald Tribune*, February 28, 1933, clipping enclosed in File 24, Box 107, Lamont Papers; Thomas W. Lamont to Robert P. Lamont, New York, February 5, 1930, File 20, Box
   102, Lamont Papers; J. W. Stimson, memorandum, Division of Latin American Affairs, November 8, 1929, 823.51/436, rl. 20, M-746, RG 59, USNA.

Figure 8. An aerial view of the four-lane Avenida Leguía stretching out into Lima's affluent suburbs. (From Peru, Ministerio de Fomento, *La labor constructiva del Perú* [1930])

venus abandoned their residences in the center of the city for the palatial mansions which private developers constructed in the suburban districts.

Refurbished or newly built parks, plazas and public monuments complemented the city's new Parisian-style boulevards. The regime also added imposing public edifices such as the Ministerio de Fomento. By 1922 the New York–based Frederick Lay Company had undertaken a dozen construction projects in Lima, including the capital's first "skyscraper," a six-story structure built of reinforced concrete, fully electrified, equipped with elevators and "designed for economy, efficiency and utility in the transaction of business . . ."[54] Leading American corporations such as W. R. Grace, National City Bank and the Cerro de Pasco company built or occupied similar modern facilities in the city. Signs of modernization seemed to emerge throughout the capital. Benz buses now linked urban districts, and Mack trucks and American automobiles rumbled through its streets, forcing the municipality to institute traffic controls and parking regulations. The Empresas Eléctricas Associadas' customer base grew from 15,000 in 1915 to 24,000 in 1924.

While American corporations reshaped Lima's physical features, the Young Men's Christian Association attempted to reshape the values of its

54 *West Coast Leader*, October 15, 1922; James Roth to secretary of state, Lima, October 6, 1920, 823.502, rl. 14, M-746, RG 59, USNA.

citizens. As in the United States, the YMCA targeted young middle-class males for its messages of hard work, individual achievement, physical health and moral rectitude. The Y made a particular effort to assist middle-class migrants from the provinces in adapting to life in the capital. The Lima YMCA's 150-person membership consisted of 26 university students, 20 professionals and 104 white-collar employees. The Lima Y placed a special emphasis on athletics as a means of attaining its goals, often organizing family excursions in which young and old alike participated in sports activities.[55]

The youthful missionaries of the Y utilized sports as a means of spreading their message to the corporate work places of the capital. The Peruvian manager of the Victoria textile mill, who also served as the president of the Lima Y, built a combination volley and basketball court at the plant and brought in Y members as coaches and referees. He subsequently enthused about the growth of American corporate culture, noting, "All this has contributed greatly, if not entirely, towards completely changing the spirit of the factory workers. There is a cohesion among them and they have become much more interested in the factory and its progress."[56] The Peru and London Bank adopted a similar sports program. The Graces' Vitarte textile mill introduced the Y athletic program as well as musical and literary programs. One observer noted, "Nowhere do we find the Y.M.C.A. held more dear than here in Vitarte."[57] The Y missionaries carried their work beyond the capital to Mollendo and Arequipa in the south and to Huancayo in the central highlands. To the north in Piura the YMCA emissary Tommy Valdez was called a "revolutionist" because he had completely transformed community forms of recreation. Back in Lima, President Leguía personally presented trophies to Y athletes and praised "the institution which wins its triumphs in the Christian spirit."[58]

Other American cultural influences proved considerably more secular. Limeños could now choose from a host of American consumer products, from Chevrolet automobiles and Westinghouse fans to Vicks Vaporub and Palmolive soap. They sought diversion in the American films that now flooded local cinemas. Cecil B. De Mille films such as *Forbidden Fruit* and *Madame Satan* suggested that the material products of American corporations could soothe the personal anxieties and crises generated in a modern society. Peruvian moviegoers could not help but be impressed by the ability of American industry to create a seemingly endless supply of material goods of apparently unlimited variety. American films reinforced those perceptions of material well-being and added to them images of a society that emphasized individual achievement and seemingly placed few re-

55 *West Coast Leader,* October 26, 1928; *El Comercio* (Lima), January 17, 1928.
56 *West Coast Leader,* October 26, 1928.
57 Ibid.
58 Ibid.

strictions on economic and social advancement. An RCA ad suggested the ultimate wish fulfillment in such a society, assuring readers that with one of its radios or record players "You can own the world!" Those images and impressions, much like the transformation of Lima, sometimes contained more illusion than reality.[59]

Public parks and Parisian-like avenues could create the physical illusion of general prosperity and social equality, but they could not obscure the harsh realities behind the oncenio. Urban renewal sent real estate prices in the capital soaring by 400 percent in the first half of the decade, creating inviting investment opportunities. The well-to-do, who sought profit and palatial homes in the southern suburbs, had segregated themselves from the city's northern districts of Rimac and Victoria, where a mushrooming population struggled for subsistence in crowded, unsanitary living conditions. That disparity symbolized the sharply increased inequalities that developed during the 1920s. As much as Lima's white-collar employees saw themselves as a class apart, with inherently greater material needs than workers, they also had come to realize that greater militancy rather than greater deference would be required to gain concessions from their employers. Lima's petite bourgeoisie and middle class represented a seemingly privileged group during the oncenio. Expanding public sector employment was concentrated in the Lima–Callao area, and the growth of the international economy offered new job opportunities in commercial enterprises. Yet even while employment opportunities grew, real incomes failed to achieve prewar levels. For most of the middle class, the array of new consumer products in Lima's shops lay beyond their reach. The capital's modernization could provide only a physical facade for mounting class antagonisms.[60]

In 1928 a young Peruvian from the provinces wrote to the leaders of the YMCA humbly thanking them for helping him to adapt to life in Lima and gain admission to the University of San Marcos. But far more middle-class migrants were like another student at San Marcos, Raul Haya de la Torre, who brought with him a strong sense of resentment over the displacement of the petite bourgeoisie resulting from the transformation of such sectors as sugar and mining. The middle class also found that the promise of opportunity contained in Leguía's assurances about educational reform remained unfulfilled. And those like Haya de la Torre who protested publicly faced arrest or exile. As elements of the petite bour-

59 *West Coast Leader,* 1919–30; Lary May, *Screening Out the Past: The Birth of Mass Culture and the Motion Picture Industry* (New York: Oxford University Press, 1980), pp. 201–36; *El Comercio,* July 4–12, 1925, November 15, 1931.

60 Thorp and Bertram, *Peru, 1890–1977,* p. 118; David S. Parker, "White-Collar Lima, 1910–1929: Commercial Employees and the Rise of the Peruvian Middle Class," *HAHR* 72 (February 1992), pp. 69–70. Increases in public sector salaries left the real incomes of government employees below levels achieved before World War I; see Thorp and Bertram, *Peru, 1890–1977,* p. 116.

geoisie turned toward leftist movements such as APRA and the Socialist party, junior army officers also became alienated from the regime.

Military officers shared with other elements of the middle and working classes a strong nationalist resentment over the predominant influence which American interests had come to play in Peruvian society. The discontent among army officers also stemmed from professional concerns. Leguía's promotion of a second security force, the Guardia Civil, and the funds which he lavished on it, posed a direct challenge to the interests of the Peruvian army.[61] When the Great Depression undermined the economic base of Leguiismo, military and civilian interests would join in a series of challenges to the alliance with American business forged during the oncenio.

The Great Depression struck at the economic foundations of the oncenio. Prices for Peruvian exports plummeted, and credit from American banks evaporated. Given the narrow social base on which Leguía stood, his regime collapsed like a house of cards when Major Luis Sánchez Cerro launched his coup d'etat. Over the next four years, local groups drawn from the petite bourgeoisie, the middle class, workers and peasants would attempt to redirect the course of Peruvian history. Each of these groups had distinct experiences and concerns with American corporate culture. U.S. companies had originally expanded the market base for small business people, only to subsequently threaten to overwhelm them in corporate efforts at vertical integration. For the middle class, American companies meant more jobs, but they found themselves ill treated by managers who viewed them as inherently inferior, and discovered that the new consumer paradise had serious limitations. Workers received higher wages but faced far more rigorous work disciplines, and experienced the same bias that white-collar employees endured. Despite these distinct experiences, these Peruvians identified American companies as the common source of their problems and would soon seek to rectify what they viewed as unjust treatment at the hands of U.S.-owned enterprises. Direct confrontations between such groups and American corporations would open and close that era and define much of its significance.

---

61 Víctor Villanueva, *Ejercito peruano del caudillismo anárquico al reformismo militar* (Lima: Editorial Juan Mejía Baca, 1973), pp. 202–3.

6

Resistance communities

. . . it is time to lift our heads, take arms, and under the red flag exercise our rights . . . We are able to govern ourselves! (Mateo Cueva, Peruvian miner)

The masses have not the proper respect for law and order and it will take fear alone to inspire this. It is further generally believed that . . . the result cannot be obtained by a few shots . . . but only by a cold blooded slaughter with machine-guns. (Julian D. Smith, U.S. assistant commercial attaché)

The collapse of the Leguía regime in August 1930 unleashed a series of challenges to the modernization of Peruvian society. Although an alliance of American corporations and the Peruvian elite had directed that transformation, U.S. companies became the focal point of protest. Peasants, workers and small business people benefited from the economic growth brought by American enterprise, but these companies also accelerated economic differentiation and social dislocation, and became identified with the repressive Leguía regime. Given their diverse roles in the national economic and social systems, these Peruvian groups expressed their community of interests through the concept of nationalism. The elite's narrow version of nationalism gave way to a popular nationalism which served as a mechanism for community solidarity and social protest.

Four years of popular protest and rebellion followed the authoritarian stability of the oncenio. The Cerro de Pasco workers, the community of interests in the Chicama Valley, the IPC oil workers, urban employees of Grace and ITT and finally the port community at Callao rallied in defense of their own interests and in opposition to the transformational process under way in Peruvian society. While impressive, this list of centers of opposition also suggests some of the limits of the protest movement. Language and other cultural differences still isolated much of Peru's rural Indian population from the westernized residents of the cities and mining centers, making it difficult to communicate the idea of a shared national community. Furthermore, as in Central America, resistance communities emerged in areas where American corporate culture had its most direct impact. Most of Peru's largely rural population did not feel the direct effects of that culture. As a result, for this group social stresses did not develop along lines dividing Peruvians from foreigners. For much of the Peruvian populace the nationalist symbols of the resistance communities did not convey the same appeal or significance. Despite these limitations, the popular unrest of the early 1930s threatened for a time to sweep away the alliance for modernization which had for so long guided national policy in Peru. Nowhere was that threat more evident than in the events which unfolded in the central highlands.

Conditions in the Cerro de Pasco mining camps became increasingly grim during 1929. Faced with burdensome debt payments for its development projects during the previous decade, the company began cutting production and laying off workers. Many of the miners who were still employed found themselves shunted into lower-paying positions, while contractors increased their demands on the miners. Workers who contemplated overt resistance to these conditions knew that they faced certain opposition from Leguía's local officials. Despite these formidable obstacles, organizational activity accelerated throughout 1929 in the company's Morococha camp.[1]

At the beginning of the year, Adrián Sovero, who had worked as a timekeeper for the company, formed the Sociedad Pro-Cultura Popular (Society in Favor of Popular Culture) in Morococha. Sovero worked in conjunction with the noted radical José Carlos Mariátegui in Lima. Mariátegui's group had begun creating a network of contacts in the region after the mining disaster at Morococha in 1928. However, it was Sovero and other local activists who led the labor protest that erupted at Morococha in October 1929. In response to the firing of fifty miners, Sovero organized a committee that staged a strike by *obreros* and empleados on October 10. Cognizant of Leguía's continuing protection of the company, Sovero addressed a letter to Dr. Augusto de Romaña, the prefect of the department of Junín. While notifying Romaña of the strike, Sovero also conveyed the strikers' congratulations to Augusto Leguía on the beginning of his third consecutive presidential term. Sovero's tactical maneuver apparently persuaded Romaña to refrain from outright suppression of the strike. The response from the company, however, proved less satisfactory.[2]

The strike committee presented a list of demands which included pay increases, an end to the contract system and the rehiring of the fired workers. Harold Kingsmill, the general manager of Cerro de Pasco in Peru, rejected most of these demands except for the reinstitution of the dismissed workers. Beyond a few such limited concessions, the strike achieved mixed results. Under Kingsmill's direct orders, mine supervisors adopted a more benevolent attitude toward workers, which allowed Sovero and his compa-

1 Martínez de la Torre, *Interpretación marxista,* 1, p. 9; "Labor Conditions," 323.114 Cerro de Pasco Corp./30, RG 59, USNA.
2 Martínez de la Torre, *Interpretación marxista,* 1, pp. 6–7.

triots to accelerate their organizational activities. However, contractors continued their excessive labor exactions and warned the miners that organizational efforts would achieve little as long as the contratistas controlled the work process. And in response to Augusto de Romaña's policy of benign neglect, Kingsmill requested the prefect's removal.[3]

In July 1930 Jorge del Prado, a member of the Mariátegui group, joined Sovero and assisted him in organizing smelter workers in Oroya. But the Lima radicals were highly critical of the skilled workers at Oroya, for whom employment at the smelter had become a long-term source of income. These workers rejected Prado's initial call for a strike, citing warnings from the prefect and other local officials that a strike would accomplish nothing. Even more ominously, the smelter workers selected Lucio Tolomeo Castro Suárez as secretary general of the union. Castro Suárez, who held a law degree and had worked in the timekeeper's office, was hardly Prado's version of an ideal proletarian leader. The proletarian credentials of the other Oroya workers were equally suspect, since they owned small shops in the town or were members of the Oroya comunidad.[4] Conditions in Oroya reflected a community of interests and ideas which the Lima radicals viewed as a major impediment to their dreams of proletarian revolution.

For Jorge del Prado the mine workers of the central highlands had an aggravating tendency to view their exploitation by the Cerro de Pasco Corporation as a problem of nationality rather than class. They had a disconcerting tendency to believe that reformist legislation would resolve their problems. Del Prado attributed this tendency to propaganda by Apristas and other nationalist radicals which the local petite bourgeoisie used to mislead the workers.[5] Eventually his suspicions came to focus on his compatriot Adrián Sovero. Before that happened, fresh evidence of an alliance between workers and the middle class based on a nationalist ideology would appear in the protests that swirled through Cerro de Pasco's labor camps.

Augusto Leguía's resignation on August 25 triggered a wave of euphoria in the central highlands. The collapse of the regime's repressive political apparatus, the end of press censorship and a widespread belief that the new government would back local demands against the Cerro de Pasco company spawned a wave of organizational activity in the mining camps. On August 29, the day of Sánchez Cerro's triumphal entry into Lima, the workers at the Goyllarisquisga coal mine staged a massive celebration, crying "Viva Sánchez Cerro" and "Death to the gringo." Leading the demonstration were Antonio Mateo Cueva and Julián Florez, employees of a local mercantile house. Cueva drew up a list of worker demands and

3 Ibid., pp. 9–25.
4 Ibid., pp. 32–34; "Labor Conditions," 323.114 Cerro de Pasco Corp./30, RG 59, USNA.
5 Martínez de la Torre, *Interpretación marxista*, 1, p. 28.

threatened the company with a strike. A detachment of the Guardia Civil arrived at the mine and carted Cueva off to Cerro de Pasco. On August 31, Julián Florez led a protest against Cueva's arrest which ended in an attack on the company's property.

In Cerro de Pasco, Cueva had to confront the new prefect of the department of Junín, Colonel Jerónimo Santiváñez. Santiváñez, a classmate of Sánchez Cerro's at the military academy, was one of a series of local officials installed by the new Peruvian leader. After a brief admonishment, the prefect sent Cueva back to Goyllarisquisga. Cueva and Florez now requisitioned several company buildings and took over the local school, social club and mutual aid society. On September 7 they formed a union and called for a strike. Santiváñez quickly arrested both men and sent them off to Lima. In response, the miners' wives, who had been among the early promoters of the union movement, initiated a two-day strike by the workers. By then Santiváñez was coping with yet another protest, this time at his headquarters in Cerro de Pasco.[6]

On September 5 R. C. Philpott, the superintendent at Cerro de Pasco, invited the workers to submit a series of requests and met with a delegation of miners the following day. After making some minor concessions, Philpott advised the delegates that issues such as wage increases and the seven-hour day would have to be resolved by Kingsmill. Philpott had acted quickly to deal with the miners' immediate demands, but he had done nothing about the subsidence problem in the town. Dr. Madrid, the newly appointed mayor of Cerro de Pasco, was a vociferous critic of the company. He had previously served as mayor, only to be dismissed by Leguía because of his insistence that the company pay for subsidence damage. Santiváñez, who enjoyed a close relationship with Madrid, now called for a new meeting between the miners and Philpott. After the meeting ended on September 7, over a thousand workers remained in the streets of the town. Urged on by town officials, they attacked the company's offices and residences. Santiváñez called in troops from Oroya, but by the time they arrived the next day the town fathers had delivered their message, and calm had been restored. The Cerro de Pasco Corporation now tried to take a broader approach to the unrest sweeping through its camps.[7]

In Lima, Harold Kingsmill recognized that the corporation faced a broad-based attack on its interests. Workers were striking throughout its facilities, backed by the Lima radicals, elements of the region's small business interests and the company's empleados. Company officials were also wary of newly appointed local authorities drawn from the middle class, such as the mayor of Cerro de Pasco and Prefect Jerónimo Santiváñez.

6 "Labor Conditions," 323.114 Cerro de Pasco Corp./30; "Report Presented by the Prefect of the Department of Junín, Mayor [sic] J. Santiváñez, to the Minister of the Interior Regarding the Miners' Congress at Oroya" (hereafter cited as "Report, Santiváñez"), n.p., n.d., 323.114 Cerro de Pasco Corp./88, RG 59, USNA.
7 "Labor Conditions," 323.114 Cerro de Pasco Corp./30, RG 59, USNA.

From the company's perspective, Santiváñez had done little to stem the uprisings at Goyllarisquisga and Cerro de Pasco. He had quickly released Mateo Cueva after his first arrest. After sending Cueva and Florez to Lima, he had conveniently failed to file charges against them, and the two were released. Kingsmill attacked these mounting problems head on, inviting workers' delegations from all of the camps to negotiating sessions in Lima. He would soon discover that his problems ranged beyond the local level to the highest reaches of the national government.[8]

After toppling Augusto Leguía, Luis Sánchez Cerro ruled Peru for six months through a military junta. A key figure in that regime, Colonel Gustavo Jiménez, was, like many of the younger military officers, from humble social origins. His frequent conspiracies against Leguía had led to his arrest and finally his expulsion from the armed forces. Stripped of his military rank, Jiménez worked for a time as a truck driver. Jiménez had played a pivotal role in the coup which brought Sánchez Cerro to power, and now served as minister of government in the junta. Despite Jiménez's initial backing of Sánchez Cerro, political ambitions and important policy differences separated the two men. Although Sánchez Cerro sought to place himself at the forefront of the popular nationalist movement, he had once referred to the Peruvian masses as "indolent and lazy rabble," and in one of his first communiqués after the coup he promised to repress "Communist excesses." In contrast, Jiménez would eventually align himself with the Apristas, and he apparently already shared their views on the labor question. He would demonstrate considerable sympathy for the working class in the challenges it now made to the Cerro de Pasco Corporation.[9]

During the month of September, delegations from the mining camps arrived in Lima to negotiate with the Cerro de Pasco company. Their leaders included Adrián Sovero from Morococha and Lucio Tolomeo Castro y Suárez from Oroya. The company refused to deal with Mateo Cueva and Julián Florez, but at Gustavo Jiménez's insistence the two were allowed to sit in on the negotiations with the Goyllarisquisga delegation. Indeed, Jiménez himself participated directly in the discussions with the various worker committees and strongly backed their demands.[10]

Despite a number of common complaints against the company, significant differences also separated the delegations. Their constituencies ranged from skilled long-term workers and empleados from the Mantaro Valley, Oroya and Cerro de Pasco to *enganchedados* and contract workers from the impoverished puna who labored in the mines and construction camps of Morococha, Goyllarisquisga, Casapalca and Malpaso. The smelter workers of Oroya demanded improvements and expansion of existing housing, a school for workers and the expulsion of workers who failed to

---

8 Ibid.
9 Luis Valcarcel, *Memorias* (Lima: Instituto de Estudios Peruanos, 1981), p. 227; Stein, *Populism in Peru*, pp. 86, 92, 190–91; Klarén, *Modernization, Dislocation,* pp. 139–40.
10 "Labor Conditions," 323.114 Cerro de Pasco Corp./30, RG 59, USNA.

cooperate with the labor movement. They also addressed regional and national concerns, demanding elimination of the smelter's toxic smoke and insisting that the work be carried out by Peruvian engineers. The Morococha miners demonstrated their continuing links to the countryside by demanding the right to licenses which would allow them to remain absent from the mines for up to eight days at a time. The demands of the Malpaso workers reflected the more primitive conditions under which they labored. They insisted on a school for their children, a bakery and butcher shops, and free access to the camp for local peddlers. Empleados sought assurances on hours of work, promotions and insurance. The corporation conceded many of these demands in the agreements with the workers and empleados. However, issues critical to the interests of miners, such as the use of contractors, remained unresolved. Furthermore, the company's concession of wage increases on a sliding scale based on the price of copper was meaningless in the face of a collapsing world market. As a result, a split quickly developed in the delegations, with some members of the Morococha, Malpaso, Goyllarisquisga and Casapalca delegations denouncing the agreements and the work of the Oroya and Cerro de Pasco representatives. The denunciation in part represented real differences between the interests of the more stable labor forces in Oroya and Cerro de Pasco and the transient workers in the other camps. But it also reflected the Lima radicals' continuing concern over petit bourgeois influence in the movement. The focus of that conflict now shifted back to the central highlands.[11]

In Morococha, Jorge del Prado had nothing but contempt for the new agreement and the man who had signed it, Adrián Sovero. Sovero wrote to his colleagues and advised against another strike. Del Prado in turn denounced Sovero to his Lima colleagues as a bourgeois opportunist. Initially the workers and empleados at Morococha backed Sovero and voted against another strike. Both Sovero's attitude and that of the workers quickly changed when the company failed to abide by the agreement. On October 10, the Morococha workers celebrated the anniversary of the 1929 strike. The work stoppage became a protest against the company's policies, and the miners demanded that the sergeant of the local Guardia Civil detachment arrest the company's superintendent and his assistant. Bowing to the demands of the workers, the sergeant arrested both men. As they were marched off to jail, a procession of miners, shopkeepers and merchants followed close behind, carrying a triumphant Adrián Sovero on their shoulders. Prefect Jerónimo Santiváñez now arrived on the scene and insisted that company officials abide by the agreement reached in Lima and specifically warned them against firing workers, only to rehire them at lower wages. As for Sovero, he suggested the company find a job for

---

11 Martínez de la Torre, *Interpretación marxista,* 1, pp. 39–40, 50–52, 55–60; Fred Morris Dearing to secretary of state, Lima, October 13, 1930, 323.114 Cerro de Pasco Corp./15; "Labor Conditions," 323.114 Cerro de Pasco Corp./30, RG 59, USNA.

him at one of its other camps. A few days later Santiváñez carried out a similar intervention at Malpaso. As he later explained, he had stepped in "because I perceived that our humble workers had been exploited for years without a single voice being raised to aid them . . ."[12]

For Jorge del Prado, these events only confirmed his opinion of Sovero. After Santiváñez's intervention, Sovero had joined with the prefect in urging the miners to return to work. Clearly Sovero represented the type of petit bourgeois element that had to be purged from the movement. By this time the Lima radicals, recently reconstituted as the Peruvian Communist Party, had decided to hold a miners' congress in Oroya in early November. The congress would provide a means for consolidating the region's various workers' groups into a single federation which would affiliate itself with the Communist Confederación General de Trabajadores del Perú (CGTP). Beyond that basic organizational goal, the congress would provide the means for purging petit bourgeois elements from the ranks of the local movement and preparing the workers for their role as the vanguard in a proletarian revolution. Meanwhile, labor militancy continued to intensify in the mines.[13]

Miners adopted a new more militant stance on the job. They engaged in work slowdowns and devoted much of the workday to discussions of the political situation. Shift foremen failed in their effort to enforce the usual work discipline in the face of a workforce that was now "disobedient, insolent and defiant." Workers bombarded managers with new demands that included equal pay with foreigners, a requirement that all shift bosses be Peruvians and time and a half for Sunday. For the corporation's management, many of these demands reflected the continuing nationalist theme which ran through the protests. Reporting on the events at Morococha on October 10, an American commercial attaché concluded, "The whole episode at Morococha was not so much a strike as a demonstration against the Company and against Americans." It is hardly surprising that workers would view the struggle as one which pitted Peruvians against gringos, given the contempt in which their U.S. employers held them. As one American concluded, "The laborers are Andean Cholos, one of the most backward races. The company has on occasion experienced labor difficulties and the workmen have, when aroused, proved bloodthirsty and dangerous." When they were not aroused, their supervisors described them as being "like cattle" or "sheeplike." The company considered its workers insufficiently civilized to appreciate or make use of the housing and sanitary facilities which it provided. Those views also extended to other elements of the community.[14]

12 "Labor Conditions," 323.114 Cerro de Pasco Corp./30; "Report, Santiváñez," 323.114 Cerro de Pasco Corp./88, RG 59, USNA; Martínez de la Torre, *Interpretación marxista,* 1, pp. 72–73.

13 Martínez de la Torre, *Interpretación marxista,* 1, pp. 67–68; Flores Galindo, *Los mineros de la Cerro de Pasco,* pp. 101–3.

14 "Labor Conditions," 323.114 Cerro de Pasco Corp./30; Dearing to secretary of state, Lima, March 19, 1931, 323.114 Cerro de Pasco Corp./113, RG 59, USNA.

The local officials who took power in the central highlands after the Sánchez Cerro coup threw their support to the workers' movement. The sub-prefect and municipal authorities at Oroya, for example, were reported to be "pouring fuel on the flames." Americans described these officials as "uninspiring in their make-up, inexperienced and for the most part . . . Indians of the 'cholo' class." Jerónimo Santiváñez was singled out as the most notorious of these "cholo" officials.[15] Santiváñez had intervened on behalf of the workers at Cerro de Pasco, Casapalca, Morococha and Malpaso. He permitted meetings and demonstrations while limiting his admonitions to calls for non-violence. He had also repeatedly stepped in to prevent the firing of workers. The Americans concluded that "he would apparently like to see them [the workers] get all they can in this struggle between his countrymen and foreigners . . ."[16] Nor were the company's problems with officials confined to the regional level.

From the company's perspective, the workers were seeking to exploit the "reformist and socialistic objectives" of "a government recruited from the middle class . . ." Sánchez Cerro and the officers who surrounded him were middle class in origin and espoused a version of populist nationalism, although "socialistic" hardly described his own attitude toward the working class. Gustavo Jiménez, on the other hand, demonstrated considerable empathy with the workers. When violence erupted at Cerro de Pasco in September, Jiménez had expressed sympathy for the workers, and he had given them strong backing in their negotiations with the company in Lima. When those meetings ended, he issued safe conducts for Antonio Cueva and Julián Florez to return to Goyllarisquisga. He also issued a safe conduct to Carlos Loayza, a school teacher who had been the principal organizer of the labor movement in Casapalca. In Loayza's case, Jiménez went even further and appointed him chief of police for the area. In the face of such actions, company officials and U.S. diplomats found the government's response to their demands for protection to be entirely inadequate.[17]

After the outbreak at Cerro de Pasco, the Sánchez Cerro government sent 350 troops to the area. These regular army forces consisted largely of conscripts from the central highlands. When they arrived in Oroya, many of them were greeted by friends and relatives. American observers expressed serious doubts whether these "cholo" soldiers would open fire on their own people. In light of what the company viewed as no more than a gesture of support, Harold Kingsmill requested the removal of Jerónimo Santiváñez. Sánchez Cerro rebuffed the request to dismiss his old classmate. The Americans also considered trying for the removal of Gustavo Jiménez, but concluded that his departure might destabilize the regime. Instead they pressed for the dispatch of more soldiers, preferably from the

15 "Labor Conditions," 323.114 Cerro de Pasco Corp./30, RG 59, USNA.
16 Ibid.
17 Dearing to secretary of state, Lima, October 22, 1930, 323.114 Cerro de Pasco Corporation/26;
     "Labor Conditions," 323.114 Cerro de Pasco Corp./30, RG 59, USNA.

Civil Guard, and a declaration of martial law, which would take effective control of the situation out of the hands of local officials.[18]

Company managers and U.S. diplomats pursued a two-pronged strategy in their efforts to push the regime toward suppression of the labor movement. Harold Kingsmill repeatedly threatened Sánchez Cerro with a shutdown of company operations, with dire consequences for the hard-pressed national economy. At the same time U.S. diplomats made it clear to the government that a direct link existed between its policy toward the company and its efforts to solve its international debt problems. Unable to meet its debt payments to J. W. Seligman and Company, the Sánchez Cerro regime had requested that the State Department intervene on its behalf. On October 21 U.S. ambassador Fred Morris Dearing informed the Peruvian foreign minister that the regime could not expect any help while the Cerro de Pasco situation remained an "open sore." Two days later, while Dearing was conveying that same message directly to Sánchez Cerro, the Peruvian ambassador met in Washington with Secretary of State Henry L. Stimson. Stimson also linked the Cerro de Pasco and debt questions, telling the ambassador that "he thought the whole army, if necessary, should be sent to quiet conditions and make it possible for legitimate business to carry on their lawful enterprises" and that "there would also be an effect on Peru's credit abroad . . ."[19] But efforts to pressure the regime into repressing the labor movement failed to prompt the desired response. On October 29 Dearing reported that "we are practically just where we were several weeks ago . . ."[20]

Sánchez Cerro's hesitancy in complying with American demands stemmed from a number of factors. Popular support for Sánchez Cerro was largely based on his reputation as an ardent foe of Leguiismo and his espousal of popular nationalism. Acting in close cooperation with an American corporation to suppress Peruvian workers would tarnish that image and his hopes of being elected president. Sánchez Cerro also personally resented the attempt of the corporation to tell him how to run the country. Furthermore, Gustavo Jiménez, the pivotal figure in restraining government action against the miners, was the most powerful individual in the junta. Overriding his policies or removing him from power also carried significant political risks for Sánchez Cerro. It was the miners' congress in Oroya which finally undermined Jiménez's position and allowed Sánchez Cerro to act.[21]

18 "Labor Conditions," 323.114 Cerro de Pasco Corp./30, RG 59, USNA.

19 Memorandum of conversation between Manuel de Freyre y Santander, Peruvian ambassador, and secretary of state, Washington, October 23, 1930; Dearing to secretary of state, Lima, October 23, 1930, 823.51/519, 524, RG 59, USNA.

20 Memorandum, "Communist Riots in the Mines of the Cerro de Pasco Copper Corporation in Peru," Washington, January 13, 1931, 323.114 Cerro de Pasco Corp./106, RG 59, USNA.

21 William C. Burdett to secretary of state, Callao/Lima, December 9, 1930, 323.114 Cerro de Pasco Corp./90, RG 59, USNA.

In the days immediately preceding the congress, workers from the various syndicates met in Oroya in an effort to hammer out a common program for the new labor federation. That effort represented a logical attempt to form a united front among the various camps, which included both permanent workers and those who still gained much of their livelihood as peasants. But those delegates themselves now became a central issue in the meetings. The syndicate representatives in Oroya rejected out of hand a list of demands formulated by Castro Suárez and submitted motions to expel all those who had negotiated with the company in Lima. The process of purging the movement of its petit bourgeois elements accelerated once the Communist delegates from Lima arrived and the congress opened on November 8.[22]

The miners' congress, while recognizing the role of empleados in the new union, specifically excluded lawyers, students and anyone who was not part of the proletarian class. The measure represented the Communists' effort to eliminate petit bourgeois elements such as the Oroya shopkeepers and the comunidad members from the labor movement. Eudocio Ravines, a representative of the Communist party in Lima, reinforced this measure by threatening to assassinate Castro Suárez and anyone else who betrayed the "sacred cause of the workers."[23] In the congress' opening session, Ravines had also declared, "To destroy Capital is to solve our problems! The authorities are the allies of Capital, and for that reason, we must destroy the authorities also." On the 10th, speakers grouped Sánchez Cerro with Leguía and earlier Peruvian presidents as "deceivers and exploiters" and called on workers to "make war without quarter on the authorities and the uniformed bourgeoisie . . ."[24] For Jerónimo Santiváñez, whose spies had monitored events at the congress, the Communist oratory offered sufficient justification to arrest the convention's leaders. In the early-morning hours of November 11, Santiváñez rounded up the convention delegates and sent them to Lima. In response, thousands of workers poured into the streets of Oroya demanding the release of the delegates. The crowd took two managers of the Cerro de Pasco Corporation hostage in an effort to enforce their demands. In addition, the railway workers went on strike, and the CGTP declared a general strike. The government released the delegates, and in turn the workers freed the Cerro de Pasco employees. The government then issued decrees proclaiming martial law in the departments of Junín and Lima and ordering the abolition of the CGTP. On November 12 some eight hundred miners attempted to march from Malpaso into Oroya in support of the labor movement. At a bridge leading out of Malpaso, a detachment of troops blocked their way and

22 Dearing to secretary of state, Lima, November 8, 1930, 323.114 Cerro de Pasco Corp./45, RG 59, USNA.

23 Martínez de la Torre, *Interpretación marxista,* I, p. 91; "Report, Santiváñez," 323.114 Cerro de Pasco Corp./88, RG 59, USNA.

24 "Report, Santiváñez," 323.114 Cerro de Pasco Corp./88, RG 59, USNA.

opened fire on the workers, killing fourteen of them. The crowd fled back to the camp. Subsequent clashes left nine more workers and two Americans dead. By the time of the massacre at Malpaso, the events in Oroya had effectively undermined the position of Gustavo Jiménez in Lima.[25]

When Jiménez met with Harold Kingsmill and Fred Dearing on the evening of November 12, he remained in a defiant mood. He pointed to the corporation's failure to fulfill its promises to the workers as the principal cause of the unrest in the mining camps. But twenty-four hours earlier the junta had met in an acrimonious session and agreed to take harsher measures in Oroya, undermining Jiménez's policy of supporting the workers' movement. Sensing the shift in the political climate, Dearing berated Jiménez, attributing the entire problem to the minister's failure to suppress the labor movement in its early stages. In response, Jiménez expressed regret over the incident at Malpaso and promised full compliance with the company's demands for additional troops and complete suppression of the labor movement. In a follow-up meeting the next day, Jiménez could only plead for a reopening of the mines for the sake of the workers. Dearing concluded that "Jiménez was most conciliatory and completely beaten."[26]

Within a few days of those conversations, Sánchez Cerro removed Jiménez from office, sent additional troops to the mining camps, imposed press censorship and initiated a wholesale roundup of labor organizers. Jerónimo Santiváñez proved to be the one obstacle in this process. He publicly advertised plans for the arrest of labor organizers, giving them ample time to go into hiding. The prefect also proved less than diligent in rounding up the labor leaders. His conduct prompted another unsuccessful demand by Kingsmill that the prefect be removed. Santiváñez's actions, however, provided only a short-term delay in the suppression of the workers' movement. Furthermore, the company had effective tools of its own to accomplish that same task.[27] The month-long shutdown of the mines proved the company's most effective weapon for disciplining the workers. As an American official noted at the beginning of the lockout, "A month shutdown of the mines would bring practically 50,000 persons to the verge of famine and would give them proper appreciation of what an actual job means in comparison to the promises of communist orators." He concluded that the shutdown provided "an example their mentality can grasp."[28] The corporation also instituted a system of blacklists

25 Dearing to secretary of state, telegram, Lima, November 12, 1930; same to same, Lima, November 13, 1930; "Report, Santiváñez," 323.114 Cerro de Pasco Corp./39, 57, 88, RG 59, USNA.
26 Dearing to secretary of state, telegram, Lima, November 14, 1930; same to same, Lima, November 13, 1930, 323.114 Cerro de Pasco Corp./42, 57, RG 59, USNA.
27 Dearing to secretary of state, Lima, December 14, 1930, 323.114 Cerro de Pasco Corp./91, RG 59, USNA.
28 William C. Burdett to secretary of state, Callao/Lima, December 9, 1930, 323.114 Cerro de Pasco Corp./90, RG 59, USNA.

throughout its camps. The lists, combined with continued force reductions over the next several years, allowed the company to effectively purge its ranks of militant workers.

The Communists' defeat at Oroya resulted in large measure from their failure to comprehend that long-term market forces operating in the region, accelerated by the arrival of the North American corporation, had created a complex social community in the central Andes. Beyond their work in the mines, Cerro de Pasco workers fulfilled a diverse range of roles, as peasants, shopkeepers, itinerant peddlers and students. In the camps themselves, workers ranged from the skilled stable communities of Oroya and Cerro de Pasco to the unskilled transient workers at Morococha and Malpaso. Given the diversity of their experiences and roles, the workers could readily identify with the demands of empleados for better working conditions, peasant complaints against smoke damage and the subsidence problems of Cerro de Pasco's residents. The sense of identity shared by workers and merchants at camps such as Morococha might be stronger than linkages between the unskilled workers of Morococha and the skilled labor force at Oroya. That identification enabled the workers to forge an alliance with petit bourgeois and middle-class elements including itinerant peddlers, shopkeepers, merchants, empleados, lawyers and teachers. Those alliances reflected the emergence of a community that defined itself in terms of its opposition to a foreign corporation that dominated and frequently disrupted the lives of local citizens. Corporate policies served to reinforce that sense of identity.

Despite growing unrest in its mines by the end of World War I, the Cerro de Pasco Corporation made only limited efforts to exercise control through policies of social welfare. Even in Oroya, where the labor requirements of the new smelter demanded a skilled and stable workforce, the corporation provided only rudimentary and overcrowded housing. The company's welfare efforts for their large unskilled and transient workforce in mining and construction camps proved virtually nonexistent. These policies reflected in part the company's continued reliance on enganche and contratista systems to secure an unskilled and temporary workforce. Creation of company stores that excluded local mercantile activity served to spread the sense of exploitation to the region's retail merchants. Corporate policy also reflected the views of company managers that even their minimalist social welfare policies were wasted on what they viewed as an uncivilized workforce. That same attitude extended to the region's petite bourgeoisie and to the local officials appointed by Sánchez Cerro. Company officials viewed all of these groups as part of the same inferior cholo race.

Given the enormous impact of a foreign corporation upon their lives, the residents of the Cerro de Pasco mining region defined their struggle in terms of Peruvians versus gringos. That definition gave their efforts a legitimizing nationalist theme within Peru's dominant culture. As a result, the Cerro de Pasco community found allies within the Sánchez Cerro regime such as Jerónimo Santiváñez and Gustavo Jiménez. The paternalism of Santiváñez and the populist political ambitions of Jiménez limited the scope of that alliance to the exploitative acts of a foreign corporation. Communist calls for internationalism and direct assaults on national political authorities pushed Santiváñez to repress the labor movement and undermined Jiménez's position within the governing junta.

The significance of the conflict in the central highlands extended beyond the crushing defeat of the labor movement and its Communist allies. Those events demonstrated the potential of emerging resistance communities which opposed the dislocative effects of Peru's modernization. Rather than precluding further resistance, the Cerro de Pasco conflict prefigured the formation of a series of resistance communities which militantly challenged Peru's alliance for modernization. Since these groups defined themselves in terms of their opposition to foreign capital, they eventually created opportunities for alliances at the national political level. Changes in the national political picture set the stage for the emergence of several such communities.

Luis Sánchez Cerro's attempt to call a snap presidential election early in 1931 triggered a series of challenges to his position from both civilian and military elements. Gustavo Jiménez, now commander of the Lima military garrison, played a central role in forcing Sánchez Cerro into exile and installing a new government junta in March. The junta's members, drawn primarily from Arequipa in southern Peru, suppressed a strike against a Peruvian sugar producer on the north coast. Their attitude toward popular protests in their own region against American corporations proved quite different.[29]

Popular resentment against Augusto Leguía's policies of repression and modernization and the economic crisis which they helped create continued to smolder long after the dictator's departure. In Arequipa those resentments erupted into a massive demonstration. In May 1931 several thousand students, workers and white-collar employees marched in protest against the alleged arrest and beating of a worker by sub-prefect Abel Salazar, a holdover from the Leguía regime. After police fired on the crowd and killed two of the marchers, a general strike by workers and shopkeepers paralyzed the city. The much-reviled Salazar sought safety in the nearby port town of Mollendo. When local citizens discovered Salazar's hiding place in a downtown hotel, they dragged him from his room, beat him senseless, tied a metal rail to his feet and threw him into the harbor.[30] Nor did the protests in southern Peru stop with this incident.

When W. R. Grace announced a 10 percent salary cut for its Peruvian employees in mid October, Grace employees in Arequipa and Mollendo struck

29 Klarén, *Modernization, Dislocation,* pp. 121–24; Stein, *Populism in Peru,* p. 95.
30 Dearing to secretary of state, Lima, May 16, 19, 1931, RG 84, USNA.

in protest. The employees of Arequipa's commercial houses, with the support of the city council, formed the Employees' Syndicate of Southern Peru and called a general strike, which spread to Cuzco and Puno. Shopkeepers and other small business people, along with maritime and railway workers in the South, joined the walkout in sympathy with the empleados. Employee associations in other cities, including Lima and Trujillo, announced their support for the Grace workers. The Aprista newspaper *La Tribuna* denounced the Grace company as "an imperialist enterprise" and declared its employees victims of "the abuses of imperialism." The southern syndicate responded by promising to "maintain its attitude against imperialism."[31]

The surge of popular support for the empleados' strike in the junta members' home base and the ability of APRA to capture the powerful issue of anti-imperialism quickly persuaded the national government to order arbitration of the dispute. The arbitrators imposed measures that ameliorated the impact of the wage reduction, guaranteed the workers protection against reprisal and assured them of salary payments for the period of the strike. The government also guaranteed strike payments to the railway workers. When the arbitration process was completed, the prefect of Arequipa congratulated the strikers on the success of their movement.[32] Meanwhile the junta had been coping with yet another strike cast in anti-imperialist terms, at the other end of the country.

After the fall of Leguía in August 1930, IPC faced growing militancy among its six thousand oil field workers in the northern towns of Talara and Negritos. In mid May 1931 workers in Negritos seized the local police chief, who had arrested their leaders. The workers threatened the chief with the same fate as sub-prefect Salazar of Arequipa. Police attacked the workers' headquarters and freed the chief, leaving two workers dead. The violent protests which ensued left seven people dead and twenty-two wounded. The junta now dispatched 250 troops to the oil fields to suppress the labor action, and IPC shut down its operations.[33]

The encounter between the American corporate culture of IPC and the community interests of its Peruvian workers lay at the heart of the conflict. The workers wanted to define both drillers and those working in the chemical labs as employees to bring them under the protective umbrella of empleado legislation instituted by Leguía. The workers demanded permanent jobs in response to the frequent layoffs or firings resulting from the company's constant reorganization of its workforce to achieve the most efficient output. They also demanded an end to contract work, which imposed a task system of labor. Rejecting the company's control over their communities, they insisted that the fences around company camps be torn down and that camp managers stop interfering with the authority of local municipalities.

31 Dearing to secretary of state, Lima, November 1, 17, 21, 23, 28, 1931, RG 84, USNA.
32 *West Coast Leader* (Lima), November 24, December 1, 1931; Merwin L. Bohan, "Economic Section," Lima, November 26, 1931, RG 151, USNA.
33 Dearing to secretary of state, Lima, May 25, 27, 1931, RG 84, USNA.

Faced with the shutdown of the strategic oil industry, the junta, at the urging of Gustavo Jiménez, issued a decree which granted the workers' demands but still left the company in charge of the work place. The junta also announced plans to increase taxes on IPC. However, Jiménez, while backing these decrees, was also desperately seeking 3 million soles to pay government employees and to meet other pressing needs. He hoped to raise those funds by selling government vouchers to foreign companies, including IPC. The company indicated it would purchase vouchers, but only if the state solved the labor problems to the company's satisfaction. IPC kept its oil operations tightly shut, and within a few days the junta retreated. The government sent security forces into the oil fields, where they opened fire on the strikers and then proceeded to arrest labor organizers. IPC, with the labor decree set aside and its facilities under military guard, reopened its fields.[34] But the junta's labor problems were by no means over.

On August 26 sixty of ITT's female telephone operators in Lima went on strike. The women struck to protest the firing of eight of their number who were being displaced by the introduction of automatic exchanges. Beyond that immediate issue, the women demanded recognition of their union, the Sindicato de Empleados y Empleadas Telefonistas de Lima. They insisted that the Sindicato be given approval on hirings and that ITT change its policy of giving operators no salary during an initial six- to twelve-month trial period. The anti-American and feminist aspects of their actions won the operators support from the Lima elite's newspaper, *El Comercio,* and from Zalia Aurora Cáceres, Peru's leading spokesperson for women's rights. Widespread popular support for the women's cause prompted ITT to offer concessions on all issues except recognition of the union. When a government intervenor finally settled the strike in the first week of October, the women won shorter hours and higher wages but did not gain recognition of their union.[35]

Much like the 1919 protests in Lima, the militant popular resistance of 1931 convinced members of the modernization alliance that the populace must be terrorized back into submission. In June 1931 Julian D. Smith, the U.S. assistant commercial attaché in Lima, expressed their views when he noted that since Leguía's fall

the masses have not the proper respect for law and order and it will take fear alone to inspire this. It is further generally believed that the time is soon coming when such action will be necessary and that the result cannot be obtained by a few shots in the air followed by a few scattered casualties; but only by a cold blooded slaughter with machine-guns. This is a general belief among the better element of Peruvians and foreigners alike.[36]

Smith's prescription for social control proved prophetic.

34 Julian D. Smith, memorandum, Lima, June 3, 1931; Dearing to secretary of state, Lima, May 25, 27, June 3, 22, 1931, RG 84, USNA.
35 Dearing to secretary of state, Lima, September 4, 15, 27, October 4, 1931, RG 84 USNA.
36 Smith, memorandum, Lima, June 3, 1931, RG 84, USNA.

The Great Depression exacerbated the tensions that had been mounting in the sugar regions of Peru's northern coast. Record low sugar prices led to workforce and wage reductions and triggered the laborers' strike in May. The depression also worsened conditions for local merchants and small landowners, whose livelihoods had already been threatened by the expansion and rationalization of the plantations.[37] Although Haya de la Torre remained in exile, the lifting of press and political restrictions in preparation for an October presidential election enabled Aprista loyalists in the North to begin an energetic organizational campaign. In May they held a regional congress in Trujillo whose program clearly reflected the coalition of local forces on which the Apristas had built their movement. The congress called for the end to piece work and the enganche system and for a minimum wage for sugar workers. The delegates demanded the cancellation of the government concession for the port of Malabrigo, which local merchants viewed as the principal source of their own economic woes. Small landowners were promised reform of the local water distribution system, which the large plantations had used to throttle the operations of independent farmers. But the platform went beyond these issues to address national concerns involving the penetration of American corporate culture. It called for the nationalization of the large mines, an eight-hour day and equal wages for Peruvian and foreign employees. With Cerro de Pasco dominating Peruvian mining and the national economy, and with U.S. companies paying Peruvian engineers half what they paid American engineers, such proposals appealed to a broad national audience.[38]

Aprismo provided the political vehicle for nationalist protests by a regional community against the economic differentiation and social dislocations brought on by the modernization of the sugar industry. Peruvians in fact controlled the plantations outside the Chicama Valley, and the Gildemeisters could claim Peruvian status. But popular attacks on foreign corporations provided a legitimizing symbol for nationwide protests against the processes of rationalization and concentration in the Peruvian economy.

Upon his return to Peru in August, Haya de la Torre played on precisely this theme in his presidential contest with Luis Sánchez Cerro. When he first returned to Peruvian soil at the northern port of Talara, in the heart of the IPC-controlled oil region, he declared the area to be under the domination of Yankee imperialism. He subsequently denounced the disruptions and dislocations which foreign sugar companies had caused and talked of nationalizing foreign corporations. Haya's personal commitment to anti-imperialism is questionable. He had already met with Harold Kingsmill in London and promised to soften his attacks on American interests.[39] Yet

---

37 Gonzales, *Plantation Agriculture*, pp. 179–81.

38 Klarén, *Modernization, Dislocation*, pp. 124–25; Dearing to secretary of state, Lima, June 10, 1931, and enclosure: *La Tribuna* (Lima), RG 84, USNA.

39 Klarén, *Modernization, Dislocation*, p. 128; Thomas M. Davies, "The Indigenismo of the Peruvian Aprista Party: A Reinterpretation," *HAHR* 51 (November 1971), pp. 26–45.

what is critical is not Haya's personal commitment to the message but its appeal among the popular forces in the North and in the capital.

The presidential election could hardly be considered a national referendum, since much of the peasant population remained disenfranchised. Yet it did provide some measure of the new forces seeking to reshape Peruvian society. Sánchez Cerro split the urban populist vote with Haya de la Torre and earned his winning edge in rural areas where issues of nationalism and anti-imperialism had little immediate significance. The workers, middle class and petite bourgeoisie of Peru's northern departments and of the Lima–Callao metroplex provided Haya de la Torre with 74 percent of his total national vote. They voted for Aprismo, its more inclusive view of the nation and its campaign against the dislocations caused by the transformation of Peru. These were ideas for which many in the north coast sugar community would soon sacrifice their lives.[40]

APRA's electoral defeat prompted demands for more militant action from the popular forces which had committed themselves to its program. After APRA's leadership repeatedly delayed plans for a general uprising, pressure from the rank and file prompted a rebellion in the city of Trujillo in July 1932. With the backing of hundreds of sugar workers, the Apristas seized the city and executed members of the military garrison. Cartavio workers, who had joined the uprising en masse, captured an army detachment composed of one officer and twenty-four enlisted men and summarily executed them. But the premature revolt prevented the scheduled return of Gustavo Jiménez from exile to lead the rebel military campaign. Government forces quickly recaptured Trujillo and wreaked their own revenge. Colonel Jerónimo Santiváñez helped lead the retaking of Trujillo, but he turned down Sánchez Cerro's offer to make him temporary prefect of Trujillo, repulsed by the massacre of Apristas which had already begun and fearing a mutiny by his own soldiers in protest against the butchery. Major Guzmán Marquina had no such qualms. After accepting the prefect's position, Marquina carried out the execution of 1,500 people. In the purge of the Cartavio workforce, the military demonstrated its own class biases as it took white-collar employees to Trujillo for court martial while summarily executing workers in the cane fields. In March 1933 Gustavo Jiménez, who had resumed his life in exile, returned to northern Peru and marched toward the Chicama Valley. Twenty thousand sugar workers prepared to join him, but a blown bridge prevented Jiménez from arriving in the valley before government troops sent from Lima. In the ensuing encounter, Jiménez died and with him the last hope for rebellion in the North.[41]

The events at Oroya and Trujillo drove both the Apristas and Communists underground. The alliance for modernization now tried to regroup

40 Stein, *Populism in Peru*, pp. 192–200; Klarén, *Modernization, Dislocation*, pp. 135–36.
41 Klarén, *Modernization, Dislocation*, pp. 137–41; Luis Alberto Sánchez, *Haya de la Torre y el Apra* (Santiago: Pacífico, 1955), pp. 305–25; Burdett to secretary of state, Lima, July 14, 1932; Burdett, memorandum, Lima, July 29, 1932, RG 84, USNA.

behind Sánchez Cerro to resume the transformation of Peru. Despite Sánchez Cerro's alignment with the coastal planter interests that formed the core of the oligarchy, his regime still gave expression to the national-ist/populist forces that had come to dominate Peru's political discourse. As one observer explained, Sánchez Cerrismo consisted of a ". . . strange coalition of aristocratic Civilistas with the labor group of the Union Rev-olucionario which is led by Sánchez Cerro . . ."[42] The former group gave vent to the animosity which had mounted over Leguía's policy of giving free rein to American investors with little regard for the interests of the old guard of the elite. Sánchez Cerro's regime also gave expression to pop-ular protests against American interests and to demands for economic jus-tice. In accord with his own populist agenda and in response to the virtual collapse of state finances, the president imposed taxes on foreign corpora-tions and pursued social welfare proposals that frequently antagonized American interests. The nationalist agenda also found expression in a law requiring companies to employ Peruvians in 80 percent of all positions and to pay 80 percent of the salaries in each job category to Peruvians. In April 1933 Ambassador Dearing declared that "anti-American feeling is constantly being stimulated by every Government agency."[43] After Sánchez Cerro's assassination in April 1934, his successor, Oscar Bena-vides, purged the regime of its populist elements, sought to reconcile the interests of the Peruvian oligarchy and American investors, and con-fronted the last significant depression-era challenge from organized labor.

On Wednesday, October 24, 1934, the Grace liner *Santa Clara* docked at Pier 3 in Callao. Both the foreign and domestic business communities celebrated the event, because it signaled the opening of the new dock-works. The facilities promised to make Callao the most efficient port on the west coast of South America. But as the *West Coast Leader* observed, "the dawn of the day was not so viewed by all. Sullenly and resentfully, stevedores watched the berthing of the 'Santa Clara' because they realized that it meant a change in the conditions under which they had previously worked."[44] The dockworkers' longstanding practice of combining labor militancy with political activism to pursue their interests was coming to an end.

The dockworkers had long represented an independent and diverse ur-ban community. Unlike miners and sugar workers, they were not depen-dent on company housing or stores. They engaged in a wide range of ac-tivities that spanned both working-class and petit bourgeois occupations but maintained solidarity through the coordinated actions of a series of gremios. The Union of Stevedores represented 850 workers who loaded and unloaded cargo ships. The Union of Launch Operators and Baggage

42 Dearing to secretary of state, Lima, April 7, 1933, 823.00/960, RG 59, USNA.
43 Ibid.
44 *West Coast Leader* (Lima), October 23, 1934.

Men numbered 82 baggage handlers and 320 owner-operators of motor launches who attended the oceangoing steamers. Their community also included the Union of Port Watchmen, the Federation of Talley Clerks, independent customs house employees and a group of launch owners who handled the produce brought by coastal freighters. The leaders of the port community had exercised considerable political influence at both the local and national levels on behalf of their members. The dockworkers maintained that relationship under Sánchez Cerro, but the depression, along with increased demands for rationalization of port operations, placed the workers under increasing strains.[45]

The stevedores had long used their influence in the selection of workers to distribute work time among a community of laborers that considerably exceeded the needs on the docks. The dramatic drop in international commerce resulting from the depression placed serious strains on the system. Even limiting each man to one day of work per week provided employment for only half of the union's members. To cope with the economic slowdown, workers adopted other techniques to distribute the increasingly scarce work opportunities. Slings for loading ships that could carry six bars of copper were loaded with only two. Stevedores started the day late, stretched their lunch hour and quit early to reduce the workday to six and a half hours. They also used a "watch and watch" system, with one man assigned to "supervise" the work of each laborer. Union members developed ingenious pretenses to stop work to protest such matters as the shape of coal shovels. An American consular official concluded, "The laborers are now virtually able to dictate their own terms with regard to knocking off work, the amount of work to be done in a specified time and the number of men needed in a gang for any special job, regardless of whether that number is needed or not."[46]

The American firms which relied on the port for their business became increasingly incensed over the ability of the Callao workers to control the work place. Companies like Grace and Cerro de Pasco unsuccessfully pressed the government to declare Callao a free port, which would allow the companies to create an open shop on the docks and impose piece work. As an alternative, the companies sought to increase the size of the individual loads to be handled and attempted to reduce the size of crews employed. When the stevedores ignored efforts at speedup, the companies occasionally resorted to employing double crews, precisely what the stevedores hoped for. As a second alternative, the company would contract with the union to load a ship in a specified amount of time and in return pay two or three times the going wage.[47] As the depression deepened in

45 J. Kenly Bacon, "Labor Unions in Peru," Callao/Lima, September 11, 1934, RG 84, USNA.
46 Burdett, "Labor Problems on the Callao Waterfront," Callao/Lima, February 3, 1932, 823.1563/1, RG 59, USNA.
47 Jukes, "Waterfront Labor Conditions at Callao, Peru," Callao/Lima, January 22, 1934, 823.1563/2, RG 59, USNA.

Figure 9. Callao's new port facilities under construction in 1930. The piers which stretched out into the harbor would allow ocean-going vessels to dock directly at the piers and be unloaded by modern equipment. (From Peru, Ministerio de Fomento, *La labor constructiva del Perú* [1930])

1930 and work at the port became increasingly scarce, the stevedores agreed to do at least some work under contract. But contract work meant higher wages in rapidly depreciating national currency, more accidents and job-related illnesses, more unemployment and more days of hunger. From the workers' perspective, they had been reduced to "simple mechanized instruments in service to and for the benefit of shipping capital . . ."[48] In January 1932 the stevedores' union announced that it would no longer permit contract work. But by 1934 technological change and shifting political realities were turning the tide against the dockworkers.

The construction of the new port facilities proved to be a protracted process, but once completed the works provided the technical means for breaking the workers' control of the docks. In the new port, four cement piers jutted out into the harbor, allowing direct docking by seagoing vessels and eliminating the need for most lightering activities. Rail lines connected the piers directly to the central railway. The port's cargo handling equipment included a 50-ton stationary crane, a 15-ton floating crane and a 25-ton traveling crane. The facilities also included gas-powered trucks and tractors for materials handling on the docks. All of these innovations would serve to speed cargo movement and reduce labor

48 Ibid.

requirements. When the docks opened in October, the community of local interests at the port found itself poorly positioned to deal with the challenge they represented. The day before the new facilities opened, the Benavides regime issued a decree establishing a new sliding pay scale based on the tonnage handled by the stevedores. When the *Santa Clara* docked on the twenty-fourth, the dockworkers laid down their tools and walked off the job, protesting the imposition of the piece work system and the use of the new facilities, which would reduce the port's labor requirements. Some 1,700 other port workers joined the strike and sent delegates to appeal to the prefect of Callao and the minister of finance. In response, the government sent troops to the docks and declared Callao a free port, allowing shippers to hire whomever they wished. With high unemployment throughout the area, nearly 300 strikebreakers were working at the docks by Saturday, October 27. On Tuesday union members began returning to work, and the strike collapsed. The union continued to negotiate with the government over wage scales, but it had already conceded on the major issue, payment by tonnage or piece work. And while union members were guaranteed hiring preference, a government commission would have to approve the registration of union members. In effect the government formed a new union. The control over the docks which the stevedores had exercised for decades came to a sudden end.[49]

A number of factors combined to break the dockworkers' control. Technological innovation introduced by the Snare Corporation dramatically reduced the labor intensity of dock work and the shippers' dependence on the stevedores. Sánchez Cerro's repression of the Communist party and APRA precluded possible alliances with national political movements. The workers' appeals for support from other unions fell on deaf ears because several months earlier the stevedores had refused to support a call for a general strike. President Benavides had also been prepared to use force, instructing the prefect of Callao to arrest seventeen labor leaders and send them to a penal colony off the coast of Peru if the port workers' protests got out of hand. The Benavides government offered more than enforced piece work to the port community. Independent operators whose launches were no longer needed because of the new facilities would receive an indemnity equal to 50 percent of the value of their launches and be allowed to keep their boats. Those *launcheros* engaged in the unloading of fruits and vegetables would continue to operate as they had in the past. As for the stevedores, the new regulations provided for an eight-hour day, overtime pay and a pension system. While breaking the union's control of the docks, the regime also offered basic economic benefits to the workers. The Benavides regime had learned important lessons from the conflicts in

49 Mason Turner, "Communication and Transportation Facilities in Peru by Highway, Rail, Ship and Plane," Lima, July 15, 1938, 823.70/6, RG 59, USNA; *West Coast Leader,* November 13, 1934.

the mining and sugar sectors. The state now recognized that minimal welfare benefits had to be offered to cope with worker resistance to the continuing process of speedup and rationalization that Peru's transformation required. Some of the basic tenets of the popular protests which had rocked Peru for five years had become legitimate issues for debate in the national political process.[50]

The direct penetration of Peru's production process by American corporations during the first third of the twentieth century brought unparalleled growth to Peru's key export sectors; helped modernize industry, communication, power and transportation facilities; and generated substantial revenues for the domestic economy and the state. American business also brought higher wages and other material benefits to workers, and the advantages of a consumer society to the middle class. But this process of transformation accelerated economic differentiation and social dislocation in the regions which it most affected. Furthermore, American companies became caught up in a struggle by Peruvians to create a more inclusive definition of nationalism than the order and progress dictums of the elite.

While American companies brought material benefits, communities comprised of workers, peasants and elements of the middle class and petite bourgeoisie resisted what they viewed as foreign domination. Their demands for social and economic justice echoed popular protest themes that had a long history in Peru. In the preceding half century alone, those issues served as symbols of popular resistance during the Chilean occupation and the uprisings of 1919. Although peasants, workers, small business people and the middle class often had distinct interests, they could rally around common resentments against American corporations.[51] Given the increasing role of foreign and specifically U.S. corporations in the Peruvian economy since the turn of the century, these communities defined themselves in terms of their opposition to the foreign corporations that disrupted the lives of their members. The nationalist theme legitimized the struggles of popular forces and enabled them to form alliances with an array of national political movements, including Aprismo and Sánchez Cerrismo. Despite the repression of the early 1930s, their struggles defined the course of popular resistance within the national political process for the next three decades.

50 Garrett G. Ackerson to secretary of state, Lima, April 18, 1932, 823.1561/42, RG 59, USNA; Martínez de la Torre, *Interpretación marxista*, 1, pp. 391–97; Jukes, "Supplement to Report on Opening of New Maritime Terminal at Callao, Peru," Callao/Lima, November 2, 1934, RG 84, USNA, and "Waterfront Labor Conditions at Callao, Peru," Callao/Lima, January 22, 1934, 823.1563/2, RG 59, USNA, and "Opening of the New Maritime Terminal at Callao, Peru," Callao/Lima, October 26, 1934, RG 84, USNA.

51 On the formation of such communities, see Craig Calhoun, *The Question of Class Struggle: Social Foundations of Popular Radicalism During the Industrial Revolution* (Chicago: University of Chicago Press, 1982); William Roseberry, *Anthropologies and Histories: Essays in Culture, History and Political Economy* (New Brunswick, N.J.: Rutgers University Press, 1989); Gould, *To Lead as Equals*.

National political movements, whether marxist or populist, would give expression to the attempts of Peruvian popular forces to come to grips with and modify the transformation of their society. The state limited the success of these efforts because during the 1920s it had become increasingly vulnerable to external pressure through the economy's increased dependence on foreign investment and foreign loans. The selectivity of foreign investment and the limited appeal of nationalism among the Peruvian peasantry further constrained popular protest movements. The primary impact of American corporations and the most notable examples of rationalization remained limited to a few specific regions in Peru. That fact, combined with the absence of a nationalist consciousness among much of the rural population, limited the appeal of popular nationalist political programs. Given the cultural divide which separated rural Indians from westernized Peruvians, support for nationalist symbols remained concentrated in the central Andes, the north coast and the Lima–Callao metroplex. Even there populist support split between the conservative populism of Sánchez Cerro and Haya de la Torre's more radical version. Yet significant segments of the Peruvian people had identified themselves as part of a common social group, defined by opposition to the role of American corporations in the process of national development. Their movements had deep roots in Peru's history of popular protest. At the same time, themes of social and economic justice in their struggles of the early 1930s shaped a new and more inclusive nationalism which displaced the elite's narrow and exclusivist vision of national development. The populist nationalism of this period provided the basis for continued resistance to the project of the alliance for modernization. Meanwhile, to the south in Chile, a similar series of nationalist protests against elite models of modernization had erupted.

PART IV

Chile

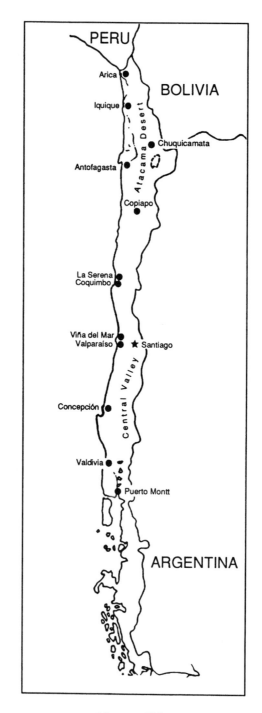

Map 7.1. Chile.

7

Salitreras and socialism

. . . nitrates will make us rich beyond the dreams of avarice! (Daniel Guggenheim, 1923)

. . . we are no longer conscious of Chilean mobs howling for the blood of American industrialists. (Hal Sevier, first secretary, American embassy, Santiago, 1934)

On May 15, 1915, a group of American and Chilean dignitaries gathered at the presidential palace in Santiago. As they watched, President Ramón Barros Luco pushed a button which started huge turbines spinning at a power plant in the northern desert port of Tocopilla. Electricity then sped eighty-six miles eastward along high tension lines to Chuquicamata, a huge open-pit copper mine and a symbol of the enormous role which American corporate culture had suddenly assumed in Chile. American culture and particularly American efficiency held a strong attraction for Chile's ruling class. Yet more than anything, President Barros Luco's symbolic act testified to the triumph of expediency over inclination for an elite whose long and prosperous relationship with British capitalism had begun to falter. During the last quarter of the nineteenth century, Chile's wheat and copper exports had disintegrated, and now the nitrate industry faced serious international competition. The elite fervently hoped that American investment would reverse those trends. At the moment when the Tocopilla turbines spun into action, U.S. investment approached the $170 million mark and would soar to $1 billion by 1929. Over half of that investment was dedicated to reviving Chile's moribund copper mines and to an attempt to salvage the nitrate industry. A further 10 percent represented the American takeover of the electrical power system. Another quarter of those capital commitments came in the form of loans to prop up a disintegrating government financial structure.[1]

American investments fulfilled much of their early promise in the first decades of the twentieth century. Between 1925 and 1931 alone, American mining companies produced $487 million worth of copper, with a

---

1 Joseph E. Maldonado, "Characteristics of the People of the United States of America," Santiago, May 5, 1920; R. de F. Boayer to chief of Bureau of Foreign and Domestic Commerce, Santiago, February 10, 1916, RG 84, USNA; Rippy, *Globe and Hemisphere*, pp. 36–39; Leo J. Keena to Joseph H. Shea, Valparaíso, October 26, 1917, RG 84, USNA.

third of that value being returned directly to the Chilean economy in the form of taxes, payments to labor and other local costs. American companies also salvaged what they could of the dying nitrate industry and began modernizing the electrical industry.[2] For the Americans, their Chilean ventures offered the opportunity to apply labor-saving technology and the labor disciplines of the second industrial revolution in an environment rich in low-cost semiskilled labor. Moreover, that opportunity had emerged in a country with a notable tradition of political stability. American interests also saw in their investments the solution to what they viewed as Chile's principal problem. For the Americans, the underlying cause of the export sector's decline lay in the social relations that dominated the productive process in Chile. As one American observed,

It is a regrettable fact but nonetheless true, that in Chili . . . , man in the eyes of the governing classes, possesses no commercial value, not even at all in comparison with the economic value of a jackass . . . the ruling classes cannot and will not appreciate that man in the economy of the nation is an automated machine representing a capital value . . .[3]

In response to this apparent irrationality of relations between labor and capital, American corporations offered the second industrial revolution's labor-saving technologies, work-place disciplines, and industrial welfare programs. American businessmen would not merely bring new machinery, they would uplift and educate the Chilean working class. In return they would achieve levels of productivity and labor discipline never before seen in Chile.

A tacit agreement underlay the American renovation of the export sector. American corporations promised substantial material rewards in return for control of the nation's principal mining resources and the right to enforce industrial discipline on their indigenous labor force. American companies appeared to offer a low-risk, high-return program for national development. In contrast to what obtained in Peru, U.S. investment would restore economic growth without directly displacing domestic economic interests. Furthermore, American investments, which focused primarily on the barren northern deserts, would not be highly disruptive to social relations in the Central Valley, where most of the population resided. But American penetration challenged an existing worker culture and fractured the complex of social and economic relationships that had evolved between European capitalists and Chilean society during the Nitrate Age. The dominant and very visible American role in the Chilean economy also raised serious questions of national sovereignty when the

2 Clark Winston Reynolds, "The Development Problems of an Export Economy: The Case of Chile and Copper," in Markos Mamalakis and Clark Winston Reynolds, *Essays on the Chilean Economy* (Homewood, Ill.: Irwin, 1965), pp. 375, 377.
3 J. Perkins Shanks, "Labour Situation in Northern Chile," Antofagasta, September 3, 1921, RG 84, USNA.

Great Depression struck. By 1930 the accelerating world economic crisis prevented American corporations from generating increased material benefits for the local economy. In the midst of a mounting social and economic crisis, those corporations added an important element to the formation of a new nationalism which had made economic and social justice its central themes. Anti-imperialism now provided an important new bond for the groups that supported popular nationalism. The roots of these dramatic events of the 1930s can be traced to the transformations that shaped nineteenth-century Chile.

The traditional peasant village, the focal point for a centuries-long struggle over land and labor elsewhere in Latin America, did not exist in Chile. The great estates either attracted labor with small plots of land in a variety of service tenant relationships, most commonly referred to as *inquilinaje,* or secured day laborers with payments in kind or cash. Despite the absence of village structures, Chilean peons accepted work on the haciendas only as a last resort. During the eighteenth century they exploited unused or unclaimed plots, and they petitioned for usufruct grants from local municipalities. Until the middle of the nineteenth century, independent campesino producers flourished, meeting their own needs and selling their surplus in the towns or to the large estates. A similar set of circumstances prevailed in the northern mining districts, where peons, working alone or with a few companions, discovered and developed small mining claims that constituted the heart of the mining industry. This vibrant small producer economy, however, began to disintegrate after Chilean independence.[4]

At the beginning of the nineteenth century the Chilean elite found themselves displaced in the international economy by Europeans. In response, they utilized their control of mills, storage facilities and local credit networks to extract increasing amounts of income from independent campesinos. While hacendados also initiated mechanization of their own estates, they focused their most intensive efforts on extracting additional labor from their tenants and from day laborers. In a similar fashion, merchants who had funded independent miners used their financial power to take increasing control of the mines and reduce the miners to wage workers. Out of the collapse of the small producer economy emerged a migratory population which gave birth to the Chilean *roto,* or worker. Many peons migrated the length of Chile's fertile Central Valley seeking subsistence in seasonal labor on the great estates or work in and around the towns. While their Peruvian neighbors resorted to African slaves, Chinese indentured workers and costly systems of enganche, Chilean hacendados and mine owners had access to peons as low-paid day workers or

---

4 Gabriel Salazar Vergara, *Labradores, peones y proletarios: formación y crisis de la sociedad popular chilena del siglo xix* (Santiago: Ediciones Sur, 1985), pp. 32–92, 173.

long-term service tenants. These production relations placed Chile in an optimal position to respond to international market opportunities that appeared by the middle of the nineteenth century. Between the 1840s and the 1860s, Chilean wheat growers and copper miners responded to expanding international markets with production increases of 1,500 and 500 percent respectively. Yet the impressive export figures of the early 1870s also marked economic growth limits set by Chile's social relations.[5]

Chilean hacendados and mine owners had not simply fashioned labor systems to their own liking. The peons and rotos through their popular culture formulated a vision of a just social order and exhibited an independence and contempt for authority which constantly challenged the elite. While Chilean peons frequently migrated from the countryside in search of work, many returned regularly to share in harvest time and the ceremonies, feasting and drinking which marked its completion. They also returned to participate in some of the numerous religious holidays and festivals that marked key events in the life of their rural society. Their return formed part of a migratory way of life, its rhythms and its values. In a rough and difficult life, aggressiveness proved an essential trait, and one which brought on frequent encounters with the local authorities.[6] While incarcerated, peons received the ministrations of churchmen such as Canon Francisco de Paula Taforó, who attempted to instill a Christian work ethic in his captive audience. As he noted:

But since we encounter people who do not love work and who also pass a good part of their time in idleness, it is necessary to instruct them on the obligation which they have to work. In a word, for those who do not work, we must make them see the obligation to work; and for those who dedicate themselves to it, let us teach them how to sanctify it.[7]

Yet an alternative religious vision also existed among the working people of the countryside and the city.

The rich mixture of Christian and Amerindian beliefs in popular religion gave rise to an autonomous religious culture. Within that popular culture, Christ became a symbol not only of the downtrodden masses but of specific values, particularly generosity and forgiveness. The Antichrist symbolized such values as ambition and treachery. The Antichrist represented the Christ killers, the Jews, who were at times identified as hereti-

5 Ibid., pp. 96–121, 156–68, 173–74, 187–89; Bauer, *Chilean Rural Society,* pp. 62, 159–61; Cristobal Kay, "The Development of the Chilean Hacienda System, 1850–1973," in Kenneth Duncan and Ian Rutledge, eds., *Land and Labour in Latin America: Essays on the Development of Agrarian Capitalism in the Nineteenth and Twentieth Centuries* (Cambridge: Cambridge University Press, 1977), p. 109; O'Brien, *Nitrate Industry,* p. 2.

6 Manuel A. Fernández, *Proletariado y salitre en Chile, 1890–1910* (London: Monografía de Nueva Historia, 1988), pp. 10–11; Isaiah Bowman, *Desert Trails of Atacama* (New York: American Geographical Society, 1924), p. 72.

7 Francisco de Paula Taforó, *El libro de las carceles: rehabilitación del presidario* (Santiago: Imprenta i Litografía de B. Moran, 1876), p. 209.

cal foreigners, such as the British, or as members of the elite. Beyond symbols of protest, popular religion also contained a vision of utopia emerging from the triumph of the downtrodden over their oppressors. That alternative world vision reinforced the peons' rejection of work disciplines.[8]

If the hacendado paid subsistence wages, it was due in part to the fact that the peon responded to increased wages by shortening his work week. For the peon, work on the estates or in the towns or mines was a means to maintain subsistence in a physical environment which imposed few demands on humans for their survival. Throughout the nineteenth century, Chilean peons continued their migratory life with its subsistence diet, rudimentary shelter, numerous holidays, and rounds of drinking and gambling at the *despacho,* or local tavern. Much the same lifestyle characterized those who worked the silver and copper mines.[9]

As the peons who discovered and worked the mines found themselves reduced to wage labor, they developed ways to continue sharing in the mine's profits, salting away silver in every conceivable crevice of their bodies before the end of the workday. In a tight labor market, peons frequently insisted on several months' advance wages, only to abscond with the funds. Chilean mine owners found it essential to secure contracts from their day laborers which committed them to at least one month of work. For the peons, their daily routine, which frequently involved dragging two- and three-hundred-pound sacks of ore up the narrow inclined mine tunnels, represented a dangerous occupation, and they frequently appealed to Christian saints such as the Virgin of Andacollo to provide safety and good luck. But no matter the degree of divine intervention, mining remained an arduous and dangerous occupation which peons undertook until a new opportunity in the towns, on the railways or elsewhere set them roaming once again.[10]

In the context of social relations that provided a low wage but a poorly disciplined workforce, Chilean hacendados and mine owners responded quite effectively to prevailing high prices for minerals and

---

8 John Miers, *Travels in Chile and La Plata* (1826), 2 vols. (New York: AMS Press, 1970), 2, pp. 266–68; Salazar, *Labradores,* p. 92; Maximiliano Salinas, "Cristianismo popular en Chile, 1880–1920: un esquema sobre el factor religiosa en las clases subaltenas durante el capitalismo oligárquico," *NH* 12 (October–December 1984), pp. 275–302; Carleton Beals, *The Long Land: Chile* (New York: Coward-McCann, 1949), p. 182; Guillermo Feliú Cruz, *Santiago a comienzos del siglo xix* (Santiago: Editorial Andrés Bello, 1970), p. 181; Nevin O. Winter, *Chile and Her People of To-Day* (Boston: L. C. Page, 1912), p. 270.

9 "Preliminary Report for the Year 1897 on the Trade and Commerce of the Consular District of Valparaiso," *PP,* vol. 98, 1899; "Report by Mr. Rumbold on the Progress and General Condition of Chile," *PP,* vol. 73, 1876, p. 393; Bauer, *Chilean Rural Society,* pp. 148–49; Miers, *Travels in Chile,* 2, pp. 385–86.

10 Juan Uribe Echeverría y Uriarte and Juan Guillermo Prado Ocaranza, "La Virgen de Andacollo en Chile y en la Argentina," *Folklore Americano* 32 (July–December 1983), pp. 5–52; Erna Fergusson, *Chile* (New York: Knopf, 1943), pp. 248–55; Bowman, *Desert Trails,* pp. 168–69.

wheat during the middle of the nineteenth century. But these labor-intensive methods eventually took their toll on Chile's export economy. Chile's agricultural export boom was disintegrating by the end of the 1870s in the face of competition from more capital-intensive, more efficient foreign producers. The crisis in mining came more rapidly and with greater impact. The sharp drop in copper prices which began in 1874 struck at the heart of the Chilean economy, in which minerals accounted for over 50 percent of all exports. The social relations which underpinned Chile's agricultural and mining systems had reached the limits of their ability to produce for the world market. While hacendados and mine owners had secured a large labor force at low wages, peons had continued to migrate, accepting wage labor as only an intermittent source of subsistence and rejecting many of the disciplines of the work place. The ability of agricultural and mining elites to add additional increments of cheap, undisciplined labor would no longer suffice against more efficient producers in the world market. The solution to the nation's worst economic crisis since independence came in the War of the Pacific (1879–83) against Peru and Bolivia. Chile permanently occupied the Peruvian province of Tarapacá and the Bolivian province of Antofagasta.[11] Those regions, particularly Tarapacá, were the home of the highly valuable nitrate industry.

At the time of the War of the Pacific, European-owned refineries, or *oficinas,* in Tarapacá represented the dominant force in the industry. Under considerable European diplomatic pressure to recognize the substantial international debts of the Peruvian government, and lacking the human, technical and capital resources to run the industry, the Chilean government quickly returned the refineries to European control. By 1886 European producers, who accounted for 75 percent of Tarapacá's output, had launched Chile on an unprecedented period of economic prosperity. While leaving the nitrate industry largely in the hands of British and German producers, the Chilean government imposed an export duty on nitrates which filled government coffers to overflowing. The nitrate tax provided over 50 percent of the state's ordinary revenues, which increased 500 percent between 1880 and 1918. In turn the state funneled an average of 30

11 Salazar, *Labradores,* pp. 173–89, 196–98; Elias Lafertte, *Vida de un comunista* (Santiago: Empresa Editorial Austral, 1971), p. 35; María Angélica Illanes, "Disciplinamiento de la mano de obra minera en una formación social en transición," *NH* 11 (1984), pp. 195–224; Benjamín Vicuña Mackenna, *El libro del cobre i del carbón de piedra en Chile* (Santiago: Imprenta Cervantes, 1883), pp. 266–69, 351; "Report on Chile as a Field for Emigration," *PP,* vol. 90, 1893–94, p. 5; "Report by Vice-Consul Mark on the Trade and Commerce of Caldera for the Year 1879," *PP,* vol. 74, 1880, p. 1508; Leland R. Pederson, *The Mining Industry of the Norte Chico, Chile* (Evanston: University of Illinois Press, 1966), pp. 117–19, 189–95; "Report on the Trade and Commerce of Chile for the Year 1887," *PP,* vol. 50, 1888, p. 7; Bauer, *Chilean Rural Society,* pp. 66–73, 155–66; "Report on the Trade and Commerce of Coquimbo," *PP,* vol. 81, 1890, p. 3; "Report for the Year 1898 on the Trade and Commerce of the Consular District of Valparaiso," *PP,* vol. 98, 1899, p. 11.

percent of its expenditures into national development, with particular emphasis on transportation.[12]

Between 1885 and 1920 the population of the nitrate provinces grew from 88,000 to 288,000 people. That population, with virtually no local source of food, represented one of the largest internal markets for Chilean agriculture. Manufacturing benefited from the expanded internal market, the introduction of foreign capital and technology, and increases in exports that financed capital goods imports for the industrial base. The short-term financing of nitrate production became a leading source of business for Chile's major banks. Members of the elite also enjoyed a more direct involvement in the industry. By 1906 Chileans controlled 22 percent of the capital invested in the industry and participated in joint ventures with Europeans that accounted for another 18 percent. A number of the investors represented mercantile houses that shipped products from central Chile to the firms in the North and served as middlemen for the sale of the companies' nitrates. Although a few large foreign commercial firms such as the British house Gibbs and Company dominated the international trade in nitrates, the Chilean firms arranged for the sale of the producing companies' product to the international dealers. Speculation in nitrates, land and corporate stocks became yet another form of wealth enhancement for the Chilean oligarchy during this gilded age. Gustavo Ross, scion of one of the nation's leading families and a renowned financier, made 15 million pesos during World War I speculating in corporate stocks and foreign exchange. But at the moment of Ross' financial triumphs, the nation stood on the brink of economic decline, social upheaval and political chaos. At the heart of that crisis lay the relationships which had developed between the Chilean peon and European nitrate capitalists.[13]

---

12 O'Brien, *Nitrate Industry,* p. 74; Chile, Ministerio de Hacienda, Sección Salitre, *Antecedentes sobre la industria salitrera* (Santiago: Ministerio de Hacienda, 1925), p. 21; Markos J. Mamalakis, *The Growth and Structure of the Chilean Economy: From Independence to Allende* (New Haven: Yale University Press, 1976), pp. 73–76; Thomas C. Wright, "Agriculture and Protectionism in Chile," *JLAS* 7 (May 1975), pp. 47–48; Guillermo Subercaseaux, *Monetary and Banking Policy of Chile* (Oxford: Clarendon Press, 1922), p. 202.

13 Carmen Cariola and Osvaldo Sunkel, "The Growth of the Nitrate Industry and Socioeconomic Change in Chile, 1880–1930," in Cortés Conde and Hunt, eds., *Latin American Economies,* pp. 165–68, 177; Manuel A. Fernández, "El enclave salitrero y la economía chilena, 1880–1914," *NH* 3 (1981), pp. 13–17; Marcello Carmagnani, "Banques étrangères et banques nationales au Chili (1900–1920)," *Caravelle* 20 (1972), p. 50; Henry Kirsch, *Industrial Development in a Traditional Society: The Conflict of Entrepreneurship and Modernization in Chile* (Gainesville: University Presses of Florida, 1977), pp. 1–20, 77–95; London and River Plate Bank to London office, Valparaíso, August 24, 1907, BOLSA; Bank of Tarapaca and London to London office, Valparaíso, December 10, 1907, BOLSA; O'Brien, *Nitrate Industry,* p. 144; Virgilio Figueroa, *Diccionario histórico y biográfico de Chile,* 5 vols. (Santiago: Establecimientos Gráfico "Balcells & Co.," 1925–36), 3, p. 372; 5, p. 869; Letters 163–67, 1894, File 11,470/15; Letters 324, 331, 1923, File 11, 470/24, Gibbs Papers. Also see the records of the Anglo South American Bank in Chile for this same period, in BOLSA; London and River Plate Bank to London office, Valparaíso, May 19, 1921, August 17, 1930, BOLSA.

Figure 10. One of the old Shanks-type refineries that still dominated the nitrate
industry's production system in the 1920s. (From Asociación de Productores de
Salitre de Chile, *Album . . . del centenario* [1930])

In 1878 the British engineer James T. Humberstone had introduced
the Shanks refining process, which dramatically increased worker productivity and decreased production costs. But the Shanks process also proved
to be the last major technological innovation in the industry for fifty
years. The failure to continue renovating the nitrate production process
stemmed in part from the producers' belief that the industry enjoyed a
natural monopoly. Yet before World War I it became clear that serious
synthetic competitors had emerged, particularly sulfate of ammonia. The
industry's failure to innovate even as European competition made a farce
of its natural monopoly lay rooted in the production process both in
Britain and in Chile.[14]

As a result of market and labor conditions, the second industrial revolution proved far less sweeping in Britain than in America. The British
chemical industry, where the Shanks process had been developed, typified
this slower technological development. The fact that innovation was not

14 O'Brien, *Nitrate Industry*, pp. 69–70; Oscar Bermúdez Miral, *Historia del salitre desde sus orígenes
hasta la Guerra del Pacífico* (Santiago: Ediciones de la Universidad de Chile, 1963), pp. 272–76;
George W. Stocking and Myron W. Watkins, *Cartels in Action: Case Studies in International Business
Diplomacy* (New York: Twentieth Century Fund, 1946), p. 126; Letters 80, 83, 85, 1913, File
11,116/2, Gibbs Papers; Fernández, "Enclave salitrero," pp. 27–31; George A. Makinson, "The
Cost of Producing Nitrate in Chile," Valparaíso, October 8, 1923, rl. 34, M-487, RG 59, USNA.

merely slow but came to a standstill in the nitrate industry can be explained by the interaction of British enterprises and Chilean society. From the moment that Chile absorbed the nitrate region, nitrate producers joined a chorus of lament by hacendados and mine owners over the scarcity of labor. An apparent labor shortage in a country with a large nomadic rural population and extremely low wages seems somewhat incongruous. In fact, agriculture, mining and nitrates had all come to rely on labor-intensive methods which could temporarily strain the local or national labor supply at harvest time, in periods of intense activity in mining or nitrates, or during the initiation of large public works projects. Despite that limitation, the nitrate industry proved quite successful in assuring itself of a large supply of cheap labor. In the mid 1880s the industry employed just over 5,000 workers. Three decades later that force had grown to over 46,000 laborers. The securing of that workforce had become an ever more systemized process based on enganche (labor contracting).[15] By the 1870s contractors for individual nitrate companies were scouring central Chile in search of likely prospects, and many later went to work for the Nitrate Producers' Association. When labor shortages became particularly acute in the 1920s, the Association reached informal agreements not to recruit in the more important agricultural and mining districts during periods of high demand. As a result, the recruitment drives continued to run with what one observer called military-like efficiency. For nitrate refiners, enganche, in addition to supplying large amounts of cheap labor, had the additional advantage of allowing them to dispense with most if not all of their workforce in hard times. For individual workers, layoffs could mean a long trek under the cruel desert sun in search of work. Industry-wide shutdowns left thousands of workers to find their own way south. By 1919 the Chilean government had begun to intervene during such crises to ensure more humane treatment for the laborers. Yet the nomadic life served not only the refiners' purposes but those of the workers as well.[16]

15 Fernández, "Enclave salitrero," pp. 34–35; Bauer, *Chilean Rural Society*, pp. 148–49; "Report by Vice-Consul Mark on the Trade and Commerce of Caldera for the Year 1879," *PP*, vol. 74, 1880; "Preliminary Report for the Year 1897 on the Trade and Commerce of the Consular District of Valparaiso," *PP*, vol. 98, 1899; "Report for the Year 1905 on the Trade and Commerce of the Consular District of Coquimbo," *PP*, vol. 123, 1906; Smail to William Gibbs & Company, Oficina Limeña, May 3, 1878, File 11,049A; Letter 26, 1911, File 11,116/1, Gibbs Papers; O'Brien, *Nitrate Industry*, p. 69; Arthur Lawrence Stickell, "Migration and Mining: Labor in Northern Chile in the Nitrate Era, 1880–1930" (Ph.D. dissertation, Indiana University, 1979), pp. 46–62; "Report on Chile as a Field for Emigration," *PP*, vol. 90, 1893–94, p. 5; Manuel Salas Lavaqui, *Trabajos y antecedentes presentados al Supremo Gobierno de Chile por la Comisión Consultiva del Norte* (Santiago: Imprenta Cervantes, 1908), p. 560; Fernández, *Proletariado y salitre*, pp. 16–17.

16 George D. Hopper, "The Labor Perspective in Chile," Antofagasta, March 3, 1926; Stewart E. McMillan, "A Brief Review for 1924 of the Nitrate Industry in the Antofagasta Consular District," Antofagasta, January 27–28, 1925, RG 84, USNA; Stickell, "Migration and Mining," pp. 60, 89; Michael Monteón, "The Enganche in the Chilean Nitrate Sector, 1880–1930," *Latin American Perspectives* 6 (Summer 1979), pp. 66–79.

In a very real sense, the Chilean peons maintained their migratory, independent ways even in the harsh northern deserts. At any one time, at least 5 percent of the workforce was in transit from one refinery to another in search of a better life. The nitrate companies attempted to combat this migratory process with a variety of tactics and institutions. The companies began recruiting whole families under the enganche system in the hope that the presence of the family would subdue the worker's wanderlust. The refineries employed company stores and *fichas,* or company scrip, in an effort to tie their laborers to the oficinas. Yet these measures had little effect on the wanderings of the workers. In addition to carrying on a migratory way of life, nitrate workers managed to retain other features of their lives in Chile's mining and agricultural regions, molding those features into an independent workers' culture.[17]

In the North the workers continued the tradition of heavy social drinking. One observer reported that in the desert "illicit stills spring up like mushrooms. Fiery and poisonous imitations of various kinds of whiskey are to be found in the north concocted for the special delectation of the nitrate workers and sold of course at a low price compared with their imported equivalents."[18] Holidays and special events at individual oficinas often became three- and four-day drunken festivals that paralyzed all work on the desert pampa. Religious holidays also played a role in the nitrate workers' culture. Workers migrated south to Coquimbo annually to join in the festival of the Virgin of Andacollo, which became an increasingly raucous expression of popular culture among nitrate workers. Church officials had sought to institutionalize and sanitize the cult, laying the cornerstone for a basilica to the Virgin in 1873. But even decades later, an attempt by the local mayor to suppress the miners' dance groups that had become a centerpiece of the festival collapsed in the face of the workers' protests.[19]

Yet many other nitrate workers had disavowed these Christian traditions. The small desert towns at the outskirts of the *salitreras* (nitrate refineries and their grounds) became focal points for a more worldly version of worker culture. These settlements were noted for their cantinas, gambling parlors and houses of prostitution. It was a culture that stood in sharp contrast to the rigid disciplines of the oficinas that attempted to

17 Bergquist, *Labor in Latin America,* pp. 38–40; Lafertte, *Vida de un comunista,* pp. 31–34; "General Outline Report on the Chilean Nitrate Industry," copy enclosed in David Blair to Earl of Curzon, Santiago, July 31, 1919 (cited hereafter as "Report on the Chilean Nitrate Industry"), Chile 132/198, F.O., PRO; McMillan to secretary of state, Antofagasta, January 17–28, 1925, rl. 34, M-487, General Records of the Department of State Relating to the Internal Affairs of Chile, 1910–29, RG 59, USNA; "Report for the Year 1913 on the Trade of the Consular District of Coquimbo," PP, vol. 69, 1913; Alejandro Bertrand, *The Chilean Nitrate Industry: Technology and Economics* (Paris: Imprimerie de Vaugirard, 1920), p. 84.

18 Vaughn to Curzon, Santiago, November 10, 1919, Chile 131/198, F.O.

19 Salas Lavaqui, *Comisión Consultiva del Norte,* p. 860; Fergusson, *Chile,* pp. 258–59; Salinas, "Cristianismo popular," p. 286; Bowman, *Desert Trails,* p. 168.

ban "illicit" entertainment. It was here that workers encountered labor agitators and itinerant merchants who peddled bootleg alcohol and radical newspapers published in the port cities. Those periodicals helped disseminate the secularist views of such noted labor leaders as Luis Emilio Recabarren. Visitors to the North noted the general disdain which workers held for religious beliefs. Yet even secularist workers revered certain cult figures. Virtually every peon's residence on the nitrate desert possessed at least one image of Chilean president José Manuel Balmaceda. Balmaceda had committed suicide in 1891 after his defeat in a civil war which pitted the president against Congress. This intra-elite struggle, and Balmaceda's crushing of worker unrest in the nitrate zone, could hardly have endeared him to the peons of the northern desert. But Balmaceda left a vital legacy which the workers recognized and honored. An ardent nationalist, he had invested nitrate revenues in an array of public works and denounced the trend toward British monopolization of the industry. Nitrate workers could easily envision Balmaceda as the martyr of a nationalist cause which pitted him against the elite and foreign nitrate producers. Such an image would strike a responsive chord among workers who defined their own struggles in similar terms. In their appeals to the Chilean government for improvement of their condition, nitrate workers depicted themselves as citizens of a republican nation who were being exploited by foreign capitalists. They protested against low wages, atrocious living and working conditions, and the introduction of thousands of Bolivian and Peruvian workers to further reduce wages. This strong sense of nationalism constituted yet another important element in working-class culture.[20]

Popular culture in the northern desert mixed the migratory patterns, social customs and religious beliefs of the Central Valley with a secularist cult that possessed a strong sense of nationalism. But in contrast to the experience of Central American and Peruvian workers, only one other group allied itself with workers in the nitrate region. The itinerant traders and merchants in the small desert towns near the oficinas held a strong sympathy for the plight of the workers who represented their principal market and from whom the nitrate companies sought to keep them. The workers in turn constantly demanded the institution of free trade in the region to break the monopoly of company scrip and stores, to the benefit of the merchants. Outside of this group, the desert environment was as short of workers' allies as it was of rain. But while the workers lacked sympathizers, they did not lack for effective militancy, a fact made clear by the fate of the refineries' piece rate system.[21]

20 Ricardo A. Latcham, *Chuquicamata: Estado Yankee (visión de la montaña roja)* (Santiago: Editorial Nascimiento, 1926), p. 76; Salas Lavaqui, *Comisión Consultiva del Norte*, pp. 558–62, 871–73; Bergquist, *Labor in Latin America*, pp. 49–50.
21 Salas Lavaqui, *Comisión Consultiva del Norte*, pp. 564, 569; Stickell, "Migration and Mining," p. 178; Bergquist, *Labor in Latin America*, p. 55.

Figure 11. This scene of nitrate workers breaking caliche (nitrate ore) with hand tools typified the labor-intensive nature of the industry before the Guggenheims' investments mechanized many of these processes. (From Semper and Michels, *La industria del salitre en Chile* [1908])

Out in the desert surrounding the refineries, field workers, or *particulares,* broke and loaded the nitrate ore, or *caliche*. Particulares were allowed to work the caliche beds according to their own design. Since they worked on a piece rate basis, they exploited only the highest-grade caliche in a haphazard manner. The irregular pattern in which the desert floor was broken up often meant that the lower-grade nitrate would never be exploited, since it could not be easily accessed or transported.[22] Although refiners subsequently insisted on a more systematic extraction process, their control continued to be contested at every step of the production process. The particulares constantly battled over the rate they were to be paid, since lower-grade beds required more time and effort to break up and select out caliche. Further trouble erupted at the oficinas when inspectors rejected cartloads of ore on the ground that the particulares had deliberately tossed in large amounts of waste material. This type of ongoing battle led to a piece work system which, rather than encouraging individual workers to exceed existing output norms, sought "to give the men an equal salary to maintain harmony amongst them."[23] Things did not go much more smoothly in the refineries themselves.

22 "Report on the Chilean Nitrate Industry," Chile 132/198, F.O.; John Smail to Henry Read, Oficina Limeña, March 13, 1879, File 11,472, Gibbs Papers.

23 Henry Daubeny to John Smail, Valparaíso, July 28, 1898, File 11,470/18, Gibbs Papers; "Report on the Chilean Nitrate Industry," Chile 132/198, F.O., PRO; Salas Lavaqui, *Comisión Consultiva del Norte*, pp. 850–52.

In 1879 an oficina manager reported a strike by *desripiadores,* workers who cleaned the refinery's boiling tanks, or *calicheras.* He was pleased to report that he had dealt with them successfully, "as the desripiadores have for years had things pretty much their own way."[24] Yet twenty years later the same individual reported that efforts to force the calichera workers to clean the tanks more carefully had set off a revolt "which apparently is costing us dearly."[25] The end result of these interactions between Europeans and Chilean peons was an industry with a remarkably cheap but highly undisciplined labor force. The essence of management in the nitrate industry had become the control of a low-cost but recalcitrant workforce. For the nitrate producers, the alternatives to continued control over a large, inexpensive labor force were not promising. A trust which introduced labor-saving devices and made permanent large-scale reductions in the labor force was certain to bring down the wrath of the Chilean government, not to mention the nitrate workers. Other alternatives were equally unpromising.[26]

One obstacle in the way of introducing new, more efficient machinery was that it was "not easy to find and train efficient and careful native operators." The creation of a pool of such workers would require higher pay levels. Increased wages, however, would violate the tacit alliance among hacendados, mine owners and nitrate refiners. Substantially higher wages, as one Gibbs official put it, "would inevitably give birth to yet another grudge against the industry, which can be better imagined than described."[27] Even the prohibition of liquor in the nitrate zone would anger the numerous hacendados who grew grapes and sold a substantial part of their wine in the northern desert.[28] Already slowed in their implementation of the second industrial revolution at home, British firms became enmeshed in Chile in a series of relationships that largely froze the process of labor discipline and halted technical innovation. The price paid in productivity would not become fully apparent until the growing militancy of Chilean workers threatened the elite's bastion of power in the Central Valley.

As the Nitrate Age progressed, workers took an increasingly militant stance toward the foreign capitalists who dominated the industry. Wildcat strikes in individual plants in the 1870s escalated into larger, more organized protests and culminated in a mass strike in 1907 which ended when government troops shot down hundreds of workers in the port of Iquique. After the turn of the century, militant labor actions erupted in the north, center and south of Chile. But these actions did not represent the work of a united national labor movement. Increasingly, socialists under Luis Emilio Recabarren came to dominate the labor movement in the North.

24 Smail to Read, Oficina Limeña, February 3, 1879, File 11,472/1, Gibbs Papers.
25 Smail to Brien Cokayne, London, June 7, 1900, File 11,115/1, Gibbs Papers.
26 Letter 192, 1919, File 11,470/22, Gibbs Papers.
27 Campbell to secretary of state, Iquique, January 20, 1927, rl. 34, M-487, RG 59, USNA; "Report on the Chilean Nitrate Industry," Chile 132/198, F.O., PRO.
28 Sir L. Strange to Earl of Curzon, Santiago, May 1, 1919, Chile 132/198, F.O., PRO.

Farther south, in Valparaíso and Santiago, anarchists enjoyed considerable success between 1902 and 1920. Furthermore, urban workers did not share the strong anti-foreign nationalism of the nitrate workers. Although as many as half of the industrial enterprises were foreign-owned, the urban setting did not reflect the clear division of foreign capitalists against Chilean workers that marked class relations in the North. As a result, urban workers rarely made foreign ownership an issue in their protests.[29] Instead workers eventually allied themselves with other urban groups to direct their protests against the national elite.

Unlike their counterparts in Central America and Peru, workers in central Chile did not find ready allies among the petite bourgeoisie. That may have been due to the relative vibrance of the latter group. Unlike small business people elsewhere in Latin America, who saw their interests threatened by large corporations, the Chilean petite bourgeoisie appeared to thrive at the beginning of the twentieth century. As late as 1927 small-scale or artisanal enterprises with fewer than five workers accounted for more than half of all industrial establishments and employed 67 percent of the industrial workforce. Only when the Great Depression inflicted considerable damage on small industry did these petit bourgeois interests join with labor to challenge American corporate interests.[30] Workers, however, had long since allied themselves with the emerging middle class.

In 1905 and again in 1918 the middle and working classes joined in massive and often violent urban protests against the rising cost of living. But demonstrations in the Central Valley against the vagaries of market forces remained focused on the Chilean elite and its exclusivist program of national development, rather than on foreign interests. Such protests proved vulnerable to state repression and the elite's nationalist rhetoric. The nationalism of the Chilean elite, sanctified in the War of the Pacific, served a useful purpose in subduing internal challenges. The state successfully portrayed movements such as the International Workers of the World as foreign conspiracies, and that portrayal became the justification for violent government repression of popular protests.[31] Interspersed with the periodic assaults on protest movements came minimalist attempts to relieve conditions that fed popular discontent. But as the nitrate industry

29 H. L. Gibbs to Vicary Gibbs, London, July 10, 1890, File 11,041/1, Gibbs Papers. The 1907 massacre has been treated in a number of works, including Michael Monteón, *Chile in the Nitrate Era: The Evolution of Economic Dependence, 1880–1930* (Madison: University of Wisconsin Press, 1982); Fernández, *Proletariado y salitre;* and Guillermo Kaempffer Villagren, *Así sucedio, 1850–1925: Sangrientos episodios de la lucha obrera en Chile* (Santiago: Imprenta Arncibia Hermanos, 1962). On the urban labor movement, see Peter DeShazo, *Urban Workers and Labor Unions in Chile, 1902–1927* (Madison: University of Wisconsin Press, 1983).

30 DeShazo, *Urban Workers,* pp. 14–15; Mamalakis, *Chilean Economy,* p. 145.

31 DeShazo, *Urban Workers,* pp. 77, 91, 183–94, 227–28; Thomas C. Wright, *Landowners and Reform in Chile: The Sociedad Nacional de Agricultura, 1919–1940* (Urbana: University of Illinois Press, 1982), pp. 102–7; Anglo South American Bank, Letter #32/26, Valparaíso, July 26, 1920, BOLSA.

began to spiral toward collapse, periodic repression and ineffectual reform would no longer suffice to maintain stability in Chile. By that time the elite had already turned to American corporations in search of a solution to the crises which gripped their society.

Chile had been the world's leading copper producer in the 1870s, but after the turn of the century Chilean output fell, and the nation's share of the world market dropped to less than 5 percent. That decline stemmed in large measure from the social relationships that characterized Chilean mining. Mine owners had continuing access to a low-wage labor force, but one that retained its migratory ways and resistance to industrial disciplines. Those relationships left Chilean mining with a series of labor-intensive, under-capitalized enterprises. American investment reversed both conditions. The Guggenheims' El Teniente mine near Santiago became the first in the world to apply the flotation process in concentrating low-grade ores. Far to the north, at Chuquicamata, huge mechanical shovels carved the mountain into the largest open-pit mine in the world. The Guggenheims subjected its ore to a new concentration process utilizing sulfuric acid and electrolytic precipitation which their engineer, E. A. Cappelen Smith, had developed. In 1916 the Anaconda Company joined the Guggenheims in Chile when it purchased copper mines in Potrerillos. A decade later the American companies had expended $170 million in developing their properties and controlled over 90 percent of Chilean copper production. That production had shot up from 41,000 tons in 1912 to over 200,000 tons in 1926, and it could be delivered in New York for 5 cents per pound less than the domestic product. But the Guggenheims did more than alter technology in Chilean mining; they also changed the pattern of social relations that existed in the mines.[32]

As of 1913 Guggenheim-controlled companies maintained a twelve-hour workday and a work place with minimal safety measures. As the brothers later admitted, "there was no official recognition of a social community of interest between the Company and the employee and his family." They also conceded that "these naturally were not the best conditions to promote the harmony and good will so essential to the efficient operation of a large industrial corporation."[33] But on the eve of the Great War,

32 Chile, Ministerio de Hacienda, *Industria salitrera*, p. 57; "Anaconda," Scudder Collection; Herman C. Bellinger to Stokely Morgan, New York, October 3, 1927, rl. 30, M-487, RG 59, USNA; C. Van Engert to secretary of state, Santiago, October 27, 1926, RG 84, USNA; Joanne Fox Przeworski, "The Entrance of North American Capital in the Chilean Copper Industry and the Role of Government, 1904–1916," *Atti del XL Congresso Internazionale degli Americanisti (Rome–Genoa, September 3–10, 1972)* (Genoa: Tilgher, 1973), pp. 397–401; Theodore H. Moran, *Multinational Corporations and the Politics of Dependence: Copper in Chile* (Princeton: Princeton University Press, 1974), pp. 22–23; Reynolds, "The Case of Chile and Copper," p. 221; Herfindahl, *Copper Costs and Prices,* p. 174; Harry F. Bain and Thomas T. Read, *Ores and Industry in South America* (1934) (New York: Arno, 1976), p. 220.
33 "American Smelting and Refining Company," Scudder Collection.

all of this changed. The Guggenheims instituted the eight-hour day along with accident-prevention programs, pensions and other welfare benefits. At the same time Guggenheim managers carried out "a 'job analysis' covering every operation in the plant so that the company might discover and take up any 'slack' existing, and so that each employee could fully understand his function in the operation." In the face of mounting labor unrest, the Guggenheims had moved beyond the rigid managerial culture of the fruteras and Cerro de Pasco and were rapidly adopting the techniques of industrial welfare and labor control of their American operations. They eventually instituted those methods in their Chilean enterprises.[34]

Chuquicamata represented a radical departure from the production methods and work relations which then existed in the Chilean mining and nitrate industries. In contrast to the nitrate industry, where extraction absorbed over half of the labor force, only a quarter of Chuquicamata's workers in 1915 were involved in extraction. And in 1926 only 40 percent of its workforce were considered common laborers. The highly mechanized operations of the American mines required a more skilled and stable workforce than that employed by Chilean-owned mines and the nitrate industry.[35] When American development of El Teniente began, the company induced workers to labor through the harsh winter months by operating a company lottery. With considerable fanfare, the corporation in 1916 created a welfare department at a cost of $2 million. The department was "to provide for housing, healing, educating and amusing a total of some 10,000 souls."[36] In 1923 the mine manager reported that he was able to secure enough workers, despite a general scarcity of labor, "by fair and just treatment of our men, by a steady improvement in their general living conditions, and by the provision of additional educational and social facilities."[37] At Chuquicamata an increasingly stable workforce was being shaped from the experienced miners in the nearby province of Coquimbo. To secure that stable workforce, the Guggenheims offered wages well above those offered in traditional mining ventures or in the nitrate industry, and inducements such as attendance bonuses paid at the end of the year.[38]

The Guggenheims sought to maintain performance levels among the more stable and experienced workforce they had created. The El Teniente mine had a safety-first department which ran classes and competitions, gave out awards, hired safety inspectors and maintained meticulous

34 Ibid.; Louis Hiriart, *Braden: historia de una mina* (Santiago: Editorial Andes, 1964), p. 228; Kruijt and Vellinga, *Labor Relations,* p. 82.
35 "American Smelting and Refining Company," Scudder Collection; George D. Hopper, "Social and Labor Conditions in the Four Great American Mining Camps in the Antofagasta District," Antofagasta, September 24, 1926, RG 84, USNA.
36 *Second Annual Report of the Braden Copper Mines Company* (New York: Author, 1917).
37 *Ninth Annual Report of the Braden Copper Mines Company* (New York: Author, 1924).
38 *Annual Report of the Anaconda Copper Company for the Year 1924* (New York: Author, 1925).

records, all with the purpose of reducing on-site accidents and thereby improving performance. By 1921 the company was reporting a 25 percent reduction in fatal accidents. From the outset, the Guggenheim brothers provided fully functional camps for their workforce, with concrete or adobe housing complete with free sewage and electrical service. A workers' village came equipped with a church, social center and movie houses. To relieve the monotony of grid-pattern streets and assembly-line housing, the companies offered prizes for the most attractive yard. They also provided an array of social organizations, including boy and girl scout troops and sports clubs. Chuquicamata alone boasted thirty-two soccer teams. The camps also had schools for children and offered adult vocational classes. The company store provided goods at cost and handled personnel matters through a welfare department, which sought to promote "proper values" among Chilean workers and their families.[39]

As a part of their welfare and safety programs, the companies provided hospitals, with the one in Chuquicamata manned by a team of five doctors. Hospital facilities served more than workers' immediate health needs; they were part of the Americans' self-conceived civilizing mission. But the benefits of that mission came with certain conditions attached. In return for higher pay, workers had to forgo many of the holidays associated with religious festivals. They found themselves confined to the workers' village, and consumption of alcohol was prohibited. Bootleggers who attempted to smuggle pisco, the local rum, into the camps were shot on sight by the *carabineros,* or federal police. Nor were all of the benefits that American workers received extended immediately to Chilean workers. Despite the creation of a welfare department at El Teniente in 1916, workers there struck in 1919 demanding the eight-hour day and an end to work on Sunday. The government sent in troops and then mediated a compromise which provided for the eight-hour day and overtime. In return the workers agreed that alcohol would remain banned on company property, that they would seek to arbitrate future disputes and that they would provide fifteen days' notice of any strike.[40] In the aftermath of the strike, the company's general manager noted:

In Chile, as all over the world, labor problems are our most serious difficulty. But under the protection of a government ready and firm in support of order and the prevention of violence we are hopeful of minimizing the difficulties by paying good wages, by providing good living conditions, by fair and considerate treatment and by getting the workmen

39 *Seventh Annual Report of the Braden Copper Mines Company* (New York: Author, 1922); *Annual Report, Anaconda, 1924;* Earl Chapin May, *2000 Miles Through Chile, the Land of More or Less* (New York: Century, 1924), p. 354; "American Smelting and Refining Company," Scudder Collection; Hopper, "Social and Labor Conditions in Antofagasta District," RG 84, USNA; Latcham, *Chuquicamata,* pp. 35–36, 147–51; Frank A. Henry, "The Copper Industry in Chile," Valparaíso, June 8, 1932, 825.6352/23, RG 59, USNA.
40 May, *Land of More or Less,* p. 351; Henry, "Copper Industry," 825.6352/23, RG 59, USNA.

themselves to cooperate with the management in the solution of difficulties as they arise in a liberal modern spirit and so preventing them from assuming serious proportions.[41]

In effect, the Guggenheims, with the cooperation of the Chilean state, had established the basis for a comprehensive labor relations system, with material rewards provided in return for a level of corporate control over worker behavior that considerably exceeded that which existed in the national mining sector or the nitrate industry. But despite the Guggenheims' success at institutionalizing labor–management techniques, the workers never fully internalized the corporate value system.

As of the mid 1920s, much of the indigenous culture of Chuquicamata's workers still survived. Workers evaded bans on drinking with heavily spiked punches served on festive occasions. Mythical interpretations of their environment still found expression in the popular legend which held that the mountain of waste created by the mine's operation was inhabited by the spirits of the dead. Resistance aspects of popular culture also remained as workers at El Teniente succeeded in having priests banned from their camp on the grounds that they brought bad luck and extracted tithes from the miners.[42] Despite the enticements which the Guggenheims created in their mining camps in the Chilean Andes, they faced many of the same problems of labor stability which the fruteras encountered on Central America's tropical coast. The copper miners continued to view work as a means of achieving subsistence. They did not share their American bosses' views of work as proof of moral rectitude and a vital step in the betterment of humanity. As one American observed, "Like most Latin American laborers they [Chilean copper miners] will work long enough to keep the wolf from the door but when the immediate future is provided for they much prefer to loaf."[43]

The miners also resisted new and more sophisticated forms of labor discipline by continuing their nomadic ways, forcing the company to continue employing enganchadores for labor recruitment. A report on El Teniente, which was owned by the Braden Copper Company, a Guggenheim subsidiary, noted in 1932:

Partly a result of the proximity of the mine to the agricultural region and to Santiago, and partly a result of the relentless driving policy of Braden coming into contact with the easygoing temperament of the Chilean working man, there is a tremendous turnover among the laborers.[44]

The Guggenheims might have added that their workers deserted El Teniente and Chuquicamata in particularly large numbers around Christmas

---

41 *Fifth Annual Report of the Braden Copper Mines Company* (New York: Author, 1920); Vaughn to Curzon, Santiago, November 14, 1919, Chile 132/198, F.O. PRO; Hiriart, *Braden,* p. 232; Henry, "Copper Industry," 825.6352/23, RG 59, USNA.

42 May, *Land of More or Less,* pp. 356–359; Hiriart, *Braden,* pp. 213–14.

43 Henry, "Copper Industry," 825.6352/23, RG 59, USNA.

44 Ibid.

time. As in an earlier day, the mine workers journeyed to the city of Coquimbo to pay homage to the Virgin of Andacollo. These actions expressed resistance to some of the transformational aspects of American corporate culture and reaffirmed the common beliefs and values shared by workers in the oficinas and mines of northern Chile. That popular culture also found more militant and pragmatic outlets.[45]

Working-class culture that linked nationalism to the defense of the freedom inherent in a nomadic lifestyle and workers' economic interests had already found expression in the labor militancy that characterized the nitrate district. It also formed the basis for workers' responses to the Guggenheims' transformation of the mining industry. In March 1925 nearly all of Chuquicamata's seven thousand workers struck in protest against the company's prohibition of workers' organizational meetings and circulation of labor publications on its property. The workers' manifestos denounced the "Yankee Company" and asserted that the workers' solidarity would show that "no hearts will support the imperialistic domination of North America from fear or a desire for money." They asserted that the only sovereignty in Chile derived from its own people and that "in this country private property cannot limit the fundamental rights of the human person." The American managers, by contrast, knew that tight control over the workforce was an essential part of their modernized operations. Nitrate companies accepted a government commission's proposal to allow labor meetings at their plants. But the managers of American copper companies asserted the rights of private property over those of free speech and assembly. The representative for the Chuquicamata interests denounced the commission's proposal as "a fresh encroachment upon private property . . ."[46] The carabineros quickly broke the strike, but by then the situation in Chile's northern provinces seemed to be spiraling out of control.

After government forces broke the Chuquicamata strike, port workers in Antofagasta boycotted all American shipping, and radical publications denounced the actions of the American company against the strikers. With American corporations rapidly restoring Chile's position in the world copper market, the state remained anxious to uphold its part in the tacit agreement which gave U.S. companies the right to discipline labor. President Arturo Alessandri sent in troops to load the ships and assured the company that he would use the army to smash any further outbursts.[47] But the prospects for social peace in Chile continued to disintegrate.

Chilean society appeared to be on the brink of revolution by 1925. Santiago and Valparaíso witnessed sixty-seven strikes that year, more than in any year since 1919. Not only laborers, but also white-collar employees,

45 Fergusson, *Chile*, pp. 248–55.

46 William M. Collier to secretary of state, Santiago, May 19, 1925; George Neut Latour to Collier, Antofagasta, March 7, 1925; Alfred Houston to Collier, Santiago, May 9, 1925, RG 84, USNA.

47 Collier to secretary of state, Santiago, May 11, 1925, RG 84, USNA.

were organizing and striking. The American ambassador described these events as "the rumblings of a coming revolution . . ."[48] Even more ominously, labor radicalism spread from the salitreras of the northern desert into the comparative calm of the haciendas of the Central Valley. With each new downturn in the nitrate industry, thousands of workers migrated south, threatening to spread the contagion of radicalism among rural peons.[49]

After 1919, unemployed nitrate workers, forced to seek work in the countryside, began organizing job actions on rural estates. Labor organizers from the southern coal mines in Lota and Coronel also began organizing farm laborers. As one ominous report concluded in 1922, "If these agricultural laborers were ever to become like the miners, stevedores and some other laborers, the future of Chile would seem very doubtful."[50] In 1925 the Gibbs office in Valparaíso offered an even gloomier perspective:

Another disquieting feature as far as the future is concerned is the tendency there appears to be in Chile today towards Communistic ideas. The lower middle classes among whom we would embrace a largish proportion of the Chilean employé – are openly allying themselves with the Workmens' [sic] federation. The Workmens' federations all seem to have ultrasocialistic leanings, and are in many cases openly allied with the I.W.W. . . .[51]

That warning reflected the emergence of the first tenuous national coalition between working- and middle-class protest movements.

Early in the century the popular classes of the Central Valley had not shared the ardent nationalism which characterized the nitrate workers' struggle against the British. But that situation had begun to change as the ever more erratic performance of the nation's principal industry contributed to the rising tide of social mobilization in the Central Valley. In particular, popular protest had begun to link foreign capital's role in the economy with the nation's social problems. The coalescing of working- and middle-class interests became apparent in the 1925 presidential election. The election pitted Emiliano Figueroa, supported by the traditional parties, against Dr. José Santos Salas, the candidate of a middle- and working-class coalition. Salas' "national salvation" campaign pressed for social welfare and the nationalization of Chile's natural resources. Although handily defeated by Figueroa, Salas and his nationalist, populist program ran well not only in the northern nitrate districts but in Santiago

---

48 Collier to secretary of state, Santiago, February 16, 1925, rl. 21, M-487, RG 59, USNA; DeShazo, *Urban Workers,* p. 215.

49 Stickell, "Migration and Mining," pp. 84–127.

50 Doyle C. McDonough, "Chilean Labor Movement," Concepción, February 11, 1922, rl. 21, M-487, RG 59, USNA; Brian Loveman, *Struggle in the Countryside: Politics and Rural Labor in Chile, 1919–1973* (Bloomington: Indiana University Press, 1976), pp. 191–92.

51 Letter 393, 1925, File 11,470/26, Gibbs Papers.

as well.[52] The elite could not afford to ignore the intensifying nationalism of the middle and working classes, and to some extent they shared its anti-American focus.

Despite the promotion of American investment, the interests of the elite and U.S. investors diverged at several points. The decline of the nitrate industry and rising social dissent accentuated those differences as the Chilean government sought to protect domestic industries and imposed taxes to support social welfare programs. As these confrontations unfolded, they led to what the U.S. ambassador described in 1926 as a "tide of anti-foreign feeling."[53] Members of the elite and conservative commentators provided an increasingly strident nationalist critique of the American role in Chile. They denounced American culture as materialist and grasping, and laid considerable blame at the door of American capitalism for the mounting social crisis in Chile. In his scathing denunciation of American operations in Chuquicamata, conservative commentator Ricardo Latcham blamed the corporation for the degradation of Chilean workers and the corruption of Chilean political figures. While these nationalist critiques of American capitalism had roots in the oligarchy's historical experiences and in the mounting economic crisis, there was also an effort to play to popular concerns. Members of the elite, identified in popular culture as the Christ-killers, the exploiters of the poor, now sought to indict foreign "Jews" as those responsible for Chile's suffering.[54]

Efforts to appeal to popular animosity toward alien exploiters suffered from two drawbacks. First, the crisis in the national economy forced repeated concessions to American interests. The copper industry now depended entirely on U.S. capital, and U.S. bank loans to the government had shot up from $500,000 in 1917 to $90 million in 1921. In turn, American diplomats and businessmen responded to Chile's nationalist economic policies with warnings about the dire consequences nationalist actions would have on Chilean–American economic relations.[55] As a result, a widening gap emerged between the nationalist rhetoric of Chile's rulers and repeated concessions to foreign capital. In addition, conservative intellectuals who critiqued American capitalists had an equally low opinion of their own population. Ricardo Latcham, while denouncing

52 DeShazo, *Urban Workers*, pp. 232–33; Monteón, *Nitrate Era*, p. 162; Paul W. Drake, *Socialism and Populism in Chile, 1932–52* (Urbana: University of Illinois Press, 1978), pp. 57–58; Philip Joseph Houseman, "Chilean Nationalism, 1920–1952" (Ph.D. dissertation, Stanford University, 1961), p. 114.

53 Collier to secretary of state, Santiago, January 26, 1926, rl. 23, M-487; Munro, "Situation of the American Nitrate Producers," Valparaíso, December 11, 1920, RG 84, USNA.

54 Latcham, *Chuquicamata*, pp. 10–34. Also see newspaper clippings enclosed in Engert to secretary of state, Santiago, October 2, 1926, RG 84, USNA; and William S. Culberston to secretary of state, Santiago, October 13, 1928, rl. 25, M-487, RG 59, USNA.

55 Collier to secretary of state, Santiago, April 30, 1926, rl. 21, M-487; Henry Stinson, "Finances of Chile," memorandum, Division of Latin American Affairs, August 13, 1929, rl. 24, M-487, RG 59, USNA; Leo J. Keena to Shea, Valparaíso, October 26, 1917, RG 84, USNA.

American corporations, also described Chilean workers as unteachable drunks lacking personal initiative, and berated Chilean employees who aped the customs of Americans and sold out to their corporations.[56] An effective attempt to link nationalism with concerns for social justice had to await the election of Carlos Ibáñez.

Ibáñez, one of several young military officers who pressured Congress for reform in 1924, ousted Figueroa in 1927 and oversaw his own election to the presidency. Ibáñez implemented an authoritarian version of the program of economic nationalism and social welfare, which had become an increasingly attractive option for not only the workers of the North but also the middle and working classes of the Central Valley. Ibáñez fashioned a regime designed to confront and control the mobilized social forces that had challenged the old order. He effectively crushed organized labor and the political left, sought to incorporate the working class into a system of state-dominated unions, and initiated an unparalleled set of public works to stimulate the domestic economy. He also designed social welfare programs and created new opportunities in the state bureaucracy for the middle class. The president welded these disparate policies together with an ardent nationalism.[57]

In 1931 an American diplomat concluded that "Chile has been and is, the most intensely nationalistic nation in either of the Americas . . ." That opinion referred to Ibáñez's efforts to place himself at the head of a popular nationalist coalition. Ibáñez in his campaign for president had billed himself as the candidate "of all groups incarnating nationalistic ideals." The coalition which had supported Salas backed Ibáñez, denouncing the traditional political parties as "puppets of North American capital."[58] Under Ibáñez the state initiated a range of protective laws aimed at encouraging domestic development of such industries as insurance, coal, shipping and nitrates. In 1927 alone, the American copper companies found their income tax rates doubled to 12 percent, American insurance companies faced the prospect of having to reincorporate as Chilean entities, and Ibáñez threatened U.S. copper companies with an import duty on fuel.[59]

---

56 Latcham, *Chuquicamata*, pp. 34–36; Wilhelm Mann, *Chile luchando por nuevas formas de vida*, 2 vols. (Santiago: Editorial Ercilla, 1935–36), 1, pp. 48–49. Chile's premier racist scholar, Francisco A. Encina, described the country's economic dilemma as stemming largely from the racial inferiority of its people. See his *Nuestra inferioridad económica: sus causas, sus consecuencias* (Santiago: Editorial Universitaria, 1912).

57 Charles A. Thomson, "Chile Struggles for National Recovery," *Foreign Policy Reports* 9 (February 14, 1934), pp. 289–90; DeShazo, *Urban Workers*, pp. 241–42.

58 Collier to secretary of state, Santiago, May 21, 1927, RG 84, USNA; Houseman, "Chilean Nationalism," pp. 117–18.

59 Gabriel Palma, "From an Export-Led to an Import-Substituting Economy: Chile 1914–39," in Rosemary Thorp, ed., Latin *America in the 1930s: The Role of the Periphery in World Crisis* (New York: St. Martin's, 1984), pp. 56–57; H. C. Bellinger to Stokely W. Morgan, New York, December 2, 1927; John K. MacGowen to secretary of state, New York, October 31, 1927; Culbertson to secretary of state, Santiago, October 13, 1928; Culbertson to Francis White, Santiago, November 10, 1928, RG 84, USNA.

Despite the strident nationalism that seemed to characterize his regime, Ibáñez, like his predecessors, found himself becoming increasingly dependent on American capital and corporations. The Chilean president not only had to grapple with the declining portion of state expenditures covered by nitrate revenues, he also had to fund his massive public works efforts. American loans to the government shot up from $170 million in 1927 to $275 million in 1930. Reflecting the growing importance of American financial institutions to the government, the National City Bank became the state's exclusive financial agent in 1927. That increasing dependence on American financial institutions forced Ibáñez to make tactical retreats in his dealings with American corporations. The Ibáñez administration amended the insurance bill to the advantage of American companies, and in return for minimal concessions from the Guggenheims it granted exemptions from the fuel tax to American copper companies. Ibáñez's retreat from strident economic nationalism became particularly apparent in his dealings with G. E.'s subsidiary, the American and Foreign Power Company, or AFP.[60]

At the end of 1928 AFP acquired a series of British-owned electric companies for $190 million and negotiated a new concession for them with a government commission. Ibáñez initially approved the agreement reached in 1930. But he quickly altered his course in the face of stormy public protests over a concession that granted AFP a virtual perpetual tax-free monopoly on electrical generation. In response, the company warned Ibáñez that Chile would face reprisals by American bankers should the concession be radically altered. Since the National City Bank served not only as the financial agent for the government but also as a major backer of G. E. and AFP, the Chilean president could not take the threat lightly. Ibáñez eventually accepted a revised version that still put the company well on the road to establishing a monopoly in the field of electrical power generation. The agreement remained a subject of deep-seated popular discontent over what was viewed as a surrender of national sovereignty.[61]

As intense as the public protest over the AFP agreement was, it paled in comparison to the uproar produced when Ibáñez entered into a joint venture with the Guggenheims to control the nitrate industry. Ibáñez's political survival came to depend on that enterprise, which in turn became the central theme in Chile's national political discourse and would remain a pivotal issue for nearly a decade. In their efforts to radically reform the nitrate industry, the Guggenheims became the central target of popular nationalist protest. The fates of the Guggenheims and Ibáñez became inextricably intertwined with that of the nitrate industry. The first

---

60 Culbertson to secretary of state, Santiago, August 26, 1929, RG 84, USNA.
61 Culbertson to Hoover, Santiago, October 3, 1930, RG 84, USNA; "Acquisitions, Chile, Mexico, Costa Rica, Guatemala," New York, December 31, 1942, Box 143981, EBASCO; Stinson, "Utilities in Latin-America, Power Companies, Diplomatic Policy of the United States," Division of Latin American Affairs, February 11, 1931, 810.6463 Electric Bond & Share Co./4, RG 59, USNA.

signs of trouble had appeared in 1919 when prices and production of Chilean nitrate plummeted in the postwar recession. In response, refiners formed the Nitrate Producers Association, which temporarily restored prosperity to the industry with its price-fixing agreements. But by the mid 1920s by-product and synthetic nitrogen had seriously eaten into Chile's foreign markets. Nitrate producers in Chile experienced an increasingly serious set of cyclical setbacks with grave consequences for the industry and the nation. While the industry had supplied 74 percent of the world's nitrate in 1894, it controlled only 35 percent of the market by 1924. Employment levels in the industry took ever more erratic swings. The 57,000 workers employed in 1918 fell to 25,000 in 1920. Employment reached 61,000 in 1925 and then dropped by 25,000 over the next two years. The industry, which supplied the state with 60 percent of its ordinary revenues in 1916, could provide only 26 percent by 1927. That collapse was rooted in more than world market conditions.[62]

Every observer of the nitrate industry concluded that it had an incredibly inefficient, labor-intensive production system, but one with such low wages that innovation was discouraged. An American study, noting the low labor costs of the industry, concluded that "so long as enough labor can be found to work according to the present methods, it will only be in exceptional places that money can be saved by introducing machinery."[63] As a result of cheap but undisciplined labor, the industry made little effort in the way of technical innovation. The process of estimating the potential of new nitrate lands remained a matter of experience and guesswork. Only occasional experiments with compressed air drills and other devices occurred. A study in 1922 concluded, "As a whole there has been less advancement and improvement in the natural nitrate industry than in any other technical–chemical process followed on a large scale."[64] The logic of the social relations which had developed on the desert pampa discouraged refining companies from hiring chemists, engineers and technicians to develop new machinery and processes and assume managerial positions. Instead the companies drew management candidates from exper-

---

62 Stocking and Watkins, *Cartels in Action,* pp. 123–41; Hopper, "Labor Perspective," Antofagesta, March 3, 1926, RG 84, USNA; Thomson, "National Recovery," p. 288; Stickell, "Migration and Mining," p. 340; Chile, Ministerio de Hacienda, *Industria salitrera,* p. 21; "Report on Compania de Salitre de Chile," prepared by Division of Latin American Affairs, September 16, 1932 (cited hereafter as "Cosach Report"), pp. 14–15, 825.6374/1054, RG 59, USNA.

63 "Report on the Chilean Nitrate Industry," Chile 198/132, F. O., PRO; H. Foster Bain and H. S. Muliken, *Nitrogen Survey, Part 1: The Cost of Chilean Nitrate,* Bureau of Foreign and Domestic Commerce, Trade Information Bulletin No. 170 (Washington, D.C.: Government Printing Office, 1923), p. 13; Bertrand, *Nitrate Industry Technology,* p. 55.

64 Homer Brett, "Nitrate Industry of Tarapaca Province," Iquique, January 11, 1922, RG 84, USNA; BFDC File #235 Chile Santiago, R. H. Squirrell to Ralph Ackerman, Santiago, August 7, 1923, File 235, Chile, RG 151, USNA; Harry Campbell to secretary of state, Iquique, September 16, 1925, rl. 34, M-487, RG 59, USNA; Bertrand, *Nitrate Industry Technology,* pp. 76–78; Fernández, "Enclave salitrero," pp. 31–34; Bain and Muliken, *Nitrogen Survey,* p. 19.

ienced timekeepers and supervisors who knew how to deal with recalcitrant peons. In selecting a manager for one of their oficinas in 1907, a Gibbs partner noted of the candidate that "Brooke Comber is very good at managing men which was always more than half the battle and nowadays must be even more important."[65]

Much as Chilean hacendados had once added land and labor, nitrate producers responded to the growing demand for their product by adding oficinas and workers, and with an increasingly complex division of labor. In 1894 Chile had 51 oficinas operating with 18,092 workers. In 1917 those figures had risen to 129 refineries and 56,981 laborers. Refiners carefully subdivided tasks within the production process. They initiated more intense supervision of the work process as the ratio of supervisory personnel to production workers increased from 3.4 per 100 in 1921 to 11 per 100 in 1929.[66] The inability of nitrate producers to respond to the competitive challenges they now faced lay rooted in the past. The integration of British industrialists into local social relationships had left them with a low-cost but independent workforce and a labor-intensive industry. Innovation would threaten the compromise between British capital and Chilean labor and the profitable commercial and financial relationship which the Chilean elite enjoyed with the industry. As early as World War I the Guggenheims proposed precisely such radical changes for the nitrate industry.

In 1916 Daniel Guggenheim met with Dwight Morrow, a senior partner in J. P. Morgan and Company, and suggested that their firms join forces to reorganize the Chilean nitrate industry "into a modern, up-to-date, American industry, capable of yielding a greatly increased profit upon a greatly increased capitalization."[67] Guggenheim suggested that they buy up most of the European- and Chilean-owned nitrate refineries, the British nitrate railways, and the Chilean government's unused nitrate grounds as well as its longitudinal railway. If possible, Daniel Guggenheim wanted to involve the Chilean government directly in the enterprise. The Morgan partners found the proposition sufficiently attractive to join the Guggenheims in forming the Panyon Corporation to explore every aspect of the venture, from its technical to its financial feasibility. The Guggenheims' immediate motivation for exploring a massive plunge into the nitrate industry – wartime disruptions that dramatically reduced prices for nitrate properties – soon disappeared as the industry rebounded to feed a war-driven munitions industry. But the increasing challenge from by-product and synthetic nitrate seemed to make the original pro-

---

65 Cokayne to Robertson, London, January 18, 1907, File 11,115/1, Gibbs Papers; Bertrand, *Nitrate Industry Technology*, p. 76.
66 Chile, Ministerio de Hacienda, *Industria salitrera*, p. 57; Stickell, "Migration and Mining," p. 246; Bain and Muliken, *Nitrogen Survey*, p. 14.
67 Daniel Guggenheim to Dwight W. Morrow, New York, January 11, 1916, File 6, Box 87, Lamont Papers.

posal all the more attractive. In 1919 the Guggenheims and J. P. Morgan and Company formed another venture, this one intended to develop a new process for refining natural nitrate. The remaining question was how to penetrate the industry itself. Despite several years of studying the industry, it still remained alien territory to the Guggenheims. They first attempted to achieve that entree through the Gibbs house, the leading British firm in nitrates.[68]

Early in 1919 Guggenheim representatives asked the Gibbs partners to prepare a thorough report on the nitrate industry, supposedly to determine if the industry's competitive problems would prompt the Chilean government to impose new taxes on copper mines. Although doubting the Guggenheims' assertions that they had no direct interest in nitrates, the Gibbs partners prepared the report as a way of probing the Guggenheims' true intentions. Not much probing was necessary. By June the Guggenheims had proposed a joint venture with Gibbs which would close all the Shanks plants and concentrate output at a few refineries using a new process. Other than that significant alteration, the scheme still called for buying up virtually the entire industry and enlisting the support and participation of the Chilean government. After much discussion, the Gibbs partners rejected the proposal. The core of the Gibbs arguments against the venture centered on its potential for rending the delicate web of relationships through which the nitrate industry operated. They noted that a trust would antagonize the Chilean directors of refineries, who made handsome profits supplying them with goods; the agents of British companies, who did the same; and a host of Chilean brokers and merchants who speculated in nitrate sales and profited from selling coal, barley and a range of other products in the region. Most importantly, it was "inconceivable that a Government would or could hand over the interest of the whole working population of a district to anything in the nature of a Trust . . ."[69] The Gibbs partners had accurately foreseen the intense opposition to the scheme that would erupt in Chile.

Daniel Guggenheim remained undeterred by the Gibbs refusal, no doubt still convinced, as he had once told Dwight Morrow, that "the [Chilean] people would favor assisting in some great undertaking which would improve their condition."[70] The Guggenheims' leading engineer, E. A. Cappelen Smith, devoted his attention to designing a new nitrate production system. By 1923 he had settled on a refining process, using refrigeration, that permitted treatment of the material in large lots. The refining method, when linked with mass extraction techniques, could treat ore with an assay of 8 percent (compared with the Shanks minimum of 15

68 Syndicate Book #10, Morgan Papers.

69 Letter 180, 1919; Letter 278, 1919, File 11,114/4; Herbert Gibbs to E. C. Grenfell, London, July 24, November 18, 26, 1919, File 11,041/3, Gibbs Papers.

70 Daniel Guggenheim to Dwight W. Morrow, New York, January 11, 1916, File 6, Box 87, Lamont Papers.

percent) and reduced production costs by 20 to 25 percent. Given those favorable prospects, Daniel Guggenheim soon exulted that "nitrates will make us rich beyond the dreams of avarice!"[71]

In 1923 the Guggenheims sold the bulk of their holdings in the Chile Copper Company, which controlled Chuquicamata, to the Anaconda Company for $70 million. That sale provided capital for the brothers' bid on a thirty-five-square-mile tract of government nitrate land known as Coya Norte. At this point the Morgan partners, still smarting from a well-publicized anti-trust investigation, withdrew from the nitrate venture because of its possible violation of anti-trust laws. Despite the departure of the Morgan interests, the Guggenheims remained convinced of the scheme's viability because of its cost-reduction potential and the relatively high price for nitrate which prevailed at that time. Even when the Producers Association decontrolled prices in 1927, the Guggenheim system still promised to compete effectively with sulfate of ammonia and synthetic nitrogen. Furthermore, the Guggenheims hardly expected to operate in a free market environment over the long term. With Chile, Germany and England controlling 88 percent of the world's nitrogen output, the prospects for an international cartel seemed excellent. Decreased production costs in both Chile and Europe would enable such a cartel to lower world nitrogen prices and still enjoy impressive profits. With these favorable conditions, the Guggenheims proceeded with their plunge into nitrates.[72]

In 1924 the brothers began construction on the Coya Norte tract of a refinery called María Elena that incorporated the new technology. The following year they purchased the Anglo-Chilean Nitrate and Railway Company, adding three refineries, a railroad and port facilities to their holdings. Finally, in June 1929, they acquired the Lautaro Nitrate Company, the most important nitrate producer in Chile. As was the case in copper mining, the Guggenheim enterprise involved not only the introduction of new technology but an attempt to reshape the workforce that manned the new machinery.

Workers at the Guggenheims' nitrate plants received wages that were 20 percent higher than those offered at the old refineries. The Guggenheims replaced the dirt-floored shacks of corrugated iron that once passed for worker housing on the nitrate pampa with wood-floored concrete houses. As in the copper mining camps, these houses included free water and electrical facilities. The company towns came complete with schools, athletic fields and central plazas graced by trees and flowers. The corporation also created social organizations such as Boy Scout troops. Once again

71 "Cosach Report," pp. 27–28, 825.6374/1054, RG 59, USNA; Hoyt, *The Guggenheims*, p. 261.

72 Vincent P. Carosso, *The Morgans: Private International Bankers, 1854–1913* (Cambridge: Harvard University Press, 1987), pp. 627–40; Vanderlip to James Stillman, New York, September 27, 1913, B-1-5, Vanderlip Papers; Syndicate Book #10, Morgan Papers; O'Brien, "Rich Beyond the Dreams of Avarice," pp. 143–46.

Figure 12. A steam shovel loading caliche at the Guggenheims' María Elena
facility. (From Asociacíon de Productores de Salitre de Chile, *Album . . . del
centenario* [1930])

the Guggenheims were attempting to mold the more stable, more disciplined workforce required by a highly mechanized production system.[73]
This herculean effort to revamp the production system and the workforce
was made possible by the Guggenheims' considerable financial power.

New York financial institutions played a pivotal role in the Guggenheims' rapid acquisition and transformation of the nitrate industry. Leading New York institutions such as Lehman Brothers and the National
City Bank raised nearly $130 million to finance the Guggenheims' initial
nitrate ventures. While this sum demonstrated the Guggenheims' financial clout, it also raised troubling questions about their scheme. The need
for outside financing derived in large measure from Cappelen Smith's discovery that he had to double the size of the María Elena plant to achieve
the level of efficiency which he had forecast. In turn he had to purchase
additional nitrate land to feed the giant refinery. As the costs of implementing the project rose, conditions on the world market worsened.[74]

The potential profitability of nitrogen which had prompted the
Guggenheim plunge into nitrates also encouraged producers in Europe to
expand their plant capacities. The so-called nitrogen rush between 1922

73 P. F. Kruger to Cordell Hull, Oficina María Elena, January 17, 1934, 825.6374/1222, RG 59,
    USNA.
74 O'Brien, "Rich Beyond the Dreams of Avarice," pp. 146–47.

Figure 13. The new Guggenheim-process refinery at the Oficina María Elena.
(From Asociacíon de Productores de Salitre de Chile, *Album . . . del centenario*
[1930])

and 1931 tripled world production capacity and sent nitrate prices plum-
meting after 1927. By 1930 Guggenheim nitrate could just barely undersell its leading competitor, sulfate of ammonia. Elimination of the $11.19-
per-ton duty became a pressing necessity. But cooperation from the
Chilean state did not come easily. Much like copper, nitrates became a
marriage of convenience between American and Chilean interests. For the
Guggenheims, a partnership with the government would thrust aside resistance by British and Chilean producers and middlemen to the long-
dreamed-of monopoly. More importantly, it would lead to abolition of the
export duty, now considered essential for the profitability of the Guggenheim nitrate enterprise. For the Chilean government, the venture held out
the promise of economic survival. By 1930 the price of nitrate had hit a
thirty-year low, employment levels had shrunk to 36,000 and the industry
could supply only 15 percent of the government's revenues. The Guggenheim scheme held out the hope that the industry could eventually return
to a competitive level. More immediately, the mere prospect of the
arrangement assisted the Chilean government in negotiating a price agreement with synthetic and by-product producers in Europe during 1929.[75]

This convergence of interests led to the formation of Cosach (Compañía
de Salitre de Chile) in March 1931. Each side owned 50 percent of the

75 Ibid., pp. 134, 144–49.

Figure 14. A Boy Scout Troop at the Oficina María Elena symbolized the efforts of
the Guggenheims to extend their industrial welfare programs into the nitrate
industry. (From Asociacíon de Productores de Salitre de Chile, *Album . . . del
centenario* [1930])

stock, but only four Chilean officials sat on the company's twelve-member
board, giving the Guggenheims effective control. In return for elimination of the nitrate duty, the Guggenheims committed themselves to cash
payments to the government totaling $80 million through 1933. After
that time, the Chilean treasury would receive 50 percent of the company's
profits. Cosach paid out $375 million in stock to the government for its
nitrate land and to private producers for their refineries. British interests
received $87 million, and the Guggenheims $92 million. The Guggenheims opted for common stock, which gave them higher risk but greater
control. The British settled for preference shares and bonds with a guaranteed return but little power. Heading a revamped and consolidated industry, the Guggenheims would be in a strong position to bargain with synthetic producers on questions of markets and prices. The announcement of
Cosach's formation in May 1930 visibly strengthened the hand of the
Chilean government, which was negotiating a cartel agreement with European producers. In August the International Nitrogen Cartel was
formed, renewing hopes of stable prices.[76]

76 Walter Edge to secretary of state, Paris, June 17, 1930; Damon G. Woods, "Features of the Euro-
     pean Cartel," Paris, September 23, 1930, RG 84 (Santiago), USNA; "Cosach Report," p. 18,
     825.6374/1054, RG 59, USNA.

Cosach remained, however, a corporation without working capital. The $375 million stock issue was based on grossly exaggerated valuations of land and refineries. Cosach had only one new refinery. The Guggenheims needed money to complete a second, build a third and cover operating expenses. In 1931 Cosach's scheduled payments on interest-bearing obligations and cash payments to the government totaled $34 million. The company expected to pay those sums by generating $38 million in net revenues. With prices and consumption collapsing, actual sales in 1931 produced only $14.5 million. The Guggenheims also expected to raise $110 million in bond flotations for working capital. The Great Depression gave the lie to that assumption as well. The Guggenheims could raise only $34 million in 1931. In July of that year the International Nitrogen Cartel collapsed in bitter disputes ignited by the depression. Cosach and the Ibáñez regime now teetered on the brink of collapse.[77]

With the disintegration of the market for nitrate and copper exports in 1930, the Ibáñez government struggled on with receipts from foreign loans. When those resources dried up in the early months of 1931, the regime's problems became insurmountable. By June the government could no longer meet its foreign debt payments. Unemployment, which had soared in the mining sector, now affected much of the Central Valley. Despite legislation requiring workforces be at least 85 percent Chilean, the middle class found itself largely excluded from the top management and technical positions in American corporations. In May the state cut the salaries of public employees, and in July it halted all public works projects. These actions triggered discontent, particularly among the middle class. Public demonstrations against Ibáñez by students and professionals erupted on the streets of the capital during the month of July. Their protests quickly found an echo in the nitrate region.[78]

Labor leaders in the northern city of Antofagasta called for a mass meeting on July 23 to express sympathy with the demonstrations in Santiago and discuss the possibility of a general strike. Government troops turned out in force that day to disperse the demonstrators. News of Ibáñez's resignation on July 26 was received "with wild enthusiasm." The next day most of the residents of Antofagasta turned out to celebrate, carrying with them signs that bore slogans such as "Chile for Sale – See Ibáñez." Labor leaders addressed the assembled crowd, denouncing Cosach and assailing Ibáñez as a tool of U.S. imperialism and a suppressor of free speech.[79] Protests also erupted farther north in Iquique. Thousands of the people who had been standing in bread lines since the creation of Cosach

77 Raul Simon, "Economic and Financial Condition of Chile," May 1932, enclosed in Culbertson to secretary of state, Santiago, June 6, 1932, RG 84, USNA.
78 Thomas D. Bowman, "The Economic Crisis in Chile in 1931," Santiago, February 27, 1932, 825.50/23, RG 59, USNA; Drake, *Socialism and Populism,* pp. 61–64; Frederick M. Nunn, *Chilean Politics, 1920–1931* (Albuquerque: University of New Mexico Press, 1970), pp. 161–63; Mann, *Nuevas formas de vida,* I, pp. 54–55.
79 Culbertson to secretary of state, Santiago, December 19, 1930, RG 84, USNA.

turned out to demonstrate in Iquique. Not surprisingly, the crowds responded most enthusiastically to those speeches that heaped verbal abuse on Cosach, for in the nitrate region "the term [Cosach] has become a synonym for poverty and misery." The popular chant "Down with the gringos" had been replaced by "Down with the Yankees!"[80]

Popular protests against Ibáñez centered on a regime which had increasingly abandoned its own nationalistic stance in the face of economic necessities and which by 1931 could no longer ward off acute economic decline. Cosach became the symbol of that popular protest. As the U.S. ambassador noted, "A list of the enemies of Cosach parallels to a large extent the list of Ibáñez enemies."[81] That convergence stemmed in part from the direct impact of Cosach on a variety of interests. In entering the joint venture with the Guggenheims, Ibáñez and his advisors convinced themselves that the drastic reduction in the nitrate labor force could be alleviated by keeping a few Shanks plants open and absorbing the rest of the workers into the agricultural sector. They also believed that the disruption of commercial and financial ties would result in only temporary dislocations. They underestimated the gravity of the problem and the impact of the Great Depression.[82]

The most obvious effect of Cosach's creation was among the industry's workforce. The new enterprise offered the same material rewards in return for labor discipline employed by the American copper companies, but that could hardly compensate for the radical decline in employment levels. Where thirty-two oficinas had operated in 1930 with 52,000 workers, there remained in 1931 six refineries with 20,000 laborers. The latter figure was maintained only by government insistence that a few Shanks plants remain open to avoid a total collapse of employment. Guggenheim managers, however, were pressing for further reductions, and by 1932 the nitrate workforce would fall to 8,500. The initial refinery closings sent a wave of 120,000 destitute workers and their families sweeping southward into Valparaíso and Santiago.[83]

Workers were not the only group to suffer from the creation of Cosach. Although the Nitrate Producers Association had tried to centralize the purchase of supplies and the sale of nitrate, Chilean middlemen had continued to enjoy a flourishing trade in both areas. Cosach completely centralized these activities, leaving the alienated middlemen carrying on an active propaganda campaign for the abolition of Cosach. Centralizing ni-

80 Edward B. Ranc to Culbertson, Antofagasta, July 30, 1931, RG 84, USNA.
81 S. L. Wilkinson to Culbertson, Iquique, July 30, 1931, RG 84, USNA.
82 Carlos Sáez Morales, *Recuerdos de un soldado: el ejercito y la política,* 3 vols. (Santiago: Ercilla, 1933), 2, pp. 109–10.
83 Report enclosed in R. Henry Norweb to secretary of state, Santiago, November 13, 1931, RG 84, USNA; Thomson, "National Recovery," p. 290; H. H. Graham, "Memorandum: Lautaro Operations Report, December 1931," Antofagasta, January 19, 1932, CNP; Stickell, "Migration and Mining," p. 340.

trate exports out of one port, Tocopilla, devastated the economies of other northern cities such as Iquique and Antofagasta. The nitrate region also depended on shipments from the Central Valley for 85 percent of its agricultural products. The dramatic reduction in the workforce severely disrupted what had been a secure domestic market for landowners and the merchants who shipped their products.[84] It can reasonably be argued that the loss of employment and markets in 1931 was inevitable given the industry's continuing decline. But Cosach brought an abrupt, dramatic and permanent diminution in both areas. Furthermore, the state had handed over the industry to a single foreign corporation with promises of resuscitating the industry which could not be fulfilled. Those aspects of the problem considerably expanded the groups who opposed Cosach.

For the Chilean middle and working classes of the Central Valley, Cosach became directly associated with the ideological and economic bankruptcy of the Ibáñez regime. That ardent nationalist had permitted American companies to take total control of the nation's most important industries and had allowed the state to become dependent on foreign banks. Yet that sale of sovereignty did nothing to stem the collapse of the state's revenues. Unable to meet its payments to foreign bondholders, Cosach further complicated the nation's international financial standing. While disrupting longstanding links to the domestic economy, it failed to halt the decay of the state's finances. That decay in turn spelled the end of public works projects and the expansion of the government's payroll. Opposition to Cosach became the basis for popular protests against the more general phenomenon of foreign exploitation of national resources. For the middle and working classes, Cosach was linked directly and indirectly with the crises that confronted and threatened them in 1931: loss of national sovereignty, international bankruptcy and internal economic collapse. Anti-imperialism and demands for social justice now became legitimated and mutually reinforcing elements of populist political protest. The dissolution of Cosach became *the* principal issue in national political discourse and the litmus test of political correctness.[85]

The presidential election that followed the collapse of the Ibáñez regime pitted Juan Esteban Montero, a Radical who had served in the Ibáñez cabinet, against Arturo Alessandri. Alessandri made Cosach his key campaign issue, denouncing it as a plot for "delivering Chile's sovereignty and economy . . . into the hands of a group of wealthy foreigners." Alessandri echoed the language of two congressional committees which had investigated Cosach, describing how the vigorous Chilean peons who once created wealth for Chile in the nitrate deserts now roamed the streets

---

84 "Cosach Report," pp. 46–47, 825.6374/1054, RG 59, USNA; Cariola and Sunkel, "Growth of the Nitrate Industry," pp. 177, 212; Thomson, "National Recovery," p. 290.
85 Sáez Morales, *Recuerdos*, 3, p. 74; Culbertson to secretary of state, Santiago, November 15, 1931, RG 84, USNA.

of the capital begging for alms. The Communists used the opportunity to resume overt organizing by presenting Elías Lafertte, a former nitrate worker, as their candidate. Among his principal issues was the dissolution of Cosach.[86] Montero handily defeated his rivals but quickly came under heavy criticism for not abolishing Cosach. With the control mechanisms of the Ibáñez regime in shambles, workers in the capital now gave overt expression to the common concerns and symbols that now linked them to the workers in the North.

On January 11, 1932, Chileans from both the working- and middle-class sectors, including shoemakers, empleados, typographers and construction, bakery and railroad workers, staged a general strike. The workers deplored the suffering of the Chilean people, which they said was due less to the world economic crisis than to the failure of the government to seek solutions that went beyond the interests of a bankrupt bourgeoisie. They denounced Chilean regimes that had given generous concessions to international capitalism and then engaged in bloody repression of workers in the North. Their first demand was for the dissolution of Cosach and the nationalization and socialization of the nitrate industry.[87]

As protests by the middle and working classes mounted, Montero received advice from the head of the air force, Marmaduke Grove, one of the young military officers who had demanded reform in 1924. Grove urged Montero to abolish Cosach. A group of conspirators who would constitute the core of the soon-to-be-created Socialist party won Grove to their cause, and on June 4 a joint civil and military coup ousted Montero and created the Socialist Republic. The new regime issued a scathing denunciation of the Chilean oligarchy which expressed the growing popular animosity toward the elite, its exclusivist concept of the nation and its long-standing alliance with foreign investors. The Socialist Republic's program denounced the elite for being "intoxicated" by luxuries provided by foreign capitalists, for which the oligarchy had exchanged the nation's national resources and permitted the exploitation of its people. Because of that experience, the elite had no respect for things Chilean. It was a powerful message which would continue to resonate through Chilean politics in the decades to come.[88]

As a step toward relieving the national crisis created by the elite's alliance with foreign investors, the Socialist Republic proposed the immediate liquidation of Cosach. However, international bankers, along with the governments of the United States and Britain, threatened a financial

---

86 Sáez Morales, *Recuerdos,* 3, p. 73; Houseman, "Chilean Nationalism," p. 135; Drake, *Socialism and Populism,* p. 67.

87 *El Mercurio* (Santiago), January 12, 1932; Ralph H. Wooten, Capt. Military Intelligence, "Report: Chile. Social, Political," Santiago, January 20, 1932, 825.5045/55, RG 59, USNA.

88 Sáez Morales, *Recuerdos,* 3, p. 71; Jack Ray Thomas, "The Socialist Republic of Chile," *Journal of Inter-American Studies* 6 (April 1964), pp. 204–8; *La Opinión* (Santiago), June 6, 1932, enclosed in 825.00 Revolutions/98, RG 59, USNA.

blockade if such action were taken. When the army ousted the Socialist Republic on June 16, plans for eliminating Cosach remained unfulfilled, but the popular outcry for dissolution could not be stilled.[89] Out of the confusing array of political events and alignments that marked this period, there emerged a more broadly defined nationalism focused on social justice, which became the dominant theme in the national political discourse. While groups across the political spectrum espoused this idea, it was most forcefully enunciated by the emerging Socialist party.

The party was an amalgam of working- and middle-class elements held together by "fragile common political beliefs, rallying symbols . . ."[90] Socialism stood for state intervention to achieve social justice and an inclusivist nationalism with strong overtones of anti-imperialism. These themes had both national and international inspiration. Concepts that linked anti-imperialism and social justice had deep Chilean roots in the cultures of rural peons and copper and nitrate workers. Like the Peruvian Apristas, Chilean Socialists drew an analogy between the exploitation of weak countries by financially powerful nations and the exploitation of workers by capitalists. Applying those concepts to their nation's immediate problems, the Socialists called for the dissolution of Cosach.[91]

The Socialists' linking of anti-imperialism and justice found numerous echoes in the tumultuous political discourse which followed the fall of Ibáñez. The leftist newspaper *El Sol* took the Socialist analogy of economic imperialism and worker exploitation a step further, focusing on the transformational and therefore intrusive quality of American capitalism. It asserted "that Yankee capitalism is the most dangerous of them all; because . . . it is a political and oppressive capitalism which always dreams of the commercial and material conquest of peoples." In explaining this point, the editorial contrasted American capitalists with British investors, who were content to collect returns on their capital and not intrude in a nation's domestic affairs. Americans on the other hand sought "to exploit, to conquer and to enslave."[92] The dominance of those themes became fully apparent in the 1932 election. With the Socialist party still in formation and its candidate, Marmaduke Grove, in prison, the Socialists managed to finish second in the balloting with a campaign heavily laced with the rhetoric of anti-imperialism. The Socialists were outdone only by Arturo Alessandri, who made the abolition of Cosach the central theme in his campaign.[93]

89 Drake, *Socialism and Populism*, p. 77.
90 Ibid., p. 155.
91 Drake, *Socialism and Populism*, pp. 147–49; Julio César Jobet, *El partido socialista de Chile*, 2 vols. (Santiago: Editorial Prensa Latinoamérica, 1971), I, pp. 69–74; Mann, *Nuevas formas de vida*, I, p. 48.
92 *El Sol* (Santiago), August 10, 1931, enclosed in Culbertson to secretary of state, Santiago, August 14, 1931, RG 84, USNA.
93 Houseman, "Chilean Nationalism," p. 157; Drake, *Socialism and Populism*, pp. 93–97.

As soon as Alessandri had taken office, his finance minister, Gustavo Ross, announced the dissolution of Cosach. Ross' plan called for the formation of a sales monopoly controlled jointly by the government and the Guggenheims. Production would fall into the hands of the Guggenheim companies, and the unsecured stocks and bonds in Cosach's debt structure would be absorbed by their owners. The plan prompted intense protests by the United States, England, Germany and the Netherlands over what was viewed as a repudiation of international debt. In an interview with the American ambassador, Alessandri "repeated on several occasions that to flatly rescind the action taken by Mr. Ross would mean the overthrow of his Government."[94] While foreign governments and investors placed intense pressure on Alessandri, they also appreciated his position. The American ambassador noted, "It is only by visualizing the internal political difficulties of the Government that one can understand why it has chosen the alternative of defying four foreign states."[95]

In 1934 the Chilean Congress approved a slightly modified version of the Ross plan. Implementation of the plan helped stem some of the most vociferous popular protests in Chilean history. As one American diplomat noted in April of that year, "The policy of transferring the industry from private hands to the Government still goes on but the process is increasingly painless and we are no longer conscious of Chilean mobs howling for the blood of American industrialists."[96] The Ross scheme, however, did not meet the standards of nationalism of the Socialist and other parties. For these groups, the Ross plan had buried not only Cosach but any hope of nationalizing the nitrate industry. They roundly criticized it for leaving much of the industry in foreign hands and applying government revenues from the industry to the foreign debt instead of to domestic problems. Ross incurred additional animosity when he reached an agreement with AFP in 1935.[97]

Although AFP had managed to secure a highly favorable concession from Carlos Ibáñez in the face of popular protest, the company's problems did not end there. Soon after the demise of the Ibáñez regime, workers at the AFP subsidiary in Santiago publicly denounced the company. They chided the company's officials for presenting themselves as the messengers of Western culture and civilization while denying their workers even the most basic of hygiene.[98] By 1933 attacks on the company had broadened as consumers, and particularly small businesses, chafed under the burden of high electricity rates. Denunciations of the company became common

94 Culbertson to secretary of state, Santiago, March 25, 1933, 825.6374/1132, RG 59, USNA.
95 Culbertson to secretary of state, Santiago, April 5, 1933, 825.6374/1138, RG 59, USNA.
96 Hal Sevier to secretary of state, April 10, 1934, 825.6374/1229, RG 59, USNA.
97 Sáez Morales, *Recuerdos*, 3, p. 77; Drake, *Socialism and Populism*, p. 166; Houseman, "Chilean Nationalism," pp. 173–76; Major John A. Weeks, "Chile Economic," Santiago, December 27, 1933, 825.6374/1216, RG 59, USNA.
98 Culbertson to secretary of state, Santiago, September 4, 1931, 825.5041/4, RG 59, USNA.

in the Chilean Congress, with one deputy referring to the company as "this tentacle of the Yankee octopus" which drained the few remaining resources of the country's humbler classes in order to slake "the insatiable thirst of North American imperialism."[99] Much like Cosach, AFP had become a popular symbol of exploitation by American capitalists, and Gustavo Ross was not insensitive to the implications of that discontent.

In July 1935 Gustavo Ross ordered a government investigation of AFP's foreign exchange operations. The company had in fact gone outside official channels to purchase foreign exchange on the black market, a common practice among U.S. companies which the government had quietly tolerated. In October the government presented the evidence of AFP's illegal exchange transactions, prompting a threat by Ross to arrest the company's local board of directors. The government newspaper *La Nación* fueled calls for nationalizing AFP, reporting that of the company's local annual payroll of 36 million pesos, 5 bosses received 8 million, 500 employees 8 million and 5,300 workers 20 million.[100] Ross' campaign against AFP struck a responsive chord among the urban populace. Workers and the petite bourgeoisie rallied against the company. The national labor federation, FOCH, along with other worker organizations, joined independent craftsmen, small merchants and neighborhood associations to form the Committee for the Nationalization of Electrical Services.[101] But Gustavo Ross had no intention of complying with popular demands for complete nationalization.

In November, Ross met with AFP president Curtis Calder and worked out a public agreement on the company which in turn was conditioned on a secret agreement the two men had reached. Under the secret agreement, the government would dismiss all charges brought against the company's officials and over a twelve-month period provide the company with $2.5 million in foreign exchange at a favorable rate. The public agreement restructured the company, creating an eleven-person board of directors, seven of whom were to be Chilean, and requiring the appointment of a Chilean president. The company would set aside up to 20 percent of its revenues for improving services and pay out two-thirds of the returns on its ordinary shares to the government, with the understanding that those returns would eventually be used to buy out AFP.

Although Congress subsequently modified the public agreement, critics pointed out that the service improvement clause allowed the company to spend as little as it wanted on improvements. Furthermore, payments to the state based on stock returns could easily be manipulated. In addition, real power in the company seemed to reside with an American man-

99 Culbertson to secretary of state, Santiago, April 15, 1933, 825.6374/1144, RG 59, USNA.

100 *La Nación* (Santiago), October 29, 1935, enclosed in Winthrop Scott to secretary of state, Santiago, October 30, 1935, 825.6463 Electric Bond & Share Co./82, RG 59, USNA.

101 On these developments, see the correspondence contained in 825.6463 Electric Bond & Share Co./63, 68, 70, 71, 73, RG 59, USNA.

ager. At least three of the Chilean directors were close associates of Ross, and the new company president was Ernesto Barros Jarpa, a friend of Ross and his go-between in the negotiations with AFP.[102] As with the Cosach restructuring, Ross' AFP scheme did little to address popular demands for the nationalization and socialization of major foreign-owned industries. Those facts returned to haunt Ross in 1938 when he sought the presidency in an election which pitted him against the candidate of the Popular Front, a center–left coalition.

Gustavo Ross' campaign for the presidency in 1938 exposed the decline of the traditional elite's version of nationalism. During the campaign Ross attempted to defend his Cosach and AFP agreements. He argued more generally that the nitrate and copper industries could not have been developed without foreign capital and that foreign companies involved in these areas had not yet earned back their investments. He also sought to redefine terms such as nationalism and imperialism, assuring listeners that foreign corporations which cooperated with the government represented no threat to national sovereignty. Ross and his political mentor Arturo Alessandri pulled out all stops in an effort to preserve the elite's now tattered version of Chilean nationalism. Albeit reluctantly, Curtis Calder agreed to help fund Ross' campaign by having AFP pay a "commission" when it bought foreign exchange from the government. The Alessandri administration withdrew the charters of the nitrate workers' unions at the Guggenheims' María Elena plant to disrupt their political organizing on behalf of the Popular Front. The regime also worked with the American copper companies in an effort to suppress similar activities among copper miners.[103] But the struggle to define the national political discourse in Chile was rapidly slipping from Ross' grasp.

Ross' opponents in the Popular Front, a coalition comprised primarily of the Radical and Socialist parties, built on the Socialist Republic's denunciation of the elite for abandoning Chilean nationalism in an alliance with foreign capitalists which impoverished the Chilean masses. The Front's spokespeople questioned Ross' nationalism. They berated the Cosach and AFP agreements and denounced Ross as an elitist who demeaned his own countrymen.[104] With the triumph of the Popular Front, nationalism defined in terms of social justice and anti-imperialism had become a central feature of Chilean political culture. Even while the presidential race was still under way, an American State Department official acknowledged this sea change in Chile's interaction with American corpo-

---

102 Phillip Hoffman to secretary of state, Santiago, November 29, 1935; September 26, 1936, 825.6463 Electric Bond & Share Co./96, 126, RG 59, USNA.

103 Houseman, "Chilean Nationalism," pp. 177–78; *Chile–American Association Bulletin,* June 8, 1938, enclosed in 825.00/1045; Norman Armour to secretary of state, Santiago, September 10, 1938, 825.6463/133; George Adams, "Economic and Political Conditions in Northern Chile, September 1938," Santiago, October 14, 1938, 825.00/1073, RG 59, USNA.

104 Houseman, "Chilean Nationalism," pp. 177–83.

rate culture. He predicted that in the future American companies would have "to give sympathetic and intelligent consideration to the necessities and demands of labor and the Chilean government and to endeavor to work out harmonious solutions so far as possible before problems reach critical phases."[105] The Guggenheims and their nitrate scheme had played a pivotal role in that development.

The American corporations that entered Chile at the turn of the century restored a moribund copper industry to global prominence, salvaged what they could of the nitrate industry, and in the process injected hundreds of millions of dollars into the national economy. In some ways, American corporations proved less disruptive in Chile than in Peru. Their mining and nitrate operations in sparsely populated desert regions did not disrupt or displace the Chilean petite bourgeoisie of the Central Valley. It would appear that the fortunes of that group in fact fed on the prosperity of the nitrate and copper industries. And while Chilean mine and nitrate workers had retained their migrant lifestyle, they were considerably more accustomed to the rigors of the industrial work place at the time of the Americans' arrival than were the peasant miners of Peru. In addition, American mine and nitrate companies, with their mass extraction techniques and high-skill labor requirements, moved more rapidly than their counterparts in Peru to institute industrial welfare programs. Chilean workers welcomed the higher wages, health care and educational benefits the American companies brought. Furthermore, widespread protests against the growing U.S. presence seemed unlikely given the distinct agendas of the popular classes. The middle and working classes of the Central Valley did not initially share the anti-foreign nationalism of the nitrate workers. Small business people benefited from the renewed economic growth brought by the Americans, while the white-collar middle class found much to support in Ibáñez's program of welfare and public employment. But the changes initiated by U.S. companies and the effects of the Great Depression soon drew these divergent groups into a common campaign.

Although American companies dramatically improved efficiency, they also destroyed a complex web of relations between British interests and Chilean society. Chilean middlemen who had prospered from commercial and financial ties to the labor-intensive nitrate industry faced ruin, and thousands of workers lost their jobs. Furthermore, while Chilean workers welcomed the material benefits the companies brought, they opposed the degree of corporate control that came with them. Daily work discipline, prohibitions on drinking and company towns that restricted their movements prompted resistance. As the workers at Chuquicamata noted in

---

105 Laurence Duggan, memorandum, Washington, D.C., July 15, 1938, 825.00/1041, RG 59, USNA.

1925, it had become an issue of control over their lives, and an issue of sovereignty. The question of sovereignty resonated through the Chilean middle and working classes as the Great Depression followed hard on the heels of the nitrate industry's decline.

When the elite's brand of nationalism, seemingly validated by the War of the Pacific, failed to address mounting domestic problems, the middle and working classes began formulating a version of nationalism which drew on popular concepts of social and economic justice rooted in Chile's past. The dominant role which American corporations achieved in the national economy and the disastrous effects of the depression popularized the anti-foreign aspects of worker culture in the northern deserts. The anti-imperialism of the northern workers provided a powerful critique of the elite's program of national development and forged a bond between them and the popular forces of the Central Valley, who were now suffering the devastating impact of the Great Depression.

The themes of popular nationalism found expression in an array of political movements in the early 1930s, including the Communists, Alessandristas and Socialists. As the triumph of the Popular Front clearly demonstrated, anti-imperialism and social justice became central themes of Chilean politics to which even the elite would have to accommodate themselves. Meanwhile, in Cuba American corporate culture had come to play an even more pervasive role in revamping productive systems and relations and shaping a consumer society. And the reaction to it had proven far more violent than in the Chilean case.

PART V

Sugar and power in Cuba

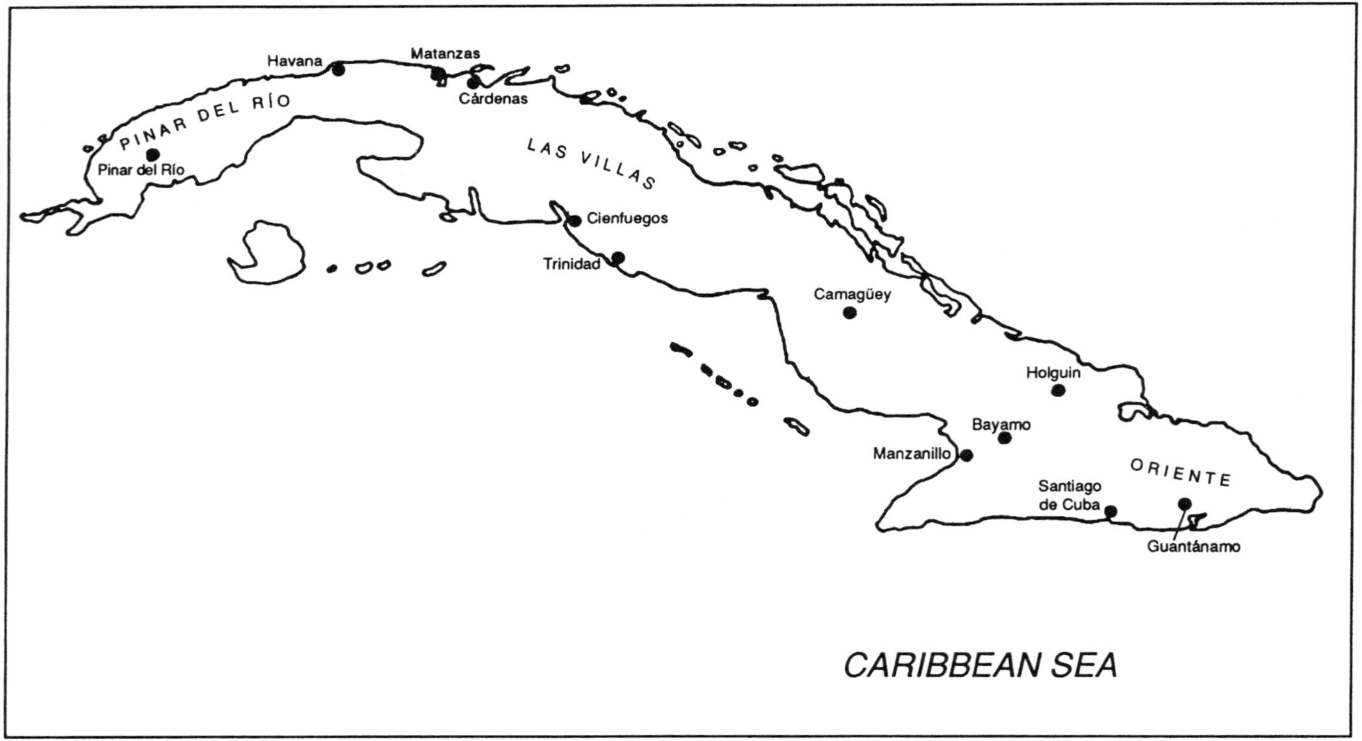
Havana
Matanzas
Cárdenas
PINAR DEL RÍO
Pinar del Río
LAS VILLAS
Cienfuegos
Trinidad
Camagüey
Holguin
Bayamo
Manzanillo
ORIENTE
Santiago
de Cuba
Guantánamo
CARIBBEAN SEA

Map 8.1. Cuba.

8

Sugar and power

We are dealing with a race . . . into which we have got to infuse new life, new principles, and new methods of doing things. (Leonard Wood)

{Edward} Deeds{'} sense of human values was also responsible for his ability to reconcile the differences between the business and working methods of the Anglo-Saxon and the Latin. The Latin and particularly one of Spanish extraction, is the world's most inveterate procrastinator. (Isaac Marcosson)

When the dictatorship of Gerardo Machado disintegrated in 1933, the winds of revolution swept across the island of Cuba. The Cuban populace rose up against domestic dictatorship, the Great Depression and foreign domination. Embedded in that process was a clash between American corporate culture and a wide range of Cuban social relations and cultural values. American investments in Cuba after the turn of the century had resuscitated a sugar industry devastated by war and helped maintain its competitive position in the world market into the 1920s. The General Electric Company brought the wonders of electricity to a quarter of a million households and introduced Cubans to conveniences like electric irons and radios. While Cubans eagerly accepted these positive aspects of American corporate culture, the rapid insertion of the technology, work processes, management and marketing systems of the second industrial revolution contributed to a wave of popular resistance. Much like the villages of Central America's Atlantic coast, the rural settlements of Cuba were of recent origin, but quickly organized to resist rationalization. That experience of resistance carried over into the industrial work place, where workers also drew on their long struggle as Cubans against their displacement by Spanish immigrants in the national labor market. Rooted in historical experiences and cast in a nationalist context, the popular resistance movement against American corporate culture proved appealing to Cuba's petite bourgeoisie and middle classes as they too faced displacement and subordination by American corporations. These groups also reacted to American corporate dominance in every major sector of the Cuban economy, from sugar to mining to finance.

In their reactions to the reshaping of the work place and to American economic domination, Cubans closely approximated the experiences of Peruvians and Chileans. Yet the Cuban experience also illustrates far more forcefully than these earlier cases the reactions of Latin Americans to the ambiguities of American consumer culture as conveyed to the island by companies like G.E. and ITT. The Cuban reaction combined concerns about work-place dislocations, U.S. economic dominance and the conflicting messages of American consumerism. As the Great Depression deepened and the Machado regime collapsed, those concerns would erupt into a series of protests which swept American corporate interests into the vortex of the Cuban revolution of 1933. Those events marked a climactic stage in the long evolution of U.S.–Cuban relations.

As the United States passed through the series of transitional phases from merchant republic to modern corporate society, Cuba became the Latin American society most consistently and intensely affected by those changes. From the outset of the relationship, Cuba's economic importance in America's international trade contributed to the intensity of that relationship. By the mid nineteenth century the United States had become Cuba's most important trading partner, and Cuba ranked among America's top sources of international commerce. When the Cubans launched their war for independence, U.S. investments on the island totaled less than $50 million, but the island also remained the leading Latin American recipient of U.S. exports. As the war dragged on, damaging U.S. investments and ravaging Cuban trade, America's corporate and financial leaders, including William Rockefeller, John Jacob Astor and J. P. Morgan, accepted the inevitability of intervention.[1] It was the work of the U.S. occupation governments which laid the foundations for the revolutionary changes which American corporate society would convey to Cuba.

The mission of the American occupiers was informed by a view of Cuban culture as fundamentally inferior to that which Americans enjoyed. General Leonard Wood, head of the first occupation regime, explained to President McKinley, "We are dealing with a race that has steadily been going down for a hundred years, and into which we have to infuse new life, new principles, and new methods of doing things."[2] Wood and his successors attempted to create a stable, quasi-independent republic and to reshape Cuban society into a more compatible environment for U.S. trade and investment. In pursuit of the former goal, the United States imposed the Platt Amendment, which gave it an unre-

---

1 Walter LaFeber, *The New Empire: An Interpretation of American Expansion, 1860–1898* (Ithaca: Cornell University Press, 1963), pp. 38, 334, 386–87. As LaFeber points out, figures on U.S. investment are probably inflated by Cuban landowners who sought the protection of American citizenship.

2 As quoted in David Healy, *The United States in Cuba, 1898–1902* (Madison: University of Wisconsin Press, 1963), p. 179.

stricted right of intervention to protect American lives and property. Leonard Wood and his aides also attempted to fashion a social order compatible with, if not identical to, the modern corporate society in their homeland. Wood later concluded that his work had created "a republic modeled closely upon the lines of our great Anglo-Saxon republic . . ."[3] Those efforts reshaped many of the institutions of Cuban society, especially its judicial system. Wood's reforms emphasized the swift administration of justice and the creation of a stable environment which would protect private property.[4]

The reforms in this last area went beyond the mere defense of property rights, to establish once and for all the supremacy of private property. In 1902 Wood issued a decree creating special court procedures for the division of *haciendas comuneras,* or communal estates. These procedures allowed large sugar estates and mills to expand by acquiring additional acreage. In Oriente province, on the eastern end of the island, where the survival of haciendas comuneras had nurtured a smallholder subsistence economy, the number of farms decreased from 21,550 to 10,854 between 1899 and 1904.[5] The restructuring of rural Cuba also affected large sugar plantations. Burdened with debt and devastated mills after the war with Spain, planters found temporary relief in the occupation government's stay law, which decreed a two-year debt moratorium. In 1900, with the expiration of the moratorium approaching, Wood rejected planters' pleas for an extension of the law or for financial assistance.[6] His new decree allowed foreclosures to resume, ensuring the collapse of the Cuban planter class. Nor did the regime restrict itself to changes affecting rural property.

The occupation government instituted patent right regulations and trademark laws which afforded invaluable protection of intellectual property to American corporations such as General Electric and Union Carbide when they entered the Cuban market.[7] Yet the protection and expansion of property interests in the form of rural landholdings, technology or trademarks would go for naught in the absence of a populace prepared for the new order. To meet this challenge, Wood began a rapid, sometimes haphazard, reform of the educational system. The occupation government

3 Leonard Wood, "The Military Government of Cuba," *Annals of the American Academy of Political and Social Science* 21 (March 1903), p. 182.

4 Healy, *The United States in Cuba,* p. 183; Herminio Portell Vilá, *Nueva historia de la República de Cuba (1898–1979)* (Miami: Moderna Press, 1986), pp. 92–96; James H. Hitchman, *Leonard Wood and Cuban Independence, 1898–1902* (The Hague: Nijhoff, 1971), p. 46.

5 Robert B. Hoernel, "Sugar and Social Change in Oriente, Cuba, 1898–1946," *JLAS* 8 (1976), pp. 223, 230; Wood, "Military Government," p. 179.

6 Wood to Root, Havana, April 12, 1900; same to same, May 18, 30, 1900, Root Papers; Louis A. Pérez Jr., *Cuba Under the Platt Amendment, 1902–1934* (Pittsburgh: University of Pittsburgh Press, 1986), pp. 63–66.

7 Copies of the decrees can be found in C. B. Curtis to secretary of state, Havana, July 29, 1929, 837.542, rl. 81, M-488, Records of the Department of State Relating to the Internal Affairs of Cuba, 1910–29, RG 59, USNA.

rationalized the educational bureaucracy and expanded physical facilities and enrollments. Wood's goals went beyond the alphabetizing of Cuban youth as "the classroom was transformed into an agent for the transfusion of cultural values . . ."[8] As a part of this effort to reshape Cuban culture, the American occupiers translated textbooks directly from American versions. They also sent 1,300 Cuban schoolteachers to Harvard, mostly for the demonstration effect of a firsthand experience with American culture. Yet Wood's attempts to transform Cuban culture did not prompt an entirely positive response. The general's efforts to impose trial by jury violated Cuban concepts of authority and the exercise of responsibility. Cubans viewed jury duty as an attempt to force them to impose punishment on their countrymen, and consistently returned verdicts of innocent. Furthermore, once direct American rule ended, Cubans quickly resorted to many of the patterns and practices which Wood saw as symptomatic of their decline. By then American corporations had assumed a leading role in transforming Cuba.[9]

Policies designed to encourage American development of Cuba contributed to an upsurge in U.S. investment from less than $50 million in 1896 to $215 million by 1914.[10] Yet the island nation still had not become the miniature Anglo-Saxon republic that Wood had envisioned. Although American policymakers successfully dictated rural property and patent laws conducive to orderly development, they failed to imprint on Cuban society the values and relations central to a modern corporate society. At the heart of their predicament lay fundamental contradictions in the policies they pursued. As American investors staked out the high ground of the Cuban economic landscape, Cuba's incipient business class found itself in a hopeless competitive struggle with powerful American interests. Government jobs, contracts and concessions constituted the one area where Cuban citizens might enjoy a competitive advantage over foreigners. Eduardo Chibás, engineer and part owner of a central sugar mill, who also dabbled in politics, was rewarded with a government concession to create the Compañía Eléctrica de Alumbrada y Tracción de Santiago.[11] In many cases, use of the state for economic gain involved directly tapping into state revenues.

The Cuban government's role as a major avenue for domestic economic advancement increasingly impaired its function as a rationalized bureau-

---

8 Louis A. Pérez Jr., "The Imperial Design: Politics and Pedagogy in Occupied Cuba, 1899–1902," *Cuban Studies/Estudios Cubanos* 12 (Summer 1982), p. 7; also Hitchman, *Leonard Wood*, p. 50.

9 Pérez, "Imperial Design," p. 13.

10 Robert W. Dunn, *American Foreign Investments* (1926) (New York: Arno, 1976), pp. 119–20; Oscar Pino Santos, *El asalto a Cuba por la oligarquía financiera yanqui* (Havana: Casa de las Américas, 1973), p. 36.

11 "Report on Examination of Compania Electrica de Alumbrada y Traccion de Santiago and Oriente Interurban Electric Company Inc.," September 30, 1922, Box 143219, EBASCO; Hugh Thomas, *Cuba: The Pursuit of Freedom, 1762–1969* (New York: Harper and Row, 1971), pp. 537, 629, 749.

cracy conducive to the development of American corporate interests. In
1914 the state employed 20 percent of Cuba's working population. By
1921 the Department of Public Works had issued contracts totaling $49
million, a sum that almost equaled the government's entire annual income. Fifteen percent of all taxes collected disappeared before they
reached the treasury, while fraudulent transactions siphoned off 25 percent of all actual disbursements. Cuban presidents used the national lottery's annual revenues of over $31 million to buy off congressmen and
newspaper editors, fund political campaigns and support no-show jobs in
the bureaucracy. These levels of corruption made efficient public administration impossible, and, combined with the collapse of sugar prices in
1920, they threatened to push Cuba into bankruptcy. American policymakers responded with yet another reform effort.[12]

In January 1921 Enoch Crowder arrived in Cuba as a special envoy
from the president of the United States. Crowder dedicated himself to re-
building "the lines of efficient and honest republican government" installed by the American occupation regimes.[13] The moralization program
which Crowder sought to impose on an uncooperative President Alfredo
Zayas included cuts in the national budget, sharp reductions in the bureaucracy, reform of the national lottery and an "honest cabinet" to implement the reforms. With enactment of Crowder's program tied to the is-
suance of a desperately needed $50 million loan from J. P. Morgan, Zayas
finally acquiesced. But as Vernon Monroe, a J. P. Morgan official, cor-
rectly predicted, the loan would stabilize Cuban finances, and as a result
"the hands of the President and politicians will be strengthened and the
hands of General Crowder a good deal weakened." After the approval of
the loan in January 1923, Zayas quickly ousted his cabinet and rolled
back the reforms.[14] The collapse of Crowder's moralization program embodied the essential contradiction in American policy in Cuba. The development of American investments on the island increased the need for a rational state apparatus. Yet the rapid growth of U.S. corporate interests
fueled the spread of government corruption. That situation was aggra-
vated by the continuing rapid expansion of American corporations in
Cuba and the changes they sought to impose on Cuban society.

If the increase in American investment down to World War I had been
impressive, its development in the following decades was nothing less

12 Pérez, *Platt Amendment,* p. 226; memorandum, Enoch Crowder to Alfredo Zayas, April 1922,
    837.51/764, rl. 65, M-488; Boaz Long to secretary of state, Havana, November 24, 1920; Enoch
    Crowder to secretary of state, Havana, May 4, 1922, 837.513/47, 50, rl. 77, M-488, RG 59,
    USNA; "Memorandum of conversation with Mr. A," n.p., March 17, 1922, File 4, Box 90, Lam-
    ont Papers.
13 Crowder to secretary of state, Havana, April 5, 1922, 837.51/750, rl. 65, M-488, RG 59, USNA.
14 Vernon Monroe, "Memorandum on Cuba," n.p., February 2, 1923, File 4, Box 90, Lamont Papers.
    U.S. efforts to reform the Zayas administration are detailed in 837.513/54, 68, 70, 76, 78, rl. 78,
    M-488; 837.51/741, 750, 756, rl. 65, M-488, RG 59, USNA; and Pérez, *Platt Amendment,* pp.
    190–245.

than spectacular. Direct U.S. investment soared from $215 million in 1914 to $1.3 billion in 1924. Paralleling events in the United States, large modern corporations dominated economic growth, with the sugar industry controlled by firms such as the United Fruit Company, the Punta Alegre Company, the American Sugar Refining Company and the National City Bank. Large American corporate interests also entered the mining industry, with the Bethlehem Steel Corporation creating the two largest iron mining operations in Cuba. The General Electric Company, establishing a pattern for its investments in other Latin American countries like Chile, invested over $50 million in Cuba during the 1920s, capturing control of 90 percent of the island's electrical generating capacity. International Telephone and Telegraph invested over $20 million in the Cuban phone system. As in the cases of the other Latin American countries we have studied, the corporate surge into Cuba represented more than a massive commitment of capital and control of the leading sectors of the Cuban economy.[15]

Men such as Gerard Swope, president of General Electric; Charles Schwab, chairman of Bethlehem Steel; Frank Vanderlip and Charles Mitchell of National City Bank; and Edward Deeds of the General Sugar Company were leading the transformation of America into a modern corporate society. Their efforts to reshape Cuban culture constituted a transformation comparable to the Spanish conquest of the island in the sixteenth century. Challenges to their mission first appeared in rural Cuba.

In the 1880s the expansion of the sugar estates rapidly eroded the haciendas comuneras in western Cuba, but in the East small family farms and haciendas comuneras would survive until World War I. But after the turn of the century rural communities and subsistence producers in the East found themselves being displaced by rapidly expanding American sugar estates. After futile attempts to defend their lands through court actions and appeals to politicians, many residents of Oriente province would throw their support to a wave of social banditry in 1917.[16] As the communities which emerged from the disruption of Cuban rural society struggled to maintain an economic independence based on access to the land, resistance also spilled over into Cuba's rural factories.

In Cuban sugar mills, where the technology and techniques of the first industrial revolution still predominated, paternalism remained an effec-

---

15 Acting secretary of state to John B. Jackson, Washington, D.C., March 16, 1911, 837.63/4; Frederick W. Hinke, "Mineral Deposits and Industries, Antilla, Cuba," Antilla, June 14, 1924, 837.63/58, rl. 89, M-488, RG 59, USNA; Lisandro Pérez, "Iron Mining and Socio-Demographic Change in Eastern Cuba, 1884–1940," *JLAS* 14 (November 1982), p. 391; Dunn, *American Foreign Investments*, p. 129; Louis Banigan to William Phillips, New York, December 6, 1933, 837.6463 EB&S Co./11, RG 59, USNA.

16 Hoernel, "Social Change in Oriente, Cuba," pp. 219–23, 239–41; Laird W. Bergad, *Cuban Rural Society in the Nineteenth Century: The Social and Economic History of Monoculture in Matanzas* (Princeton: Princeton University Press, 1990), pp. 256–57; Louis A. Pérez Jr., *Lords of the Mountain: Social Banditry and Peasant Protest in Cuba, 1878–1918* (Pittsburgh: University of Pittsburgh Press, 1989), chaps. 1 and 7.

tive means of control. Cuban mill owners gave favored employees work during the dead season when the mills shut down, helped with personal emergencies such as family illness, and used their favorites to replace better-paid but less obsequious workers. Sugar workers came to understand the manipulative nature of a system that forced "honorable and hardworking people" to beg for work and benefits. Out of the experience, workers also established a baseline for just treatment. As one striking worker expressed it in 1917, every worker who did his duty was entitled to fair treatment.[17] A part of that same struggle was the effort to control the national labor market.

At the beginning of the twentieth century Cuban workers actively engaged in strikes for higher wages and union recognition. Yet unionization efforts proved weak and ephemeral, in part because so much of Cuba's workforce consisted of immigrant, often temporary, laborers. Cuban workers had long found themselves displaced in the national employment market by Spaniards, Chinese and other immigrants. Cuban workers reacted with nationalistic fervor to displacement. As early as 1902 the tobacco workers' Liga General de Trabajadores Cubanos found support among both working- and middle-class Cubans with its calls for full national independence and an end to exploitation of Cubans by foreign corporations. That nationalist theme would reemerge as a part of renewed labor activity after World War I. By 1919 a rising national birth rate and a decline in Spanish immigration provided a more coherent base for the labor movement. A wave of labor actions swept the island between 1919 and 1920. Over the next five years, labor leaders formed a national labor federation. A soaring cost of living and efforts to rationalize the work place fueled labor actions demanding increased wages and worker control. In Cuba's incipient industrial plants, a thin line still separated skilled workers from owners. As rationalization threatened worker control, anarchosyndicalism became a dominant influence in the Cuban labor movement, with workers turning to its direct action philosophy to defend the workday and the pace of their labors within it.[18] The growing role of

---

17 Ana Núñez Machín, *Memoria amagra del azúcar* (Havana: Editorial de Ciencias Sociales, 1981), pp. 50, 62, 72; John Dumoulin, *Azúcar y lucha de clases, 1917* (Havana: Editorial de Ciencias Sociales, 1980), pp. 199–200, 207.

18 José Rivero Muñiz, *El movimiento obrero durante la primera intervención (1899–1902)* (Havana: Universidad Central de Las Villas, 1961), pp. 79, 91–93, 107, 202–5, 217; Olga Cabrera, *El movimiento obrero cubano en 1920* (Havana: Instituto Cubano del Libro, 1970), pp. 45–98; Hobart Spalding Jr., "The Workers' Struggle: 1850–1961," *Cuba Review* 4 (July 1974), pp. 3–10; Louis A. Pérez Jr., *Cuba: Between Reform and Revolution* (New York: Oxford University Press, 1988), pp. 201–5, 239–44; Instituto de Historia del Movimiento Comunista y de la Revolución Socialista de Cuba, *El movimiento obrero cubano: documentos y artículos*, vol. 1: *1865–1925* (Havana: Editorial de Ciencias Sociales, 1975), pp. 177–98; Jules Robert Benjamin, *The United States and Cuba: Hegemony and Dependent Development, 1880–1934* (Pittsburgh: University of Pittsburgh Press, 1974), p. 53; Andrés García Suárez, *Los fundidores relatan su historia* (Havana: Departamento de Orientación Revolucionaria del Comité Central del Partido Comunista de Cuba, 1975), pp. 7–12; Dumoulin, *Azúcar y lucha de clases*, p. 59; Cabrera, *1920*, pp. 55, 63–68, 104, 115.

American corporations brought them into increasing conflict with labor over the issue of rationalization.

Under the leadership of Sosthenes Behn, president of ITT, the Port of Havana Docks Company had modernized the port of Havana with labor-saving equipment. As in Peru, the workers fought to protect the subsistence levels of a community whose numbers exceeded the labor requirements of the port's modern dock facilities. They limited their work week to two or three days, and the workers' own delegates decided on the number of laborers to be employed.[19] The activities of American corporations also renewed the struggle over the displacement of Cubans in the work place. Unskilled Cuban workers faced displacement when American sugar companies in 1912 promoted the first government decree allowing Haitian and Jamaican immigration. By 1929 West Indians constituted one-third of the field workers in the sugar industry. Most skilled Cuban workers did not find themselves displaced, but they found their job knowledge called into question and subordinated to the expertise of American engineers. At the Matahambre mine in Pinar del Río province, the American Metals Company introduced dry drilling, air compressors and the use of concentrators, while Cuban miners learned that now only Americans could be gang bosses and managers.[20]

As U.S. investment in Cuba soared to over $1 billion in the early 1920s and American corporations captured effective control of Cuba's sugar, mining and transportation industries, direct labor conflict with American corporations intensified. Between 1919 and 1924 Havana port workers and sugar workers in the eastern provinces struck against American companies over issues of wages and workers' control. The national labor congresses of the 1920s called for higher wages and preferential treatment for Cuban workers, and denounced "American imperialism." The issues of worker control and wages now merged with earlier concerns about control of Cuba's labor market to form a nationalist agenda which had a strong appeal among the middle class.[21]

At the beginning of the 1920s the Cuban middle class had not yet experienced the full impact of professionalization which had swept American society. The use of family and personal ties to secure white-collar posi-

---

19 Boaz Long to secretary of state, Havana, February 10, 1920; Philander L. Caben to secretary of state, Havana, December 6, 1921, 837.504/169, 221, rl. 58, M-488, RG 59, USNA.

20 Roberto Branly, *MINAZ-608: coloquios en el despegue* (Havana: Girón, 1973), p. 57; García Suárez, *Los fundidores*, p. 18; Cabrera, *1920*, pp. 36–37; Pérez, *Reform and Revolution*, p. 204; Salvadore Morales, Gloria García and María Sánchez, *Matahambre: empresa y movimiento obrero* (Havana: Instituto de Libros, 1971), pp. 13–50.

21 On U.S. investment, see Pino Santos, *Oligarquía financiera*, pp. 36, 76. For examples of workers' control, see García Suárez, *Los fundidores*, pp. 7–12; Dumoulin, *Azúcar y lucha de clases*, p. 59. On the port workers' struggle, see Boaz Long to secretary of state, Havana, February 10, 1920; Philander L. Caben to secretary of state, Havana, December 6, 1921, 837.504/169, 221, rl. 58, M-488, RG 59, USNA. The sugar workers' demands and their significance are discussed in *Facts About Sugar*, December 6, 1924.

tions still played a central role in Cuban corporations. Such practices clashed directly with the emphasis in American companies on rationalization of management functions. Cubans who did possess the necessary professional credentials for white-collar positions found themselves shunted aside in favor of Americans or subordinated to them within the managerial hierarchy.[22] For many middle- and working-class Cubans, the conflict between their values and practices and those of American corporations provided a common bond for action.

In the 1920s middle- and working-class Cubans who came into conflict with American corporate culture shared a common nationalist theme that gave them a legitimizing symbol. As the newly formed Communist party with its national political ambitions replaced the abstentionist anarchosyndicalists as the leading force in the labor movement, it sought to build on that coalescence of middle- and working-class interests. In 1925 the Communist Anti-Imperialist League argued that "Cuba should be for Cubans. This does not mean hate *foreigners;* it means hate *foreign capital* which disregards the needs of merchants, of colonos, of workers, of employees . . ."[23] Yet the coalitions which the Communists envisioned did not pervade Cuban society. They tended to develop among skilled workers and middle-class professionals, who still occupied comparable positions in the social and economic hierarchy, and were found most frequently in those industries or segments of industries where the introduction of the new technologies, work systems and management methods was most intense. As American companies accelerated their penetration of the sugar and power sectors, they rapidly effected such changes in these industries.

Sugar

The sugar industry which American companies invested in after the turn of the century had already undergone considerable change. In response to the end of slavery and the ensuing labor shortage, Cuban sugar planters had introduced machinery into the mills which expanded grinding capacity and reduced labor requirements. To cope with the shortage of field hands, planters leased their crop lands to renters (dependent *colonos*) who received a percentage of the sugar from the cane delivered to the mill. Despite these dramatic changes, the process unfolding in rural Cuba in the closing decades of the nineteenth century did not thoroughly modernize the sugar industry. The new technology consisted of products of the first industrial revolution, available on the world market since at least the 1870s. Many of the processes in the mill remained labor-intensive, and labor relations in the *ingenios* largely retained their patriarchal character.

22 Morales, García and Sánchez, *Matahambre,* p. 50; Núñez Machín, *Memoria amarga,* pp. 62–63; Branly, *MINAZ,* p. 66; Mirta Rosell, ed., *Luchas obreras contra Machado* (Havana: Instituto Cubano del Libro, 1973), pp. 44–45, 62.

23 Rosell, ed., *Luchas contra Machado,* p. 108.

The widespread adoption of the colono system ensured the persistence of traditional methods in the agricultural sector. Neither the independent growers nor renters of estate land enjoyed the capital resources to renovate the manual methods of planting and harvesting. Furthermore, both large colonos and mill owners relied on contractors to secure and supervise their field hands, thus removing them from the direct management of labor. The creation of *centrales,* or central mills, controlling vast amounts of acreage awaited the creation of a fluid national labor market and the massive infusion of American capital.[24]

The ravages of war and Leonard Wood's policies concerning the stay law and haciendas comuneras set the stage for the direct penetration of the Cuban sugar industry by American capital. By 1914 U.S. investments in the Cuban sugar industry had reached $95 million. American interests controlled 36 of the 179 mills in Cuba and accounted for 36 percent of Cuban sugar production. The American sugar corporations, concentrated in the eastern provinces of Las Villas, Camagüey and Oriente, accounted for 31 of the U.S.-owned mills. But American investment had not yet radically transformed the Cuban sugar industry.[25] The impressive flow of U.S. dollars into Cuban sugar mills after 1898 did not totally revamp the industry. Sugar technology remained firmly planted in the steam-driven machinery that Cuban planters had begun to introduce in the 1880s. Engineers and chemists still played marginal roles in the mills. In agriculture, the machete, hoe and ox cart remained the crude implements of field work. Independent colonos who owned their own land still controlled one-third of all sugar acreage. Contractors still supervised the work of field hands, whether they labored for colonos or directly for the centrales.[26] Nevertheless, the increased efficiency of the American mills created a competitive challenge for Cuban-owned mills which eventually affected their work-place relations.

On the western end of the island, where Cuban mills continued to predominate, work relations still had a patriarchal character. Even after the Cuban Cane Sugar Company bought the Cuban-owned central Mercedes Carrillo in 1916, Antonio Carrillo, the son of the owner, remained as manager. When wartime conditions created a food shortage, Carrillo personally went to the mill to distribute bread to the workers. Cuban workers understood that this patriarchal order served as a mechanism of con-

---

24 Bergad, *Cuban Rural Society,* pp. 277–78, 283, 284, 289, 327; Fe Iglesias García, "The Development of Capitalism in Cuban Sugar Production, 1860–1900," in Manuel Moreno Fraginals, Frank Moya Pons and Stanley L. Engerman, eds., *Between Slavery and Free Labor: The Spanish-Speaking Caribbean in the Nineteenth Century* (Baltimore: Johns Hopkins University Press, 1985), p. 70; Foreign Policy Association, *Problems of the New Cuba: Report of the Commission on Cuban Affairs* (New York: Author, 1935), pp. 289–90.

25 U.S. Department of Commerce, Bureau of Foreign and Domestic Commerce, *The Cane Sugar Industrial, Agricultural, Manufacturing and Marketing Costs in Hawaii, Porto Rico, Louisiana and Cuba,* Miscellaneous Series #53 (Washington, D.C.: Government Printing Office, 1917), pp. 401–2.

26 Foreign Policy Association, *Problems of the New Cuba,* pp. 270–72.

trol. Nor did they hesitate to mobilize against it when their own economic conditions worsened. In 1917 a rising cost of living and the efforts of anarchosyndicalist labor organizers helped trigger a strike by sugar workers on the west end of the island. An important factor contributing to the labor action in Cuban-run mills was the speedup of work processes in an effort to compete with the newer and more efficient American mills in the East. The strikers drew support from local rural communities and couched their criticisms of owners in terms of workers' rights in a civilized and democratic country and owners' obligations to the *patria* and the workers.[27] Community support for labor actions and a national discourse that combined the issues of national interest and social justice intensified as American corporations continued to reshape the sugar industry.

The transformation of sugar mills by American companies raced forward in the two decades after the outbreak of World War I. First, American enterprises poured investment into the industry to take advantage of high wartime prices for sugar. Then, in the face of a postwar price collapse, corporate reformers set about revamping the sugar mills' management, production and labor systems. Although the United States imposed wartime price controls on sugar, Cuba's principal product sold at twice its prewar average between 1914 and 1919. J. P. Morgan, the National City Bank and the Chase National Bank financed corporations such as the Punta Alegre Sugar Company and the Cuban Cane Sugar Company. By 1916 American investments in the sugar industry had reached $400 million, and American companies owned 71 of the 210 mills in Cuba and accounted for nearly 50 percent of national output. Imports of sugar mill machinery, which averaged just over $2 million annually in the prewar decade, shot up to over $12 million during the war. The average production of mills on the island rose by 40 percent during the war. American mills led the way in this expansion with production averages twice those of non-U.S. ingenios. But American investment did not follow a smooth upward course.[28]

Control of Cuban sugar prices ended in December 1919 with the fixed price standing at just over 7 cents per pound. By May 1920 the price had rocketed to over 23 cents; it then plummeted toward 3 cents by December. The following year, a wave of bankruptcies swept the industry, threatening the investments of major American banking institutions. National City Bank, with its own solvency at stake, resuscitated eight bankrupt centrales with the formation of the General Sugar Company. While other financial institutions such as J. P. Morgan and Chase National Bank took less dramatic steps, they too poured in additional capital and became

27 Núñez Machín, *Memoria amarga*, pp. 50–51, 62–63, 72–73; Branly, *MINAZ*, pp. 65–66; Dumoulin, *Azúcar y lucha de clases*, pp. 57–58, 95, 199–200, 207–8.
28 Syndicate Books 8 and 9, Morgan Papers; Dunn, *American Foreign Investments*, p. 120; U.S. Department of Commerce, *Cane Sugar*, pp. 401–2, 405; Foreign Policy Association, *Problems of the New Cuba*, pp. 220, 222, 265.

more directly involved in the management of Cuban sugar mills.[29] In the wake of the 1920 price collapse, American investors accepted the fact that Cuban sugar faced a highly competitive world market. They believed, however, that a more efficient industry could prosper even if prices remained at prewar levels. That more efficient industry would emerge from a restructuring of centrales into large holding companies, increased productive capacity, the application of new American technology and the introduction of scientific management techniques.

By 1923 the ten largest American holding companies, including Cuban Cane Sugar, Cuban American, General Sugar and Punta Alegre, controlled 54 of the 182 mills in Cuba and accounted for over half of the island's sugar production. With the refinancing and reorganization of Cuban centrales, U.S. investment in Cuban sugar reached $750 million by 1924. Part of those capital commitments flowed into a further increase in productive capacity.[30] As a result of the competitive strategy of American companies, imports of sugar mill machinery continued to average over $12 million between 1919 and 1925 and helped push total Cuban production up from 4.1 to 5.3 million metric tons. The new equipment investments did not aim simply at increasing total production. As an industry publication noted in 1925, "It is noteworthy that under the conditions such as now prevail interest centres less in the construction of new mills than in the improvement of existing plants, . . . the introduction of new processes that economize labor or improve yields."[31]

With an assured market and price, American sugar companies had directed wartime investments toward expanded grinding by mills in a harvest season which could stretch out to seven or eight months. Cane left standing in fields for months and then quickly ground in the mills reduced the percentage of sugar extracted from the cane. In the competitive postwar environment, sugar companies focused on speeding up production and improving rates of extraction. Sugar companies in the 1920s transformed sugar milling into a modern continuous-process manufacturing system that would accelerate output as well as extraction rates. Technological renovation of the industry in the 1920s built on developments that had begun during the war years. The Cuban American Sugar Company took an important step in the direction of efficiency in 1912 by adopting electric power in its new central Delicias in Oriente province.[32]

29 Pino Santos, *Oligarquía financiera,* pp. 106–8; van B. Cleveland and Huertas, *Citibank,* pp. 109–10; National City Company, *Sugar* (New York: Author, 1922), pp. 25–29.

30 Dunn, *American Foreign Investments,* pp. 120, 122–23; A. B. Gilmore, *Manual de la industria azucarera cubana/The Cuban Sugar Manual* (Havana, 1928); Foreign Policy Association, *Problems of the New Cuba,* pp. 218–32.

31 *Facts About Sugar,* April 25, 1925; Dunn, *American Foreign Investments,* p. 120; Foreign Policy Association, *Problems of the New Cuba,* pp. 220, 222.

32 Alejandro García and Oscar Zanetti, eds., *United Fruit Company: un caso del dominio imperialista en Cuba* (Havana: Editorial de Ciencias Sociales, 1976), p. 137; U.S. Department of Commerce, *Cane Sugar,* pp. 400–13; J. G. Davies, *The Principles of Cane Sugar Manufacture* (London: Norman Rodger, 1938), p. 17.

Electric equipment offered significant advantages over steam-driven equipment. Since steam power had to be conveyed by drive shafts or belts, the location of motive power in mills was constricted, and stages in the production process had to run at the same speed as the steam engine. With electrical generators housed in a single power house, energy could be applied at critical points of the milling process through motors. This allowed distinct parts of the process to operate at variable speeds. It made possible rapid starting, stopping and reversing of machinery, reduced the number of operators needed and increased fuel efficiency. Cuba led the way in the electrification of sugar mills with the first two completely electrified mills built in 1918. By 1928 seventeen centrales used electric roller tandems, the industry's installed electrical capacity had reached 170,000 kilowatts, and 70 percent of the island's sugar was being produced by mills that used electrical power in their refining process.[33]

Electrification of Cuban sugar mills symbolized a general renovation of the sugar manufacturing process during the 1920s and early 1930s. American corporations proceeded to revamp virtually every element of the milling process. Side-discharge railway cars replaced endless-chain rakes and other less efficient systems of unloading cane at the factory. Increased use and improvement of cutters and shredders made higher extraction possible from cane now being ground with new high-speed rollers. Centrales employed new, more efficient crystallizers, centrifuges and boilers. The introduction of electric regulators and instrumentation provided more precise control over each stage of the milling process.[34]

As the decade of the 1920s came to a close, the dramatic impact of the technological renovation of sugar milling became fully apparent. Average mill production shot up from 16,000 tons in 1913 to 63,000 tons in 1933, with most of the increase coming after 1919. The grinding period, which had once stretched over eight months, had been reduced to 136 days by 1926. Mills which once recovered 80 percent of the sugar from cane now extracted 90 to 95 percent. Under the aegis of American corporate control, Cuban sugar milling was now a modern continuous-process manufacturing system. Part of that technological renovation involved the introduction of scientific management techniques.[35]

The formation of the Association of Cuban Sugar Technologists in 1926 reflected the growing control that engineers and chemists exercised in Cuban sugar mills. The president of its engineering section would later describe some fifty control functions which engineers now carried out in

33 *Facts About Sugar,* March 5, 1927, November 1930; L. A. Tromp, *Machinery and Equipment of the Sugar Cane Factory* (London: Norman Rodger, 1936), p. 575; Gilmore, *Sugar Manual,* p. xiii.

34 García and Zanetti, eds., *United Fruit Company,* pp. 137–40; *Facts About Sugar,* April 25, 1925, March 5, 1927; Tromp, *Sugar Cane Factory,* pp. 562–64.

35 U.S. Tariff Commission, *Sugar: Report to the President of the United States* (Washington, D.C.: Government Printing Office, 1934), p. 103; Foreign Policy Association, *Problems of the New Cuba,* pp. 242, 266.

the mills. By 1928 the Association had begun standardizing Cuban mill terminology.[36] As the industry journal *Facts About Sugar* noted in 1929:

> Time was not so long ago . . . when the average estate superintendent or factory manager looked upon the deliberations of technological organizations as having little relation to his own work, but as being a sort of harmless diversion for those who busied themselves with abstract theories and academic conclusions . . . Today these men . . . are eager listeners to, or readers of such proceedings if not active participants in them.[37]

Paralleling the efforts of their colleagues in the United States, technicians addressed the human factor in productivity. Their efforts included the use of objective criteria in the selection of employees and the creation of competitive work situations. Cuban workers soon responded to these dramatic changes in the work place.[38]

As early as 1924 Cuban mill workers struck out against the increased rationalization of American-owned mills. As the process of technification swept those plants in the early twenties, workers struggled to retain their control of the work place. In September of 1924 a wave of strikes spread across the sugar industry in eastern Cuba. American companies owned eighteen of the twenty-three mills that were struck. The Cuban Cane Sugar Corporation negotiated a settlement with its workers which recognized their union and the principle of seniority in hirings and firings. The company, however, still maintained an open shop. Despite the Cuban Cane agreement, other sugar companies refused to negotiate with their workers. As the Sugar Planters' Association explained, recognition of the unions "means in reality participation by the union delegates in the management of the sugar mills."[39] In confronting the planters, the mill workers had to cope with a hostile government in Havana and a divided constituency in the countryside.

President Alfredo Zayas, who acknowledged that union recognition and the union shop lay at the heart of the dispute, warned that the government would defend the hiring of non-union workers by the mills. Although the experience of some Spanish mill workers with anarchosyndicalism and union movements aided the strike efforts, many foreign workers still held Cubans in contempt, and mill workers looked down upon unskilled field hands. While some railway workers supported the strike, the Brotherhood of Railway Employees, an affiliate of the American Federation of Labor's Pan-American Federation of Labor (PAFL), promised to back the government in case of violence. Cuban professional employees in the sugar industry through their organization, the National Sugar Industry Association, acknowledged that the workers' demands coincided with their own interests, but most of them stopped short of join-

36 *Facts About Sugar*, March 27, 1926, April 14, 1928; Tromp, *Sugar Cane Factory*, p. 562.
37 *Facts About Sugar*, August 10, 1929.
38 Ibid., December 14, 1929.
39 Ibid., December 6, 1924.

ing the labor action. Colonos at seven of the centrales supported the owners and called for government assistance. By Christmas the strikes had collapsed, and the workers returned to the mills without having won recognition of their unions.[40] But their lukewarm middle-class allies had already begun to regret their timidity.

When President Zayas had called for a meeting between the strikers and mill owners in early December, the National Sugar Industry Association objected to its exclusion and asserted that its members were indeed workers. At the same time, the Association's members continued to reject the more radical goals of the strikers, certain that an extreme course of action would bring swift U.S. intervention.[41] Despite these differences, a common theme of nationalist protest would link the Cuban working and middle classes in the sugar industry as American companies accelerated their rationalization of the sugar mills.

National City Bank's creation of the General Sugar Company embodied the effort of American corporate reformers to fully introduce scientific management. When National City encountered problems with its Cuban sugar loans, Charles Mitchell brought in Colonel Edward Deeds to salvage the bank's interests. Deeds, an electrical engineer, had worked for National Cash Register, a firm renowned for its efforts in scientific marketing and industrial welfare. With Charles Kettering, Deeds established the Dayton Engineering Labs (DELCO), which later formed part of the General Motors Research Laboratory.[42] Deeds' tenure at General Sugar was marked by "the introduction of American business methods and modern machinery . . ." Deeds emulated American experiments in industrial relations, offering workers improved health care and sanitary conditions, for "with better health came happier workers and a corresponding increase in efficiency." He also imposed more rigorous standards of performance on his Cuban labor force. In noting that innovation, his biographer also pointed to an assumption about Cubans that constituted a central part of the American corporate mindset:

The Deeds sense of human values was also responsible for his ability to reconcile the differences between the business and working methods of the Anglo-Saxon and the Latin. The Latin and particularly one of Spanish extraction, is the world's most inveterate procrastinator. With him there is always time to do the job tomorrow. Deeds's technique of prompt, direct and forceful procedure created something akin to consternation at the start.[43]

Much like Deeds' biographer, other American sugar companies minimized the issue of Cuban resistance to these changes and plunged ahead

40 Ibid., October 11, 18, 25, November 1, 6, 15, December 6, 20, 1924; Ursinio Rojas, *Las luchas obreras en el central Tacajo* (Havana: Ciencias Sociales, 1979), pp. 51–52.

41 Rosell, ed., *Luchas contra Machado*, pp. 44–47, 61.

42 Isaac F. Marcosson, *Colonel Deeds: Industrial Builder* (New York: Dodd, Mead, 1948), pp. 66, 70, 90–91.

43 Ibid., pp. 308, 310.

with their own installation of modern technology and management techniques.

The United Fruit Company's strategy during the 1920s closely paralleled that of General Sugar. The firm installed new equipment at every stage of the milling process and electrified all functions in the mills except the tandems. These monuments to American corporate technology came under increasing control of professional technicians. As the company reported in 1931, "systematic control over the entire [milling] house is maintained by the chemists."[44] This thoroughgoing technification and rationalization of the sugar factory by American corporate reformers stood in marked contrast to the work relations that still predominated in many Cuban-owned mills.

American corporations' accelerated rationalization of sugar mill operations further depersonalized the work place. As a report in 1936 concluded, " . . . the larger milling aggregations do not lend themselves so readily to relationships of loyalty and paternalism . . . The most successful large mills substitute an elaborate administrative machinery with checks and balances, and emphasis on fair dealing and punctual fulfillment of obligations."[45] In that depersonalized work place, the workers demanded a role in corporate decision making and protested against their displacement in the national labor market. A secret report by the Cuban military in 1925 concluded that Cuban workers, preoccupied a quarter century earlier with achieving political independence, now focused on union recognition – recognition which would give workers considerable influence in the management of companies.[46] Moreover, in the American sugar mills Cubans continued to encounter displacement and subordination.

Cuban workers had long found themselves displaced in the national labor market by Spaniards, Chinese and other immigrants. That problem intensified with the growth of American influence. As one Cuban sugar worker noted, a different nationality seemed to dominate each aspect of the production process, from Haitians who cut the cane to Chinese who ran the boiling houses. Cubans were the one exception. As he ruefully concluded, "The Cuban was displaced everywhere."[47] Where skilled workers did not find themselves displaced, they found their job knowledge called into question and subordinated to the expertise of American engineers. Such concerns helped link mill workers to white-collar employees and at least some of the colonos.

In 1925 the middle-class National Sugar Industry Association's members voiced their complaints to the head of the American-owned Cuban Cane Sugar Corporation. They noted that American sugar companies were

44 *UNIFRUTCO*, February 1931; García and Zanetti, eds., *United Fruit*, pp. 138–39; Gilmore, *Sugar Manual*, passim.
45 Foreign Policy Association, *Problems of the New Cuba*, pp. 289–90.
46 Rosell, ed., *Luchas contra Machado*, p. 87.
47 Branly, *MINAZ*, p. 57; García Suárez, *Los fundidores*, p. 18.

systematically replacing Cuban engineers, managers, doctors, nurses, chemists and even typists with Americans, causing "hunger and misery" in Cuban homes.[48] They pointed out that the American companies imported almost all their material inputs; prohibited colonos from growing foodstuffs, making them dependent on the company stores; and in sum failed to develop the national economy. As a result ". . . we Cubans are condemned to vegetate like pariahs in our own country."[49] After a decade of repression, mill workers, white-collar employees and elements of the petite bourgeoisie would join together in revolt. Yet they could not necessarily rely on most of the rural population, including many colonos and field hands, to join them in resistance to a process of rationalization and displacement. Work relations in the cane fields had been only marginally affected by rationalization, and one-third of the field hands were immigrants who had benefited from the displacement of Cuban cane cutters.

As the 1920s progressed, the penetration of American corporate culture touched the agricultural sector of the industry. By the end of the decade American sugar companies had begun to introduce mechanical devices to reduce the labor intensity of operations in the cane fields. They began employing steam and then gas and diesel tractors to replace oxen in plowing and hauling. They also experimented with mechanical loaders and even combine devices that would cut, strip and load cane. Paralleling technical innovations came changes in work relations as well. American sugar companies sought to create the broad wage labor market that had failed to emerge in the decades after abolition by recruiting Haitians and other West Indians to work on their centrales. The vast expansion of their landholdings proletarianized many smallholder agriculturists, adding to the wage labor population in the East. As labor became more readily available, some American companies reduced their dependence on labor contractors and involved themselves more directly in the management of their field hands.[50]

Yet experiments in labor-saving technology and the growth of a rural wage labor market did not transform Cuban sugar fields into modern factory systems. Of forty centrales in Oriente province responding to a survey in 1928, fewer than half reported any use of tractors, mechanical haulers or other modern field devices. The use of such equipment supplemented rather than replaced the use of oxen and was almost always restricted to fields directly administered by the mills. The United Fruit Company in its reliance on sugar cane from fields which it directly administered stood out as the exception rather than the rule among American sugar corporations. In the survey, only United Fruit noted that "mod-

48 Rosell, ed., *Luchas contra Machado*, pp. 44–45, 62.
49 Ibid., p. 63.
50 Gilmore, *Sugar Manual*, passim; García and Zanetti, eds., *United Fruit*, p. 144; *Facts About Sugar*, July 11, 1925, February 16, 1929; Hoernel, "Social Change in Oriente, Cuba," pp. 234, 239; Cabrera, *1920*, pp. 36–37; Pérez, *Reform and Revolution*, p. 204.

ern field methods play an important part in maintaining production and increasing cultivated areas . . ."[51] Other respondents explained their limited use of modern field technology as resulting from physical conditions in the fields, or wrote wistfully of the future use of mechanical devices. These observations reflected problems which cane growers around the globe had encountered in mechanizing operations. In rough, muddy cane fields, oxen often proved more efficient than tractors, and sugar cane did not lend itself to the use of mechanical harvesters. But beyond these universal obstacles to mechanization, the problem most frequently cited by growers in Cuba was the persistence of the colono system.

The growth of the dependent colono system appeared to fly in the face of economic rationalization, which sought to replace human labor with machinery. American corporations loaned large sums to colonos which might have to be written off in times of falling sugar prices. The experience of the United Fruit Company indicated that administration cane could be produced more cheaply than colono cane. Finally, American producers readily admitted that the capital-poor colono system stood as the principal barrier to modernization of the agricultural sector. The American commercial attaché in Havana concluded in 1931, "The whole [colono] system seems illogical . . ."[52] However, colono production possessed an advantageous logic for American mills operators.

By the 1920s payments to colonos came in the form of cash or credit based on the price of sugar. Any sharp downturn in prices left the colono with the resulting losses. Furthermore, centrales could choose to process colono cane during periods of low prices and hold their own cane until a recovery occurred, further shifting the cost of production to the colonos. While United Fruit's commitment to administration cane had paid large dividends during the war when sugar prices remained high, the sharp downturn in prices during the twenties allowed mills relying on colono production to transfer those losses to their tenants.[53] Unlike the impact of the Grace operations in the Peruvian sugar industry, which wiped out small producers, the growth of American centrales and their landholdings actually accelerated the growth of the dependent colono system. In 1905 fields directly administered by mills, those managed by colonos renting mill land, and fields owned by independent colonos each accounted for approximately one-third of Cuba's cane area. By 1930 cane produced by the mills accounted for only 18 percent of the total; by independent colonos, 17 percent; and by dependent colonos, 65 percent.[54] Thus the re-

51 García and Zanetti, eds., *United Fruit Company,* p. 144; Gilmore, *Sugar Manual,* p. 196.

52 Frederick Todd, "Production Costs and Prices of Sugar in Cuba," Havana, August 14, 1931, RG 151, USNA.

53 U.S. Department of Commerce, *Sugar Cane,* pp. 360–65; García and Zanetti, eds., *United Fruit Company,* pp. 119–23, 154–55; Todd, "Production Costs and Prices of Sugar in Cuba," August 14, 1931, RG 151, USNA.

54 Foreign Policy Association, *Problems of the New Cuba,* p. 270; Todd, "Production Costs and Prices of Sugar in Cuba," August 14, 1931, RG 151, USNA.

lationship between modern American sugar mills and tenant farmers offered an additional impediment to the existing physical obstacles to renovation of the agricultural sector. As a result, sugar would remain a bifurcated industry with a modernized manufacturing sector and a highly traditional agricultural branch.

Small dependent colono producers who lived at the mercy of the centrales comprised an important rural petite bourgeoisie with deep-seated resentments toward American companies. Small merchants in the countryside added their numbers to this group as they found the centrales' company stores monopolizing the rural consumer market. Yet the resentment of American sugar companies which they shared with sugar mill workers and employees did not necessarily make for a close-knit alliance. American corporate culture, while it impacted every aspect of the sugar industry, established distinct relationships with important segments of Cuban rural society. Sugar mill workers and employees shared the experience of a rationalized and depersonalized work place in which they were clearly subordinated to Americans. For these groups, control of the work environment became a central issue. But unlike the small banana growers of Central America or sugar growers in northern Peru, who saw their role diminish as a result of American companies, Cuban colonos saw their role in the industry expand when American corporations increased their investment. Their concerns centered on a more equitable economic relationship with the American centrales. Field workers and shopkeepers might share the resentment of subordination, but their concerns remained at the level of wages, prices and markets. Ethnicity divided the sugar workers themselves as the Cubans reacted against the West Indians' English-language culture and their willingness to accept lower wages than their Cuban counterparts. Those differences would have important consequences as Cuban workers responded to American corporate culture.

Although important divisions existed within the rural sugar community, Cuban workers and employees as well as some members of the rural petite bourgeoisie found a common nationalist cause in displacement and subordination by American corporate culture as the industry's fortunes worsened at the end of the 1920s. These groups would find willing allies among other workers and employees with a shared experience of American corporate culture. The Cuban workers and employees of the General Electric Corporation stood at the forefront of those potential allies.

Power

As a direct extension of G. E., American and Foreign Power conveyed not only the technology but the full range of systems and values of American corporate culture to Latin America. In 1922, when G. E. began acquiring Cuban electric companies, Gerard Swope assumed the presidency of the company. Under Swope, an engineer by training, G. E. initiated "the modernization of methods and machinery . . ." and introduced a full range of industrial relations programs which "established an enviable record of labor peace . . . and by so doing maintained the high productive efficiency of its personnel." Swope also launched a campaign to introduce a wide range of consumer products, which by the end of the 1920s accounted for half of G. E.'s business.[55] G. E.'s emissary of change in Cuba also carried impressive credentials for his mission.

Henry Catlin had arranged for G. E. to acquire a German-owned electric company in Guatemala. Although Catlin's dealings with the Guatemala dictator Manuel Estrada Cabrera led to a public outcry which forced Catlin to flee Guatemala, his ability to insinuate himself into the good graces of Latin American dictators would prove useful as G. E. invested in Cuba.[56] Armed with $8 million of the company's money, Catlin arrived in Cuba in 1922, and in less than two years acquired most of Cuba's electric power companies. Cuba's small, undercapitalized electric firms that employed outdated equipment to service limited local markets represented an excellent opportunity for the introduction of advanced technology, management techniques and marketing practices.

Shortly after Catlin acquired Eduardo Chibás' Compañía Eléctrica de Alumbrada y Tracción de Santiago in September 1922, a team of American accountants arrived to examine its books. The auditors found many of the company's ledgers in a smoldering heap. Poring over the remaining materials, the American accountants quickly discovered the reasons for the ledger bonfire. The company's directors had disposed of debit accounts by creating non-existent credits. The cash account came up short by over $10,000, most of it stolen by the company's cashier. The firm hadn't bothered carrying out an inventory since 1917. Similar if less dramatic problems awaited the auditors in other companies AFP acquired.[57] Other surprises awaited them in the Cuban companies' management systems and work places.

In the Cuban electrical industry, many of the informal managerial and work practices that had once characterized American industry still persisted. Control of the work process remained largely in the hands of workers and managers who operated with a considerable degree of independence. The accountants at times found these managerial and labor systems surprisingly effective, but they insisted on rooting them out. This insistence on imposing scientific management practices came across clearly in their discussion of the Compañía de Electricidad de Cárdenas:

55 "Two Decades of General Electric Leadership," pp. 3, 6–8, in "General Electric," Scudder Collection; Noble, *America by Design*, p. 279.

56 "Mr. Henry A. Catlin at Present Representing the Electric Bond and Share Company in Cuba," memorandum, Division of Latin American Affairs, September 23, 1930, 837.6463 EB&S/1, RG 59, USNA.

57 "Report on Examination: Compania Cubana de Electricidad S.A. Santa Clara Cuba," June 30, 1923, Box 143219; "Report on Examination: Camaguey Electric Co. S.A. and Predecessor Companies, Camaguey, Cuba," September 30, 1923, Box 143116, EBASCO.

There was no system for purchasing and the various chiefs of departments made purchases as they felt the need for them and had the bills sent to the office or paid them out of pocket and collected from the company. The mayordomos [supervisors] and chiefs of departments were necessarily persons of integrity and enjoying the confidence of their employers but the system was open to abuse and so deeply infixed that it was found very difficult to break.[58]

The auditors expressed even greater distress over the Cuban companies' systems for billing their customers.

At the Cienfuegos Light and Power Company, customer billings ran a month in arrears. The billing system placed considerable power in the hands of the meter readers and collectors, who could easily cover up the delinquent bill of a friend or relative, and it left the collectors idle for as much as a week each month. AFP personnel set about diligently redesigning the system to ensure timeliness, accountability and the elimination of the collectors' free time. Those changes prompted considerable resistance from the Cuban employees. As the accountants noted:

This procedure had become so firmly fixed in the minds of the local office employees that it took months of intensive hammering to change it. However, by changing the meter reading date, installing some up-to-date office machines and thoroughly drilling employees all billings in the future will be completed no later than the last day of each current month.[59]

And AFP introduced far more than office machinery into the Cuban power system.

By 1924, AFP had already invested over $4 million to increase the power-generating and transmission capacities of its Cuban subsidiaries. In addition to upgrading power equipment, AFP automated its substations, replacing their full-time operators with part-time inspectors, thereby cutting its operating costs in half. By 1926 plans were under way to mechanize the coal-handling and crushing equipment at the company's main generating plant in Havana. In addition to saving labor, automation helped underwrite rewards for workers.[60]

By improving productivity, managers reduced labor costs and passed part of the savings on to workers. In 1926 when a $1 a day minimum wage remained an unfulfilled goal of the Cuban labor movement, common laborers at G. E. plants earned $2.48 for eight hours' work. In comparison with mining and agricultural enterprises, the company developed

58 "Report on Examination: Compania de Electricidad de Cardenas S.A.," January 31, 1923, Box 143116, EBASCO.

59 "Report on Examination: The Cienfuegos Electric Light and Power Company," January 31, 1923, Box 143219, EBASCO.

60 "Havana Report," March 2, 1926 (hereafter "Havana Report"), Box 147071, EBASCO; Louis Banigan to William Phillips, acting secretary of state, Washington, D.C., December 6, 1933, 837.6463 Electric Bond & Share Co. (hereafter EB&S)/11, RG 59, USNA.

Figure 15. Baseball players for AFP's Havana Electric Company subsidiary
celebrating the traditional "first pitch." Competitive team sports formed an
important part of AFP's efforts to Americanize its workers. (From *Diario de la
Marina* [Havana], December 17, 1933. Library of Congress)

a sophisticated managerial culture to deal with its relatively skilled labor
force. G. E. promoted the idea of a workforce composed of ambitious individuals loyal to the company. It published a monthly employee magazine,
formed a social club and athletic teams, and offered self-improvement
classes. But high pay and courses of study did not prove to be synonymous
with respect.[61]

The drive toward technological improvement and automation derived
not only from efforts to achieve efficiency but also from the company's estimate of the quality of Cuban workers. One report concluded, "The natives are rather excitable by nature and therefore do not make high class
station operators."[62] At the Havana Electric Railway, Light and Power
Company, AFP also had to deal with a union. But the firm's managers expressed optimism about the labor situation. As they reported, "The relations between the company and the Union de Obreros are conducted on a
strictly 'Open shop' basis. The native workers are very excitable and have
a tendency to be antagonistic toward the Americans, and therefore have to
be handled very diplomatically."[63]

61 "Havana Report," Box 147071, EBASCO; "Compania Cubana de Electricidad, General Review of
   Company Affairs," January 16, 1933 (hereafter "Compania Cubana, 1933"), Box 147068,
   EBASCO.
62 "Havana Report," Box 147071, EBASCO.
63 Ibid.

Internal management procedures and work-place relations were not the only areas affected by AFP's investments in Cuba. In order for the company to generate sufficient revenues from its massive investment in capacity, it had to rapidly widen and deepen the Cuban market. The electrification of sugar refining and mining operations and government buildings offered only a partial answer. Cubans had to become consumers of electrical appliances. Gerard Swope's drive to create a consumer market for G. E.'s products provided the solution. AFP introduced the latest in American marketing techniques, including mass advertising campaigns. Each AFP subsidiary operated its own store where employees, working on commission, pressed upon the Cuban public every conceivable electrical appliance, from radios to washing machines. Time-payment schemes allowed consumers to purchase the items with down payments that often did not equal the commission paid to the sales person. While attempting to infuse Cuban society with American corporate culture, AFP also incorporated Cuban power brokers into the new order.[64]

In 1923 Henry Catlin acquired the Compañía Cubana de Electricidad in Santa Clara. Through that purchase Catlin solidified his ties with the company's owner, General Gerardo Machado, an ambitious local politician. Catlin used $500,000 of G. E.'s money to finance the general's successful 1924 presidential campaign. When President Machado visited the United States in 1925 and 1927, he was accompanied by his good friend Henry Catlin, greeted by the highest-ranking government officials and toasted at banquets hosted by AFP and National City Bank officials. Catlin used his relationship with Machado to serve his own interests as well as those of AFP and other American firms.[65] Between 1927 and 1930 Catlin received $55,000 from the Chase National Bank for services in connection with its loans to the Machado regime. As one bank official described the situation, "He [Catlin] runs in and out of the [presidential] palace every little while, and is trying to get his own taxes reduced, and would be delighted to play Lady Bountiful with the funds of the Chase Bank."[66] Yet Catlin reserved his most significant services as an intermediary for the benefit of AFP.

President Gerardo Machado generally favored American businesses, encouraging them to expand their investments on the island and providing them with labor peace by suppressing strike actions. But Machado reserved

64 "Memorandum to Frank D. Mahoney, Vice President, Cia. Cubana de Electricidad," New York, October 19, 1932, Box 142197, EBASCO.

65 On the company's payments to Machado, see Carleton Beals, *The Crime of Cuba* (Philadelphia: Lippincott, 1933), p. 242. The AFP records make no direct mention of contributions to the Machado campaign, but as of December 1924 Catlin had expended $8,200,000. Of this sum, he lumped $650,000 under the heading "Cuban Investigation Expenses," a sum which the company's attorneys later concluded "could not be justified as part of depreciable property in the property acquisitions to which they relate . ." (E. R. Gilpin to Cowden Evans, New York, April 13, 1938, Box 144339, EBASCO); Robert Freeman Smith, *The United States and Cuba: Business and Diplomacy, 1917–1960* (New York: Bookman Associates, 1960), p. 115; Benjamin, *The United States and Cuba,* pp. 50–51; *Facts About Sugar,* April 30, 1927.

66 *New York Times,* October 24, 1933.

special consideration for the G. E. subsidiary. AFP encountered considerable problems in most of its Latin American operations because local officials impeded the condemning of rights-of-way for the construction of power lines. With Machado in power, local government officials made every effort to accommodate the company. As Machado later assured Henry Catlin, he always looked after Catlin's business interests "as if they were my own . . ."[67] Yet the company's close ties to Machado and other Cuban politicians contributed to the outbreak of consumer protest against the company.

Electricity rates in Cuba varied between 15 and 17 cents per kilowatt, or about twice the rates prevailing in major American cities, because of much higher costs. These rates remained in effect during the first three decades of the twentieth century, despite tremendous strides made in productivity. Higher costs in Cuba stemmed from a poor load factor and the expense of political influence. In electrical generation, optimum load factor refers to a power plant operating at maximum capacity, thereby lowering its costs of production per kilowatt hour. AFP generated most of its output in Cuba for lighting purposes, a source of demand that suffered from sharp daily fluctuations. As a result, the company achieved maximum usage for only about one hour per day. Even given the problem of load factor, however, Cuban electricity rates were excessive.[68] AFP's purchase of political influence comprised a hidden expense that contributed to those high rates.

By 1931 the national and local governments of Cuba owed AFP $7 million in unpaid bills. Local politicians and other influential Cubans owed the company another $1.7 million. Actions against the municipalities would bring legal problems, and public exposure of free service to prominent individuals would trigger a populist outcry. Instead the company assumed the position that its high rates resulted from insufficient usage by customers in outlying areas. Thus the actual problem of load factor became an excuse to cover up the high cost of AFP subsidies to influential political figures. Eventually these difficulties sparked a consumer rebellion in which Gerardo Machado gamely defended the interests of the company.[69]

AFP's 250,000 Cuban customers became increasingly disenchanted with the company's high rates during the decade of the twenties, setting the stage for alliances between the local middle class, the petite bourgeoisie and AFP workers. Periodically groups or entire communities boycotted the firm's electric light services. Since rates had been set under agreements with municipalities, local governments began passing rate reduction resolutions. Between 1922 and 1929 Cuban municipalities passed forty-six such resolutions, only to have them vetoed by President Machado. When local governments appealed to the Supreme Court, the

67 Rosell, ed., *Luchas contra Machado*, p. 175; Henry Leslie Robinson, "American and Foreign Power Company in Latin America: A Case Study" (Ph.D. dissertation, Stanford University, 1967), p. 35; "Havana Report," Box 147071, EBASCO.

68 Foreign Policy Association, *Problems of the New Cuba*, pp. 401–2, 411–16.

69 F. T. F. Dumont to secretary of state, Havana, July 18, 1931, 837.6463/6, RG 59, USNA.

Machado-appointed court consistently rejected their appeals.[70] When the Great Depression cast its shadow across the world economy, the gross earnings of AFP's Cuban operations fell from $18 million in 1929 to $12 million in 1932. Heavy investment in power generation and transmission capacity now placed an intolerable burden on the company, which derived 25 to 30 percent of its revenues from its Cuban operations. Cuban consumers, with their own incomes severely squeezed by the depression, now became incensed by high electricity rates, high-pressure sales tactics and sale of repossessed and repaired appliances represented as new.[71]

The number of community-based consumer strikes increased sharply in 1930 to twenty-four and jumped again in 1931 to twenty-eight. The latter figure included a nationwide consumer strike which began in June and cost the company 40,000 customers. Henry Catlin explained to a sympathetic minister of the interior that the company might be able to reduce rates 2 or 3 cents per kilowatt, but not the 30 to 50 percent demanded by the boycotters. And so, with Gerardo Machado's support, AFP managers grimly clung to the high rates. By the time the boycott ended in June 1932, the company's desperation over its falling revenues led it to strike out at the municipalities. With the cooperation of the Interior Ministry, AFP cut off service to twenty-three towns and cities in July 1932. As they ran out of funds to fight AFP in court, Cuba's urban governments began signing new contracts that maintained the existing electricity rates.[72] By early 1933 AFP had successfully weathered the national consumers' strike and was aggressively attacking the problems of municipal indebtedness and rate reduction resolutions. Yet these successes came against a backdrop of mounting social, economic and political turmoil in Cuba. The country stood poised on the brink of an upheaval that would force AFP's principal political ally from office.

As the Great Depression tightened its grip upon Cuba, workers, the middle class and small business people would join forces against giant American corporations such as AFP and the General Sugar Company. They rebelled in part against low wages, job displacement, job losses and high electricity rates. Workers and white-collar employees who experienced American corporate culture most intensely also reacted against American managers who viewed them as inherently inferior but still attempted to transform them into well-regulated corporate functionaries. These protesters had diverse causes and goals, but their common nationalist theme welded them into a powerful national movement which would affect not only AFP but all major American corporations in Cuba.

70 "Memorandum to Frank D. Mahoney, Vice President, Cia. Cubana de Electricidad," New York, October 19, 1932, Box 142197, EBASCO; Foreign Policy Association, *Problems of the New Cuba*, pp. 401–2.

71 "American and Foreign Power Company Inc. Annual Reports," 1929–33, Box 320999, EBASCO.

72 Harry Guggenheim to secretary of state, Havana, August 10, 1931, 837.5045/8, RG 59, USNA; Beals, *Crime*, pp. 243–44; "Compania Cubana, 1933," Box 147068, EBASCO.

9

Revolution and reaction

{T}here was a red flag waving from the highest point of the mill. And there were workers taking the barrio La Hilda, and forming the Mabay soviet. And there was José Angel feeling proud to be a man, to be a worker . . . (José Angel, sugar worker)

In the eyes of most American statesmen and business executives, Gerardo Machado proved to be the Cuban president for whom they had been searching for a quarter of a century. While appealing to and partially appeasing Cuban nationalism, Machado respected and protected American investments, providing the stable political environment in which American companies could thrive. Most importantly, Machado proved his value to American corporations by meeting and mastering the challenge presented by resistant workers and local elites.

In the same year that Machado assumed office, the Cuban Communist party was founded, and it soon gained a leading role in the country's most important labor federation, the Confederación Nacional Obrera Cubana (CNOC). Machado responded with a carrot-and-stick approach to increasing labor militancy. He used armed force to break strikes, deport émigré labor organizers and assassinate union leaders. At the same time, Machado acquiesced in the creation of the Cuban Federation of Labor, which quickly affiliated itself with the AFL through the anti-Communist Pan-American Federation of Labor.[1] Like Leguía in Peru and Ibáñez in Chile, Machado also borrowed tens of millions of dollars from American banks to fund a massive public works program which partly offset worsening conditions in the national economy. But those deteriorating conditions eventually undermined Machado's rule and triggered a revolution that gave vent to popular protests against dictatorship and depression, and to a nationalist outcry against American corporations. In fact, the Americans became the principal targets of the popular uprising.

The year 1932 had proved to be a grim year for Gerardo Machado. Sugar prices, which had begun falling in 1924, were headed toward their lowest

---

1 Thomas, *Cuba*, pp. 579–80; Memorandum of conversation between Gerardo Machado and Calvin Coolidge, Washington, D.C., April 23, 1927, 033.3711/73, RG 59, USNA; Foreign Policy Association, *Problems of the New Cuba*, p. 187.

point in history. His close friend Henry Catlin died, and the flow of international credits slowed to a trickle. American banks recognized that loans to the Cuban government had not financed a rational program of development. The state had simply poured funds into projects to offset rising inflation and falling wages. As a J. P. Morgan official noted in 1927, "I visited Secretary [Carlos] Céspedes at the Public Works Office and am satisfied that he is crazy. He is anxious to do a lot of work, and does not, I think, care very much whether he ruins Cuba or not."[2] Yet such candid observations did nothing to slow the flow of international bank credits, provided in light of the stabilizing effect which state largesse had on Cuban politics. But by 1932 the continuing collapse of the sugar market made it impossible for the government to finance additional loans. American banks now limited their disbursements to short-term refunding of the existing debt. Even government workers and contractors could not squeeze overdue salaries and payments from the Machado regime. As the national economy disintegrated, Cuban society rapidly advanced toward undeclared civil war. As a general strike spread across the island in early August 1933, U.S. ambassador Sumner Welles perceived the outlines of a social revolution that threatened American hegemony. Welles gave Cuban military commanders a choice of U.S. intervention or a coup d'etat. They chose the latter course and toppled Machado. Yet a mere change of command did not slow the upheaval.[3]

The interim regime of Carlos Céspedes proved incapable of harnessing the revolutionary forces which the struggle against Machado had unleashed. Strikes continued, with sugar workers seizing mills, taking managers hostage and organizing "soviets." A revolt by army sergeants, led by Fulgencio Batista, on September 3 put an end to the hapless Céspedes government and led to the installation of the reformist Ramón Grau San Martín as president. Yet the revolution continued, and as it took on a nationalistic tone, the American sugar companies and AFP rapidly emerged as two of its principal targets.

In 1933 near starvation wages prevailed in the Cuban sugar industry. The modernized American centrales still produced sugar but not profits. Mill owners cut output, reduced working hours and slashed wages, driving their workers to desperation. The mill workers and office and company store employees then attempted to take control of the situation. On August 2 workers at the Chaparra and Delicias mills of the Cuban American Sugar Company struck, triggering a wave of strikes that engulfed Cuba's principal industry. On August 21 the mill workers at the central Punta Alegre went beyond striking and seized the plant. Within a month, the workers occupied thirty-six mills, most of them U.S.-owned. They

2 Vernon Monroe, "Memorandum on Public Works Situation in Cuba," Havana, July 8, 1927, File 4, Box 90, Lamont Papers. On Catlin, see *New York Times*, September 28, 1932.
3 Pérez, *Platt Amendment*, pp. 265–317.

Figure 16. Fulgencio Batista (left) and Ramón Grau San Martín (right) with
Colonel Juan Blas Hernández, a famed anti-Machado guerrilla leader, Havana,
October 1933. (United States National Archives)

formed "soviets" and "red guards" and extended their control to nearby
towns and port facilities.[4]

Events at the American-owned central Homiguero typified the revolutionary upheaval in the eastern sugar region. On August 27 two thousand
armed workers surrounded the central, presented the manager with a list
of demands and gave him five minutes to sign it. After the manager
signed, the workers dispersed, but armed strikers returned the next day.
At this point the central's owners secured the protection of a twenty-five-
man contingent of the Rural Guard. But members of the Guard proceeded to fraternize with the workers, and the armed strikers extended
their presence into the surrounding countryside. At the Chaparra and
Delicias mills, the strike spread to the Cuban American Company's Chaparra Light and Power Company and Chaparra Railway Company. The
company managers fled to a British steamer anchored off the Cuban coast.
On August 27 the workers at the central Boston of the United Fruit Company took control of the mill and raised a red flag over the company's

4 Samuel S. Dickson to secretary of state, Havana, December 28, 1933, 337.1153 Cuban American
  Sugar Company (hereafter CAS)/1, RG 59, USNA; Foreign Policy Association, *Problems of the New
  Cuba,* p. 183; Lee R. Blohm, "The Labor Situation in the Cuban Sugar Industry," Havana Con-
  sulate, November 20, 1933, RG 84, USNA.

properties.[5] The euphoria and spontaneity of these actions was captured by one worker at the central Mabay who recalled that "there was a red flag waving from the highest point of the mill. And there were workers taking the barrio La Hilda, and forming the Mabay soviet. And there was José Angel feeling proud to be a man, to be a worker . . ."[6]

The workers at the Baguanos and Tacajo mills of the Punta Alegre Company struck and placed two managers under house arrest. After the company conceded their initial demands, the workers struck again to gain further concessions. By early October the workers had agreed to return to work, but the Punta Alegre's manager, Maurice Leonard, reported that there was "no attempt by the large body of men to do an honest day's work . . ." Soldiers were again fraternizing with the strikers, and Leonard decided to call for the personal intervention of Fulgencio Batista "to drive off our properties those Communistic elements." But Batista, fearful of a possible coup in Havana, refused to travel to the eastern end of the island.[7]

Despite the Communistic aspects of the upheaval, the Communist party actually had little role in its early phase. Although the CNOC had been organizing in the mills since at least 1932, the Communist party frankly admitted that it had been caught off guard by the events in August and September. Most of what transpired in the sugar mills sprang directly from white- and blue-collar discontent. Given the dire economic circumstances which triggered the rebellion, the workers' aspirations included minimum wages and overtime, and were directed at Cuban as well as American-owned mills. Yet many of their demands focused on working conditions and control of the work place. The demands of the Hormiguero laborers presented on August 28 included the eight-hour day, recognition of their union, protection from mistreatment by overseers, free speech and assembly, and the right to strike. They insisted on a company-supported social and sports club but one which would be "under the direction of young laborers and their elders."[8] The United Fruit Company strikers also wanted union recognition and the eight-hour day, as well as prohibition of firings without just cause. The Chaparra mill workers later repeated these demands and added the union shop and an end to piece work and the constant reassignment of workers to new tasks, as well as equal pay for equal work.[9]

5 Knox Alexander, "Strikes by the Sugar Workers in Province of Santa Clara," Cienfuegos, August 28, 1933, 837.5045/44, RG 59, USNA; George Rublee to Cordell Hull, Washington, D.C., December 30, 1933, 337.1153 CAS/5; memorandum, L. H. Woolsey for Mr. Wilson, Washington, D.C., August 30, 1933, 837.00/3791; memorandum, L. H. Woolsey, Washington, D.C., September 5, 1933, 837.00/3840, RG 59, USNA.
6 Núñez Machín, *Memoria amarga*, pp. 71–72.
7 Sumner Welles to secretary of state, Havana, October 11, 1933, 837.00/4207; E. R. Leonard to secretary of state, Washington, D.C., October 21, 1933, 837.00/4270, RG 59, USNA.
8 Alexander, "Strikes by the Sugar Workers in Province of Santa Clara," August 28, 1933, 837.5045/44, RG 59, USNA.
9 H. Freeman Matthews to secretary of state, Havana, February 13, 1934, 337.1153 CAS/50, RG 59, USNA.

The Cuban sugar mill workers defined the clash of cultures that had been destabilizing Cuban society for more than a decade. They reacted strongly to an American corporate culture that challenged worker control through increased technology in the work place, strove to speed up work through the task system, assigned workers according to the needs of production, and replaced patriarchal work relations with administrative rules. Workers insisted on increased control through unions that would determine hiring, firing and work assignments. Their demands went beyond simple control of the work place and extended to social values, as indicated by the Chaparra workers' demand for a social club controlled by the elders of the working-class community. Concerns about equal pay also expressed an ongoing resentment against their subordination to Americans. Yet at the same time the workers also drew upon concepts held dear by Americans, such as freedom of assembly and freedom of speech, to counteract what they found objectionable in American corporate culture. Nor were the upheavals at the sugar mills confined strictly to mill workers.

At the central Mabay, Haitians and Jamaican field hands joined the strike. Many of the mills' supervisors, office workers and company store clerks as well as independent shopkeepers supported the strikes. The sugar workers at the central Tacajo provided support for campesinos threatened with the loss of their land. At the central Río Cauto in Oriente province, the striking workers received the support of campesinos and local merchants, with Jamaican field hands also recruited into the strike movement. At the Santa Lucía central, colonos provided cash payments to help support the strikers. These popular protests that crossed class lines found a strong echo in events involving the American and Foreign Power Company.[10]

With the collapse of the Machado regime, a new consumer boycott erupted against AFP. Slogans painted on walls urged Cubans not to pay their electricity bills. Newspaper editorialists and radio commentators echoed these sentiments. In a scene repeated across the island, hundreds of local citizens attended a rally in Cienfuegos to hear the company denounced as a foreign exploiter of the Cuban people and an ardent supporter of Gerardo Machado. Well aware that its principal political ally had fled the scene, the company agreed to the creation of a government commission to study the rate issue, with the understanding that customers would resume paying their bills. Yet the boycott continued, and the commission never issued its report. Instead, on December 6 President Grau issued a decree reducing electricity rates by 45 percent. The company protested vigorously, strongly suggesting that the decree violated the Platt Amendment.[11] Even as the decree was being issued, the company faced a labor rebellion that led to worker control of the company.

10 Rojas, *Tacajo*, pp. 71, 185–89; Instituto de Historia del Movimiento Comunista y de la Revolución Socialista de Cuba, *El movimiento obrero cubano: documentos y artículos*, vol. 2: *1925–1935* (Havana: Editorial de Ciencias Sociales, 1977), p. 625.
11 Foreign Policy Association, *Problems of the New Cuba*, pp. 402–5.

Despite the substantial material rewards AFP offered its workers, a variety of factors fed a deep and growing resentment toward the company. American managers held Cuban workers in low regard, and Americans received clearly preferential treatment over Cuban employees. Furthermore, the company attempted to eradicate informal work habits and accounting methods that provided workers with a significant degree of leisure time and considerable authority in the work place. Automation of plants and substations threatened workers with the loss of their jobs or control over them. Increased pressures in the work place affected white-collar employees as well. The company installed office machinery, insisted that employees devote some of their "free hours" to working in appliance stores on a commission basis and subjected them to "pep meetings." What American managers viewed as self-improvement training for ambitious individuals, Cuban employees often viewed as a barrage of service bulletins, magazines and Berlitz classes designed to instill in them values and attitudes that ran contrary to their own beliefs and interests. One AFP executive "went to unprecedented lengths in prying into the personal affairs of many employees outside of office hours and attempting to regulate the conduct of their private lives."[12] Even university-educated Cuban professionals who appeared to fit the corporate mold were told that they did not have sufficient technical training to occupy management positions.[13]

The experiences of workers and white-collar employees reflected a complex cultural interaction that had developed within AFP. On the one hand the company offered monetary incentives and the promise of continuing material improvement in an environment that encouraged individual achievement. But Cuban workers found that automation challenged their job control and the existence of the jobs themselves. Workers and employees objected to attempts to control them through scientific management. Professionals resented a supposedly objective career ladder which was in fact biased in favor of Americans. When the Great Depression undermined the material incentives G.E. had previously offered, it served as a catalyst for Cubans to launch a nationalist protest against their status within American corporate culture.

In the face of Cuba's depressed economy, AFP reduced its Cuban workforce from over four thousand to under two thousand between 1929 and 1933 and instituted a 25 percent pay cut for all those making more than $60 per month. These cutbacks and the end of Machadista repression triggered an uprising by AFP workers. On August 20 eight hundred of AFP's Cuban workers and employees merged their separate organizations to form the Federación Sindical de las Plantas Eléctricas y de Agua. Sensitive to the new environment in Cuba, the company sought an accommodation

12 Ibid., p. 407; "Compania Cubana, 1933," Box 147068, EBASCO.
13 Instituto de Historia, *Movimiento obrero*, pp. 845–46.

with the new union by offering it the use of one of the company's offices as a headquarters. The union declined and instead submitted an escalating series of demands over the next several months.[14]

In articulating their grievances against the company, AFP's workers argued that because of the firm's close association with Machado "it did . . . whatever was convenient to its interests without taking into account the rights of the Nation at all . . . Tariffs were established which stole the scarce wages of people ground down by poverty and tyranny."[15] Describing their own plight, the workers also referred to AFP's management as a tyranny which robbed them of "fair wages" and in which their American bosses humiliated them. While American managers justified the imposition of their management systems in terms of efficiency, AFP workers defended their actions in terms of social and economic justice: "Those whose positions had been usurped in order to give their places to the imported privileged ones . . . demanded the reorganization of the departments. The laborers . . . demanded that they be given a chance to live . . ."[16]

Couching their language in terms of a "just" and "free" society, the electrical workers rejected the harsher aspects of American corporations. They also rejected the social differentiation essential to scientific management, calling instead for an alliance of professionals and workers.[17] Given the impact of the depression and AFP's pay cuts, wages had become a leading issue. Yet the union's demand of equal pay for equal work also represented a response by Cuban workers to the preferential treatment accorded Americans and the scientific management policy of enforcing individualized wages to maximize output by workers. In a similar vein, the union demanded that piece work be prohibited if it reduced employment of permanent personnel.

The AFP workers made clear their intention of asserting a significant degree of control over the work place through the federation. The union would serve as the legal representative of the workers, and new employees were to be hired from a union-approved list. The union must be consulted on any reductions of staff, and seniority would be the first criterion considered in promotions or layoffs. Union leaders also sought to limit AFP's attempts to transform workers into interchangeable cogs in its apparatus. Workers could not be required to carry out tasks which lay outside their specific job responsibilities, they could not be demoted into lower-level

14 Foreign Policy Association, *Problems of the New Cuba,* p. 404; "Compania Cubana, 1933," Box 147068, EBASCO; José Ignacio Rovira and Rodolfo Fraginals, "Historia de un centro de trabajo: la antigua Compañía Cubana de Electricidad, hoy Empresa Consolidada de la Electricidad Antonio Guiteras," in Comisión Nacional de Activista de Historia, Departamento de Orientación Revolucionaria del Comité Central del Partido Comunista de Cuba, *Los obreros hacen y escriben su historia* (Havana: Author, 1975), pp. 296–300.

15 H. Freeman Matthews to secretary of state, Havana, January 26, 1934, 837.6463 EB&S/45, RG 59, USNA.

16 Ibid.

17 Instituto de Historia, *Movimiento obrero,* pp. 672–73.

positions, and work in the much-despised appliance stores would be limited to a specifically defined sales force. Furthermore, the entire administrative structure of the company was to be reorganized.

Item number thirty-eight in the union's list of forty-one demands clearly articulated resentment of the attitude which American managers adopted toward Cuban workers. It demanded that "every workman or employee shall receive from the Company dignified treatment of his person and the courtesy to which he is entitled, and no executive can lessen his standing by acts, words or notes of an objectionable nature, going beyond his functions."[18] These provisions represented the workers' vision of labor relations, couched in terms which deliberately idealized labor relations under the old patriarchal order. They also reflected a view shared by thousands of other Cuban workers impacted by American corporate culture.

In the iron mines of Oriente province where the Bethlehem Steel Company had introduced mass extraction and processing technology, the miners struck and demanded recognition of their union as a means of controlling the work process. As Bethlehem's local general manager noted, "This is why they insist on the abolishment of the task work, the pace would be that of the slowest worker."[19] In early September, International Telephone and Telegraph Company workers demanded recognition of their union, union control over the hiring and classification of employees, promotion based on seniority and reorganization of the company's departments on the basis of collective contracts. The company's Cuban engineers echoed the nationalist theme of the AFP activists, protesting their subordination to American experts. Like their AFP counterparts, the ITT workers appealed for support from consumers. To customers outraged by the company's installation of pay stations in place of phones in neighborhood stores and cafes which residents had used free of charge, the workers promised improved service and an end to the pay station system.[20] When the company rejected many of their demands, the workers struck.

In the ITT strike, as well as in the other labor actions at AFP and in the sugar industry, Cuban workers and elements of the middle class demonstrated considerable cohesion in protesting the radical transformations wrought by American corporate culture. Such alliances crossed the skill-level and sectoral boundaries defined by modern industry. For example, Rafael Giraud, the accountant leading the electrical workers, provided direct assistance to the organizational efforts of the striking workers at the Cuban American Sugar Company. On a broader scale, the electrical workers' union asserted that its goal was the creation of a new, free and just society shaped by an alliance of technicians with industrial and agricultural workers. Such aspirations expressly rejected the social differentiation that was an

18 Matthews to secretary of state, Havana, January 26, 1934, 837.6463 EB&S/45, RG 59, USNA.
19 "Mineral Deposits and Industries," Antilla, Cuba, June 14, 1924, rl. 89, M-488; E. R. Leonard to secretary of state, Washington, D.C., October 21, 1933, 837.00/4270, RG 59, USNA.
20 Foreign Policy Association, *Problems of the New Cuba*, pp. 416–32.

essential part of scientific management. Yet in rejecting what they viewed as the exploitative aspects of American corporate culture, these workers drew upon concepts of a "just" and "free" society that were so much a part of the American ideal.[21] But the desire to capture control of the productive process and shape a new social order was not universally shared by the working- and middle-class groups that joined together to topple Machado and pursue an agenda of economic nationalism. Many in that group would have been content with the reformism of the Grau administration.

In response to radicalization of the protest movement at the end of 1933, the Grau regime issued a series of decrees guaranteeing the eight-hour day, the right to unionize and strike, and workmen's compensation. In addition, it required that Cubans compose at least 50 percent of the workforce in every company. The government also sought to mollify the rural petite bourgeoisie. On January 2, 1934, it issued a decree creating the Asociación de Colonos de Cuba. All colonos would have to join the organization, which ostensibly would give them a greater voice in their own affairs. While acquiescing to some of the workers' and colonos' most strident demands, the government also sought to control them. The new decrees required unions to register with the government and prohibited strikes until union demands had first been submitted to government arbitration boards controlled in effect by the judiciary. With the same purpose in mind the Grau administration had created the Asociación de Colonos to incorporate small growers into government mechanisms for regulating the sugar industry.[22] Despite the reformist character of these measures, Americans viewed them as further evidence of the revolutionary nature of the Grau administration. As Grau attempted to implement his reformist program in late 1933 and early 1934, U.S. corporate and government leaders pursued their own program of containment, in which Fulgencio Batista came to play a critical role.

In response to the wave of strikes and plant seizures, many American sugar companies signed short-term agreements with their workers which they intended to revise once conditions had returned to normal. Fulgencio Batista arranged for military commanders to serve as mediators in other mill disputes. This usually resulted, as in the case of the Cuban American Company, in thirty-day cooling-off periods during which the workers returned to the mills while the companies reviewed their requests. By late November an uneasy truce had been negotiated between the workers and the corporations.[23] However, Cuban American's subsequent rejection of

21 Instituto de Historia, *Movimiento obrero*, pp. 672–73; Jefferson Caffery to secretary of state, Havana, February 2, 1934, 337.1153 CAS/40, RG 59, USNA.

22 Lee R. Blohm, "Labor Notes," Havana, December 11, 1933, RG 84, USNA; International Bank for Reconstruction and Development, *Report on Cuba* (Washington, D.C.: Author, 1951), p. 817.

23 Rublee to Hull, Washington, D.C., December 30, 1933, 337.1153 CAS/5, RG 59, USNA; Blohm, "The Labor Situation in the Cuban Sugar Industry," Havana, November 20, 1933, RG 84, USNA.

its workers' demands drove the Grau regime to more extreme actions to resolve its labor dispute.

On November 1, 1933, the management of Cuban American rejected its workers' demands and offered instead a return to conditions that existed prior to the strike. When the workers refused this "offer," the company closed its mills on December 1. Less than three weeks later, the government ordered the seizure of the company's properties. However, the Grau administration did not act out of some revolutionary motivation. As the secretary of agriculture explained to the American chargé, "If they [Cuban American] do not grind and we do not do anything about it, you can easily understand that the one hundred thousand inhabitants of the district will take matters into their own hands."[24] Meanwhile, a similar course of events was unfolding at AFP.

While a relative air of calm settled over most of the sugar industry, AFP had rejected all of its workers' initial demands except the eight-hour day which Grau San Martín had already put into effect. On December 5 the union presented its list of forty-one demands and gave the company forty-eight hours to accept them or face a strike. Long before that ultimatum, the AFP management had turned to the U.S. government and Fulgencio Batista for assistance. A week after union leaders had asked for company recognition on September 28, company officials went to see F. T. F. Dumont, the American consul general, who in turn kept Fulgencio Batista advised of developments. When the union presented its forty-one demands, Dumont went to see Batista in his headquarters at Camp Columbia. In a two-hour conference the two agreed that a strike at the company would quickly paralyze business and government, as well as creating intolerable sanitary conditions. Batista then met with union officials and persuaded them to delay the strike for one week. As the new deadline approached, union and company officials as well as Batista joined in an all-night bargaining session at the American Consulate. As a result, the company accepted thirty of the forty-one demands and received a thirty-day grace period to consider the remainder. AFP's rejection of most of the outstanding demands led to a strike by the workers on January 14, 1934. The Grau administration immediately intervened in the company and placed Rafael Giraud, a company auditor, in charge of the firm. Giraud, a union leader, proceeded to fire every one of the company's top executives, including the general manager. The union now took full control of the company, with Giraud serving as general manager. The workers would face serious challenges in their efforts to manage the company.[25]

24 Dickson to secretary of state, Havana, December 28, 1933; Rublee to Hull, Washington, D.C., December 30, 1933, 337.115 CAS/1, 5, RG 59, USNA.
25 Foreign Policy Association, *Problems of the New Cuba*, pp. 406–7; F. T. F. Dumont to secretary of state, Havana, December 16, 1933; Matthews to secretary of state, Havana, January 26, 1934; same to same, Havana, January 5, 1937, 837.6463 EB&S/20, 45, 91, RG 59, USNA.

The National City and Chase National banks enjoyed close ties to AFP. Charles Mitchell of National City had sat on the AFP board for eight years. Curtis Calder, president of AFP, and Gerard Swope of G.E. both served as directors of the bank. Henry Catlin had been Chase's principal agent to Machado. In 1930 the two banks had taken $20 million of a $50 million bank loan to AFP. In the face of the worker takeover, the banks refused to cash any checks collected in payment of consumer bills or to accept new deposits of company funds. General Electric and Westinghouse also instituted a boycott of the company. Yet the worker-controlled enterprise survived.[26]

AFP workers proved quite capable of running the company without American executives, and the Cuban middle class rallied to their support. With union officials depicting the seizure as a historic act of nationalist revolution, consumers abandoned their boycott and flocked to pay their bills. This provided the company with an adequate cash flow during the three weeks that the workers maintained control. However, events were rapidly moving against the more radical elements of the revolutionary movement.[27]

Despite the radical and aggressive action taken by Cuban workers in 1933, they were by no means a united force. Serious divisions existed among organized labor. Some rail unions, for example, gave their full support to the sugar workers, but the Railway Brotherhood, with its close ties to the AFL, rejected cooperation with the strikers. Some of these differences stemmed from the degree to which modern American corporations had penetrated the Cuban economy. At ports such as Havana, where American companies had modernized the docks with labor-saving equipment, workers had assumed a radical stance in defense of their interests. Conversely, in more traditionally run ports such as Santiago and Cienfuegos, the docker-backed unions focused strictly on bread-and-butter issues.[28] Given the manner in which American capital had reshaped the sugar industry, even that sector suffered from segmentation. American corporations had supported the growth of the dependent colono system, contributing to the survival of traditional technology and work relations in the agricultural sector. Mill workers often held the unskilled field hands in low regard and believed that they had little in common with them. Ethnicity also divided sugar workers. Haitian and Jamaican migrant workers had few if any ties to Cuban rural society. In turn, their strange language and culture, abject poverty and willingness to accept low wages alienated Cuban workers.[29]

26 "National City Bank Annual Report, 1934," Scudder Collection; "History of the Company," pp. 11a, 18, Box 145445, EBASCO; Foreign Policy Association, *Problems of the New Cuba,* p. 409.

27 Foreign Policy Association, *Problems of the New Cuba,* pp. 409–10.

28 Welles to secretary of state, telegram, Havana, September 6, 1933, 837.00/3770, RG 59, USNA; Blohm, "Cuban Labor Notes IV," Havana Consulate, March 15, 1934, RG 84, USNA; Foreign Policy Association, *Problems of the New Cuba,* pp. 187–90.

29 Rojas, *Tacajo,* pp. 23–24; Foreign Policy Association, *Problems of the New Cuba,* p. 285.

These divisions became apparent during the strikes and plant seizures in August and September. While the strikers at the Homiguero central appended a separate list of demands for field hands to their agenda, workers at the Cuban American centrales made no mention of this group. The Sindicato Nacional de Obreros de la Industria Azucarera readily admitted that mill workers held disparaging attitudes toward field hands and had failed to incorporate them into the strike movement. The lower level of participation of field hands, most of whom worked for colonos, was reflected in Grau's eight-hour-day decree, which specifically excluded agricultural workers. Grau's nationalization decree further divided workers over whether they should defend the rights of immigrant laborers as a matter of class solidarity.[30]

Mill workers and colonos failed to cooperate in a consistent fashion. The Homiguero workers had also presented a brief list of demands for colonos, but the Cuban American union did not. Colonos generally formulated and acted on their own programs, reflecting a very different agenda from that of the mill workers. Colonos sought the stabilization of their leasing arrangements with centrales, forgiveness of debt and revision of the methods for determining payments for cane. Many found in Grau's Asociación de Colonos de Cuba the means for resolving these concerns. For the mill workers, acts of solidarity would also be difficult when they involved the middle class, itself a highly fragmented group.

Part of the challenge to Machado in 1933 had come from a growing group of new professionals that included lawyers, teachers, engineers and accountants. Much of the middle class depended on jobs and contracts from a now bankrupt state apparatus. A smaller element had experienced American corporate culture and its marked preference for Americans in middle and upper management positions. The Cuban middle class and workers agreed on a program of economic nationalism and the need to change the political power structure. But even for many of those directly exposed to American corporate culture in the work place, their objections were to the bias against them as Cuban professionals, not a general rejection of capitalist rationalization. Most middle-class activists stopped far short of endorsing the workers' desire for revolutionary social transformations.[31] Some of that fragmentation became apparent at the level of national politics.

Grau San Martín's own supporters subscribed to a reformist line that sought to contain and control the revolutionary upsurge. But Antonio Guiteras y Holmes, Grau's interior minister, espoused a militant nationalism and promoted the AFP intervention. Later his short-lived Joven Cuba movement tried to build on worker radicalism. The ABC, a right-wing

---

30 Instituto de Historia, *Movimiento obrero*, pp. 626, 633; Foreign Policy Association, *Problems of the New Cuba*, pp. 184, 211.

31 Pérez, *Platt Amendment*, p. 290.

student movement, advocated a strong corporatist philosophy and harbored a deep suspicion of worker radicalism. The Communist party generally rejected cooperation with any of these elements and even failed to appreciate the momentum of revolutionary forces in Cuba. This fragmentation of the middle class, which left the Grau regime in a highly vulnerable position, and divisions in the working class would eventually frustrate many of the more radical aspirations of the revolutionaries as external pressures came to bear on the revolution and the regime.

The Grau administration's policies of economic nationalism and social welfare generated suspicion and finally outright opposition from the U.S. government. As Sumner Welles chronicled events such as the rate reduction imposed on AFP, he became convinced that the Cuban president intended to eliminate U.S. investments on the island. The United States isolated Grau diplomatically, encouraged his domestic opponents and befriended the ambitious Fulgencio Batista, who demanded Grau resign on the same day that the president ordered the intervention in AFP properties. Carlos Mendieta, a member of Cuba's old political elite, succeeded Grau San Martín and served as Batista's willing servant and a defender of U.S. interests.[32]

By early February 1934 Mendieta had begun returning control of the sugar mills to American companies. At mills, soldiers went house to house arresting strikers, including managers who had supported the labor action. Hanging over these actions was Batista's warning that there would be a harvest or there would be blood. The government then relied on the presence of soldiers at the centrales and on mediation to resolve other strikes in the sugar industry.[33] The Mendieta regime also returned the AFP plants to company control on February 3. The AFP workers had greeted Mendieta's selection as president with a brief strike, lasting until the regime agreed to set up a commission to study the labor dispute. Despite that concession, the workers struck again to protest the return of the plants to AFP. Mendieta dispatched troops to AFP's Havana facilities and issued a decree requiring compulsory arbitration of labor disputes and prohibiting strikes that threatened the public welfare, including strikes in the electric power industry. A new wave of strikes was then broken, "ostensibly by the penalties provided in the decrees but actually through the use of armed forces in making these threats effective."[34] In response to these harsh measures, the AFP workers engaged in a work slowdown, and

32 Ibid., pp. 323–33; Benjamin, *The United States and Cuba,* p. 169.

33 Caffery to secretary of state, telegram, Havana, February 2, 1934; Caffery to secretary of state, Havana, January 31, 1934; Matthews to secretary of state, Havana, February 6, 1934, 337.1153 CAS/40, 47, 49, RG 59, USNA; Rojas, *Tacajo,* pp. 89–98; Blohm, "Cuban Labor Notes IV," Havana Consulate, March 15, 1934, RG 84, USNA; Blohm, "Cuban Labor Notes III," Havana, February 15, 1934, 837.5045/137, RG 59, USNA.

34 Matthews to secretary of state, Havana, January 5, 1937, 837.6463 EB&S/91, RG 59, USNA; Blohm, "Cuban Labor Notes IV," Havana Consulate, March 15, 1934, RG 84, USNA.

the dispute was not completely settled until the end of May, when the company acceded to the workers' eleven remaining demands.[35]

In reporting the end of the strike, an American consular official described it as "one of the greatest threats at organized government in Cuba during the recent period of political upheavals."[36] Yet the strike, when considered with the electricity boycott and other confrontations, was more than a pivotal political event. It represented the most overt reaction of Cuban society to the sudden insertion of American corporate culture. Even with the settlement of the dispute in May 1934, the company's vice president complained that "the company was faced with the constant intervention of a committee of the Federation . . . though the labor agreement had specifically provided against the intrusion of the Federation in matters of administration."[37] Yet much of the workers' success proved to be ephemeral. In February 1935 the Mendieta regime faced a strike by teachers and students demanding the restoration of democracy. When the sugar and electrical workers gave their support to the general strike in March, the Mendieta regime crushed the movement with force, shooting workers, arresting their leaders, occupying factories and importing strikebreakers. By March 13 the strike had collapsed, and workers returned to plants which were now surrounded by Cuban troops.[38]

With the backing of the Mendieta regime, AFP purged its workforce of 121 union activists, while the government declared the federation dissolved and closed its offices. By the end of 1936 the company's general manager reported that the federation could not drum up enough support to get a quorum for its annual meeting. Even when the union expelled the employees who had been fired in March 1935, the company still refused to deal with it. Yet despite these harsh measures, the Batista/Mendieta regime could not simply return to the labor policies of the Machadato.[39]

Although the Cuban American Company received its mills back in February 1934 as a direct result of military mediation and intervention, its manager soon found that Batista was no Machado. After breaking up the wave of strikes in March 1934, Mendieta proceeded to declare an amnesty for all violators of his decrees forbidding strikes. When the Cuban Telephone Company resisted accepting returning workers who it claimed had damaged property, Mendieta ordered the company to accept them. By November the regime had established minimum wages for industrial and agricultural workers and a maternity fund for working women. The managers of AFP soon learned a hard lesson in the new real-

35 Foreign Policy Association, *Problems of the New Cuba,* pp. 202–3, 410–11; Rovira and Fraginals, "La antigua Compañía Cubana de Electricidad," pp. 305–10.
36 Blohm, "Cuban Labor Notes VI," Havana, June 5, 1934, RG 84, USNA.
37 Matthews to secretary of state, Havana, January 7, 1937, 837.6463 EB&S/91, RG 59, USNA.
38 Blohm, "Cuban Labor Notes IV," Havana, March 15, 1934, RG 84, USNA.
39 "Compania Cubana de Electricidad, General Review of Company Affairs," January 20, 1937 (hereafter "Compania Cubana, 1937"), Box 147068, EBASCO.

ity. In August 1935 AFP received an order from the secretary of labor to reinstate nine of the employees fired in March. The trickle soon became a deluge. By the end of 1936, the secretary of labor had issued reinstatement orders for all but nine of the fired employees. Mendieta consistently rejected the company's appeals to override the orders, leaving it with the long and costly task of fighting each case through the courts.[40]

As the labor policies of the Batista/Mendieta regime took shape, one American official concluded that "it might be said (confidentially) that the present government of Cuba is a labor government and is closely following the extremely nationalistic tendencies rapidly developing in other Latin American countries."[41] Batista later described these policies more accurately, asserting that it was the role of the army "to teach the masses that capital and labor both are necessary and should cooperate."[42]

Despite the failure of the 1933 revolution, a new era had dawned in Cuba, in which the state provided at least minimal guarantees to labor and placed some constraints on corporations. Paralleling events in much of Latin America at this time, the Cuban state under Batista now pursued a policy of accommodation. Many of the rights won by workers and incorporated in decrees of the Grau administration became functional elements in the new relationship between the state, American companies and labor. The state now functioned as a mediator between U.S. firms and their Cuban workers and the colonos. Corporations also played an active role in the process of cooptation and control.

AFP coopted new union leaders, elevating them to well-paid management positions where they could continue to control their members. The AFP, propagating its faith in professionalization and efficiency among the Cuban middle class, opened management positions to Cubans and offered more generous terms to its sales force. Understanding its past problems, AFP nationalized its marketing strategies, Hispanicized its corporate symbol to "Listo Kilowatt" and injected its advertising into local events, including carnival parades.[43] American companies also developed more

---

40 Blohm, "Cuban Labor Notes V," Havana Consulate, April 25, 1934, RG 84; Rublee to Lawrence Duggan, Washington, D.C., March 3, 1934, 337.1153 CAS/58, RG 59, USNA; "Compania Cubana, 1937," Box 147068, EBASCO; Matthews to secretary of state, Havana, January 7, 1937, 837.6463 EB&S/91, RG 59, USNA.

41 Blohm, "Cuban Labor Notes V," Havana Consulate, April 25, 1934, RG 84; memorandum, n.p., ca. December 1934, File 344 Cuba, RG 151, USNA.

42 R. B. Wood to secretary of state, Havana, February 6, 1934, 337.1153 CAS/49; Benjamin, *The United States and Cuba*, p. 81.

43 International Bank for Reconstruction and Development, *Report on Cuba*, p. 817; Samuel Farber, *Revolution and Reaction in Cuba, 1933–1960: A Political Sociology from Machado to Castro* (Middletown, Conn.: Wesleyan University Press, 1976), p. 91; Brian Pollitt, "The Cuban Sugar Economy in the 1930s," in Bill Albert and Adrian Graves, eds., *The World Sugar Economy in War and Depression* (London: Routledge, 1988), pp. 97–108. For a detailed account of the reforms' potential effects on American companies' relations with the colonos, see 337.1153 Cuban Cane Products Company, RG 59; memorandum, n.p., ca. December 1934, File 344 Cuba, RG 151, USNA; "Compania Cubana, 1937", Box 147068, EBASCO; Rovira and Fraginals, "La antigua Compañía Cubana de Electricidad," p. 315.

refined methods of labor control in the sugar industry. Sugar companies created company-controlled rather than worker-controlled social clubs for employees, organized baseball teams for the workers and instituted company unions. The rules and tactics of conflict had now changed. This approach combined accommodation and cooptation, a method which grew out of the clash between American corporate culture and Cuban society.[44]

American companies offered real material incentives to Cuban workers and employees. They held out the promise of increasing prosperity in an open competitive environment that encouraged individual initiative and self-improvement. At the same time these corporations conveyed new science-based technology and management systems, which homogenized work processes and curtailed the independence of middle and lower management. Convinced of the superiority of their corporate culture and the innate inferiority of Cubans, U.S. businessmen viewed and treated their workers as inferior beings while offering incentives designed to coax more work from them.

The reality of higher wages and the promise of continuing prosperity within an open meritocracy appealed to Cuban workers and employees. But in response to loss of control in the work place and discrimination, those Cuban workers most deeply affected by American corporate culture initiated a program of overt resistance. In formulating that response, they drew on a diverse range of experiences, including past resistance to rationalization, control of the work place by skilled workers, the long struggle over displacement in the national labor market and those aspects of American ideology that stressed freedom and justice.

Drawing on those experiences, they sought not just wage increases but wage equalization to limit the process of speedup inherent in incentive pay schemes. They attempted to forestall management efforts to transform them into interchangeable parts of a modern corporate machine, by controlling hiring and promotions and through strict job classifications. This program paralleled many of the responses by American workers to the same corporate revolution. But a similar process of rationalization inserted into Cuba by modern American corporations allowed workers there to define their struggle as a nationalist crusade against foreign exploitation. That theme struck a responsive chord among elements of the middle class.

At the time that American corporations introduced scientific management to their Cuban operations, the Cuban middle class had not undergone the same pervasive process of professionalization which had been sweeping American society for decades. Despite the material rewards that accompanied them, many of the concepts of scientific management remained alien to middle and lower managers, accustomed to considerable independence in their jobs. Furthermore, Cuban professionals, viewed as

44 García Suárez, *Los fundidores*, p. 21; Rojas, *Tacajo*, pp. 113–20.

inferiors by their American counterparts, frequently found themselves shunted aside to make way for American "experts." As a result, Cuban engineers and other employees made common cause with workers in confrontations with American corporations in the electrical, telephone and sugar industries.[45] The dominant role of U.S. companies in the national economy and their close association with Machado gave another common cause for discontent among working- and middle-class Cubans.

Beyond the American domination of the national economy and changes in the work place, Cubans also responded to the ambiguities of American consumerism. General Electric, for example, brought consumer electrical services and products which purported to offer not only a materially better way of life but the happiness which Americans had come to associate with a consumer society. Yet Cubans learned that the convenience and happiness of a consumer society came at a considerable price. They endured high prices for electricity service and soon learned the hidden dangers of time-payment schemes which allowed them to immediately satisfy their desire for the latest consumer products. Finally, the depression cruelly exposed the ephemeral nature of the happiness offered by consumerism. Yet despite the common themes around which Cubans could rally, serious fissures existed in this nationalist front.

Middle- and working-class support for the more radical aspects of the revolution often depended on the degree of exposure to American corporate culture. Even for many members of the middle class exposed to the American work place, the issue was not rejection of professionalization and the social hierarchy it implied, but rebellion against discrimination which distorted the objective standards of the professional career ladder. And for both the middle class and workers, the consumerist aspect of American corporate culture remained immensely attractive. For workers in sectors largely untouched by new technology and scientific management, basic bread-and-butter issues remained paramount. For much of the middle class, still dependent on state patronage, control of the state and its resources represented the goal and purpose of the revolution. The theme of nationalism gave the workers' movement legitimacy in the national political arena, but it also had divisive effects, particularly among the sugar workers with their large immigrant component.

Despite its limitations, the Cuban response to American corporate culture enabled the Cuban middle and working classes to rally around shared values and play a pivotal role in shaping their society. The widespread appeal of their nationalist agenda forced Batista and American corporations to acknowledge the legitimacy of issues such as union recognition, union work rules and the nationalization of the work place.[46] Modern Cuban so-

---

45 During the time they managed the company, the AFP workers explicitly stated that theirs was an experiment fraught with revolutionary social consequences and made possible by the strong bonds between technicians and industrial workers; see Instituto de Historia, *Movimiento obrero*, pp. 672–73.

46 See for example Rojas, *Tacajo*, pp. 118–37.

ciety emerged in part from the activities of middle- and working-class groups which selectively incorporated elements of American corporate culture into their own value systems while rejecting its harsher aspects.

As we have seen, similar processes were shaping events in other regions of Latin America. In response to the intrusion of American corporate culture, workers and elements of the middle class defined their reaction to that culture in their own terms. Their response found expression in nationalist symbols already sanctioned by the elite and the syncretic adoption of American values of freedom, mobility and democracy. Popular resistance to the negative elements of American enterprise had now become a legitimate issue in the national political arena. It gave expression to a complex cultural interaction that was playing a pivotal role in shaping Latin American societies and their relations with the United States. At the time of the Cuban revolution of 1933, that interaction was entering a climactic phase in Mexico.

PART VI

Mexico: patriotism and capitalism

Map 10.1. Mexico.

10

The Americanization of the Mexican

. . . it takes just four years to complete the Americanization of the Mexican . . .
(Ralph Ingersoll, Phelps Dodge)

I am tired of your rules, the Presidente Municipal has told us what we can do to
you damned gringos. (Mexican miner)

In January 1917 as revolutionary upheavals shook Mexico, emissaries of
President Venustiano Carranza journeyed to the Wall Street office of
Thomas W. Lamont, a senior partner in J. P. Morgan and Company. Carranza, in desperate need of a loan to shore up his regime, had sought
credit from the Continental National Bank in Chicago, only to have the
deal quashed by the Morgan interests. Carranza's representatives, who included his brother-in-law Niceforo Zambrano and an American entrepreneur, W. E. Brock, then traveled to America's money center to plead for a
loan directly from Morgan. What they received instead was a lecture from
Lamont on the necessity of Mexico's revolutionary government's honoring
the financial obligations of previous regimes. The rebuff intensified Carranza's animosity toward J. P. Morgan, whom the Mexican president
blamed for most of his financial woes. Yet if Carranza despised Morgan as
the presumptuous messenger, the message itself was not new.[1]

In March 1916 Judge Delbert J. Haff, who represented Phelps Dodge
and American oil companies in Mexico, had met with Carranza's finance
minister and close friend Luis Cabrera in El Paso. As the talks stretched
on for over a week, Haff warned Cabrera that new mining taxes would be
suicidal, a warning Mexican leaders would hear time and again about
policies designed to rein in foreign investment. In a broader context Haff
advised Cabrera that Mexico must honor its foreign debt, respect existing
foreign concessions and put an end to rumors concerning the nationalization of the petroleum industry.[2]

These meetings set the agenda and the tone for interaction between the
Mexican revolutionary elite and American banks and corporations for the

---

1 W. E. Brock to Lamont, Durango, November 9, 1933, File 24, Box 192, Lamont Papers.
2 Haff to Luis Cabrera, El Paso, n.d., File 6, Box 1371-0348, Phelps Dodge Papers.

next decade. The revolutionary elite envisioned a revised version of the development process which had reached its apogee under Porfirio Díaz. Under that process, the doors had been opened wide to American business, which had revamped much of the productive process in Mexico and sent its export economy soaring. Those developments had meant new economic growth for the elite, an expansion of the small business class and higher wages for workers in American companies. But that same process challenged specific economic interests of the elite, threatened to overwhelm much of the petite bourgeoisie and assailed worker and peasant control of the work place and the land. The revolutionary elite's revised plan involved enhanced taxation and increased state control over foreign investment.

American financiers and corporate leaders working in close cooperation used threats of international economic isolation to deter the elite from enacting some of the more advanced aspects of this nationalist agenda. Yet the Americans also offered a carrot with the stick. Carranza and his ally Alvaro Obregón had already demonstrated their reliability during the most violent stages of the revolution by protecting American investments and subduing some of the more radical elements of the revolutionary movement. After 1917 the Americans clearly understood that the new elite required their assistance to stabilize conditions in Mexico and consolidate its power. That stabilization was an essential countermeasure to the continuing popular protest against the transformation of Mexican society by American corporate culture.

Efforts to reach an accommodation between the Mexican elite and American corporations were played out against the backdrop of ongoing social upheaval. The revolution which American penetration helped trigger in 1910 seemed to subside with the writing of the Constitution of 1917, which promised protection for peasants and workers. As it became apparent that reality fell far short of constitutional principles, popular forces resumed their struggle. During the early 1920s workers continued to resist the disciplines of the modern work place. In response, American corporations pursued intensified capitalization to reduce labor requirements and launched complex efforts at social control to pacify their workers. Workers responded with efforts to recapture control of their work environment. In this process they often found allies among members of the petite bourgeoisie who faced displacement by American companies and those who were discovering the dark side of the new consumer society. Together these groups forged a nationalist agenda which went beyond the elite's plans to control foreign investment, with demands for control of the work place and social and economic justice. Mexican nationalism in the 1920s assumed several distinct forms as different groups of Mexicans struggled to accommodate aspects of American corporate culture which promised material wealth, while others rejected those aspects of the culture which threatened their way of life. The decade was marked by intense struggles to determine the course of Mexico's national development. Those struggles grew out of unresolved conflicts in the 1910 revolution.

In the decades preceding the reign of Porfirio Díaz (1877–1911), Mexican efforts to promote commercialization of agriculture and overall development enjoyed only marginal success. The prevalence of systems such as debt peonage, service tenantry and share cropping reflected the fact that commercial agriculture remained labor-intensive and that labor still proved difficult to secure and costly to control. Those problems obstructed attempts at capital accumulation, which in turn stalled efforts to resolve other difficulties such as a woefully inadequate transportation system.[3] When Porfirio Díaz took power, Mexico had only 666 kilometers of railway. Wagons and mules still provided the principal – extremely expensive – means of moving goods across the national territory. The inadequate transportation system proved particularly burdensome for the development of mining, with its heavy, bulky ore cargoes. Moving one ton of ore by mule team was six times as expensive as moving it by rail. Mining also suffered from the same problems of labor supply and control that existed in agriculture.[4]

Labor problems in mining reflected in part the problems of securing a labor force. To entice workers away from agriculture, mine owners supplemented wages with a share system which gave workers a portion of the ore produced, and they worked less promising sites with independent prospectors, or *gambusinos*. These methods reduced both the mine owners' control over the production process and their profits, impeding the capital accumulation required for mechanization. This resulted in labor-intensive exploitation techniques, with production costs triple those of more modern methods.[5]

When Porfirio Díaz decided to seize power, he cast his lot with American businessmen who were already aggressively pursuing solutions to the types of obstacles that impeded economic growth in Mexico. That position won Díaz considerable support among American business interests when he rose in rebellion against President Sebastian Lerdo in 1876. The

3 David Brading, "Hacienda Profits and Tenant Farming in the Mexican Bajio, 1700–1860," and Jan Bazant, "Landlord, Labourer, and Tenant in San Luis Potosí, Northern Mexico, 1822–1910," in Kenneth Duncan and Ian Rutledge, eds., *Land and Labour in Latin America: Essays on the Development of Agrarian Capitalism in the Nineteenth and Twentieth Centuries* (Cambridge: Cambridge University Press, 1977), pp. 23–58, 59–82.
4 James Douglas, "Notes on the Development of Phelps, Dodge & Co's Copper and Railroad Interests," n.p., January 1906, Phelps Dodge Papers; American Institute of Mining and Metallurgical Engineers, *Transactions* 32 (1902), p. 132.
5 American Institute of Mining and Metallurgical Engineers, *Transactions* 32 (1902), pp. 132, 463, 475; Percy F. Martin, *Mexico's Treasure-House (Guanajuato): An Illustrated and Descriptive Account of the Mines and Their Operations in 1906* (New York: Cheltenham Press, 1906), pp. 64, 197; Juan Felipe Leal and José Woldenberg, *La clase obrera en la historia de México: del estado liberal a los inicios de la dictadura porfirista* (Mexico City: Siglo Veintiuno, 1980), pp. 13–36.

broad network of American financiers, landowners and railroad tycoons would be amply rewarded for the funds they channeled into the Díaz rebellion. At the same time their investments carried the promise of breaking down internal barriers to the development of Mexico.[6]

By the time Porfirio Díaz fled into exile, American direct investment in Mexico had soared to nearly $900 million. With generous concessions including land grants to American railroad companies, Díaz launched a frenzy of railway construction which boosted track mileage in Mexico from 666 kilometers in 1876 to 14,573 in 1900. By 1902 U.S. investment in Mexican railroads had reached $305 million, but once the Díaz regime began acquiring an interest in the lines, it dwindled to $100 million in 1911. American investors had also committed $200 million to 100 million acres of land acquired under Díaz's generous land policies. American petroleum companies, including Edward L. Doheny's Mexican Petroleum Company, had invested $50 million in Mexican oil fields. But with nationalization of the railroads, it was mining which attracted the largest infusion of American capital. American investment in Mexican mining, much of it concentrated in the northern border states of Sonora and Chihuahua, reached $250 million by 1911.[7]

A handful of multinational corporations controlled the bulk of U.S. mining investments. The Guggenheim brothers led that group, operating after 1900 through the American Smelting and Refining Company (ASARCO). In 1911 ASARCO constituted the largest American mining corporation in Mexico, with a total investment of approximately $100 million. Anaconda's investment of $70 million stemmed from its 1907 takeover of William E. Greene's Cananea copper mines in the state of Sonora. In addition to Anaconda, another American multinational, the Phelps Dodge Company, was also operating in Sonora. Phelps Dodge had purchased the Moctezuma Copper Company from the Guggenheims in 1897. The Moctezuma's mines were located south of Cananea in the Nacozari mining district. The $8 million value of the Phelps Dodge holdings placed it in the second tier of American mining companies, which included the properties of Robert Towne ($13 million), the Batopilas Mining Company ($9 million) and the Guanajuato Reduction and Mines Company ($11 million). Together these half dozen American mining companies accounted for two-thirds of all investment in Mexican mines and smelters at the end of the Porfiriato. American corporations also established close ties to much of the Mexican elite.[8]

---

6 Hart, *Revolutionary Mexico*, pp. 105–26.

7 For statistics on U.S. investment, see José Luis Ceceña, *México en la órbita imperial: las empresas transnacionales* (Mexico City: Ediciones El Caballito, 1979).

8 Hart, *Revolutionary Mexico*, pp. 103–37; Marcosson, *Anaconda*, pp. 51–53, 251–55; Ceceña, *México en la órbita imperial*, p. 66; George Young to Ygnacio Bonillas, Cananea, September 2, 1915, File 21, Box 1371-0348, Phelps Dodge Papers; *Annual Report of the Phelps Dodge Corporation for 1912*, Phelps Dodge Papers; D. C. Brown to Robert Lansing, San Luis Potosí, July 8, 1916, 312.11/8011, RG 59, USNA; Bernstein, *Mexican Mining*, p. 75.

Figure 17. Mexican workers prepare to take the swift but dangerous trip by cage to the mine face at the Phelps Dodge operations at Nacozari. (From Ingersoll, *In and Under Mexico* [1924])

The elite benefited along with foreigners from legislation that facilitated the acquisition of village and public lands and eased restrictions on the exploitation of mining claims. Prominent Mexicans also enjoyed the rewards of directorships in the American railroad companies. Such linkages did not occur in mining, but profitable relationships did develop. The Guggenheims hired two of Díaz's closest associates as their Mexican representatives. The brothers also purchased the concession to build a smelter in Ciudad Chihuahua from the powerful Terrazas family. A member of the clan owned the company store at the smelter, while another headed a syndicate of attorneys that represented ASARCO and other large American mining companies. Beyond seemingly secure ties to the elite and the Porfirian state, the most inviting prospect for both the state and the American corporations was the potential for renovating the technology and work processes of Mexican mining.[9]

The American mining corporations essentially replaced human, animal and steam power with electrical power. Most companies set up diesel-driven power stations to supply electricity, while the Guanajuato Company created the allied Guanajuato Power and Electric Company, which generated hydroelectric energy from the Duero River, one hundred miles

9 Mark Wasserman, *Capitalists, Caciques, and Revolution: The Native Elites and Foreign Enterprise in Chihuahua, Mexico, 1854–1911* (Chapel Hill: University of North Carolina Press, 1984), pp. 88–91.

from the mine. Electrification made possible the widespread implementation of mechanical devices, including electric pumps to drain the mines, trams to move ore underground, pneumatic drills that replaced hand drills and electrically powered hoists that moved men and ore swiftly up and down the shafts. The Phelps Dodge operation proved fairly typical of these developments.[10]

In just over a decade, Phelps Dodge transformed the mines at Nacozari. The company began construction of a power plant in 1904 that generated over eight million kilowatt hours by 1909. It largely replaced steam engines with a dozen electric engines. Electrical power made possible the use of electric hoists and high-speed cages. The company installed a compressor plant to power pneumatic drills, now utilized for most of the excavation work. These dramatic changes in mining operations constituted economies of scale and resulted from the transformation of ore processing.[11]

The mechanization of extraction responded to the rapid improvements in the treatment of ores once they reached the surface. The mechanization of ore crushing and sorting, the development of gravity-based methods for separating ore from waste material (concentrating) and the development of reverberatory furnaces, the convertor method of smelting, and the cyanide treatment of silver ore largely preceded and necessitated improvement in mining methods.

Robert Towne built the first modern smelter in Mexico, a thousand-ton mill which began operations in San Luis Potosí in 1892. ASARCO dominated the transformation of ore processing, with its plants accounting for 60 percent of Mexico's copper smelting capacity by 1913. While Cananea and Phelps Dodge focused primarily on their mines, the companies complemented these efforts with local concentrating and smelting operations.[12] These changes, combined with the revamping of mining methods, became steps in the creation of a continuous-process manufacturing system that would run from the ore face through the smelter. Development of that process had directly confronted the problem of transforming Mexican labor in the mines themselves.

American investors and engineers became convinced that their work force of 100,000 Mexican miners constituted the principal obstacle to the accelerated development of the industry. The Mexican elite's own views of the Mexican popular classes as physically and morally degenerate reinforced the racist perspective of American corporate managers. According to both these groups, Mexican peons drank too much, gambled to excess, smelled bad, took too many days off, had little or no ambition, were

10 Bernstein, *Mexican Mining*, p. 42.
11 *Annual Report of the Phelps Dodge Corporation for 1909*, Phelps Dodge Papers; "Statistics," Box 1371-0417, Phelps Dodge Papers.
12 D. C. Brown to Robert Lansing, San Luis Potosí, July 8, 1916, 312.11/8011, RG 59, USNA; Bernstein, *Mexican Mining*, pp. 41, 53, 57–58; J. S. Williams, "The Moctezuma Copper Company History," 1922, File 2016, 1928–30, Box 1371-0331, Phelps Dodge Papers.

seemingly immune to physical punishment and hardship, and had child-like mental processes. But unlike the elite, American corporate leaders did not simply condemn the world of the peon, they intended to transform it. The Americans' racist rhetoric offered an emotionally compelling justification for the transformation of a set of social relations in Mexico which represented serious impediments to development.[13]

During the last quarter of the nineteenth century, when mining remained a comparatively unattractive income source for most Mexicans, companies turned to the rudimentary exercise of control and the use of force to cope with these problems. But given the difficulty in accessing labor, mine workers had to be attracted with the dual inducements of wages and production shares. Even then, Mexican workers, who were focused on the maintenance of subsistence, preferred to limit their time in the mines with its mind-numbing routine. As the manager of the American Metals Company noted, "It usually happened that a man given a particular job would work for a certain length of time and then quit if he had made enough to keep him for several days and you could never rely upon his coming back to the same post . . ."[14] While on the job, workers enjoyed wide latitude in how they performed their tasks.

Experienced miners exercised considerable control in the work place, since their know-how in seeking out and efficiently extracting the richest ores largely determined the success of a mining enterprise. As a result, these experienced workers determined the pace and method of work. The challenges of retaining and disciplining Mexican workers became the central preoccupation of the American businessmen, whose redesigned mines, electric hoists and compressed air drills required miners who worked regular hours and remained on the job on a long-term basis, and whose activities in the work place could be closely monitored and controlled. Managers found a partial solution to that problem in mechanization.

As the Phelps Dodge managers explained, their increased use of compressed air drills helped them cope with the uncertain supply of labor, since the new technology reduced skill requirements. However, the technology also tended to create more jobs rather than displace labor. As Phelps Dodge intensified the revamping of its mines between 1906 and 1909, total employment grew from 1,010 to 1,582.[15] To attract workers, mining and petroleum companies continued to pay high wages while extending the workday to as much as twelve hours. High wages linked to

13 Rodney D. Anderson, *Outcasts in Their Own Land: Mexican Industrial Workers, 1906–1911* (De Kalb: Northern Illinois University Press, 1976), pp. 69–73; Barry Carr, *El movimiento oberero y la política en Mexico, 1910–1929* (Mexico City: Sep-Setentas, 1976), p. 17; T. A. Rickard, *Journeys of Observation* (San Francisco: Dewey, 1907), pp. 99, 103–6; Martin, *Treasure-House*, pp. 62–63, 67; Ralph M. Ingersoll, *In and Under Mexico* (New York: Century, 1924), pp. 45, 58, 81, 149–60.

14 "An Interview with Dr. Kuno Heberlein," Albert Bacon Fall Collection, Huntington Library, San Marino, Calif.

15 "Statistics, 1906–1909," Box 1371-0417, Phelps Dodge Papers.

longer hours proved insufficient to retain an adequate workforce, and the companies initiated a series of control mechanisms institutionalized in the company town.[16]

American corporate reformers viewed company towns as material expressions of their civilizing mission and as mechanisms for labor retention and control. Edward L. Doheny provided the following description of the Mexican Petroleum Company's towns to its stockholders:

> Telephones and electric lines, automobile roads, good brick, stone and lumber houses for offices and dwellings, stores to accommodate the needs of the population, good bathing facilities, absolute absence of any liquor vending establishment, a school house for children, an officer to maintain peace and order – these are the things which distinguish the oil camps established by your Companies in these hitherto primitive regions.[17]

In creating its company town at Nacozari, Phelps Dodge built a planned community, with a rectangular town square lined by public buildings and stores and dominated by the company's edifice. Housing and a school for Mexican workers were erected adjacent to and surrounding the core. By 1910 the company had constructed two new schoolhouses, and it used the old one for an entertainment center. The town offered a further inducement, since the Phelps Dodge mining concession from the state of Sonora exempted its workers from state military service. The Cananea company town proved equally elaborate. Both companies supplied their populaces with water, electricity and other utilities. Yet the most important town institution in the struggle to retain workers was the company store.[18]

While the company store frequently served as a source of profit, its greatest value was as a retention device. With most of their wages paid in the form of credits at the company store, workers had to remain on the job, and as the Batopilas Mining Company noted, "the rougher and roving population were not attracted to the place by the mode of payment."[19] Company stores also enhanced on-the-job performance, since less cash was available for liquor. That aspect of company store operations reflected the larger purpose of the company towns: the creation of a disciplined workforce.

Corporations employed a variety of control mechanisms in the towns. The most overt form of enforcement was the local police force supple-

---

16 "Annual Report of Mexican Petroleum Company for 1913," p. 15, Scudder Collection.

17 Ibid., pp. 15, 17. For a very different view of the oil companies' dealings with their workers from the one presented in this book, see Jonathan Brown, *Oil and Revolution in Mexico* (Berkeley and Los Angeles: University of California Press, 1993), pp. 307–65.

18 *Annual Report of the Phelps Dodge Corporation for 1910,* Phelps Dodge Papers; George Young to Ignacio Bonillas, September 2, 1915, Cananea, September 2, 1915, File 21, Box 1371-0348, Phelps Dodge Papers.

19 Memorandum, Office of Solicitor, Department of State, June 3, 1915, 812.5041/3, rl. 167, M-274, Records of the Department of State Relating to the Internal Affairs of Mexico, 1910–29, RG 59, USNA.

mented by rurales – the armed enforcers of the Porfirian regime. However, American managers usually relied on more subtle methods of discipline. In the older towns in central Mexico, generous payments to the local priest could make him an exponent of company policy. In the northern
states such as Sonora, the key individual was the local mayor, or *presidente
municipal*. The Díaz regime steadily reduced the power of local municipalities to the point where prefects appointed by the state governor selected
mayoral candidates, who were then subject to a perfunctory popular vote.
These municipal officials proved anxious to accommodate the needs and
interests of American mining companies.[20]

With its institutions safely under the control of the corporation, a company town, as the Cananea manager noted, served to advance "the moral
welfare of the people in a well-ordered prosperous community where ample school facilities and other moral advantages are provided." That effort
was part of a "definite policy of the company . . . to develop skill, as well
as habits of industry among the native employees."[21] Phelps Dodge executives concurred in that approach, arguing, "It seems quite possible to
raise a native community to a commendable standard of living, and to educate a selected number in modern methods of work."[22] That effort extended directly into the work place itself.

The mining companies relied on a cadre of supervisors and foremen or
shift bosses to oversee the work underground. However, direct control of
the workers was left to contractors, who hired a gang of peons to carry out
a specific task under agreement with the company. While this relieved the
corporations of a considerable burden in terms of attendance and close supervision of the work, it left most underground operations under the control of workers. The gangs shared mining know-how among their members and determined how each job would actually be carried out. The
contract system which came to be used throughout mining operations was
a compromise which left labor in control of much of the work place. In an
effort to reduce such control, the companies installed piece rate systems to
speed up the production process.[23]

Simple bonus systems proved inadequate, since the workers earned
wages more rapidly and could afford to take more time off. In response,
managers developed an alternative bonus system tied to job numbering. A
worker could earn a bonus, but only if he provided a replacement worker
for his specific job when he chose to take time off. Both mining and oil
companies used piece work methods which based pay on work accom-

20 Bernstein, *Mexican Mining*, pp. 85, 90; Ramón Eduardo Ruiz, *The People of Sonora and Yankee Capitalists* (Tucson: University of Arizona Press, 1988), p. 207.
21 George Young to Ignacio Bonillas, Cananea, September 2, 1915, File 21, Box 1371-0348, Phelps
Dodge Papers.
22 *Annual Report of the Phelps Dodge Corporation for 1915*, Phelps Dodge Papers.
23 José Luis Trueba Lara, *Cananea: 1906* (Hermosillo: Gobierno del Estado de Sonora, 1989), pp.
86–87; Ingersoll, *In and Under Mexico*, pp. 38–45.

plished. No pay system or combination of systems which the corporations employed ever proved totally effective. Companies regularly kept a work-force which was 20 percent or more in excess of their daily needs to compensate for absenteeism. Such efforts reflected ongoing struggles between workers and the corporations as Mexicans sought to protect and expand their own interests in the face of intensifying efforts at rationalization by American companies.[24]

In the waning days of the Porfiriato, Mexican mine workers had a lengthy agenda which bore a strong resemblance to the program of American miners subjected to similar processes of rationalization. Workers demanded safer working conditions, particularly relief from the dust destroying their lungs; improved housing; and an end to the control which company stores exercised over their lives. They also opposed efforts at rationalization which extended the workday, challenged their control in the mines and threatened to reduce their incomes. Like their counterparts in the United States, they opposed the foreign corporations that tried to radically revamp their lives. However, for the Mexican worker, the term foreign had a far more powerful meaning.[25]

American businessmen's demeaning attitude toward Mexican workers provided a rationalization for differential pay scales. Mexican workers received half or even one-third the pay of Americans who carried out the same jobs. In addition, the American companies had little motivation to shower the benefits of industrial welfare on the large number of unskilled workers still required for underground excavation. While company towns provided amenities such as housing, it was grossly inferior to that provided to Americans. Physical and verbal abuse could readily be meted out to Mexican workers, who supposedly lacked the sensibilities of Americans.[26] Unequal pay and inhumane treatment from gringos became inextricably linked with the process of rationalization which American corporations inserted into Mexican society. Protest against the foreigner became a method of protesting against American corporate culture and its attempt to reshape much of Mexican society. Once the social and political control mechanisms of the Porfirian state began to disintegrate in the first decade of the twentieth century, those protests and the workers' agenda became part of a revolutionary movement that would shape three decades of Mexican history.

The Porfirian development model had proven a two-edged sword for even the most privileged members of Mexican society. While the elite profited from Porfirian policies and linkages to foreign interests, regional power brokers found themselves excluded from the political process in

24 "Annual Report of Mexican Petroleum Company for 1913," Scudder Collection; Rickard, *Journeys of Observation*, p. 106; Ingersoll, *In and Under Mexico*, p. 81.

25 Anderson, *Outcasts*, p. 78.

26 Trueba Lara, *Cananea*, pp. 72–84; Martin, *Treasure-House*, pp. 61, 67; Ingersoll, *In and Under Mexico*, pp. 57–59, 81, 116–17.

Mexico City and in hopeless competitive situations with foreign corporations. Regional elites waged competitive struggles against foreign interests which possessed vast capital resources and close connections to the regime in Mexico City. The Madero family of Coahuila typified the dilemma faced by such groups as they found themselves in direct competition with the Guggenheims' mining and smelting operations in northern Mexico. Increasing resentment against foreign domination prompted Francisco Madero's electoral challenge to Díaz in 1910 and secured additional support from the petite bourgeoisie.[27]

Rancheros, shopkeepers and members of the professional classes shared the provincial elite's experience with the Porfirian order. The numbers of the petite bourgeoisie had exploded during the Porfiriato as the Mexican economy expanded. But when the economy entered a severe decline in 1907, these groups faced economic hardship in addition to the direct competition from foreign corporations and exclusion from the political process which they already endured.[28] Led by such figures as Alvaro Obregón Salido, these groups merged with provincial elites to vie for power after Madero's assassination by Porfirian general Victoriano Huerta. Peasants and workers who had lost lands or faced increased exploitation within the Porfirian developmental model had already rallied to Madero's cause. Under the leadership of Pancho Villa and Emiliano Zapata and of anarchists from the Casa del Obrero Mundial and Partido Liberal Mexicano (PLM), these groups played a pivotal role throughout the revolutionary struggle.

Mexican workers shared a long tradition of revolutionary anarchism. In the years before the revolution the petit bourgeois PLM represented the Communist wing of anarchism, while the Casa del Obrero served the cause of anarchosyndicalism. The PLM and IWW organizers from the United States found a responsive audience among the popular classes in Mexico's northern mining districts. Revolutionary anarchism's calls for direct confrontation with capital and the state and for workers' control of the production process enjoyed a special appeal for those struggling to come to grips with the capitalist transformation of mining. The response to anarchism was the continuation of protests over the rationalization of mining which had emerged as early as the 1880s. After the turn of the century, those protests erupted in the modern mining enterprises of Sonora and set the stage for revolution.[29]

Mine laborers and white-collar workers in Cananea found themselves at odds with a large American corporation. Mexicans, whether they labored with picks and shovels or served as timekeepers and supply clerks, earned half what their American counterparts did. Itinerant peddlers from

27 Hart, *Revolutionary Mexico,* pp. 96–100.

28 Ruiz, *Sonora,* p. 48.

29 Ibid., pp. 108–12; Manuel J. Aguirre, *Cananea: las garras del imperialismo en las entrañas de México* (Mexico City: Libro México, 1958), pp. 65–68.

Cananea found themselves prohibited from selling food at the company's work sites. A local branch of the PLM led by Manuel M. Diéguez, a supply clerk in one of the mines; Esteban B. Calderón, a mine timekeeper; and Francisco M. Ibarra, a small merchant, had begun organizational work among the miners. In 1906 the company converted from a system of paying contractors and their gangs on a time basis to a piece work system. Cognizant of the speedup aspect of piece work, which they were certain would reduce the number of workers, the miners demanded an eight-hour day, wage increases, the firing of two supervisors and the provision that Mexicans fill 75 percent of all jobs at the company. When the company rejected their demands, the workers struck, violence erupted, and the governor of Sonora permitted Arizona rangers to cross the border to crush the strike. The common struggle against foreign corporations had elicited a nationalist response from a mining community.[30]

As the old order crumbled, new opportunities developed for strike action in the mining sector. In July 1911, 11,000 workers at the mines in the El Oro district of central Mexico seized the British- and American-owned mines, demanded the ouster of all foreigners from the district, placed a bounty on the heads of company managers and announced that they would run the mines. As in the case of Cananea, members of the PLM had involved themselves in organizational efforts. The area's *jefe político* denounced the gringos, and the local community voiced its support of the workers and their anti-gringo stance.[31] As conditions stabilized at El Oro, a new strike broke out in Cananea. Workers demanded the firing of three American bosses who treated them in a cruel and insulting manner. The company suppressed the strike after four days. But the local community soon exhibited its support as a local judge arrested two of the Americans for using abusive language to Mexicans and held them in lieu of 12,000 pesos' bail. By the time of the second strike, Esteban Calderón and Manuel Diéguez had returned to the Cananea area. Calderón became a schoolteacher, while Diéguez won election as mayor of Cananea. In December 1912 the Cananea workers struck for shorter hours and higher wages. The workers only returned when the company finally agreed to a half-hour shift reduction and free water service. As mayor, Diéguez had promised to protect non-striking workers, but his secretary Juan José Rios issued a broadside in support of the workers' demands. Calderón handled the negotiations for the strikers. After the settlement, the governor of Sonora arrested Calderón and Rios. Diéguez was spared arrest because of the public office he held.[32] A variety of indirect and direct

---

30 Ruiz, *Sonora*, pp. 113–15, Antonio G. Rivera, *La revolución en Sonora* (Mexico City, 1969), p. 139; Aguirre, *Las garras del imperialismo*, pp. 48–51, 73–84, 91–93, 105, 116; Hart, *Revolutionary Mexico*, pp. 65–68.

31 On the El Oro strike, see the reports contained in 812.5045/10–17, rl. 167, M-274, RG 59, USNA; Rickard, *Journeys of Observation*, pp. 55–100.

32 George Young to L. D. Ricketts, Cananea, December 23, 1912, 812.5045/49, rl. 167, M-274, RG 59, USNA; Aguirre, *Las garras del imperialismo*, pp. 177–78.

protests by miners continued throughout the years of revolution as many fled the mines to join the revolutionary armies and others struck for higher wages and shorter hours.[33]

During this period the breakdown of central control over municipal governments allowed communities to act in support of workers' actions. Freed of direct intervention from state governors, workers now elected pro-labor candidates as mayors, undermining an important mechanism for corporate social control. Phelps Dodge noted in 1917 that a cause contributing to rising mining costs was "the general inefficiency of the Mexican labor due to the interference of local officials and the injection of politics into the industrial life of the community." Yet the company went on to state that "this . . . condition is greatly improved at the present time, and labor conditions may be regarded as more normal."[34] That change in conditions reflected the stabilization of Mexican society by social groups that now dominated the Mexican state.

Out of the multi-class forces which rallied against economic dislocation, political exclusion and displacement by foreign corporations, an alliance of the provincial elites and petit bourgeois groups led by Venustiano Carranza and Alvaro Obregón pitted themselves against the more radical forces led by Zapata, Villa and the Casa. Carranza and Obregón's forces would prove their "reliability" time and again to American investors. In 1914, for example, Obregón's lieutenant Plutarco Elías Calles intervened in a strike by pro-Villa workers at Cananea.[35] The reputation of the Carranza–Obregón forces prompted intervention on their behalf by American interests, who perceived them as the only viable alternative to radicalized peasants and workers.

In the revolutionary struggle, American corporations had been a prime target of workers and peasants who blew up mines and burned estates. As losses from such attacks mounted into the tens of millions of dollars, pressure grew on the Wilson administration to intervene.

In August of 1913, National City Bank's Frank Vanderlip explained the administration's dilemma to James Stillman, chairman of the board:

We were very close to war with Mexico a few days ago, but the situation there has improved somewhat. There is still a chance that we will become involved, but the Administration is entirely awake to the reason for not becoming involved. Military authorities estimate that it would cost $1,000,000 a day and take two years to entirely subdue the country. It would be certain to be an unpopular venture after the first few months. It would be hard work getting up any patriotic views in regard to such a war, and the expense and the difficulties of it would quickly turn any enthusiasm into criticism. If it is possible to avoid war, I feel certain the Administration will do so.[36]

33 *Annual Report of the Phelps Dodge Corporation for 1913 and 1916*, Phelps Dodge Papers.
34 *Annual Report of the Phelps Dodge Corporation for 1917*, Phelps Dodge Papers.
35 Hart, *Revolutionary Mexico*, p. 297; Federico Besserer, *El sindicalismo minero en México: 1900–1952* (Mexico City: Era, 1983), p. 19.
36 Vanderlip to Stillman, New York, August 15, 1913, B-1-5, Vanderlip Papers.

The U.S. occupation of Veracruz in April 1914 proved to be the Wilson administration's alternative to war. When the Americans departed, they left shiploads of armaments for the Carranza–Obregón forces, which proved decisive in their struggle against the revolutionary forces led by Villa and Zapata.[37]

As the revolutionary elite consolidated its power, it turned to the task of state building. The Constitution of 1917 gave formal expression to the interests of this new elite. Reflective of their nationalism, it established a strong central government and reclaimed the nation's subsoil rights from foreign corporations. Cognizant of the continuing revolutionary potential of peasants and workers, it affirmed the legitimacy of the peasant village and provided guarantees on the length of the workday and minimum wages for workers. At least in theory, it legitimized many of the goals which popular forces continued to struggle for in Central America, Peru, Chile and Cuba. In reality, it was simply a phase in an ongoing encounter with American corporate culture that continued to be carried on at both the level of the revolutionary elite and the popular classes. Over the next decade both of these groups sought to define their relationship to American corporations as those companies continued their transformation of Mexican society. The elite's approach to this issue proved considerably different from that of other Mexicans.

In late 1918 J. P. Morgan and Company, with the approval of the State Department, formed the International Committee of Bankers on Mexico. Chaired by Thomas W. Lamont, the committee included leading American and European banks and served as an informal policy arm of the State Department. Officially the committee acted on behalf of Mexican bondholders only. A number of other groups emerged at this time to protect direct American investments, but only the Association of Petroleum Producers in Mexico remained an active and effective organization. In fact the bankers' committee represented both bondholders and corporate interests in Mexico.

At this time the money center banks stood at the apex of the American corporate organizational system. Financial houses and banks like J. P. Morgan and Company and National City Bank funded the creation of corporate giants such as U.S. Steel, General Electric and Anaconda and financed the expansion of firms like Phelps Dodge and the Guggenheim brothers. Together J. P. Morgan and Company, National City Bank, Guaranty Trust Company, First National Bank of New York City and Bankers' Trust Company held 341 directorships in major American corporations.

---

37 Hart, *Revolutionary Mexico,* pp. 290–97; Haff to J. S. Williams Jr., El Paso, March 16, 1916, File 6, Box 1371-0348, Phelps Dodge Papers; Homer Coeu to secretary of state, Durango, May 15, 1915; W. D. Thornton to Col. M. M. Parker, Washington, D.C., June 7, 1916, 812.63/99, 116, rl. 210, M-274, RG 59, USNA.

In turn the banks' boards of directors included the heads of America's largest corporations. The board of the National City Bank included such moguls as Cleveland H. Dodge, William Rockefeller and Joseph P. Grace. The membership of the bankers' committee reflected this intertwining of financial and corporate interests. Individual members represented their own financial institutions and specific corporate interests. Mortimer Schiff served not only as the representative of Kuhn, Loeb but also as a representative of American Smelting and Refining because of Kuhn, Loeb's close association with the Guggenheim brothers. Albert H. Wiggin of Chase National would represent not only the bank but the Texas Company as well.[38]

The oil companies proved the most aggressive interest group in their treatment of Mexico and the most at variance with the policies of the bankers' committee. In 1921, for example, the committee rejected a petroleum association plan to pay Mexican taxes with depreciated Mexican bonds. Yet what is far more striking is the unanimity of purpose and policy that marked the actions of American banks and corporations in cooperation with the American state. Called on by the oil companies to protest a proposed petroleum law in 1922, Thomas Lamont warned Adolfo de la Huerta, the minister of finance, that passage of the law meant "economic suicide for Mexico."[39] Lamont also acted in accord with State Department policy. In 1921, at the request of the State Department, the banker refused to visit Mexico. The department was denying recognition to the Obregón government until it provided recognition of American property rights as they existed before the revolution.[40] In simple terms, the Mexican government would receive neither recognition nor credits until it guaranteed the rights of American investors.

The message from the American state and corporate interests was not lost on Alvaro Obregón. The new president had acknowledged that he was Mexico's last chance to achieve an accommodation with the Americans and avoid a Cuban-style intervention. Within a year of Obregón's taking office, the Supreme Court began issuing decrees favorable to the foreign oil companies.[41]

---

38 Morgan Syndicate Books, Morgan Papers; van B. Cleveland and Huertas, *Citibank*, pp. 314–15; Ron Chernow, *House of Morgan: An American Banking Dynasty and the Rise of Modern Finance* (New York: Atlantic Monthly Press, 1990), p. 314; record of meeting of American Group of International Committee of Bankers on Mexico, offices of J. P. Morgan, March 13, 1919, File 2, Box 192; memorandum, AMA to Lamont, August 9, 1918, File 17, Box 195, Lamont Papers.

39 On Lamont's statement to de la Huerta, see Lamont to W. C. Teagle, New York, September 19, 1921, File 5, Box 197, Lamont Papers. On the oil companies, see Lorenzo Meyer, *Los grupos de presión extranjeros en el México revolucionario, 1910–1940* (Tlateloco: Secretaría de Relaciones Exteriores, 1973), pp. 29–32; Ira Patchin to Teagle, New York, November 10, 1922, File 8, Box 197, Lamont Papers.

40 Lamont to D. E. Pomeroy, New York, June 29, 1921, File 4, Box 192, Lamont Papers.

41 Memorandum of conversation between Lamont, Sir William Wiseman and Rodolfo Montes, New York, February 25, 1921, File 4, Box 192, Lamont Papers; Meyer, *Grupos de presión*, p. 85.

While Obregón came to office cognizant of the need to make concessions to the Americans, American corporate interests were equally aware of the need to bolster Obregón. In 1921 an unnamed prominent Mexican shared with leading American investors and financiers his views on the Obregón regime, which closely reflected their own thinking. From his perspective,

the present President is a prisoner of his own party . . . He is bound hard and fast to certain radical ministers because he has not the money to satisfy them . . . At the present moment it is not the despotism of Obregon but of the ministers, governors, generals and laborers upon whom he depends. This force can only be removed from [them] and returned to the President himself by putting him in such a financial position as to give him dominance. Money will change his cabinet, make over his congress, give him domination over his governors and allow him to abrogate or modify present unsatisfactory laws.[42]

In 1922 the need to bolster the regime and ensure its ability to deal with social upheavals that threatened American corporate interests helped bring about an agreement between Lamont and Adolfo de la Huerta on Mexico's foreign debt. The following year the Obregón government essentially guaranteed the non-retroactive character of Article 27 of the Constitution, which had reclaimed the state's subsoil rights. U.S. diplomatic recognition quickly followed.[43]

The policy of bolstering the regime to suppress domestic resistance reflected the views of not just the State Department and the bankers but the entire American investment community in Mexico. American electric companies, cognizant of the need to stabilize Mexican state finances in order to restore social stability, unanimously backed the granting of diplomatic recognition to the Obregón government. In September 1923 the oil companies, the most bitter critics of the regime, loaned it $1 million and six months later offered another $1 million conditioned upon the government's suppression of militant oil workers in Tampico.[44] A year later Walter Douglas, president of Phelps Dodge, decided not to make a claim for repayment of export taxes that apparently violated the company's concession. He explained that "the Mexican Government had to have the money to prevent a condition of civil chaos and that we benefited through the condition of comparative order which has prevailed through the Republic from their ability to partially finance their administration."[45]

---

42 Statement enclosed in Teagle to Lamont, New York, December 15, 1921, File 7, Box 197, Lamont Papers.

43 "Agreement between the Minister of Finance of Mexico and the International Committee of Bankers," n.p., June 16, 1922, Lamont Papers; Robert Freeman Smith, *The United States and Revolutionary Nationalism in Mexico, 1916–1932* (Chicago: University of Chicago Press, 1972), pp. 207–13.

44 "Guanajuato Power and Electric Company," Scudder Collection; Guy Stevens to Alberto Macarenas, New York, March 21, 1924, File 11, Box 197, Lamont Papers.

45 Douglas to Haff, July 10, 1925, File 2044, Box 1371-0334, Phelps Dodge Papers.

After Plutarco Calles assumed the presidency in 1924, the effects of American policy became apparent. While Calles still insisted on taxing and regulating foreign investment, he also sought social stability – a scarce commodity for American corporations in the 1920s. Because while the bankers' committee could effectively coordinate a corporate strategy toward the Mexican government, it also provided convincing evidence for popular nationalists that, despite the revolution, Mexico remained subordinated to an American corporate monolith.

Between 1920 and 1924 hundreds of strikes broke out each year in Mexico. The spiraling protests culminated in 1924 when workers seized the Tampico Light and Power Company, oil workers struck and a general work stoppage gripped Tampico.[46] Workers were joined by white-collar employees of foreign corporations who organized against low wages and discrimination, consumers and small business people who protested high utility costs, and renters who protested exorbitant rates for housing. American corporations, the targets of many of these protests, had a great deal at stake.

The 1920s were a time of consolidation rather than expansion for American business in Mexico. The rapid depletion of Mexican oil reserves during the 1920s caused the oil companies to halt all fixed capital investment. The total of American investment in mining did not increase between 1911 and 1929, because of the collapse or absorption of a number of smaller operations. The larger corporations, however, poured millions of dollars into improving their facilities. Raw materials producers, whether logging in the Pacific Northwest, grinding sugar in Cuba or mining copper along the U.S.–Mexico border, were seeking increased productivity in the face of sharp increases in the costs of labor and materials. Equally troublesome was the rise of revolutionary syndicalism, through which workers turned to direct action to resist discipline in the work place and reassert the concept of workers' control. Efficiency now became the watchword for survival. The Mexican mining industry reflected that trend.[47]

Central to improvements in efficiency throughout the industry was the widespread introduction of the flotation system for concentrating ores. In 1925 alone, mining companies in Mexico completed four new flotation plants and began construction of five others.[48] The Phelps Dodge Com-

46 Norman Caulfield, "Mexican Labor and the State in the Twentieth Century: Conflict and Accommodation" (Ph.D. dissertation, University of Houston, 1990), pp. 142–87.

47 Meyer, *Grupos de presión*, p. 97; Ceceña, *México en la órbita imperial*, p. 117; Lorenzo Meyer, *Mexico and the United States in the Oil Controversy, 1917–1942*, trans. Muriel Vasconcellos (Austin: University of Texas Press, 1977), pp. 6–11; Robert J. Holton, "Revolutionary Syndicalism and the British Labour Movement," in Wolfgang J. Mommsen and Hans-Gerhard Husung, eds., *The Development of Trade Unionism in Great Britain and Germany, 1880–1914* (London: Allen and Unwin, 1985), pp. 280–81; U.S. Department of Commerce, Bureau of Mines, *Recent Developments in the Mining Industry* (Washington, D.C.: Government Printing Office, 1930), pp. 1–4.

48 Bernstein, *Mexican Mining*, pp. 143–45; *EMJ* 121 (February 13, 1926).

pany pursued this same policy of intensified investment in physical plant to improve efficiency. Through 1917 the company had invested $2.4 million in its facilities at Nacozari. Between 1918 and 1922 it invested an additional $4.3 million, including a remodeling of its concentrator, expansion of its electrical power house and changing over from coal to oil-fired turbines.[49]

In addition to consolidation and intensification of mining operations, electrical generation emerged as a rapidly expanding field in the 1920s. The British-owned Mexican Light and Power Company dominated power generating in the capital at the beginning of the decade. Three American-owned companies, Guanajuato Power and Electric, Michoacan Power and Central Mexico Light and Power, had consolidated to give American capital a substantial presence outside Mexico City. In 1928 the American and Foreign Power Company began acquiring most of the electrical power network north and east of Mexico City. Over the next two years, the company invested $50 million in making those acquisitions. The 1920s also witnessed a continuing shift in the power industry's market. The electrical industry had largely grown up in partnership with mining, with the three American companies relying on mining for 75 percent of their business. Yet in 1921 manufacturing and consumer use already accounted for 75 percent of their sales. During the 1920s electricity became a major consumer industry.[50]

By the end of the decade, American corporations had intensified capital investments to combat worker resistance and improve efficiency and had entered a new field in which the creation of a consumer society became central to success. These aspects of American corporate culture represented fundamental challenges to the Mexican working class and the petite bourgeoisie. Both groups faced the threat of displacement and the further penetration of their everyday lives by market forces. To cope with popular resistance, American corporations attempted to diversify and enhance the control they exercised in the work place and in Mexican society as a whole. The origins of this process can be found in the workers' response to the charter of rights contained in Article 123 of the 1917 Constitution.

The afterglow of working-class enthusiasm for Article 123 faded quickly. The federal government failed to enact enabling legislation for nearly a decade and a half, leaving individual states to pass their own labor laws. When the state of Sonora passed a labor law in 1920, representatives of leading mining companies, such as George Young of Cananea and

49 Ledger No. 5, File 94, Box 137 75; J. S. Williams, "The Moctezuma Copper Company History," 1922, File 2016, 1928–30, Box 1371-0331; *Annual Report of the Phelps Dodge Corporation for 1920*, Phelps Dodge Papers.

50 "Acquisitions, Chile, Mexico, Costa Rica and Guatemala," Box 143981, EBASCO; "Guanajuato Power and Electric Company," and "Mexican Light and Power Company," Scudder Collection; Ernesto Galarza, *La industria eléctrica en México* (Mexico City: FCE, 1941), p. 88.

T. A. Hamilton of Phelps Dodge, met at the Hotel Evans in Nogales to formulate a request to the state legislature for changes in the law. By the time of that meeting the American managers had already "influenced" a majority of the legislature to modify the original bill before it was passed, and Young had been using his connections in Mexico City to pressure Governor Adolfo de la Huerta for that same purpose. In states such as Chihuahua where these tactics failed, the companies managed to negate the impact of the laws with legal injunctions. By 1924 corporate legal actions had crippled Chihuahua's labor law, and labor advocates abandoned any serious attempts to enforce its most important provisions. At the same time that American companies turned back the most objectionable aspects of local labor legislation, they accelerated rationalization.[51]

American mining companies set to work ever more Mexican supervisors to oversee expanding contract and bonus systems. They also replaced the "carload" system, which paid contratistas by the carload of ore produced. Contratistas had frequently bribed Mexican inspectors to count worthless loads of rock. The companies now paid on the basis of work assignments that had been carefully laid out and measured by a growing number of American engineers. As for the Americans' opinion of Mexican workers, that had changed little as a result of the revolution. While conceding that peons could no longer be treated roughly, American managers still regarded their workers as indolent, careless and childlike – an opinion they also applied to the Mexican petite bourgeoisie. Under the contract system, which supposedly encouraged and rewarded individual initiative, even contratistas found themselves struggling to rise above the level of bare subsistence. Ralph Ingersoll, an engineer for Phelps Dodge, visited the home of one of the company's contractors and was shocked to find that he lived the same subsistence-level existence as the mine workers.[52] Such individuals eventually joined the workers in their resistance to American mining companies.

In response to low pay and discrimination, many workers opted for indirect forms of resistance. In 1924 alone the manager at the Phelps Dodge operations reported an annual labor turnover of 100 percent. That same year, one-third of Cananea's workers also abandoned their jobs. Many migrated north to the mines and ranches of the American Southwest, while others found opportunities within Mexico. Miners in Sonora often sought

51 Thomas McEnelly to secretary of state, Chihuahua, November 16, 1924, RG 84, USNA; Stewart to secretary of state, Chihuahua, April 25, 1924, 812.504/344, rl. 163, M-274; Francis J. Dyer to secretary of state, Nogales, March 25, 1920, 812.504/208, rl. 165, M-274, RG 59, USNA. The companies' influence at the state level was particularly effective, since President Obregón generally avoided intervening in local labor disputes; see Ramón Eduardo Ruiz, *Labor and the Ambivalent Revolutionaries: Mexico, 1911–1923* (Baltimore: Johns Hopkins University Press, 1976), p. 79. *EMJ* 114 (August 5, 1922).

52 Ingersoll, *In and Under Mexico*, pp. 37–45, 113–15; David J. D. Myers to secretary of state, Durango, April 14, 1924, 812.504/557, rl. 164, M-274, RG 59, USNA; *EMJ* 114 (September 30, 1922).

work in the state's cotton region. Agricultural wages were lower than those in mining, but an entire family could find employment on the cotton plantations – and under considerably safer working conditions. Others, however, took far more direct action to ameliorate their condition.[53]

The actions of Mexican workers at the beginning of the 1920s still focused on basic economic issues as they struck for higher wages, shorter hours and better working conditions.[54] Yet if the issues had changed little since the days of Porfirio Díaz, workers now had a far greater ability to protest and pressure for their demands. In October 1920 the Cananea miners struck over hour and wage issues. When Adolfo de la Huerta, now interim president of Mexico, sent a commission to investigate, the workers largely ignored it. Flavio A. Bórquez, the governor of Sonora, visited Cananea, invited three of the strike leaders to meet with him in the state capital and arranged to meet in El Paso with T. A. Evans of the Cananea Company. The strikers showed little faith in Bórquez. Fearing a trap, only two of their leaders went to the capital. Despite the presence of fifty troops in Cananea, the strikers pressured the mine superintendent into signing an agreement on hours and pay. As these events unfolded, Raymundo Navarro, a contratista working for the company, shot and killed a mine foreman. After firing the fatal shots, Navarro cried out, "That is where all of you damned gringo sons of bitches belong!" At the company clinic, the American doctor demanded that a worker show him his employee identification before treating his child. The miner pulled a gun and told the physician, "I am tired of your rules, the Presidente Municipal has told us what we can do to you damned gringos."[55] The worker's statement only confirmed the Americans' mounting suspicions about the mayor of Cananea, Salvador Taylor. Originally Taylor had cooperated with the company and kept things quiet in the town. However, during the strike Taylor backed the workers' pressure on the superintendent for an agreement. As the strike neared an end, he arrested a non-union worker who was trying to arrange for the company to keep strikebreakers on its payroll.[56]

The Phelps Dodge Corporation encountered similar problems. In October of 1920 Venturo Lujan, the mayor of Pilares, a Phelps Dodge company town, accepted an invitation to visit the mayor of Mexico City. When Lujan set out on his trip, J. S. Williams, the Phelps Dodge manager, wrote to Minister of War Plutarco Calles and asked him to arrest Lujan. Williams explained to Calles that Phelps Dodge was having labor problems because the union at Pilares was a branch of the IWW-controlled Cananea union. Lujan's election as mayor a few months earlier

---

53 Alexander V. Dye to American ambassador, Mexico City, April 5, 1924; Monnett B. Davis to secretary of state, Coahuila, March 20, 1924, rl. 164, M-274, RG 59, USNA.
54 On the numerous strike actions of the early 1920s, see rl. 163, M-274, RG 59, USNA.
55 Dyer to secretary of state, Nogales, October 25, 1920, rl. 163, M-274, RG 59, USNA.
56 Ibid.

had added to that problem. After taking office Lujan began a frontal assault on the network of mechanisms which the company used to control its workforce. He denounced unsafe conditions at the company school and arrested the manager of the company store for selling rotten produce. When a worker on the night shift broke his leg, Lujan rushed to the mine and told the workers that the company didn't care about Mexican workers but would make a great fuss if the injured employee was some "cabrón gringo." Lujan then arrested the night-shift supervisor. After a company superintendent posted a notice that miners arriving late to work would lose a day's pay, Lujan arrested him as well. Williams felt Lujan had to be gotten rid of because of his "decidedly red tendencies" and because he hated "anything that is foreign."[57]

ASARCO faced control problems at its operations in Santa Bárbara, Chihuahua. The former presidente municipal of Santa Bárbara, Eduardo Modesto Flores, headed the Ricardo Flores Magón Syndicate, which challenged the company union for influence among local workers. The former mayor made a point of threatening to shoot the gringo superintendents at the smelter in order to break the company's influence. Flores' campaign against the company was not suppressed until the federal government sent in one hundred troops.[58]

When the workers at the American-owned Tampico light company struck repeatedly in 1923, they enjoyed the backing of the local police inspector and the presidente municipal. The Camara Nacional de Comercio also stepped into the dispute, offering to pay the difference between the wages the workers demanded and those the company was willing to pay.[59] During the 1925 strike against the Huasteca Petroleum Company, the mayors of local towns such as Tempache, Tantima and Tepetzintla ordered the company's camp bosses to halt work because they were employing scab labor. The local towns' affinity for the workers' cause no doubt stemmed in part from the concentration of workers there, but rural communities also had reason to support the effort. During the strike, the residents of the Hacienda and Community of Juan Felipe, municipality of Tepetzintla, filed a formal protest, complaining that the Huasteca company had been closing old community roads, particularly the road to the port of Tuxpan, and that the company's white guards would not let them use the road to the municipality of Tepetzintla.[60]

57 James Williams to Plutarco Elías Calles, Nacozari, October 26, 1920, File 21, Box 1371-0348, Phelps Dodge Papers.

58 Thomas McEnelly to secretary of state, Chihuahua, November 8, December 5, 1923, RG 84, USNA.

59 S. Lief Adleson, "Casualdad y conciencia: factores convergentes en la fundación de los sindicatos petroleros de Tampico durante la decada de los veinte," in Reunión de Historiadores Mexicanos y Norteamericanos, *Labor and Laborers through Mexican History* (Tucson: University of Arizona Press, 1979), pp. 646–49.

60 Charles A. Bay to secretary of state, Tampico, August 18, 1925, 812.504/694, rl. 164, M-274, RG 59, USNA. Huasteca had become a subsidiary of Standard Oil in 1925.

The events at Cananea, Pilares, Santa Bárbara and Huasteca revealed that Mexican popular classes had derived from the revolution a concept of nationalism considerably at variance with that of the new elite. Far from accommodation, their version of nationalism called for continuing confrontation with Americans to protect their vested interest. In addition to that common nationalist theme, workers now enjoyed enhanced political power at the local level. Prior to the revolution, towns such as Pilares held the status of *comisarías,* in which state officials appointed the mayors, or *comisarios.* The emergence of such towns as free municipios with elected mayors placed town government in the hands of workers and petit bourgeois elements.

By 1924 workers' political power at the local level and shared concepts of nationalism among the petite bourgeoisie and the working class gave them a formidable role in the changes sweeping Mexican society. Furthermore, syndicalism provided a direct-action strategy and offered a vision of the future with a strong grounding in the Mexican past. While the concept of workers' control had roots in the self-sufficiency of craftsmen, peasants and petty commodity producers, it also offered an alternative to increased corporate control in the work place. As a result, labor actions came to involve more than demands for better hours and wages.

The six months of intermittent strike activity by the workers at the Tampico Electric Light Company in 1923 had more than wages as its goal. The workers' demands included control over hiring and firing and various management phases of the company's operation. Before the strike was settled with partial concessions to the strikers in February 1924, 250 armed workers seized the plant and faced down federal troops who had been sent to dislodge them.[61] In an effort to control the growing protests in the Tampico area, Alvaro Obregón appointed a provisional governor for the state of Tamaulipas in February. However, labor leaders took umbrage at the selection, and someone attempted to shoot the new appointee. Obregón quickly withdrew his choice and substituted a candidate more acceptable to labor. His actions did nothing to stem the tide of protest.[62]

Workers at the British-owned El Aguila Petroleum Company in Tampico initiated a strike in late March that dragged on into July. They demanded no hiring or firing of workers without union approval and the dismissal of any foreman to whom the union objected. In turn, "the Company maintained that the conceding of these points would mean that control of the refinery would pass into the hands of the Union and that this was really the main object of the strike, and that the question of wages and working conditions was secondary . . ."[63] When their demands were

---

61 James B. Stewart to secretary of state, Tampico, March 24, 1924, rl. 164, M-274, RG 59, USNA.

62 Guy Stevens to Charles Evans Hughes, New York City, February 19, 1924, 812.504/533, rl. 163, M-274, RG 59, USNA.

63 James B. Stewart to secretary of state, Tampico, March 24, 1924, rl. 164, M-274, RG 59, USNA. See also J. A. Brown to Henry Hall, Mexico City, February 11, 1924, RG 84, USNA.

not met, the workers had seized the company's facilities in March. Again government arbitration brought a partial victory for the union.[64]

The Tampico electrical workers' strike which served as a catalyst for the oil workers' actions was only one example of militant actions by electrical workers. The electricians' union in Veracruz had also staged a strike. Then in April of 1924 the workers at the Central Mexican Light and Power Company in San Luis Potosí went out demanding the firing of the company's thirty-four non-union workers. The company responded by organizing its non-union employees into a labor syndicate, hoping to confront the government with the dilemma of appeasing two competing unions. But with the blessing of Governor Aurelio Manrique, the strikers seized the plant and won partial control over hiring and firing. After their victory the electrical workers paraded through the city on trucks, chanting "invectives against capitalists in general and the United States in particular."[65]

In the face of these events, the U.S. consul general concluded, "Syndicalism is the ruling ideal in Mexico today." His analysis of conditions in Mexico defined the ongoing struggle as a contest between the progressive and productive forces of American capitalism and the unreasoning and anarchic forces of syndicalism and the Mexican working class. According to his report, economic issues were invoked "only as bait for continued blind unreasoning support of the plans of syndicalism for wresting all productive factors from the control of capital for political ends." Reflective of American views, the consul ascribed this phenomenon to the intellectual makeup of the Mexican worker, who "ranks low in intelligence" and is "incapable of working out for his own benefit advanced theories of the just rights of labor."[66] The American commercial attaché pointed out that popular nationalism gave exceptional power to the working class' militant actions. As he explained, labor conflicts nearly always assumed "the feature of Mexican against foreigners where patriotism is involved on the side of labor."[67] Nor did the problems end with syndicalist tendencies among Mexican workers.

As market forces increasingly impacted the various aspects of their lives, Mexican workers, the petite bourgeoisie and an emerging middle class struggled to impose controls on the process of modernization. Urban tenants formed renters' associations and launched rent strikes demanding government controls over rates. When electrical workers struck in the early 1920s, they found sympathetic audiences among the local commu-

64 Stewart to secretary of state, Tampico, March 31, 1924, 812.504/549, rl. 163, M-274, RG 59, USNA.

65 Walter F. Boyle to secretary of state, San Luis Potosí, April 23, 1924, RG 84, USNA; Walter F. Boyle to secretary of state, San Luis Potosí, April 9, 1924, rl. 163, M-274, RG 59, USNA.

66 Charles B. Warren to secretary of state, Mexico City, April 11, 1924, rl. 164, M-274, RG 59, USNA.

67 Alexander V. Dye to American ambassador, Mexico City, April 5, 1924, rl. 164, M-274, RG 59, USNA.

nities which they served. Parallel with the workers' strike actions came protests by small businessmen and consumers against the high rates charged by the companies.[68] White-collar employees also had specific complaints against the emerging corporate society.

During the oil workers' strike at the American-owned Huasteca Petroleum Company in 1925, Ruben Cid, a member of the company's accounting department, headed the strike committee. Cid took a militant stance against the company and denounced the anti-Mexican biases of its superintendent, William Green.[69] At the time of the oil workers' strike, the employees' union in Mexico City demanded recognition, the union shop and the eight-hour day from the country's leading foreign banks. But this expression of white-collar militancy was soon squelched. The clerical workers' union formed part of the Confederación Regional Obrera Mexicana (CROM), a state-supported labor federation which represented the cooptive aspect of the government's labor strategy. When the foreign financial institutions began restricting credit in Mexico, Calles ordered Luis Morones, head of the CROM, to halt the strike, and the labor leader quickly complied.[70]

Calles' action in the bank strike and his use of federal troops against the Huasteca strikers clearly defined the limits of the state's cooptive labor strategy. The elite's efforts to control the labor movement in the 1920s accommodated the interests of American corporations and signaled a growing recognition of the need to push ahead with the process of rationalization. An editorial in *Excelsior* in 1929 noted that Mexico was in a period of "industrial transition" and needed to follow the American example of introducing labor-saving machinery to increase efficiency and lower prices.[71] That perspective neatly matched the labor strategy being pursued by American corporations.

A distinguishing feature of American investment after the revolution was its labor-displacing aspect. A Phelps Dodge official explained in 1927 that the increased adoption of labor-saving devices and techniques became part of a conscious strategy of social control:

With the radical wave throughout the Mexican Government the general policy has been to adopt any device or practice which will break even on cost and do away with men. In other words the Company should be operated with the very fewest number of men possible. Gradually, as jobs are combined, we will have a better, higher paid, and more satisfied organization.[72]

68 Galarza, *Industria eléctrica*, pp. 102–5.
69 William Green to Licenciados Calero, Castelazo and Charles, Huasteca Petroleum Company, June 29, 1925, 812.504/698, rl. 164, M-274, RG 59, USNA.
70 James R. Sheffield to secretary of state, Mexico City, May 18, 1925, 812.504/15, rl. 167, M-274, RG 59, USNA.
71 *Excelsior* (Mexico City), April 20, 1929.
72 Frank Ayer to H. H. Horton and E. Leland, Nacozari, May 26, 1927, File 2055, Box 1371-0334, Phelps Dodge Papers.

This smaller workforce would receive better treatment from the company.

As early as 1918 the company had begun upgrading worker housing in the company towns, plastering the walls of workers' shacks and laying floors in them. It enlarged the schools for Mexican children and began providing entertainment, including motion pictures. The company encouraged the development of a local sports club composed of the "better element," and actually built a gymnasium for the club. In 1928 Phelps Dodge began construction of a combination theater and dance hall in Pilares to accommodate motion pictures and local social events. Diversions such as motion pictures and company-supervised sports improved worker retention and upgraded performance by weaning workers away from traditional forms of recreation, especially social drinking. The company ran an intensified campaign, with booklets, posters and monthly lectures from managers on the evils of alcohol. In addition, the employment office received instructions to gradually purge the payroll of habitual drinkers.[73] Ralph M. Ingersoll, a Phelps Dodge engineer, explained the company's perception of its workforce which lay behind these reforms:

> . . . it takes just four years to complete the Americanization of the Mexican – to teach him to bathe every day, to sleep in clean rooms with plenty of air, and to curb, in a measure, his ferocious appetite for spirits. Also it is an accepted fact that the results are highly satisfactory, and that increased output goes hand in hand with physical and mental improvement.[74]

Ingersoll captured the American corporate reformers' vision of their role in Mexico. The dirty, drunken, dissolute Mexican would be transformed into the Americanized Mexican, a clean, sober, productive worker. That more efficient worker, however, carried added costs. Since the company was now tying up additional time and money in training Mexican workers, retention became a leading priority for Phelps Dodge. As one official noted, "A man who has been here a year or two has tied up in him a lot of valuable information regarding our policy regulations, safety campaign, etc., and in losing him we lose a certain amount of money."[75] The company arranged to have the U.S. consulate at Agua Prieta send it a monthly list of Phelps Dodge workers who had migrated to the United States. Company officials would then attach a note to each name explaining the reason why the worker had left. Managers kept an eye on the top workers to try and identify any causes for possible discontent. The com-

---

73 Memorandum, Nacozari, March 24, 1928, File 2020, Box 1371-0331; *Annual Report of the Phelps Dodge Corporation for 1918;* Frank Ayer to H. H. Horton and E. Leland, Nacozari, May 26, 1927, File 2055, Box 1371-0334; *Annual Report of the Phelps Dodge Corporation for 1929,* Phelps Dodge Papers.

74 Ingersoll, *In and Under Mexico,* pp. 116–17.

75 Frank Ayer to H. H. Horton and E. Leland, Nacozari, May 26, 1927, File 2055, Box 1371-0334, Phelps Dodge Papers.

pany also attempted to upgrade its workforce through a safety campaign. The company had begun a "Safety First Campaign" in all its mines in 1925. The program came none too soon in its Mexican operations, which in 1923 suffered a catastrophic twelve fatal accidents among a total workforce of 1,500. The company kept careful records of all accidents and provided training and pamphlets on safety as well as carrying out safety inspections and offering awards for improved safety records. Through the cultivation of workers' contentment, along with measures to ensure their safety, the American overseers transmitted corporate values and culture.[76]

As a part of the upgrading process and the extension of social control, Phelps Dodge made strenuous efforts to preempt strikes by its workers. Managers placed the subsidiary which ran the company stores under strict orders not to make any changes which would affect the corporation's relations with its Mexican workers. The accounting department compiled a record of pay scales for each job classification since the mine had opened. Managers combined this data with cost-of-living information for the average family so adjustments could be made before labor troubles started. Should that effort fail and a labor action begin, managers were instructed that "all operating should be forgotten and the complete attention of the Management given to meeting the situation and not allow the Sindicato to carry out Anti-Company schemes."[77] Phelps Dodge went beyond reactive strategies and formed a workers' committee designed to preempt union challenges to company work rules. The management insisted on "establishing it [the committee] as *the* place where every man in our employ will take his suggestions and grievances."[78] The policies and experiences of the Phelps Dodge Corporation in the 1920s were not unique.

As early as 1913 ASARCO had initiated an industrial relations program that included accident prevention, welfare activities and worker–management committees. ASARCO applied these policies directly to its Mexican operations, creating the position of welfare representative at its plants and setting up company unions in attempts to control its workforce. The company pointed to the impact of better industrial relations in the improved efficiency of the crushing operations at its Durango plant, where output per man-day rose by over 60 percent between 1914 and 1921.[79] In general American companies undertook welfare work, including building schools, hospitals and athletic fields and running programs to combat alcoholism. Beyond a smaller and more disciplined labor force on which to build Mexico's development, American corporate reformers

---

76 "Moctezuma Copper Company Statistics," File 1091, Box 1371-0331, Phelps Dodge Papers; *EMJ* 122 (November 27, 1926).

77 Frank Ayer to H. H. Horton and E. Leland, Nacozari, May 26, 1927, File 2055, Box 1371-0334, Phelps Dodge Papers.

78 Ibid.

79 "American Smelting and Refining Company," Scudder Collection; Thomas McEnelly to secretary of state, Chihuahua, November 8, 1923, 812.504/520, rl. 163, M-274, RG 59, USNA.

envisioned a new professional class with the appropriate values to create that modern corporate society.[80]

Given the highly technical nature of its operations, G. E.'s subsidiary American and Foreign Power Company began sending its more promising employees to the United States for training.[81] Elsewhere the efforts were somewhat more subtle. As labor relations at the Huasteca Petroleum Company worsened in 1925, members of the company's engineering department in Tampico were approached by their supervisor, engineer Yarza. Yarza made it clear to the employees that they would be far better off resolving their problems through direct talks with management than by remaining members of the oil workers' union. William Green later explained that Yarza's efforts reflected a fundamental affinity of cultural values and goals between corporate management and technicians: "Work of a confidential nature of course demands greater confidence and closer identification than those tasks which are entirely manual and without any great responsibility, the artisans of which can easily be substituted without detriment to the work."[82] Green also pointed out that this affinity was matched by a fundamental division between the working class and these professionals. He noted that, while the union bore the name of laborers and employees,

the ideals and tendencies of the former and the latter are widely different, and notwithstanding that there are apparently many points of contact, the differences are also very great as to enlightenment, culture, education, social demands and more responsibility under which they live, preventing their amalgamation into a body of radical and impetuous tendencies.[83]

Green's statements addressed a dual problem. Corporations required a new professional class with the technical skills to manage modern production processes, yet elements of that emerging middle class had acted in alliances with workers. In response, the oilman had set out to redefine the term "worker," which in Mexico as in the United States had long encompassed a broad array of groups from independent craftsmen and industrial artisans to day laborers in agriculture and industry.

Green's comments also reflected a set of policies pursued by Standard Oil after it purchased Huasteca from the American oil entrepreneur Edward L. Doheny. Standard accentuated differences between Mexican employees and workers by placing employees in separate company camps

80 "Anaconda," Scudder Collection; George Wythe, "Brief Review of Labor Movement in Mexico," Mexico City, April 9, 1928, 812.504/930, rl. 165, M-274, RG 59, USNA; *EMJ* 121 (February 13, 1926); Galarza, *Industria eléctrica*, p. 165.

81 Wythe, "Brief Review of Labor Movement in Mexico," April 9, 1928, 812.504/930, rl. 165, M-274, RG 59, USNA.

82 William Green to general secretary of petroleum syndicate, Tampico, April 28, 1925, Document 24, Huasteca Petroleum Company Documents, 812.504/698, rl. 164, M-274, RG 59, USNA.

83 Ibid.

known as *campos americanos*. The homes in the "American camps" came equipped with window screens, fans and furniture. Workers' housing in the *campos mexicanos* possessed none of those features.[84] Standard's policies illustrated the growing need for American corporations to professionalize the Mexican middle class and separate it from the working class in the ongoing struggle over the future of Mexican society.

American corporate efforts to shape that future went beyond the work place itself to encompass municipal, state and national political institutions. The ability of workers to elect municipal governments remained a thorn in the side of the Phelps Dodge Corporation. Although it tried to influence elections, it did not enjoy the success of companies like the El Tigre Mining Company which had smaller towns to deal with. The company also found the state and federal governments difficult to deal with at times, particularly on the issue of taxation. However, by 1925 the governor of Sonora, Alejo Bay, was proving more cooperative, backing company policies and promising to expand the contingent of state troops stationed at the Phelps Dodge mines.[85]

In 1927 the Phelps Dodge assistant manager H. H. Horton observed a refreshing pro-business trend in state politics. He noted that recently elected state officials "seem to be a better class of men than have been in the office for a long time, and they all seem anxious to do anything which will bring new business to the State."[86] This was particularly true of the newly elected governor, General Fausto Topete. In a meeting with Horton, the governor-elect assured Horton that he intended "to see that justice is done, not only to Labor but to Capital as well." Horton impressed Topete with his description of company safety programs. The governor in turn promised Horton "full support in our program of elimination of worthless workmen . . ."[87]

Not surprisingly, company officials showed a distinct preference for dealing with local officials on labor matters. In 1927, when the federal government ordered the creation of conciliation boards to deal with labor problems in mining, Phelps Dodge managers expressed concern that this would take labor matters out of the hands of the state government and circumvent state labor laws. But state bureaucrats who had been swayed by American corporate concepts of efficiency served as important allies on the conciliation boards. The local inspector and board member D. M.

---

84 "Dictamen de los Peritos," Mexico City, May 19, 1935, RG 84, USNA; Watts, *Order Against Chaos*, p. 4; John Mason Hart, *Anarchism and the Mexican Working Class, 1860–1931* (Austin: University of Texas Press, 1978), pp. 17, 86–87; Hart, *Revolutionary Mexico*, pp. 56–58.

85 John Jones, "Political Conditions in the Agua Prieta Consular District," Agua Prieta, November 2, 1927, rl. 165, M-274, RG 59, USNA; "Memorandum for the Directors," Nacozari, September 6, 1926, File 2044, Box 1371-0334, Phelps Dodge Papers.

86 Horton to R. G. Beckett, Nacozari, April 4, 1927, File 2055, Box 1371-0334, Phelps Dodge Papers.

87 Ibid.

Gardillo proved quite cooperative. Horton explained the company's problems with labor efficiency, and Gardillo promised that "he would lend us all the assistance possible in finding some means of getting better attendance of the workmen, knowing that the interests of the Government, workmen and ourselves are mutual, and that increased efficiency would result in benefit to all concerned."[88]

The state government also lent a sympathetic ear to the company's complaints about municipal government. Horton explained to Topete the problems occasioned for the company by the elected officials of the company towns, particularly Pilares. Defining the problem as one of impartiality and law and order, Horton asked that Pilares be reduced again to the status of a comisario, "as the government of the Camp will then be in charge of a responsible man who will not feel that in enforcing the law, he will incur the enmity of his friends or political associates."[89] Topete assured Horton that state officials were considering reducing the number of municipalities. In the meantime, Topete began to intervene directly in municipal politics on the company's behalf.[90]

Phelps Dodge also worked to develop a sympathetic attitude at the federal level. The company had a strong base to work from in Mexico City, since Obregón and Calles had been instrumental in protecting the company from Villa's forces during the revolution. Company officials continued to curry favor in the capital during the 1920s, sending government agencies favorable propaganda about their safety program and other positive aspects of their operations. At the end of the decade, Phelps Dodge officials still preferred to deal with state officials on labor matters, but federal involvement had proven quite benign. Despite the creation of the conciliation boards, local labor inspectors still held the deciding vote on the boards, and the Calles regime insisted that labor problems be resolved in accordance with state laws. Yet despite favorable government policies and their own efforts to control the work place and encourage the development of a modern society, American corporate efforts to encourage efficiency fell far short of expectations.[91]

American efficiency programs in mining showed mixed results during the 1920s. Output per man had risen dramatically, but as of 1927, despite considerable consolidation in the industry, the number of workers remained essentially at the same level as before the revolution. At Phelps Dodge, the total workforce actually increased slightly in this period, and more importantly the company's own measures of mining efficiency showed nearly a 50 percent decline between 1922 and 1930. The limited ability of American corporations to transform the work place and Mexican

88 Horton to Beckett, Nacozari, April 25, 1927, File 2041, Box 1371-0331, Phelps Dodge Papers.
89 Horton to Beckett, Nacozari, April 4, 1927, File 2055, Box 1371-0334, Phelps Dodge Papers.
90 Ibid.; Horton to Ayer, Nacozari, May 3, 1927, File 2053, Box 1371-0334, Phelps Dodge Papers.
91 Ayer to Horton and Leland, Nacozari, May 26, 1927, File 2055, Box 1371-0334; Horton to J. H. Davis, Nacozari, October 14, 1930, File 2041, Box 1371-0331, Phelps Dodge Papers.

society in the 1920s exposed the limits of American corporate culture and the ability of Mexicans to resist those aspects of it which they found unacceptable.[92]

William Green's vision of a professionalized Mexican middle class bound closely in values and interests to American corporations fell considerably short of reality in the 1920s. In 1925 the federal government enacted the responsible engineer law, which in effect required mining companies to hire at least one Mexican engineer. American corporations like Phelps Dodge complied, but they placed the Mexican engineer in the non-strategic position of safety engineer. Outside of that single engineer, the highest-ranking white-collar Mexican employees at Phelps Dodge in 1930 were clerks.[93] So too consumers and small business people who had formed protest groups against the high utility rates charged by foreign companies had little to show for their efforts. They had achieved minimal reductions in charges and received little but interminable delays from a government system ostensibly designed to regulate the industry. The discontents of the petite bourgeoisie and middle class made them natural allies of workers who continued to face low wages and exclusion within American corporations.[94]

The American corporate strategy of the 1920s which envisioned a more stable and more efficient work force also assumed that the system would extract more work from the labor force. In the same memo in which company managers discussed creating "a better, higher paid, and more satisfied organization" they went on to state, "On account of inattendance, it would be advisable to gradually bring in more Italians and Japs, who will work harder and more regularly, thus maintaining our present contract prices and stabilizing conditions underground at Pilares."[95] And while Phelps Dodge had an elaborate set of wage scales for every job classification under its contract system, the company advised its engineers that "under favorable conditions" a lower wage should be paid than that quoted in the scales. Throughout this period, mining and petroleum companies continued to rely on contract work and task systems to extract greater output from their workers.[96]

If American managers instituted industrial welfare policies, they remained convinced that they were wasting much of the effort on a Mexican

92 Meyer, *Grupos de presión,* p. 44; Anderson, *Outcasts,* p. 342; Bernstein, *Mexican Mining,* pp. 161–62; "The Moctezuma Copper Company Statistics," File 1091, Box 1371-0331, Phelps Dodge Papers.

93 *EMJ* 121 (February 13, 1926). On Phelps Dodge's employment of Mexicans in non-labor positions, see File 2003, 1928–30, Box 1371-0331, Phelps Dodge Papers.

94 Galarza, *Industria eléctrica,* pp. 4–6.

95 See File 2003, 1928–30, Box 1371-0331, Phelps Dodge Papers.

96 Federico Besserer, José Díaz and Raul Santana, "Formación y consolidación del sindicato minero en Cananea," *Revista Mexicana de Sociología* 42 (October–December 1980), p. 1334; File 2003, 1928–30, Box 1371-0331, Phelps Dodge Papers.

labor force which they viewed as ignorant, improvident and lacking in ambition. Ralph Ingersoll explained how this ambivalence shaped corporate actions:

They [Phelps Dodge] built the men houses, but houses such as [these] . . . were very sorry improvements on the native ones. They tried to teach safety-first and gave medical service, but paid little or no attention to the living-conditions of the so-called healthy. The first encounter with evidence of traditional influence and of Latin American temperament seemed to discourage any further attempt.[97]

Limited material rewards and American biases helped promote new challenges by the workforce to American corporate culture.

In light of poor improvements in productivity, Phelps Dodge managers prepared a memo in 1926 which ascribed the rise in production costs to the existence of democratically elected municipal governments in Nacozari and Pilares. Unlike the malleable comisario regimes of an earlier time, these governments insisted on raising taxes on the company store and ranch. Furthermore, "the law is only enforced when there is a chance to sting the Company, the clandestine sale of liquor is allowed to go unchecked and criminals unpunished. In fact, there is less regard for law and order at the present time than at any time in the history of the camp."[98]

The presidentes municipales also went beyond taxation and lax enforcement of the law. One company official described William Yates, the mayor of Nacozari in 1927, as the "reddest Bolshevik I ever saw" because of his strong backing for the miners' union.[99] Juan Solórzano personified the strong links between the community and the union. Solórzano, a local merchant and leader of the union, became a candidate for mayor in 1928.[100] In an oft-repeated complaint, company manager Frank Ayer reported in 1926, "We have spent the last few days doing practically nothing but treat with the most rabid, red, bolsheviki members of the Sindicato whom we have ever seen . . ." The managers reported that they frequently had to neglect their technical duties to attend to endless complaints by the union.[101]

Throughout the latter part of the decade, company managers bemoaned the challenges they faced from their Mexican workers. As one reported in 1926, "Our men not only are failing to report to work, but when they do go to work they are not doing very much. They are independent and im-

---

97 Ingersoll, *In and Under Mexico*, p. 117.
98 "Memorandum for the Directors," Nacozari, September 6, 1926, File 2044, Box 1371-0334, Phelps Dodge Papers.
99 John Jones, "Political Conditions in the Agua Prieta Consular District," Agua Prieta, November 2, 1927, rl. 165, M-274, RG 59, USNA.
100 Horton to Davis, Nacozari, May 29, 1928, File 2041, Box 1371-0331, Phelps Dodge Papers.
101 Ayer to Beckett, Nacozari, August 31, 1926, File 2044, Box 1371-0334, Phelps Dodge Papers.

pudent and make it plain to all concerned that they do not have to exert themselves. They even insult the bosses in public."[102] In one effort to speed up their recalcitrant labor force, Phelps Dodge required workers to bring their lunches with them into the shafts rather than having hot lunches sent in at noontime. Juan Solórzano, with the backing of the municipal government, headed a workers' protest. Phelps Dodge finally settled for carting five of the labor leaders off to Hermosillo to be lectured by Governor Topete on the need for greater efficiency if hot meals were to be continued. The following year the company issued a warning to the workers that they were not working hard enough and that if they did not improve, lower copper prices would force layoffs.[103]

At times the workers also found support from federal bureaucrats. In 1926 the union at Pilares managed, with the help of a federal labor inspector, to get the minimum wage raised in the municipality to 3.50 pesos. However as the Great Depression gripped the mining region in 1930, another labor inspector concluded that a cut in the minimum wage was justified and recommended that Phelps Dodge petition the Department of Industry, Commerce and Labor for a reduction to 2.50 pesos. When the department's emissary met with the workers, he was greeted by jeers and insulting remarks about the government, the company and himself. In return for any reduction, the workers demanded a return to the carload system of measurement, use of meters instead of feet for measuring and a reduction in house rentals. The company rejected the demands, and H. H. Horton went to see the governor of Sonora to gain his backing for the wage reduction. He also pressed for the elimination of elected government in the company towns, which allowed the local petite bourgeoisie to act in concert with the workers. The governor agreed to send fifty troops to Pilares to back up the company. However, when Horton arrived with the troops, the workers at Pilares had already gone out on strike.

The company locked out the workers, and the troops arrested three union leaders. Town officials quickly released the union men, only to have them rearrested by the military. Federal authorities declared the strike illegal because the workers had struck without giving prior notice. The federal government also authorized local officials to settle the matter according to state law. The Sonoran secretary of state announced the wage reduction to the strikers, who threatened to shut down the mines. The company fired those workers who continued to resist the new wage and threw them out of their homes. The governor lured union leaders to Hermosillo and arrested them. The crushing of the strike in October 1930 did not end all resistance to the company's policies. In December four men were arrested in Pilares for plotting to assassinate the company's em-

102 Ayer to Beckett, Nacozari, August 26, 1926, File 2044, Box 1371-0334, Phelps Dodge Papers.
103 "Statement of Moctezuma Copper Company to its Workers," Nacozari, November 20, 1929, File 2041, Box 1371-0331, Phelps Dodge Papers.

ployment agent. Two of them had been active participants in the strike, and a third was a local newspaper correspondent who had published articles critical of the company. As was the case with its efficiency policies, Phelps Dodge's experience with labor resistance was not unique.[104]

Despite state intervention against them in 1920, the Cananea workers continued their organizational efforts, creating a new labor organization in 1926. Although the union enjoyed little success against the company, its branch in Pilares was considered the center of militant action against Phelps Dodge. In 1930 the Cananea workers formed the Sindicato Nueva Orientación, which secured recognition from the company and at least limited concessions on the drastic cutbacks which the company was making.[105] Electrical workers threatened a general strike in 1925 in an effort to obtain an industry-wide collective contract. The unions failed to carry through on the strike threat, perhaps deliberately, since electric company managers planned to use the strike as an excuse to break the unions. But the workers at the Mexican Light and Power Company succeeded in gaining an agreement that put an end to individual contracts and gave union members preference in hiring. Elsewhere electrical workers continued to engage in militant actions, including plant seizures and sabotage.[106]

The 1920s marked a period of consolidation but also one of substantial achievement by American business in Mexico. Large mining companies as well as G.E. made significant advances in expanding important sectors of the Mexican economy. While their industrial welfare policies were often driven by pragmatic efforts to cope with labor radicalism, the companies and the state did make headway in improving working and living conditions, at least for the higher-skilled and better-organized members of the working class. American companies had also successfully joined the debate on Mexico's future. They portrayed the interests of corporations as those which represented enlightenment and progress for Mexico, as opposed to the ignorance and violence of the working class. They also redefined the working class itself, excluding white-collar employees as "professionals" or employees of confidence whose interests in individual achievement and progress closely aligned them with management. Yet that corporate strategy for development meant continued intrusion by foreign companies allied with the state into the lives of workers and local governments, and it continued to reflect the demeaning attitude which corporate reformers still held toward Mexicans.

State and corporate policies enjoyed only limited success in the 1920s in part because of the self-limiting aspects of American corporate culture

---

104 Horton to Davis, Nacozari, May 29, 1928, File 2041, Box 1371-0331, Phelps Dodge Papers.

105 Tureba Lara, *Cananea,* pp. 20–21; Besserer, Díaz and Santana, "Sindicato Minero," p. 1336.

106 F. J. Miller to Whitehall Securities Corporation, Mexico City, November 24, 1925, Box 143122, EBASCO; Mark Elliot Thompson, "The Development of Unionism Among Mexican Electrical Workers" (Ph.D. dissertation, Cornell University, 1966), pp. 81–83, 122, 131–36.

and the Mexican state. Despite policies of industrial welfare and an emphasis on individual achievement within a meritocracy, American corporate reformers still viewed Mexicans as members of an inherently inferior race. They therefore limited their policies of corporate welfare and continued to exclude the Mexican middle class from advancement. As for the Mexican revolutionary elite, their efforts to accommodate American corporations called into question their legitimacy as nationalists. At the same time, Mexico's working and middle classes found the common ground for an alternative vision of the future in the concept of nationalism.

While syndicalist direct action strategies gave way to trade unionism, syndicalism still provided workers with a critique of welfare capitalism and offered socialization of the means of production as an alternative. Working-class nationalism strengthened that vision. It served as a powerful critique of a course of progress which depended on the continued intrusion of foreign capital. It also provided a bond between Mexican workers and much of the petite bourgeoisie. Together they formed resistance communities which challenged American corporate culture's transformation of their society. Even the blows of the Great Depression could not subdue popular resistance to the transformation of Mexican society. In fact, the depression undermined the material rewards from the welfare policies of the Mexican state and American companies, and would prompt new and more widespread debate on the course of national development.

11

Nationalism and capitalism

{The YMCA} is creating a new and infinitely better young Mexican manhood. It is improving morals and physical standards . . . and is undermining and will ultimately exterminate revolutions . . . (Delbert Haff)

In the fall of 1931 thousands of families in the towns of Nacozari and Pilares stripped the corrugated metal roofs and doors from their shacks and piled them along with their few personal possessions on waiting wagons and trucks. By the end of December the workers' diaspora had reduced the two Sonoran mining camps to ghost towns. Phelps Dodge had closed its Mexican mines. The Great Depression had begun. Want and desperation stalked the mining regions of Mexico. The story of collapse repeated itself throughout the national economy, threatening to destroy the process of development which Mexico had so recently resumed.

During the 1920s communities of Mexican workers and elements of the petite bourgeoisie had rallied behind a version of Mexican nationalism with strong populist themes. Meanwhile, the revolutionary elite and American businessmen were pursuing the ideal of capitalist development and a consumer society. Material rewards played a central role in their conception of national development. The depression which crippled private enterprise and impoverished the national government undermined their ability to provide such material compensation. Economic collapse also gave new life to the syndicalist concept of workers' control as the means by which to achieve social and economic justice.

In the 1930s the Mexican state and American corporations had to confront reinvigorated syndicalism among popular forces with diminished resources to fund programs of industrial welfare. Their success in coping with this challenge derived from a number of different policies and factors. The revolutionary elite continued to expand the control which the state exercised over the country's regional power centers. That development paralleled and reinforced the renewed ability of American corporations to influence events at the local level. The state and corporations also began to address concerns of the petite bourgeoisie in terms of regulating large enterprises and creating opportunities for this group through the formation of a new professional class. Perhaps most significantly, the elite under Lázaro Cárdenas recaptured control of the issue of Mexican nationalism, sharply curtailing the ability of workers to define their struggles in patriotic terms. By the end of the Cárdenas era the revolutionary elite had firmly established control of Mexican society. It could once again assert its claim as the standard-bearer of Mexican nationalism while pursuing a process of development in conjunction with American corporations. Yet, as with any hegemonic class, it based its success on the ability to absorb demands for change from popular forces while stripping the popular agenda of its more radical items. This process unfolded during the 1930s.

Mexico's economic recovery from the destruction and disruptions of the revolution began disintegrating in 1930. That year the country's gross domestic product fell by 12.5 percent. By 1932 exports had fallen by one-third, as had public revenues, and imports dropped to levels last seen at the turn of the century. Manufacturers, oil producers and mining companies cut wages and hours and then initiated mass layoffs. Mining, probably the hardest-hit sector, reduced its labor force by 50 percent. Phelps Dodge became one of scores of companies that completely shut down their operations. If workers were the hardest hit in the crisis, the middle class was not far behind. The Mexican revolution dealt a devastating blow to what has been termed the traditional petite bourgeoisie. The class of artisans, shopkeepers, small merchants and industrialists, which had doubled in size during the waning years of the Porfiriato, had shriveled during the most physically destructive phases of the revolution. While the decade of the twenties brought economic recovery and halted the decline in the size of these groups, the renewed growth of large capitalist enterprises further diminished the role of the traditional petite bourgeoisie. Battered by the revolution and facing an uncertain future within a modern society, these groups made a major American corporation the focal point of their protests during the early 1930s.[1]

Between 1928 and 1930, G. E.'s American and Foreign Power Company (AFP) acquired electric power companies in cities such as Mérida, Veracruz, Tampico, San Luis Potosí and Puebla, giving it control of a power grid that stretched in a great arc from the Yucatan in the Southeast to Chihuahua in the North. By 1935 its acquisitions and investments totaled $85 million. AFP's operations in Mexico reflected the changing structure of the electrical industry. Its contract with ASARCO to supply electricity for the company's mining and smelting operations in the state of San Luis Potosí reflected the close identification between the mining and electrical industries, while its agreement with the Atoyoi Textile

---

1 Arnaldo Córdova, *La clase obrera en la historia de México: En una época de crisis (1928–1934)* (Mexico City: Siglo Veintiuno Editores, 1980), pp. 81–85; José Calixto Rangel Contla, *La pequeña burgesía en la sociedad mexicana, 1895–1960* (Mexico City: Universidad Nacional Autónoma de México, 1972), p. 93.

Company in Puebla indicated the increased use of electricity by manufacturing enterprises. AFP's upgrading of sales rooms at its offices in Veracruz, Tampico, Córdoba, Torreón, León and Aguascalientes signaled the rapid growth of electricity as a consumer industry, reaching one-fourth of the Mexican population.[2]

The development of AFP operations came amid growing protests against the power industry. At the heart of the protest movement were small businessmen. As the Puebla daily *El Comercio* explained in 1928, high electricity rates were seen as a matter of life or death for the national economy. Rates in Mexico were one-third higher than in the United States, and in Mexico small industrialists, businessmen and consumers paid rates that were ten to twenty times those charged large mining and manufacturing enterprises. Protests by consumer leagues formed by small business interests finally pressured Plutarco Elías Calles in 1928 to implement regulations for the 1926 national electrical code. Government regulation of the industry, however, remained minimal, and the hard times of the depression sparked a new and far more militant protest movement. While unemployment rose and incomes shrank in Mexico, the foreign power companies continued to maintain the same high rates they had been charging for two decades. In response, the Camara Nacional de Comercio called for public protests against the foreign electric companies. In 1930 consumers and small business interests in Saltillo formed the Unión de Consumidores de Luz y Fuerza Motriz. The consumers' union demanded a 60 percent rate reduction and reform of existing concessions for electrical generation. Protests and organizational efforts quickly spread through the rest of the country.[3]

Protests against AFP in Mérida emerged in the spring of 1930. The AFP experience with the Compañía de Electricidad de Mérida was fairly typical of its operations in Mexico. After acquiring the British-owned company in 1928, AFP initiated a program to upgrade its operations, switching the system over to alternating current from its previous AC/DC mix, and installing new power lines. These changes required a new concession from the municipality of Mérida. The company obtained the concession by canceling the municipality's outstanding debt of 300,000 pesos. The company's modernization program prompted strong popular protests. The new steel posts now formed an unsightly web of power lines over the downtown district. The shift to AC current forced businesses to

---

2 "Acquisitions," Box 146548, EBASCO; memorandum of conversation, Edward L. Reed and James S. Carson, Division of Latin American Affairs, Department of State, March 28, 1935, rl. 157, M-1370, RG 59, USNA; "Annual Report of American and Foreign Power Company for 1929," Box 320999, EBASCO; Miguel S. Wionczek, "Electric Power: The Uneasy Partnership," in Raymond Vernon, ed., *Public Policy and Private Enterprise in Mexico* (Cambridge: Harvard University Press, 1964), pp. 36–37.

3 Wionczek, "Electric Power," pp. 44–45; Galarza, *Industria eléctrica*, pp. 97–102; *El Universal* (Mexico City), February 4, 1932.

buy new equipment. AFP installed bare transmission wires because insulation tended to rot in Mérida's tropical climate. In May of 1930 evidence of popular discontent came with the arrest of several American engineers overseeing the installations. In July the governor of Yucatán intervened to halt the revamping of the system as local protest continued to mount.

AFP's lack of employee and consumer safety programs brought on ever greater protests. On July 17 a Mérida woman died when she brushed against an exposed wire on the patio of her home. Five days later a laborer working on the facade of a building perished in a similar accident. As a result of the second death, the local authorities in Mérida temporarily detained Henry Payne, the manager of the electric company. On the night of the twenty-third, a crowd of several thousand protesters listened to the governor of Yucatán denounce the company and explain his efforts to obtain federal intervention in order to restrict its operations. With Henry Payne facing criminal charges in the deaths of the two electrocution victims, the company withdrew its construction crews from Mérida. Then in September yet another Mérida workman died by accidental electrocution. An angry crowd met Payne when he visited the scene of the accident, and that evening a former company employee tried to shoot him. A temporary calm settled over the city, only to be broken in late October by a fourth fatal accident. That incident led directly to the formation of the Liga de Consumidores de Luz y Fuerza Eléctrica and renewed calls for state control of the power company. AFP soon faced challenges at its other operating centers.[4]

On April 21, 1931, the people of Veracruz commemorated the American invasion of the city in 1914. That evening, city officials struck out at a new symbol of American domination, the Veracruz light company. The chief of police and a group of citizens occupied and shut down the company's power station. Six weeks later the municipal council of Veracruz canceled the concession of the local AFP subsidiary and issued a call for bids on a new concession. These actions were in keeping with a campaign against the company by the League of Consumers of Electric Light of Veracruz. The Veracruz Chamber of Commerce and the city's pro-labor mayor, Mario Díaz, had played key roles in the creation of the association. Its membership also included more radical figures such as Heron Proal, who had led renters' strikes in the 1920s and who now headed the Sindicato Revolucionario de Inquilinos. Salvador Roquet, an associate of Proal, headed the Liga. At one point in the battle with AFP, Roquet was arrested and whisked off to Mexico City, accused of being one of the "dinamiteros" who were bombing the homes of well-to-do citizens. Local politicians, who derived their power from Veracruz's petit bourgeois and working-class communities, soon secured his release, and the struggle against AFP continued.

4 Rufus Lane to secretary of state, Progreso, July 29, August 7, October 16, November 5, 1930, 812.6463 EB&S Co./2–5, rl. 157, M-1370, RG 59, USNA.

Under the Liga's direction, the company's seven thousand customers refused to pay their bills. Local merchants supported the Liga, and those who failed to cooperate found their windows tarred and their stores boycotted. The league also conducted its own version of urban guerrilla warfare against the company. It assisted consumers too poor to pay for electricity in tapping into the company's lines for the first time. It also reconnected electrical service for customers who refused to pay their bills. When company workers tried to disconnect service to a small stand at a public market, an angry crowd surrounded them. The police arrested company employees for trying to enter residences to shut off service. The company's Mexican lawyer and assistant manager found the electricity to their homes shut off, and squatters occupied company-owned land. When F. J. Miller, AFP's Mexico City representative, visited the city, the police arrested him for the failure to repair defective equipment on the company's streetcar system. The state government threw its backing to the Liga, increasing taxes on AFP's showrooms and seizing appliances from the stores when the corporation refused to pay. In a meeting with AFP officials, Mario Díaz made clear that the Liga's agenda included the forgiveness of all delinquent light bills and the firing of several company officials. The Liga's demands extended beyond consumer issues. They also required AFP to pay sums to workers whom it discharged and to pay the fines which had been assessed against the company's workers. Even the U.S. consul warned the AFP managers that some rate reduction would be necessary in order to achieve peace with local officials. Yet another threat to the company's interests came in early 1932, when some of Veracruz's leading businessmen created the Nueva Planta Eléctrica, an enterprise designed to compete directly with AFP. As the struggle in Veracruz dragged on, new challenges erupted throughout the AFP network.[5]

The Veracruz liga organized a consumers' league in Córdoba. On November 22 more than three thousand people, including a large labor contingent, marched through the streets of Córdoba protesting against the American-owned electric company. Small-scale industrialists, merchants and shopkeepers in San Luis Potosí formed a consumers' league, and demonstrations erupted in Saltillo. As protests continued to mount in the early months of 1932, L. P. Hammond, vice president of AFP's parent firm, the Electric Bond and Share Company, visited with ex-president Plutarco Calles, who still wielded the real power in the Mexican state. Calles began his meeting with Hammond by noting that if a consumers' league were organized in Mexico City he would be among the first to join it because the electric bill at his home in Cuernavaca was outrageous. He argued that the company had created a monopoly on electric power and charged exorbitant rates. Yet Calles went on to assure Hammond that any

---

5 "Political Reports for April, June, July, September 1931," 812.00 Vera Cruz/18, 22, 23, 26, rl. 21, M-1370, RG 59; "Political Report for May 1932," Veracruz, May 31, 1932, RG 84, USNA.

reductions ordered in rates would be minimal and limited to charges for lighting.[6]

Although the federal government delayed real rate reductions with interminable studies, the consumers' movement did possess allies within the state's Ministry of Industry, Commerce and Labor. The ministry's technical staff, members of the emerging group of new professionals in Mexican society, were anxious to see strong federal control over the electrical industry as a part of their larger vision for national development. To that end they passed confidential data on company rates and costs to the leagues. That information helped fuel a continuing series of consumer protests.[7]

The San Luis Potosí Liga called a consumers' strike in October. Some six thousand customers boycotted company services, refused to pay their bills, denounced uncooperative merchants as traitors to their country and called for the nationalization of the industry. In November leaders of consumers' leagues, government técnicos and Mexican intellectuals met in Mexico City and formed the Confederación Nacional para la Defensa de los Servicios Públicos. The new organization announced its support for local actions and called for the nationalization of the power industry. The continuing consumer boycotts of the company's operations finally forced rate reductions in cities such as Mazatlán, Saltillo, Córdoba and Veracruz. In July 1933 Plutarco Calles publicly congratulated the national confederation for its work in bringing about such rate reductions. Federal pressure for rate reductions remained, however, highly selective.[8]

In the city of Mazatlán in 1935 consumers formed the Sindicato Revolucionario de Inquilinos de Mazatlán. Members refused to pay their rent or bills from the American-owned electric company that controlled both the electrical and water utilities. After an accidental stoppage of the water supply, sindicato members seized the electric company's manager and only released him when he convinced them that the shutdown was unintentional. As the sindicato movement carried its activities on into 1936, its members seized an electric company bill collector and refused to release him to the local police chief. They finally relented when federal troops intervened. When municipal workers struck in February, the sindicato backed them, forcing a declaration of martial law in the city. The federal government now stepped in and reduced house rents while also reducing property taxes to appease landlords. However, it left electricity rates untouched, pointing out that legally they could be adjusted only once every five years.[9]

6 Galarza, *Industria eléctrica*, p. 103; "Political Report for October 1931," Veracruz, November 1, 1931, 812.00 Veracruz/26, rl. 21, M-274, RG 59, USNA.

7 Wionczek, "Electric Power," pp. 50–51; Galarza, *Industria eléctrica*, pp. 97–105.

8 Galarza, *Industria eléctrica*, pp. 104–63.

9 "Political Reports for November 1935, January and February 1936," Mazatlán, 812.00 Sinaloa/85, 87, 88, rl. 18, M-1370, RG 59, USNA.

As consumer protests continued through the mid 1930s, the Cárdenas regime finally established a federal electricity commission in 1937, and in 1938 Congress passed a national electrical law. The law limited new concessions to Mexican companies, gave the government broad powers over rates and required electric companies to undertake expansion programs to meet the demand for electricity. AFP expressed particular concern about the last provision, which might require it to engage in unprofitable operations, and about the possibility that the law would provide the basis for expropriation. However, in a personal interview with Curtis Calder, the president of AFP, Cárdenas assured him that he had no intention of nationalizing the industry. At the same time the law provided for the earning of reasonable profits by companies, which largely precluded the danger of forcing companies to engage in unprofitable expansion.[10]

The regulation of the electrical industry marked a major triumph for the small business people who had led the consumer leagues and the new class of government técnicos who had assisted them. Increasing state intervention to regulate the capitalist economy on behalf of the petite bourgeoisie, to control the working class, and generally to promote economic growth created new opportunities for the técnicos and other new professionals drawn from the ranks of the petite bourgeoisie. By the beginning of the 1930s, Mexico's revolutionary elite recognized the need to create a new professional class to meet the needs of a modern economy. In 1932 sub-secretary of education Luis Padilla Nervo spoke of the need to rationalize education to create technical professionals with practical minds who could meet the demands of the national economy.[11]

By that time university faculties were busy designing distinct curriculums to meet the needs of professional career paths in areas such as engineering and architecture. By the end of the decade, the Mexican university system, once devoted almost exclusively to the liberal professions, still graduated nearly three hundred lawyers each year, but it also generated over two hundred engineers and chemists. Between 1928 and 1938 professional degrees as a percentage of all university degrees granted in Mexico rose from 27 to 42. In turn the government formulated legislation to regulate the professions. The state also acted to enhance opportunities in the private sector. In addition to the responsible engineer regulation, the Cárdenas regime began restricting the immigration of engineers and other foreign professionals. New positions created in this manner could be filled by the growing number of technicians trained in national and foreign universities.[12]

10 Josephus Daniels to secretary of state, Mexico City, December 6, 1938, 812.6463 EB&S Co./37, rl. 157, M-1370, RG 59, USNA; Wionczek, "Electric Power," pp. 57–67.

11 *Excelsior* (Mexico City), February 16, 1932.

12 *EMJ* 138 (February 1937), pp. 76–77; *Excelsior* (Mexico City), February 2, 5, 1932; David E. Lorey, *The Rise of the Professions in Twentieth Century Mexico: University Graduates and Occupational Change Since 1929* (Los Ángeles: UCLA Latin American Center Publications, 1992), p. 91.

Figure 18. A crowd gathers in the main square of the Phelps Dodge company town at Nacozari for the annual celebration of the local hero, Jesús García. (From Ingersoll, *In and Under Mexico* [1924])

Although engineers and accountants played a pivotal role in modern American corporations, the deep-seated racism of American managers had led them to resist the employment of Mexican professionals down into the 1920s. Those attitudes had begun to change by the 1930s. American managers began to recognize that the Mexican middle class could and in fact should be incorporated into American corporate culture. If lawyers remained one of the leading products of Mexican higher education in the 1930s, their roles had begun to change. Where Mexican lawyers had once acted primarily as influence peddlers for foreign corporations, they now served as experts on the complex web of legislation regulating foreign companies. They were now recognized as professional experts in highly technical fields. American engineers still dominated corporate positions, but Mexicans continued to make inroads as draftsmen and in other low-level technical positions. After resuming its operations in 1937, Phelps Dodge hired a young American-trained engineer named Ramos. As it had done in the past, the company assigned the Mexican professional to the position of safety engineer; however, it also began training him to take charge of all underground operations.[13]

Changing attitudes about the employment of Mexican professionals were accompanied by a new sensitivity toward Mexican nationalism. In

13 *EMJ* 137 (August 1936), pp. 379–416; H. M. Lavender to Louis Cates, Nacozari, April 9, 1937, File 1095, Box 1371-0334, Phelps Dodge Papers.

1932 Plutarco Calles solicited a contribution from the Phelps Dodge Company for a fund-raising drive by the elite in Hermosillo. The Sonoran capital's leading citizens planned to build a monument to Jesús García. García, a young worker, had sacrificed his life in 1919 to save the town of Nacozari from a trainload of explosives. Although it had shut down its mining operations, the company, cognizant of García's status as a local and national hero, made the donation.[14]

Besides making concessions to grass-roots Mexican nationalism, American corporations and the Mexican elite sought to instill in the new middle class values compatible with their plans for Mexican society. That shared vision found one of its expressions in the Young Men's Christian Association of Mexico. For decades the YMCA had trained young American middle-class males in the proper attitudes of ambition and dedication to the work ethic. American corporate leaders such as Dwight Morrow, the former Morgan partner who served as U.S. ambassador to Mexico, and Mexican political leaders such as Plutarco Calles envisioned the same role for the YMCA in Mexico. Their specific target market for the Mexican branch was "the employees of every big employer."[15]

In 1929 Walter Douglas, president of Phelps Dodge, approved a contribution of $5,000 to the Young Men's Christian Association in Mexico City. The contribution was more than corporate beneficence. As Douglas' colleague Delbert Haff explained, the YMCA "is creating a new and infinitely better young Mexican manhood. It is improving morals and physical standards . . . and is undermining and will ultimately exterminate revolutions . . . Through its steadily increasing membership, now over 4,000, [the YMCA] is actually americanizing the Mexican youth."[16] President Calles was equally enthusiastic about the project, explaining to Walter Douglas "his desire to have the young people become interested in athletics, both from a point of view of improving their physical condition and also he hinted, to give them something to think about except politics."[17] Such views continued to prevail during the Cárdenas administration. An editorial in *El Universal,* one of Mexico City's leading dailies, noted in 1938 that future generations of Mexicans must be taught that revolutions are not synonymous with progress and that such upheavals are in fact detrimental.[18]

Throughout the 1930s the Mexican elite continued to pay homage to the new professional class and praise its role in a corporate society. The in-

14 Walter Douglas to Beckett, Mexico City, January 17, 1932, File 2014, Box 1371-0331, Phelps Dodge Papers.
15 Haff to Douglas, Mexico City, September 5, 1929, File 2013, Box 1371-0331, Phelps Dodge Papers.
16 Ibid.
17 Douglas to Haff, New York, September 16, 1929, File 2013, Box 1371-0331, Phelps Dodge Papers.
18 *El Universal,* November 1, 1938.

auguration of a modern office building in downtown Mexico City in 1932 prompted the press to describe it as a beehive of activity for the engineers, financiers, lawyers and doctors who directed the city's life. The resurgence of revolutionary symbolism under Cárdenas caused many teachers and writers to describe themselves as educational or literary "workers." *El Universal* lashed out at the practice as denigrating to the professions.[19] The stridency of the editorial reflected the vital importance of professionalization to the elite's vision of Mexico's future.

The urgency of state and corporate efforts to accommodate the traditional petite bourgeoisie and forge a new class of professionals grew out of the repeated working-class and petit bourgeois challenges to the transformation of Mexican society. During the 1920s the working class and elements of the petite bourgeoisie had repeatedly and often violently challenged that process, which threatened them with displacement or subordination. The state and American companies now offered assurances that there was a place in the new Mexico for small business people, who would be protected from large enterprises by state regulation, and for the middle class, who received the assurance of a professional career ladder in business and government. Such guarantees became important as the new Mexico faced a growing challenge from workers.

If the depression limited the ability of American corporations to offer material incentives, it provided fresh opportunities to discipline the workforce. When the Cananea company began a new round of layoffs in the first quarter of 1932, it specifically targeted union members. Phelps Dodge reopened the mines at Nacozari and leased the San Carlos mine in Chihuahua in 1937. Once initial construction work was completed at San Carlos, Phelps Dodge began firing the union members among the construction crew. H. M. Lavender, the company's general manager, explained the firm's labor strategy this way:

> In the San Carlos district there are available a large number of unskilled men who are relatively untouched by the radicalism prevalent in Chihuahua, especially where A. S. & R. operations are carried on. It is the plan to recruit our operating force locally and while it will take a little time to make underground miners, we can better afford a period of reduced production than be loaded up with some of the dynamiters whom we would have to employ if hiring experienced miners from the interior.[20]

The deliberate use of layoffs to purge the workforce and the overall impact of firings and reduced wages made the 1930s a decade of mounting labor turbulence. Officially sanctioned strikes had fallen off dramatically after 1925, but labor conflicts had not. As workers experienced wage reductions and layoffs, the number of labor conflicts skyrocketed from

---

19 Ibid., December 28, 1932, March 28, 1938.
20 Lavender to Cates, Nacozari, November 29, 1937, File 1095a, Box 1371-0334, Phelps Dodge Papers.

13,000 in 1929 to over 36,000 in 1932. They responded angrily to the paralyzing of production in many industries. The number of officially recognized strikes rose from 13 in 1933 to 833 in 1937.[21]

Miners and petroleum and electrical workers led this wave of labor actions. Miners at ASARCO's coal mines in Coahuila began serious organizing efforts in 1931, defeated a company union and pressured the corporation into signing a collective contract in 1934. Cananea workers followed a similar course, combating a company union and securing a collective agreement in 1932. These actions helped lay the foundations of the first national miners' federation, the Sindicato Industrial de Trabajadores Mineros Metalúrgicos y Similares de la República Mexicana (SITMMSRM). In 1937 the federation launched a campaign to secure a company-wide labor contract from ASARCO. Oil workers had formed thirty-five independent unions, and through a series of labor actions in the mid thirties they forged a single labor organization, the Sindicato de Trabajadores Petroleros de la República Mexicana, and pressed for an industry-wide contract. Electrical workers created two federations and began pressing AFP and Mexican Light and Power for a company-wide collective agreement. When AFP began violating existing agreements with the workers, they went out on strike in Veracruz, Tampico and Puebla in 1936 and Mérida in 1937.[22]

The rising labor unrest of the early and mid 1930s clearly represented an effort to regain some of the ground lost by workers as a result of the depression. Trade union activity also demonstrated that Mexican workers had come to accept and work within some of the basic parameters and values of modern culture.[23] But in the face of the material failures of capitalism, workers also drew upon their earlier syndicalist concepts to demand workers' control of the means of production.

In 1935 ASARCO workers in Chihuahua struck, protesting against violations of their collective contract signed in 1934. The strike demands included economic issues such as a 50 percent pay increase, but the union focused on issues of control, particularly with its claim that the company had exceeded the allowed number of confidential employees. Confidential employees included technicians and other supervisory staff who did not belong to the union. The ASARCO managers concluded "that the underlying cause of the labor disturbances is the common belief among the

21 William Galbraith, "Statistics of Labor Strikes: Mexico," Mexico City, September 19, 1938, rl. 66, M-1370, RG 59, USNA; Córdova, *Época de crisis,* p. 87.

22 Victoria Novelo, "De huelgas, movilizaciones y otras acciones de los mineros del carbón de Coahuila," *Revista Mexicana de Sociología* 42 (October–December 1980), pp. 1357–58; Besserer, *Sindicalismo minero,* pp. 30–41; Caulfield, "Labor and the State," pp. 216, 228; "Miscellaneous Data About the Labor Problems of Six American Owned Electric Power and Light Companies," 812.5045/778, rl. 66, M-1370, RG 59, USNA.

23 Charles B. Warren to secretary of state, Mexico City, April 11, 1924, rl. 164, M-274 RG 59, USNA.

workers that they are mentally and technically equipped to take over control of this as well as other industries."[24] The oil workers' union raised the issue of workers' control with petroleum companies during negotiations in late 1936. As company officials noted, the workers sought "a complete reorganization of their relationships to the organizing companies based upon the desire . . . to place labor and Government in control of the industry."[25] That same year, during an eighty-day strike, the Cananea workers demanded an end to piece work and the right to oversee the operations of contractors. The union also insisted on an exclusionary clause which would require the company to fire workers who had been expelled by the union. Most importantly they demanded that the exclusion clause apply to all supervisory personnel up to the level of superintendents of departments. The company finally conceded many of these points, though the exclusionary clause was limited to the lowest-level foremen.[26] Striking electrical workers in Mérida sought to enforce a similar exclusionary clause, demanding the firing of a non-union sales manager.[27] Labor actions and demands for worker control reached a decisive stage in 1938.

Some of the conflicts which erupted in this period reflected the same array of forces that had existed in the previous decade. In Zacatecas in 1937 workers, with the support of the SITMMSRM, presented a collective contract to the Laja mining company. The company rejected the contract and fired half of its union workers before a petition to strike could be filed, replacing them with non-union workers. In February of the following year the federal government sent a labor inspector to oversee a strike vote which the company, with its purged workforce, felt certain it would win. In light of the upcoming vote, the national elites aligned with the foreign business interests, while local elites, tied to the workers through community heritage and intimate contacts, sided with them. The governor of Zacatecas, General Francisco B. Panuelos, agreed to send armed guards to protect the company's interests. The guards arrived as part of a delegation of municipal officials from several nearby towns who immediately threw their support to the union and called on the other workers to join the struggle against "foreign capitalists." The union men also received moral support from workers at other nearby mines who arrived to witness the vote. An important part of the local union consisted of *fleteros*, who had utilized their mule-drawn wagons to haul the company's ore until the firm replaced them with a fleet of company-owned trucks. Members of the union who were also local *ejiditarios* challenged the company's

24 Pierre de L. Boal to secretary of state, Mexico City, August 12, 1935, 812.5041/95, RG 59, USNA.
25 Daniels to secretary of state, Mexico City, December 20, 1937, 812.5045/600, rl. 64, M-1370, RG 59, USNA.
26 "Collective Labor Contract between Cananea Consolidated Copper Company and Union, May 23, 1936," File 2041, Box 1371-0331, Phelps Dodge Papers.
27 Boal to secretary of state, Mexico City, July 26, 1937, 812.5045/480, RG 59, USNA.

right to control the road which ran from the mine through their properties. With many of the fired workers voting, the company's 109-person workforce voted in favor of a strike, which dragged on until May. Only then, with the national labor board about to overturn the original favorable ruling on the strike vote, did the union issue a return-to-work order.[28]

The struggle at the Laja mine reflected the persistence of a community of local alliances and interests that rallied under the banner of nationalism to oppose what they saw as abuse by foreigners and detrimental aspects of rationalization. Yet the Laja conflict involved a community that developed around a small American corporation in a remote setting. Elsewhere that community of interests had begun to break down as American corporations and the Mexican state marshaled their forces to modernize Mexican society.

As the revolutionary elite began to centralize control during the Calles years, it became increasingly possible for the state and federal governments to intervene effectively in the affairs of municipios. As early as 1928 Fausto Topete, the governor of Sonora, had removed municipal officials at Nacozari who challenged Phelps Dodge interests. Topete's assistance in gaining direct control of municipal governments, however, came about in an entirely unintended manner. In 1929 Topete, as well as the mayors of Nacozari and Pilares, joined an unsuccessful Sonoran rebellion against the federal government and had to flee the state. The Phelps Dodge manager, H. H. Horton, received authorization from the Mexican consul at Douglas, Arizona, to fill both municipal posts. Horton commented on his two appointments that "both Sr. Peraza and Sr. Contreras are strong men, and I believe that we will get along nicely . . ."[29] The provisional state governor proceeded to suppress all municipal elections. A year later Horton reported, "The municipal officials in our locality are appointed by the Governor and this manner of handling has avoided a great deal of unrest among the residents of this District."[30]

In 1931 candidates of the PNR, Calles' official party, swept the municipal elections in Sonora, thanks to a total lack of opposition candidates. The predetermined election results led to a voter turnout of only 10 percent. When presidentes municipales failed to toe the line, Rudolfo Elías Calles, the former president's son and the newly elected governor of Sonora, did not hesitate to replace them. In 1935 cooptation and intimidation of potential opposition candidates proved so successful in predetermining the outcomes of local balloting that newspapers did not bother publishing the election results.[31]

---

28 A detailed account of the strike is contained in 812.5045/754, 763, 787, rl. 66, M-1370, RG 59, USNA.
29 Horton to Beckett, Nacozari, May 2, 1929, File 2503, Box 1371-0331, Phelps Dodge Papers.
30 Lewis V. Boyle to secretary of state, Agua Prieta, September 25, 1930, 812.00 Sonora/1042, rl. 18, M-1370, RG 59, USNA.
31 "Political Reports, April 1931, September 1932, April 1935," 812.00 Sonora/1067, 1146, 1254, rls. 18, 19, M-1370, RG 59, USNA.

In 1937, when the Phelps Dodge Corporation learned that the town of San Carlos had secured the status of a free municipality, it knew in advance of the election that the new mayor would be a Señor Orsate, known to be favorable to the company. The next such "election" prompted an armed insurrection by the townspeople which was quelled by federal troops. American interests were relieved to see an end to local democracy, which they viewed as nothing more than "turmoil and bloodshed." As for the dispatch of federal forces, it was only one small sign of the increasingly solicitous attitude taken by the central government toward foreign corporations.[32]

From the outset of his administration, Lázaro Cárdenas came under considerable pressure to accommodate American investors in Mexico. The depression-battered economy was particularly dependent on American mining companies because of their contributions to employment levels, state revenues and the earning of desperately needed foreign exchange. In March of 1938 the U.S. Treasury Department agreed to advance Mexico $13.5 million on future purchases of silver. But the workers at the ASARCO smelter in Monterrey launched a series of rolling one-hour work stoppages that cut the facility's silver output by half. Desperate federal officials fell all over each other in their frenzied efforts to get the workers to call off their job action. Yet such direct pressures were not the principal determinant of the regime's labor policies.[33] The Cárdenas administration's pro-labor policy represented an attempt to resolve both short- and long-term problems in the Mexican economy. First, Cárdenas sought to redress the largely repressive measures of recent administrations and the material losses inflicted by the depression in order to revitalize the productivity of the Mexican working class. The longer-term effort focused on remaking the Mexican worker.

In 1932, *El Universal,* certainly no pulpit for working-class ideology, argued in favor of state support for secondary education. The paper's reasoning was clear:

Illiterate and coarse peons of whom one can only ask submission and the resilience to work fourteen or sixteen hours daily no longer meet the needs of nascent capitalism. The development of industry demands the existence of a working class with a somewhat higher level of culture . . .[34]

Excelsior, the capital's leading daily, captured the subtleties of the question more effectively, noting that mechanization demanded a social process of

32 Horton to Beckett, Nacozari, June 23, 1928, File 1001, Box 1371-0331; Ormsbee to Horton, Nacozari, December 1, 1937, August 7, 1938, File 1095a, Box 1371-0334, Phelps Dodge Papers; "Political Report for April 1935," Guaymas, May 1, 1935, 812.00 Sonora/1254, rl. 19, M-1370, RG 59, USNA.
33 Telegram, Mexico City, 812.5045/712, rl. 66, M-1370, RG 59, USNA.
34 *El Universal* (Mexico City), December 5, 1932.

"perpetual renovation" and that therefore the culture of the masses must be transformed to overcome disorientation caused by change and the resistance to capitalism which it prompted.[35] President Calles, however, had continued to back American corporations which responded to the depression with lower wages and stricter discipline.

The deepening social and economic crisis in Mexico during the 1930s finally provided the popular pressure to initiate policies to meet the immediate material needs of workers and undertake the transformational process which the elite had long promoted. Much like American progressives, the regime sought to create a better-educated working class which received greater material rewards. But these better-educated and better-fed workers would not be allowed to take control of their industries. When he intervened on behalf of striking workers against the Monterrey business community in 1936, Cárdenas explicitly stated that he did not consider the working class intellectually, technically or financially equipped to control the productive process. Again like American progressives, Cárdenas envisioned a professional state bureaucracy that would intervene to ameliorate the most serious problems in terms of benefits and better working conditions without denying corporations their control of the means of production.[36]

The Cárdenas policy of accommodating the needs of corporations became apparent to Phelps Dodge when it began operating at San Carlos. In order not to threaten the financial viability of the mine, the Department of Labor decided that it would not strictly enforce laws requiring the construction of housing for all workmen. The Commissioner of Labor in Mexico City advised the firm to set up a local union before any significant number of workers were hired. The company could then negotiate a highly favorable contract with this small group which would be legally binding on any subsequent hires. A few weeks later, H. H. Horton met the federal labor inspector for Nacozari, who offered to round up half a dozen men and head to the mine immediately to set up a union. Horton politely declined the offer, fearing that the inspector was assuming the position of employment agent for the company.[37] In fact, based on their behavior, it would at times be rather difficult to distinguish between company officials and federal labor bureaucrats. Yet the effort to create a state bureaucracy that would mediate relations between labor and capital was only partially successful. Even Phelps Dodge's raw recruits continued to challenge the company, and across the country the number of strikes continued to mount as the fateful year 1938 approached.

35 *Excelsior* (Mexico City), September 5, 1932.

36 Caulfield, "Labor and the State," p. 226; Joe C. Ashby, *Organized Labor and the Mexican Revolution under Lázaro Cárdenas* (Chapel Hill: University of North Carolina Press, 1963), pp. 34–35.

37 José Cantu to Eugenio Caballero, Mexico City, January 1, 1937, File 1020, Box 1371-0334; Lavender to Cates, Nacozari, April 9, 1937; Randall Ormsbee to H. H. Horton, Nacozari, April 19, 1937, File 1095a, Box 1371-0334, Phelps Dodge Papers.

Between 1936 and 1938 relations between the foreign petroleum companies and their workers steadily deteriorated. The Sindicato de Trabajadores Petroleros de la República Mexicana (hereafter the Oil Workers' Union) drew up an industry-wide collective contract in 1936. The oil companies rejected the proposed contract because of one key issue, control. The workers had insisted that all foreign technicians be replaced by Mexicans within a year. They also wanted a sharp reduction in the number of confidential employees – managerial and technical staff who did not belong to the union and whose loyalty therefore lay with the company.

The companies offered to substitute Mexican for foreign technicians but insisted that the change could not be accomplished in only a year. They also objected to the union's prohibiting Mexican engineers from working directly with their foreign counterparts. The union's insistence on the latter point stemmed from the workers' awareness that for over a decade companies like Standard Oil had provided preferential treatment to Mexican white-collar employees in an attempt to create a group of new professionals who would identify with American managers rather than with Mexican workers. The workers, through their insistence on Mexican technicians and reduction in the number of confidential employees, challenged corporate control as exercised through technical staff and managers loyal to the corporation.[38] That issue remained at the heart of the conflict between the workers and the oil companies.

The federal Labor Department entered the dispute, launching a mediation effort which dragged on to the end of May 1937. When the talks failed, the Oil Workers' Union declared a strike, and the federal Board of Conciliation and Arbitration intervened. The companies rejected the board's findings in favor of the union and the Supreme Court's decision backing the board. Cárdenas then ordered the expropriation of the oil companies on March 18, 1938.

The issue of workers' control triggered the final confrontation between the workers and the corporations. In their ongoing negotiations, the workers and the companies had clashed on two fundamental issues, wages and control. But the latter issue proved the real stumbling block. In early March 1938, after nearly two years of bitter dispute, American oil executives explained to Ambassador Josephus Daniels "that even if they could pay the money [for wage increases], the administrative sections of the contract would remove the operations of their properties from their hands and give it [sic] to the representatives of the syndicate."[39] On March 11 the oil companies accepted the workers' wage demands but still insisted on modifying the administrative clause of the contract. The issue of confidential employees remained at the heart of the administrative section of

38 "Petroleum Labor Code in Mexico," Mexico City, November 17, 1936; "Dictamen de Los Peritos," Mexico City, May 19, 1935, RG 84, USNA.
39 Daniels to secretary of state, Mexico City, March 11, 16, 1938, 812.5045/688, 691, rl. 66, M-1370, RG 59, USNA.

the proposed contract. The union's original proposal limited the entire in-dustry to 114 confidential employees, or *puestos de confianza*. Under that arrangement, Standard Oil's Huasteca operations would have a limit of 35 confidential employees. The corporation argued that with so few puestos de confianza "virtually the management of the Company is turned over to the union."[40] The companies had consistently defended their right to em-ploy a large number of workers under this heading, charging that with each succeeding strike they had been forced to reduce the number of puestos de confianza.

The oil corporations argued that union workers owed their first loyalty to the syndicate and that union seniority rules prevented them from using the best-trained personnel. The companies' rejection of a proposal that they train Mexican technicians for positions controlled by the union made clear what the central issue was. At stake was the corporations' ability to train a staff of new professionals who would manage operations and who owed their first loyalty to the corporation. The union quickly rejected the oil companies' March 11 offer to raise wages in return for a modification of the contract's administrative clause. One week later, Cárdenas national-ized the industry, but his policy on the issue of control did not differ markedly from that of the companies.[41]

From the outset of the oil workers' struggle, the federal government provided strong backing on the question of wages. That support did not extend to workers' control. As the dispute dragged on, Section 30 of the Oil Workers' Union at the Poza Rica field, one of the divisions most strongly influenced by syndicalist concepts, called for expropriation of the industry and workers' control. Specifically the section called for creation of a cooperative in which the industry would remain a private corporation, with the workers becoming shareholders instead of assuming managerial roles in a state-owned enterprise. Cárdenas rejected that request, prefer-ring to rely on the state's mediation process to achieve a solution. The ac-tions of the federal Board of Conciliation and Arbitration indicated what the state had in mind for the industry. As required by law, the board ap-pointed a Commission of Experts to study the dispute. That commission included Professor Jesús Silva Herzog, counselor of the Department of Fi-nance and Public Credit, and a host of other professionals and technicians. The creation of such panels pointed to a continuing effort to utilize the emerging group of new professionals as the principal mechanism for har-monizing the interests of labor and capital.[42]

When the continued recalcitrance of the oil companies pushed Cárdenas to expropriate the industry, some concessions to the oil workers' demands for control had to be made in order to ensure continued production. The

40 "Petroleum Labor Code in Mexico," Mexico City, November 17, 1936, RG 84, USNA.
41 "Objections of the Petroleum Industry to the Reports and Opinions of the Comision Perecial," August 3, 1937, 812.5045/506 1/2, rl. 62, M-1370, RG 59, USNA.
42 Caulfield, "Labor and the State," pp. 222–31; Ashby, *Organized Labor,* p. 214.

union accepted a government proposal that placed actual production management under local workers' councils. This step brought a significant degree of stratification within the workers' movement, as illustrated by the case of Eduardo Pérez Casteneda, head of Section 30, who became manager of the Poza Rica field. The rank and file quickly rejected his attempt to fill other posts without a vote by union members. Yet elevation of Pérez Casteneda to manager marked part of a trend within the union as a whole. The new manager had previously held the confidential post of assistant to the field superintendent. His promotion typified a process in which white-collar workers who held leadership positions in the union moved into professional management posts in the expropriated industry. It was a trend which accelerated under direct state intervention.[43]

In July 1938 the government created Petroleos Mexicanos, or PEMEX, which abolished the workers' councils and was empowered to name all management personnel. The oil workers "thereby saw vanish what they thought [had] been one of their principal points gained by developments in the last two years i.e. control of the industry."[44] That new reality became apparent when Section 1 of the Oil Workers' Union at the former Aguila operations in Tampico demanded the firing of two sub-managers. The general manager of PEMEX refused to fire the two officials, and President Cárdenas personally intervened to denounce the attitude of the Section 1 workers. Local sections of the Oil Workers' Union responded to the increasing centralization of power in the industry by pressing for a general convention in which they could address the issue of control. PEMEX officials worked with the union's executive committee to stall off the convention. If those efforts failed, the government's labor department was prepared to arrest the section leaders to prevent the convention from being held.[45] The stalling tactics worked, and the process of centralization continued.

The national oil company moved union leaders into permanent management positions. For example, Juan Gray, who had previously served as the union's administrative secretary, became the personnel director of PEMEX. At the same time, PEMEX's senior managers, such as Jesús Silva Herzog, sought to weed out subordinates who failed to meet their criteria for technical competence and who owed their positions to election by their fellow workers. When workers complained about their loss of control, the state and the media denounced their challenge as treason, picturing it as an attack on a national institution fomented by a conspiracy of foreign companies.[46]

43　Ashby, *Organized Labor,* p. 247, Jesús Silva Herzog, *Petroleo mexicano* (Mexico City: Fondo de Cultura Económica, 1941), pp. 219–20; Caulfield, "Labor and the State," p. 234.

44　Josephus Daniels to secretary of state, Mexico City, August 12, 1938, RG 84, USNA.

45　Daniels to secretary of state, Mexico City, August 12, October 10, 21, 1938, RG 84, USNA.

46　Daniels to secretary of state, Mexico City, October 10, 1938, RG 84, USNA; Silva Herzog, *Petroleo mexicano,* pp. 219–20; Caulfield, "Labor and the State," pp. 235–37.

The oil nationalization clearly defined Cardenismo. The state, through an expanding group of technocrats or new professionals, would continue to promote what it saw as modernization through rationalization and the harmonizing of relations between labor and capital. That harmonization entailed assuring material rewards to militant workers and rejecting the syndicalist agenda of workers' control. Most important of all, the nationalization allowed the Mexican elite to reassert its claim as heir to the nationalist traditions of the Mexican revolution. After two decades of seeking a partnership with foreign capital, the revolutionary elite had struck out at a major symbol of foreign corporate power. The near universal support within Mexico for that act of militant nationalism allowed Cárdenas to add nationalism to a set of devices which he now used to rein in militant workers in mining and the electrical industry.

In 1936 the national delegates of the Mine Workers' Union had rejected the union leadership's decision to join the state-controlled labor federation, the CTM, headed by Lombardo Toledano. But at the end of March 1938 Cárdenas' prestige was sufficient to ensure the union's incorporation into the Partido de la Revolución Mexicana, the new corporatist political institution of the revolutionary elite. The union's national officers had now become part of the state bureaucracy dedicated to controlling labor and its allies in local government. The combined efforts of these formal and informal state bureaucrats played a pivotal role in determining the outcome of labor conflicts in the mining industry.[47]

The day of the petroleum industry's expropriation, workers seized the ASARCO smelter in Chihuahua. Their action, along with the ongoing work stoppages by ASARCO's Monterrey refinery workers, which inhibited silver exports, constituted part of a larger effort by the Mine Workers' Union to secure a company-wide contract from ASARCO. By fall the struggle had spread to the Phelps Dodge operations, the Cananea mines and the ASARCO complex at Nueva Rosita.[48]

The workers' challenge to the American corporations had been accelerating throughout the preceding year. Productivity at the Chihuahua smelter had fallen by 70 percent, forcing the managers to ship 10,000 tons of ore a month to the ASARCO smelter at El Paso. It was reported that "the discipline at the plant became deplorable and many workmen would scoff at the bosses when required to carry out orders. In fact the plant had practically fallen into the hands of insubordinate workers . . ."[49]

In the months between March and September 1938, continuing battles raged between capital and labor. Workers engaged in sitdown strikes, full-scale stoppages and plant seizures. The companies fired union organizers, locked out workers and pressured the Mexican government for a

47 Besserer, *Sindicalismo minero*, pp. 38–39.
48 *EMJ* 143 (February 1939), pp. 60–61.
49 Lee R. Blohm to secretary of state, Chihuahua, March 21, 1938, 812.5045/711, rl. 66, M-1370, RG 59, USNA.

solution that favored them. As with the oil workers' strike, the principal issue at stake in this struggle was the attempt of workers to assert control over the productive system.

Throughout the mining industry, union contract proposals included provisions for wage increases, but the focus of conflict with the companies was the issue of control. Contract requirements involving confidential employees lay at the heart of this issue. The Nueva Rosita workers proposed reducing the number of such employees from fifty-three to fifteen and specified that positions such as general superintendent and chief clerk were to be removed from the confidential category. The Cananea workers proposed similar reductions and listed the specific positions, such as president, vice president, manager and chief electrician, which could be retained in this category. Consistently the companies agreed to meet the basic wage demands but refused to negotiate the issue of confidential employees. From the perspective of corporate managers, compromise on this item meant surrendering control of their operations. It meant union control over the middle-management positions essential to corporate control of technology and the work process.[50]

Workers also found other ways to express concern over their loss of control of a constantly changing work environment. The Cananea miners insisted that neither the company nor contractors could require a worker to perform drudgery, specifically defined as the bonus system. Any adjustments due to economies from the introduction of new technology were to be discussed with the union, and any reductions were to be made in work hours, not in pay. Promotion was to be based on seniority, and among workers with equal seniority it would rest on "the best social record and attendance of workmen." Having lost control of the implements and processes of production under the concept of private property, the miners now asserted their own property rights, arguing that the "rights of length of service and seniority are the exclusive property of the workmen and the patrimony of their families."[51] C. J. Kelly, the president of Anaconda, cut to the heart of the issue, complaining that "the Union was interested in the rights of the workmen more than in economic benefits."[52] Kelly and other American executives conveyed their complaints to the Mexican ambassador, who passed them directly to Cárdenas.

The miners' strikes placed enormous pressure on Cárdenas. They threatened to curtail vital silver shipments at a time when the state faced severe pressures from an international oil boycott. In the larger economic context, the mining companies were quite different from the petroleum corporations. Unlike the oil companies, the mining interests had poured

---

50 Daniels to secretary of state, Mexico City, March 26, 1938, 812.5045/715, rl. 66, M-1370, RG 59, USNA.

51 Memorandum of conversation between Bruce Kremer, C. J. Kelly and Sumner Welles, June 8, 1938, 812.5045/792, rl. 66, M-1370, RG 59, USNA.

52 Ibid.

tens of millions of dollars into their operations before the depression, and no other foreign-controlled sector played such a large role in generating foreign exchange, government revenues and employment. Beyond these economic pressures, the president had made clear that the goal of his pro-labor policy was to secure material benefits for workers while rejecting syndicalist concepts that threatened his plans for capitalist development. As with the oil workers, Cárdenas strongly supported the economic demands of the workers but flatly rejected their attempts to assert control over the work process. The effects of that stance became apparent when miners, who struck during the fall of 1938, suddenly changed tactics. In late September ASARCO executives noted that the unions had suddenly taken a more conciliatory tone with their company and Anaconda. The following month a visitor to the Phelps Dodge operation reported that the workers told him they had no further complaints against the company and that they were "well disposed towards doing all in their powers so that the company attain better results in the operations."[53] By that time the union had called off virtually all of the labor actions, and negotiations were under way to settle the disputes. Notably absent in the tentative agreements were any further efforts by the union to control confidential employees. The sudden change of heart by the workers reflected the fact that their position had been considerably weakened on two fronts. First, the expropriation seemed to legitimize the state's nationalist credentials and cast further labor actions within a beleaguered economy in a new light. Second, the state employed all the agencies and devices at its disposal to rein in labor militancy.

In the weeks after the oil expropriation, Phelps Dodge workers made clear their support for the nationalization. However, local merchants and ranchers were worried about the expropriation's impact upon the precarious condition of the national economy. Labor actions against foreign companies were no longer necessarily a matter of patriotic solidarity.[54] When the San Carlos workers made their demands to the Phelps Dodge Corporation, the federal labor inspector for Chihuahua hurried to the mine. His ostensible mission was to deal with reported strife inside the union section. Before he departed he warned the workers about their obligations under the federal labor law, and dismissed many of their complaints as groundless. Shortly after the inspector's visit, delegates from the national union arrived in San Carlos to deal with the internal disputes in the local section. During their visit the delegates "helped the more conservative element . . . in their efforts to get control of the local section."[55] The shift-

53 Eugenio Caballero to Cates, Chihuahua, October 10, 1938, File 1004, Box 1371-0334, Phelps Dodge Papers; memorandum by Pierre de L. Boal, Washington, D.C., September 23, 1938, 812.5045/819, rl. 66, M-1370, RG 59, USNA.

54 Memorandum of conversation between Herman H. Horton and Governor Ramos, Agua Prieta, April 6, 1938, 812.6352/20, rl. 19, M-1370, RG 59, USNA.

55 Ormsbee to Horton, Nacozari, June 4, 1938, File 1095a, Box 1371-0334, Phelps Dodge Papers.

ing position of the union was quite apparent to company officials in the May Day speech delivered in San Carlos by a member of the local section. The speech had been written by the company's personnel relations manager.[56]

Elsewhere the methods of control took on a more overt form. As the Cananea strike dragged on into September, Ramón Yocupicio, the governor of Sonora, promised "to take drastic measures, if necessary to induce the syndicates at Cananea to accept the Company's terms and return to work."[57] The chief of the federal Department of Labor, Antonio Villalobos, intervened personally to arrange a suspension of the strike at the Monterrey refinery. Cárdenas himself warned the miners that he would not accept industrial warfare. Yet the apparent labor peace proved to be a temporary respite rather than a lasting truce.[58] By the end of 1938 workers at the ASARCO operations in Chihuahua and Monterrey were back on strike. Sitdown strikes erupted throughout much of the mining sector, with labor actions dragging on into the spring of 1939. By that summer even the seemingly docile San Carlos miners were voting overwhelmingly in favor of a strike if the company refused to consider the collective contract they had proposed.

Lázaro Cárdenas responded directly to these challenges from labor. In a March 17 letter to the secretary general of the Miners' Union, he pointed to the positive negotiations going on at such mines as Cananea, then denounced the labor actions at Monterrey and Chihuahua and other mines as "revolutionary paros," or strikes, and examples of "illegal syndicalist measures." He contrasted his own policies, such as the expropriation of the oil companies, with the "unpatriotic" acts of those who fomented the miners' strikes.[59] The message was not lost on the labor bureaucracy. On March 25 the ASARCO unions announced their willingness to compromise. An agreement was reached in a matter of days, and ASARCO officials pronounced themselves "very well satisfied over their present labor situation." Workers at the Fresnillo mining company refused to heed Cárdenas' warning and threatened a strike over the issue of confidential employees. Cárdenas sent a special emissary to explain that the president disapproved of labor actions based on non-economic issues.[60]

When the San Carlos workers voted to strike, the company responded by filing a request with the federal government to shut down the mine.

---

56 Ormsbee to Horton, Nacozari, May 13, 1938, File 1095a, Box 1371-0334, Phelps Dodge Papers.
57 Thomas H. Robinson to secretary of state, Nogales, September 30, 1938, 812.5045/811, rl. 66, M-1370, RG 59, USNA.
58 Memorandum of conversation with N. W. Rice and Charles Wyzanski, October 7, 1938; Daniels to secretary of state, Mexico City, October 29, 1938, 812.5045/828, 832, rl. 66, M-1370, RG 59, USNA.
59 Enclosed in James B. Stewart to secretary of state, Mexico City, April 5, 1939, 812.5045/872, rl. 66, M-1370, RG 59, USNA.
60 James B. Stewart to secretary of state, Mexico City, April 5, 1939, 812.5045/872, rl. 66, M-1370, RG 59, USNA.

The government quickly dispatched a group of delegates from the national union to San Carlos. The delegates proceeded to browbeat a meeting of workers into voting to expel some of their fellow union members. Phelps Dodge then obligingly fired the former union members. The delegates also warned the workers that "they had to cooperate with the company closer and that they would not be allowed to try to interfere with the administration of the Company . . ."[61] With the local section properly cowed, Phelps Dodge proceeded to negotiate a contract that provided for a 10 percent wage increase. In turn the section agreed to drop all lawsuits and allowed the company to employ as many confidential employees as it wished.[62] The state had effectively prevented Mexican miners from asserting control over the work place and redirecting the course of development in their sector of the economy.

The Cárdenas regime had dealt just as effectively with similar aspirations held by electrical workers. Among the Mexicans who labored for foreign corporations, those who toiled in the electrical industry demonstrated the most pervasive and persistent commitment to syndicalism. A number of factors accounted for that phenomenon. The electrical workers' expression of syndicalist tendencies dated back to their role in the creation of the Casa del Obrero Mundial and their support of the Casa's two general strikes in Mexico City in 1916. Although electrical generation was a modern, science-driven industry, its workers continued to function as highly independent master craftsmen. AFP, for example, did not have direct supervisory control over its electricians. The company's labor contracts allowed the electricians to take on outside jobs provided they did not perform them during regular working hours. In practice, electricians assigned their helpers to do the company's tasks while they went off to do the private jobs – a custom which considerably increased the company's labor costs.[63]

While the petroleum companies pursued a policy of disinvestment after 1924 and American mining companies halted development in the face of the depression, investments in electrical generation had raced ahead. After expending some $50 million acquiring properties in Mexico, AFP poured over $22 million into upgrading them between 1928 and 1938. The British-owned Mexican Light and Power Company spent over $14 million improving and expanding its facilities. These efforts increased Mexico's generation capacity by 73 percent and, as in Cuba, subjected the independent craft workers of the industry to an intense process of technification,

61 James F. Berry to Horton, Nacozari, June 23, July 28, September 29, 1939, File 2041, Box 1371-0334, Phelps Dodge Papers.

62 James F. Berry to Horton, Nacozari, September 29, 1939, File 2041, Box 1371-0334, Phelps Dodge Papers.

63 Hart, *Revolutionary Mexico,* pp. 317–18; Thompson, "Mexican Electrical Workers," p. 29; Edmund B. Montgomery, San Luis Potosí, November 14, 1938, 812.5045, rl. 66, M-1370, RG 59, USNA.

with its inherent threats of deskilling and displacement.[64] The industry's rapid expansion also threatened its engineering professionals.

In 1932 Mexican Light began laying off engineers and other white-collar employees as some of its major construction projects reached completion. The company's underlying motive was to circumvent anticipated legislation which would guarantee long-time employees retirement and other benefits. The employees' actions at this point illustrated the dilemma of a middle class struggling with divergent visions of the future. One group eventually formed the Sindicato Nacional de Ingenieros Mecánicos y Electricistas, an association that stressed the professional interests of its members. A second group of employees responded by joining the workers' union, the Sindicato Mexicano de Electricistas. Through the SME and its national federation, the Confederación Nacional de Electricistas y Similares (CNES), the engineers pushed for a more militant stance on control of the work place and the avoidance of government interference in labor matters. In 1936 the SME issued contract demands that focused on non-economic issues, including no layoffs due to technological changes and sharp limits on the number of confidential employees. The union won major concessions on these issues, particularly a drastic cut in the number of confidential employees.[65] Two years later the union members formulated a dramatic proposal for shaping the industry's future.

Weeks before the oil nationalization, the SME's Central Committee proposed creating a cooperative to buy out Mexican Light. Workers, consumers and government representatives would comprise the cooperative, which would then run the company. The union promoted the idea of a cooperative as a socialist concept which would overcome antagonisms between workers and owners. Profits from the operation of the industry would be directed toward lowering rates and improving working conditions. Much like the oil workers with their proposal for a cooperative, the electrical workers had gone beyond demands for workers' control to formulate ideas for the management of a modern company.[66] The AFP workers split off from the SME's national federation, the CNES, in 1934 to form their own organization. But the same militant stance displayed by the SME characterized the AFP workers' actions, leading to a direct confrontation with the state.

In March 1938 the Federación Nacional de Trabajadores de la Industria Eléctrica (FNTIE) prepared to strike six AFP subsidiaries, including those in Veracruz, Tampico and Torreón. Beyond the usual economic demands, the workers' contract proposals centered on issues of control. They pro-

64 Daniels to secretary of state, Mexico City, November 7, 1938, 812.6463 EB&S Co./29, rl. 157, M-1370, RG 59, USNA; Cristóbal Lara Beautell, *La industria de energía eléctrica* (Mexico City: FCE, 1953), p. 42; "Mexican Light and Power," Scudder Collection.

65 Galarza, *Industria eléctrica*, p. 166; Thompson, "Mexican Electrical Workers," pp. 151–73.

66 *El Universal* (Mexico City), March 11, 1938.

posed that only the manager and superintendent at each subsidiary be exempt from union membership and that all other management positions be filled by union members as they became vacant. Furthermore, "the adoption of modifications or new systems of work as well as new machines or apparatus which simplify doing the work shall not in any case be a motive for reducing the number of workmen . . ." In a new effort to assert their independence, the workers also demanded that the company allow them to cultivate the vacant lands it owned.[67]

The militant stance of the FNTIE brought it under intense pressure from a number of different directions. By April the company and the press had launched a campaign to discredit the workers. The media campaign led by *El Universal* in Mexico City pursued two closely related nationalistic themes. The first argued that it would be unpatriotic for electrical workers to strike at a time when the oil nationalization had placed such intense strains on the national economy. The larger theme sought to define strikes in general as essentially unpatriotic. According to the newspaper, since strikes served the interests of only one class, while the nation was composed of several classes, strikes sacrificed the national interest for the selfish interests of one group. The Mexico City daily argued that if labor leaders were truly nationalists, they would allow the state to settle labor conflicts without resort to strikes.[68] The FNTIE responded to the media barrage, accurately identifying their opponents' attempts to turn the concept of nationalism against the labor movement. As the federation explained, ". . . our companions of Tampico, Veracruz, Puebla, Zacatecas, Gómez Palacio, Mazatlán, Ixtepec and Cuautla are accused of incomprehension, stupidity, madness, and anti-patriotism, and so it is that they are represented to the . . . functionaries of the Government as making illegitimate proposals and having counter-revolutionary attitudes . . ."[69]

Cárdenas met with the union leaders in March and asked them not to threaten a strike, but they proceeded to vote in favor of the labor action. In April the government-controlled CTM, the FNTIE's parent federation, criticized the union's leadership and pressed for cancellation of the strike threat. Antonio Villalobos, whose Department of Labor was mediating the talks between the union and AFP, assured the company's negotiator that the Labor Department official involved in the meetings would be removed because of his pro-union position. Finally Villalobos made it known that if the federation struck as planned on April 30, the government would dispatch federal troops to arrest its leaders. Under the threat of arrest, federation leaders canceled the strike deadline, and by the end of May they had

---

67 "Miscellaneous Data About the Labor Problems of Six American Owned Electric Power and Light Companies," 812.5045/778, rl. 66, M-1370, RG 59, USNA.

68 *El Universal* (Mexico City), March 28, April 9, July 7, 1938.

69 "Miscellaneous Data About the Labor Problems of Six American Owned Electric Power and Light Companies," 812.5045/778, rl. 66, M-1370, RG 59, USNA.

negotiated contracts which largely conceded the issue of workers' control. But the electrical workers' resistance had not totally subsided.[70]

In November 1938 workers struck the AFP subsidiaries which provided power to the central mining region, including the states of Guanajuato and San Luis Potosí. They demanded the firing of non-union workers and continued freedom from close supervision. The press quickly reported that local mines were flooding and being forced to lay off workers. An editorial in *Excelsior* attacked the strikers for harming the national economy and therefore the interests of the masses.[71] While the petite bourgeoisie and workers had once made common cause against AFP, the Chambers of Commerce of the state of Guanajuato now demanded government intervention against a strike which they claimed was harming the national interest. The National Confederation of Chambers of Commerce and Industry sent a message to President Cárdenas reminding him of his statement at the time of the oil nationalization that the country must not endure strikes that threatened the national interest. The Confederation also called for a one-day lockout to protest the strike. In the city of León the nationalist message was reinforced by anti-strike demonstrators who marched behind the national flag and sang the national anthem. The marchers concluded their proceedings by sending a telegram to Lombardo Toledano of the CTM which read, "The people of León en masse are manifesting their hatred for your unpatriotic act, and ask for a settlement of the electric strike."[72] Cárdenas intervened personally and helped bring settlement on a contract that focused on economic benefits. The electrical workers had been effectively isolated and subdued.

American corporate culture was probably more pervasive in Mexico than in any other Latin American country. In the half century after Porfirio Díaz assumed power, American companies played a major role in mining, railroads, agriculture, petroleum and power generation. Not only did American companies dominate key economic sectors, but American goods poured into Mexico, and American companies came to play a central role in creating a consumer economy. By the same token, Mexican responses to American corporate culture spanned that same half century and assumed a variety of forms, from the revolution of 1910 to the syndicalism of the 1920s to the consumer movements and trade unionism of the 1930s.

---

70 Boal to secretary of state, Mexico City, April 29, May 3, 1938, 812.5045/752, rl. 66, M-1370; Sumner Welles to James Carson, Washington, D.C., June 7, 1938, 812.5045/781, rl. 66, M-1370, RG 59, USNA.

71 *Excelsior* (Mexico City), November 13, 1938. Details of the strike can be found in the documents contained in 812.5045/836-51, rl. 66, M-1370, RG 59, USNA.

72 *El Universal* (Mexico City), November 13, 16–18, 20, 1938; *Excelsior* (Mexico City), November 15, 1938; E. Wilson to secretary of state, San Luis Potosí, November 16, 1938, 812.5054/846, rl. 66, M-1370, RG 59, USNA; Thompson, "Mexican Electrical Workers," p. 199.

By the 1930s Mexico represented the most successful Latin American effort to incorporate elements of American culture into national life. Part of this was due to the sheer enormity of the American presence during the Porfiriato, which helped give birth to a revolutionary elite committed to greater state controls over American companies. As a part of that process the Mexican elite energetically sought to accommodate petit bourgeois and middle-class concerns about the new order in Mexico, with policies to protect small business and consumers as well as promote professionalization. Those efforts helped accelerate a process of social differentiation between the middle and working classes by the late 1930s. Popular pressures that pushed Cárdenas to nationalize the oil industry also restored the elite's claim to represent true Mexican nationalism and gave it a powerful weapon in its struggle to rein in the more radical responses to the American-aided process of modernization.

Out of the struggles of the 1920s and 30s had emerged a dominant ideology which fused Mexican nationalism and capitalism into the patriotic project of Mexican development. In response to the popular protests of the 1920s and 1930s, that new national discourse included an acknowledgment of workers' rights to certain minimal standards of material existence. In turn workers, as they were incorporated into a system of trade unionism, accepted certain precepts of the new culture, especially values such as individualism and personal achievement. Within that same ideology the elite and the new professional middle class had defined themselves as the promoters of rational, orderly development against the irrationality and violence of Mexican workers. The Mexican system became a model for other Latin American elites in succeeding decades as they sought to pursue a course of national development heavily influenced by American corporate culture.

Conclusion and epilogue

In undertaking their self-conceived mission of reform and revitalization in Latin America, U.S. corporate leaders gave birth to an era of American global influence – in Henry Luce's words, the American century. Luce, a strong proponent of American overseas power, coined a phrase that defined the era in terms of the sheer size and impact of American military and economic power. Yet the passing of the cold war has made it apparent that American cultural influence, particularly as conveyed by American corporations, may well represent the most pervasive and enduring legacy of the American century. Furthermore, the full significance of American culture lies not only in its global reach but in how people around the world have responded to it. That process was one of interaction: of incorporation and rejection of American corporate culture which bears similarities to events that unfolded in the United States. American corporate culture evolved from the interaction of the second industrial revolution with features of American society to create the first modern corporate society. The new industrialism of science-based industries, dramatic increases in production and reduced worker control on the shop floor found a particularly receptive environment in the United States. Long-held American values of individualism, self-denial and competitiveness, the cult of the new, and the ideal of the self-made man combined with a government intent on promoting private initiative and a vast, uniform internal market to give an impetus to the second industrial revolution unmatched anywhere else in the world. At the same time, corporate America contributed to substantive social changes. A society of small business people and farmers, self-employed craftsmen and independent-minded workers gave way to a society of middle-class professionals and disciplined industrial workers. If America offered diminished opportunities for independence in the economic sphere, it now provided a new "democratization of desire." Corporate America offered an array of products which purportedly satisfied every imaginable human need, physical as well as psychological. In place of self-denial, Americans now focused on acquisition of material goods as a means of achieving happiness. But more than a consumer society, this new culture promoted a concept of humanity which argued that "what is most 'human' about people is their quest for the new, their willingness to violate boundaries, their hatred of the old and the habitual . . . and their need to incorporate 'more and more' – goods, money, experience, everything."[1] But this new society did not develop without a struggle.

American entrepreneurs' efforts to create a modern corporate society had prompted deep-seated resentment and often violent conflict. They had faced intense resistance from labor in their attempts to capture control of the work place, eliminate casual work practices and create sober, individualistic competitive workers. Local communities often threw their support to workers in these struggles and battled against the alien corporations and their new order. The conflicting forces joined battle not only on the shop floor and in city streets but in the minds of Americans as businessmen postulated a vision of an America driven by individual competition and efficiency, in contrast to their opponents' values of mutualism and community interests. Modern American society emerged as the outcome of this struggle rather than as the simple imposition of some model designed by corporate reformers such as Frank Vanderlip. As much as America came to symbolize modern society, with its huge corporations, science-based industries and consumerist market strategies, much of its reality, including mass culture and industrial welfare policies, represented concessions to popular agendas which differed sharply from those of the business elite. This struggle created a society which bore characteristics with tremendous appeal for much of humanity in the twentieth century.

America came to symbolize material wealth and individual freedom. One gifted human society appeared to have devised the means for perpetually expanding the boundaries of material production within a social milieu which promoted and even idolized individual betterment and freedom. The potential for replicating that social order overseas gave American business leaders like Daniel Guggenheim a powerful argument for the internationalization of American companies as a means of sharing the benefits of this new order. Beyond its material benefits, that new society carried a vision of human beings as relentlessly competitive, consumption-oriented individuals who scorned the old and restlessly sought out the new. That perspective reflected the narrowness of corporate culture's conception of humanity – a conception which rejected what was "also 'human' about human beings; their ability to commit themselves, to establish binding relationships, to sink permanent roots, to maintain continuity with previous generations . . . to remain loyal to community or country . . . to seek spiritual transcendence beyond the self . . ."[2] Furthermore, business leaders attributed the failure of large segments of the population to prosper in an environment of accelerating economic differentiation to the racial inferiority of these groups. In the discourse of business executives, this unwashed amorphous mass of inferior human beings threatened to disrupt the course of orderly progress which corporations had set for America.

---

1 Leach, *Land of Desire*, p. 385.   2 Ibid., pp. 385–86.

These complex aspects of American corporate culture were carried to Latin America by a diverse range of corporations with distinctive characteristics. Among the differences were distinctions in the types of managerial cultures, which ranged from those stressing maximum extraction of effort from labor through stern discipline to those which sought to institute industrial welfare programs. American agricultural enterprises and many mining companies continued to face heavy demand for large numbers of unskilled workers. On the other hand, more advanced mining firms like the Guggenheim interests stressed capital intensity and a smaller, more skilled work force. Science-based industries like General Electric stood at the extreme end of this spectrum in terms of high-tech industries with highly skilled workforces. Those distinctions affected the degree to which they attempted to implement industrial welfare policies.

Different types of enterprises also encountered Latin Americans in different contexts. While mining and agricultural companies' effects would be felt in the larger sphere of the national economy and the work place, firms such as G.E. also affected Latin Americans in their attempts to promote the development of a consumer society. In addition, American companies also conveyed their culture to Latin America in a variety of ways. The introduction of rudimentary consumer goods, the domination of important natural resources, the intensification of wage labor and industrial discipline, the provision of advanced consumer services and markets, American films and the promotion of American institutions like the YMCA all represented avenues by which companies conveyed a culture with two important themes.

American business leaders carried two powerful messages of liberation to Latin American societies. The first contained a promise of an end to material want. In a few short decades, the United States had made itself the world's leading industrial power and created a system in which most of its citizens gained some share in that new wealth. A second and equally compelling message promised to liberate and uplift human beings. Individual betterment through the rationalization of human functions contained within it the promise of a new social order grounded in educated, materially prosperous citizens free to make choices in both the marketplace and the political arena. These visions of prosperity and freedom made American culture compellingly attractive. From Peruvian basketball players and Cuban baseball teams to enthralled audiences at Cecil B. DeMille films and proud owners of American automobiles, the enthusiasm for American culture manifested itself at all levels of Latin American society. American material achievements and American values of individualism and freedom represented accomplishments and values which many Latin Americans sought to emulate. Yet within those very appealing elements lay requirements and contradictions that triggered consternation and resentment among Latin Americans.

The new age of prosperity promised by the American corporations required the creation of a workforce disciplined in the demands of the modern work place, and one which internalized the values of a consumer society. The American work place demanded not only punctuality and
adaptation to machine pacing, it required workers to accept competitiveness and, most importantly, constant adaptations in their behavior to
meet the ever changing demands of the modern corporation. Much like
Americans at the beginning of the Gilded Age, many Latin Americans
faced social dislocations and challenges to their economic interests from
modern companies. Many felt that corporate stress on individual achievement, unremitting competition and constant change threatened deeply
held values that emphasized community, mutualism and values sanctified
by history and experience. Latin America's popular classes also reacted
strongly against the racist perspective which helped legitimize the Americans' "civilizing mission" while at the same time it justified their often
harsh treatment of Latin Americans. Ultimately these groups possessed a
powerful weapon of resistance which their counterparts in the United
States had lacked – the appeal to nationalism. Nationalism became the
binding ideology for the multi-class alliances which resisted American influence. The roots of that nationalist outcry and much of what defined the
American corporate encounter with Latin Americans can be traced to the
region's history.

The liberal development policies of the Latin American elite, while enjoying considerable success, also encountered substantial obstacles. Their
policies often expanded or perpetuated monopolistic aspects of their
economies, and they generally failed to create a political and judicial system which encouraged individual rights and initiative. Many peasant
communities resisted commercialization and survived to provide an alternative to wage labor for much of the population. In the face of these conditions, Latin American entrepreneurs settled for labor-repressive mechanisms that created a low-paid but poorly disciplined workforce. Those
mechanisms reflected not only a social compromise but the low opinion in
which Latin American oligarchies held their largely non-white populations. Those attitudes led the elite to fashion an exclusivist nationalism.
Under that credo, the elite created societies in which most of the national
population had few if any political rights and gained a miserably small
share in national prosperity. As some of the internal obstacles to further
development began to threaten the growth of their export economies,
Latin American elites also faced a growing challenge from an evolving
popular nationalism which projected a more inclusive vision of the
nation – a nationalism focused on social and economic justice. In response
to the economic crisis, the elite invited in American corporations, which
soon became enmeshed in the nationalist struggles that began to grip the
region. But at the outset the invitation to American enterprise seemed to
represent a no-lose strategy.

For Latin American leaders, American investments appeared to represent an optimum strategy from a cost–benefit perspective. U.S. corporations would bring the capital and technology to develop sectors with high risk and little local investment, like bananas, electrical generation and petroleum, or they would assist in resuscitating areas, like copper mining, which had failed to maintain their international competitiveness. From a domestic standpoint, the use value of undeveloped or moribund economic sectors was minimal, and the Americans would be shouldering the risks. Those strategies proved highly effective. Central America became the world leader in banana exports, Chilean copper recaptured its position in the world market, Mexico became the world's second leading producer of oil during the 1920s, and Mexicans and Cubans came to enjoy a modern electrical system and its related appliances and leisure-time devices. Beyond a general increase in national economic growth, other segments of Latin American society also stood to gain from U.S. investment. At least initially, local banana growers and merchants in Central America and small merchants as well as labor contractors in Peru flourished as a direct result of American investments. During the latter stages of the Porfiriato, the overall growth of the economy which U.S. companies helped stimulate promoted a doubling in the size of Mexico's petit bourgeois class. For the emerging middle class in countries like Cuba and Mexico, American corporations offered the concept of professionalization with its promise of a career ladder free from the arbitrariness of paternalism. There was also the promise of an emerging consumer society in which material goods would offer them rewards for their toil and fulfillment of their dreams. For Latin American workers from miners to electrical workers to those who labored in the cane fields and on the banana plantations, American corporations brought higher wages, rudimentary consumer products, housing and basic forms of medical services. For some of the more privileged, those benefits also included education, sports teams, movies and even consumer luxuries like electric lights and running water.

Just as different social classes derived different benefits from American corporate investment, the national experience of American corporate culture varied from country to country. While Nicaraguans were watching American movies long before Sandino led his rebellion, the effects of the fruteras in Central America tended to center on more basic changes. The banana companies brought the disciplines of the industrial work place and a greater dependence on wages and the market to secure subsistence goods. In nations like Peru and Chile, American mining companies brought the new industrial technology, and particularly in Chile they introduced some of the most advanced elements of industrial welfare. At the far end of the spectrum stood Cuba and Mexico, where American interests like G.E. not only introduced advanced technology and welfare systems but coupled that with some of the most intense promotions of a consumer society. By the mid 1930s U.S. companies were also making significant opportunities available to the new professional classes.

The differences in the national experiences of American culture resulted from a variety of factors. The degree to which Americans focused on the agricultural sector versus mining enterprises or utilities played a role. Differences in corporate type – that is, capital- versus labor-intensive – were also significant. Such differences often appeared within the same industry, as suggested by the relatively rudimentary technology and labor systems of Cerro de Pasco versus the more advanced equipment and methods of the Guggenheims in Chile. Factors within the host countries proved equally important. Higher levels of national income and infrastructure development in nations like Chile and Mexico made it possible for American corporate culture to have a more pervasive effect in those countries than in Central America.

Just as diverse as these experiences were the negative consequences of American corporate culture. Despite the role of Latin American elites in inviting in American companies to revive their liberal development models, they often held highly ambivalent attitudes toward U.S. interests. Admittedly in a few instances little direct opposition developed. In Cuba the planter class had been swept away by the end of the Stay Law, and in Central America the fruit companies focused on a sector to which domestic elites had made a minimal commitment. But elsewhere the direct clash of interests was unmistakable. The most striking case was Mexico, where Díaz opened the floodgates and American capital poured in. The sheer size of the U.S. investment surge threatened to overwhelm elite interests in several sectors, most notably mining. Elite animosity toward a policy of development carried out at their expense helped undermine the Díaz regime. Elsewhere the relations between local interests and the Americans were less violent but still tempestuous. Cerro de Pasco's encounter with the tunnel company, and U.S. bankers' with José Payan, illustrated the intention of the Peruvian upper class to protect its turf. Chileans who enjoyed profitable relations with British nitrate interests would wreak their vengeance on Cosach.

Domestic opposition was even more obvious at the level of the petite bourgeoisie and the middle class. Although many U.S. companies like the fruteras had an initial positive effect on small business, over time they came to threaten those interests. Local planters and merchants in Central America found their interests subordinated to the fruit companies. Shopkeepers and peddlers throughout Latin America faced narrowing markets with the installation of company stores. Independent colonos in Cuba and small growers in Peru viewed U.S. sugar companies as the bane of their existence. As for the emerging middle class of new professionals, they frequently discovered that the material dreams of consumer society lay beyond their grasp. In the work place, the arrival of Americans often brought dislocations and, more importantly, racial bias that distorted the promised professional meritocracy.

Concerns of work-place dislocation and racial bias also stirred resentment and resistance by workers. American companies provided Latin American workers with higher wages, housing and medical services, but there was a price to be paid for those benefits. American corporations demanded a more disciplined workforce with the consciousness of time that prevailed in the United States. The new workers must surrender the casual work place of the past, with its intermittent work habits and ideas of mutuality. Workers would now be competitive individuals, completely dependent on wages and on the marketplace for subsistence. Racial bias and in some cases a reliance on large numbers of unskilled laborers led some U.S. companies to pay Latin American workers less than their American co-workers and to make minimal efforts to introduce industrial welfare.

Clearly these varying reactions to American corporate culture among distinct segments of Latin American societies produced different agendas. The elite's new approach became clear in the actions of the Mexican revolution's leadership cadre. American investors were welcome in Mexico, but they must accept higher taxation and in general greater state intervention, which would ensure that the elite shared in the new economic development. Petit bourgeois interests also sought state protection, but in their case protection to prevent them from being overwhelmed by large U.S. corporations. Some of the leading concerns of the middle class centered on the exclusionary nature of American professionalism and on incomes which limited their participation in the consumer market. Workers demanded not only better wages and living conditions but greater control of the work place. Despite the differing agendas of these groups, many of them coalesced in the 1930s to support popular nationalist movements which offered an alternative to the liberal development schemes of the past.

Communities of workers, peasants, petit bourgeois interests and the middle class provided the starting point for the events which unfolded in the 1930s. By the turn of the century such groups had begun to call into question the elite's exclusionary nationalism. Initially invoking often idealized versions of their own past, they formulated a nationalism which espoused the social and economic well-being of all the nation's citizens. The social and economic clauses of Mexico's 1917 Constitution gave the clearest Latin American expression to the new principle that the nation consisted of all its people and that the state was responsible for their well-being. Yet even in Mexico those concepts remained largely ideals rather than realities. In the continuing struggle to redefine the nation, the increasing presence of American corporations played a central role. Many communities composed of distinct social classes had already found a common cause in their opposition to American companies which fed into popular nationalism. In the economic power of American companies, in the disruptions and dislocations they

brought and in their bias against Latin Americans could be discerned a foreign threat to the community and the nation.

While many of their concerns were quite different, both middle- and
working-class groups shared a very real fear of losing their national sovereignty to U.S. corporations. American companies controlled most of the
leading export products of Central America, Peru, Chile, Cuba and Mexico. American banks funded their national debts, and companies like G.E.
and ITT dominated vital segments of their economic infrastructures.
Members of the middle and working classes most directly exposed to U.S.
companies shared concerns about the reshaping of the work place and discrimination against them. Finally these Latin American communities differed strongly with a culture which grounded its definition of human in
ideas of acquisitiveness, the constant quest for the new and the competitive individual. Such ideas often ran contrary to Latin American concerns
with community, values stressing mutualism and strong connections to
the past. The activities of American corporations helped solidify these
communities, giving them a common nationalist rallying point. The
Great Depression served as a catalyst for the growing resentment against
American companies, triggering the nationalist reactions of the 1930s.

The depression made a cruel joke of American promises of perpetual
prosperity and of the elite's liberal development strategies. Sandinismo,
the Honduran banana strikes, Aprismo, Chilean socialism, Cardenismo
and the Cuban revolution of 1933 all gave vent to popular nationalism
which demanded a greater role for the state in assuring social and economic justice and in reining in the American corporations which had
played a central role in the liberal development programs of the elite.

Some of the more radical goals of these movements, such as the dream of
G. E.'s Cuban professionals and workers of a new society free of the social
differentiations of modern capitalism and grounded in popular control, did
not come to pass. The appeal of such a project was limited by the fact that
most Latin American professionals and workers had not experienced the
rigors of the new American work place. That factor limited the spread of
radical ideas in movements such as the Cuban revolution and Sandino's rebellion. Furthermore, the policies of Cardenismo exemplified new state
strategies to protect the petite bourgeoisie, appease the middle class and
offer skilled workers in major industries better wages and living conditions
in return for abandoning their more radical goals. Popular nationalism itself was also limited by the local environment. Cultural differences, particularly language, which segregated Indians in their own societies; low levels
of literacy; and the initially superficial penetration of modern communications, often limited the impact of popular nationalism in rural areas. Yet
for all its limitations, the new nationalism had enormous influence.

The movements of the 1930s established a new and more inclusive definition of nationalism in which the state would be responsible for regulat-

ing foreign corporations, ensuring that they returned a greater share of wealth to the nation and that the state would protect its own citizens from some of the harsher aspects of American corporate culture. To American companies, government involvement in labor negotiations, social security systems, regulations on the power industry, laws protecting colonos and others requiring national quotas in their workforces, and of course outright nationalization of foreign interests all constituted unwarranted intrusions of the state into the arena of private enterprise. They represented clear evidence of Latin America's continuing backwardness. But for Latin Americans they were deliberate choices they had made which defined on what terms and to what extent they would interact with American corporate culture.

The struggles of the 1930s in Latin America erupted at several levels. Internally the working and middle classes fought for a new, more inclusive nationalism. At the same time, they struggled to shape a new agenda for national development to replace the failed model of liberal internationalism. Ultimately that new agenda acknowledged a major role for American enterprise, but at the same time it regulated those companies to secure more wealth for the nation and preserve local interests. If direct state intervention for workers and legislation to protect small producers seemed economically irrational to the Americans, it made perfect sense to the Latin American communities which struggled to survive while adapting to the new order that Americans were helping to shape. Nevertheless, there were limits to popular nationalism, particularly in its failure to incorporate most of the rural population in its plans for the future. At the same time, its protectionist economic policies, designed to defend local interests, often obstructed development. Those policies and popular nationalism's compromises with American corporations and the domestic elite sowed the seeds for a renewal of discontent that would erupt in the 1960s and 70s. Again some of the roots of those movements can be traced to changes in American society.

By 1938 a coalition of large capital-intensive, internationally oriented corporations such as G.E., United Fruit and Standard Oil had thrown their political support to the Roosevelt administration. These capital-intensive firms supported industrial welfare policies to conciliate domestic labor and an aggressive international program to exploit their competitive advantages on a global scale. Their partnership with the federal government rapidly evolved into a coalition that included large labor organizations and farm groups. At the heart of the relationship lay a historic compromise between corporations and the labor movement. In return for freedom to continue reshaping the work place, corporations promised continued enhancement of the material conditions of their workers. In this relationship the federal government assumed a mediating role. For

the next three decades this New Deal coalition promoted private enterprise, international economic expansion and domestic social welfare programs. The emergence of this new political alignment, the effects of popular protest on state policies in Latin America and the ravages of the Great
Depression combined to alter the course of American corporate interaction with Latin America.[3]

By the end of the thirties, American corporations had begun to modify
their policies in Latin America. They responded to changing conditions at
home as well as to Latin American nationalism and cultural sensibilities by
making concessions on new taxes and regulations, integrating local symbols into their marketing strategies and presenting themselves as partners
with local governments in the project of national development. They also
"nationalized" their mid-level management positions by increasing their
hirings among the Latin American middle class, stepped up programs of
industrial welfare and worked to create a stable system of labor–management relations. The changing environment also promoted a shift in the relations between the corporations and their own government.[4]

Battered by the Great Depression and the wave of popular protests in
the early 1930s, U.S. corporations turned increasingly to their own government for assistance. The United States government played a major role
in trying to protect American companies, from the oil nationalization in
Mexico, worker occupations in Cuba and Sandinismo in Nicaragua to the
miners' strikes in Peru and the dissolution of Cosach in Chile. At the
same time the Roosevelt administration established trade agreements and
government financial agencies designed to revive trade and investment after the great collapse. In the process the federal government abandoned its
reactive policy of responding only to immediate crises and began working
directly with corporations to shore up and strengthen their economic base
in Latin America.[5] But despite these adaptations and changes by corporations and governments, many of the conflicts arising from the interaction
of American corporate culture and Latin American societies had yet to be
resolved. Furthermore, groups which challenged U.S. companies now possessed powerful ideological arguments in the form of popular nationalism.

Some of the problems for American corporations stemmed from the fact
that the popular nationalism of the 1930s had established the principle that
governments had the right and the obligation to regulate, tax and even na-

---

3 Thomas Ferguson, "From Normalcy to New Deal: Industrial Structure, Party Competition, and
   American Public Policy in the Great Depression," *International Organization* 38 (Winter 1984), pp.
   41–94.

4 The documents and company publications in the Electric Bond and Share archive clearly document
   this trend for G.E.

5 Efforts to give the federal government a larger role in shaping international economic policy date
   back at least to World War I; see, for example, Burton I. Kaufman, *Efficiency and Expansion: Foreign
   Trade Organization in the Wilson Administration, 1913–1921* (Westport, Conn.: Greenwood Press,
   1974).

tionalize foreign corporations in the public interest. General Electric found itself particularly vulnerable to these policies as foreign exchange controls seriously impaired its ability to repatriate profits from Latin America and government pronouncements made clear the intention of Latin American nations to control their own public utilities. By the beginning of the 1960s G.E. had begun to sell off many of its Latin American holdings to local governments.[6] But regulation and the threat of nationalization were only the most overt expression of deeper conflicts that still troubled the interaction of American corporate culture and Latin American societies.

A variety of issues more complex and troubling than increased state control over foreign corporations evolved from the confrontations and compromises of the 1930s. In Central America the dictatorships which emerged, such as the Carías regime in Honduras, made little effort to accommodate the popular protests of the early 1930s. As a result, popular discontent continued to mount beneath the surface of an imposed social peace. Between 1944 and 1946 a new wave of popular nationalism promoting working-class interests and democracy swept much of Central and South America. But in countries such as Peru, Chile, Cuba and Mexico, a conservative backlash gave birth to flawed versions of the historic compromise that underpinned the New Deal coalition.[7] These Latin American coalitions usually consisted of a triadal relationship between corporate interests, the state, and the urban middle and working classes.

The Latin American coalitions typically neglected conditions in the countryside and the interests of the rural population while providing protection for organized labor, which sacrificed worker participation and innovation in the work place to preserve wages and jobs for a small portion of the working class. The unreformed agrarian sector hindered productivity and increased inflationary pressures. Furthermore, these coalitions did little to ease the grip of American corporations on many of Latin America's leading export sectors. While retaining a predominant position in primary export products, U.S. companies also began to invest in the industrial sector and achieved a dominant position in international telecommunications systems and airline services. As a result Latin Americans found themselves exposed to an ever expanding array of American consumer products and American images and ideas conveyed through film, radio and television. Constraints on national development, the failure to achieve social justice and new challenges to concepts such as nationalism and community set the stage for a wave of new confrontations over the course of development and the role of American corporations in that process. Not surprisingly, the new era of crises began in Central America, where the fewest concessions had been made to the populist movements of the 1930s.

6 See the Electric Bond and Share financial reports in Box 152370, EBASCO.
7 Leslie Bethell and Ian Roxborough, "Latin America Between the Second World War and the Cold War: Some Reflections on the 1945–8 Conjuncture," *JLAS* 20, pt. 1 (1988), pp. 167–89.

Prior to World War II, a harshly authoritarian government had re-
pressed banana workers in Honduras, with little effort at compromise by
either the government or United Fruit. By the 1940s the workers and
their allies returned to active protest. After sixteen years of dictatorial
rule, Tiburcio Carías relinquished his grip on the presidency in 1949.
Many Liberal party exiles, including Zuniga Huete, the failed presidential
candidate of 1932, returned to the country. Meanwhile banana workers
quickly resumed overt organizational efforts. With a presidential election
looming in October 1954, the banana workers struck in early May. Some
30,000 workers joined the strike, which quickly expanded into a general
strike along the north coast. The Standard Fruit Company settled with its
labor force after two weeks, but the strike at United's facilities dragged on
for two months. The workers demanded a number of improvements, including higher wages, an end to contract labor and better medical services. The strikers eventually won on most of their points except contract
labor, but more importantly they had forced the fruteras to acknowledge
the legitimacy of their organizations and of collective bargaining. Their
ability to sustain a two-month strike resulted in part from the outpouring
of support which they received from local merchants and shopkeepers.
The survival of the Somoza regime forestalled similar dramatic developments in neighboring Nicaragua.[8]

Authoritarian rule in Nicaragua did not suffer the dislocations which
occurred after World War II in Honduras. Instead the Somoza dictatorship survived until a revolutionary movement which laid claim to the nationalist, anti-imperialist legacy of Sandinismo toppled the family from
power in 1979. Yet these events do not mark a simple historical trajectory
of Sandinismo fulfilling its popular nationalist goals. The martyrdom of
the Sandinistas of the 1930s gave a mythic quality to their anti-imperialist
nationalism. Anti-imperialism reverberated more widely through Nicaraguan society after 1934, fed by the symbolism of Sandinismo and the obvious subservience of the Somozas to U.S. interests. Yet a disparity still
existed, as it had in Sandino's day, between the anti-imperialist consciousness of many Nicaraguans and the reality of their own social environments, where American influence had a minimal effect. Despite the Somoza family's accommodating policies toward foreign capital, U.S.
investments totaled only $76 million by 1969. Furthermore, when threat-
ened by challenges from the elite and middle class after World War II, the
family patriarch, Anastasio Somoza García, turned to populist policies,
providing the working class with a labor code and freedom to organize
unions. Only when workers and campesinos had experienced the limits of
Somocista populism and found that it masked what remained of a labor-

8 On the 1954 strike, see Robert MacCameron, *Bananas, Labor, and Politics in Honduras: 1954–1963*
(Syracuse, N.Y.: Maxwell School of Citizenship and Public Affairs, Syracuse University, 1983), and
Meza, "Historia del movimiento obrero en Honduras."

repressive system fostered by a U.S.-backed regime did they combine anti-imperialism with a rejection of Somocismo and support the 1979 revolution.[9]

In Peru no such revolutionary coalition ever emerged. After their repression by the government during the 1930s, both APRA and the Communist party returned to active labor organizing during the 1940s. APRA enjoyed considerable success in organizing workers in the mining and sugar regions. As a result of these successes, the Communists and particularly the Apristas assumed a trade unionist philosophy stressing top-down control over worker democracy, and hours and wages over larger social issues. Anxious to protect these hard-won gains and to earn full readmission into the national political arena, the Aprista leadership pursued an increasingly cautious agenda, throwing its support to conservative presidential candidates, dropping its criticisms of American corporations and giving no more than lip service to calls for sweeping land reform in the sugar industry.

With the radical political forces of the 1930s pursuing more conservative courses, U.S. investment in Peru continued to increase, reaching $600 million by the early 1960s. Large haciendas expanded their position in the North, while a new agrarian bourgeoisie of peasant origins gained power in the central Andes. At the same time Peru suffered from acute inequality in the distribution of national wealth. Two percent of the nation's estates controlled 85 percent of its land. The poorest 25 percent of the population received only 3 percent of national income. As the social crisis intensified, the more radical elements of the Communist and Aprista parties broke away to form splinter movements, peasants mobilized and engaged in insurrection, and union dissidents staged militant actions. Deteriorating economic conditions, social unrest and political paralysis triggered a military coup in 1968 which led to the enactment of much of the Aprista agenda of the 1930s.

That the military, the Apristas' sworn enemy, would serve as the instrument to fulfill APRA's original program is not at all incongruous. Like Gustavo Jiménez, Peru's new military president, General Juan Velasco, was the scion of a provincial lower-middle-class family. Velasco and many of his fellow officers were influenced in their thinking on national development by civilian intellectuals, including Aprista dissidents. Moreover, many of Aprismo's original goals represented not just the platform of a particular political party but ideas deeply held among many Peruvians. During Velasco's tenure, the military regime nationalized IPC, Cerro de Pasco, W. R. Grace, ITT and foreign-owned sugar plantations. In addition the government distributed land to 360,000 families. However,

9 Carlos M. Vilas, *The Sandinista Revolution: National Liberation and Social Transformation in Central America* (New York: Monthly Review Press, 1986), pp. 82–119; Gould, *To Lead as Equals*, pp. 294–95.

much like the Cardenist regime in Mexico, the military had no desire to drive foreign investment from Peru. The regime made significant concessions to foreign corporations such as ITT, providing them with compensation and new opportunities to invest in Peru. And much like the Cardenista regime, the Peruvian military attempted to rein in popular protests by creating state-run umbrella organizations such as SINAMOS, the National System to Support Social Mobilizations.[10]

In Chile, populist mobilization went considerably further in achieving the goals of the 1930s. There the success of popular nationalism took on concrete form in the triumph of the Popular Front in the 1938 presidential election. The next two decades of Chile's history came to epitomize the accomplishments and the limitations of the historic compromise in Latin America. The electoral success of the Popular Front affirmed the legitimacy of participation by working- and middle-class parties in the political process and in power sharing within the Chilean state. The Socialists and Communists now had considerable freedom to organize workers, while the middle class used the state to expand their employment opportunities and social benefits. Those accomplishments, however, had required the tacit acceptance of continued elite control in the countryside. The effects of that concession eventually undermined the new political relationship.

The parties of the left had in effect abandoned rural labor as the price of their participation in the political system. That price proved to be a high one as the unreformed agrarian sector fueled inflation and placed market constraints on industrialization. At the same time, U.S. economic dominance, symbolized by American control of the copper industry, continued with little change. As the national economy faltered and inflation raced ahead, middle- and working-class parties abandoned the compromise, intensifying their efforts to mobilize the rural population. That process brought the Socialists and Communists to power under the Popular Unity government in 1970. The new regime pursued much of the popular nationalist agenda around which workers and the middle class had rallied in the 1930s.

The new government acted on a program that carried strong echoes of the 1930s populism that linked anti-imperialism, social justice and attacks upon the national elite. While its efforts at actually socializing the industrial economy proved timid, the government did nationalize the U.S.-controlled copper and nitrate industries, seized domestically controlled monopolies and engaged in a policy of massive income redistribution. Exceeding the scope of the 1930s populist program, the Popular Unity government broke the strictures of the historic compromise, responding to rural mobilization with a widespread land reform program.

10 Klarén, *Modernization, Dislocation,* pp. 154–55; Kruijt and Vellinga, *Labor Relations,* pp. 106–7; James D. Cockcroft, *Neighbors in Turmoil: Latin America* (New York: Harper and Row, 1989), pp. 401–2, 409; Abraham F. Lowenthal, ed., *The Peruvian Experiment: Continuity and Change Under Military Rule* (Princeton: Princeton University Press, 1975), p. 23.

Events in Chile were preceded by even more radical actions in Cuba. Given the dimensions of the revolutionary threat in 1933, Batista's new order exceeded the ad hoc populism of Somoza, but, unlike Chile's, Cuba's historic compromise represented a form of authoritarian populism. The dimensions of the new order emerged fairly quickly after 1933 as Batista codified legislation on wages and hours for workers, gave the state a central role in protecting colonos and oversaw an economic recovery that appeased much of the middle class. In this new order, the state assumed the task of extracting wage concessions from American corporations for politically favored unions. At the same time American corporations showed greater sensitivity in hiring middle-class professionals, and worked actively to create cooperative unions. Yet much like the Chilean case, that compromise set in motion forces that undermined Cuban economic development and triggered a new and more radical revolutionary uprising.

Under Batista's authoritarian populist order, organized labor, especially the Communists, became a highly conservative force protecting a relatively narrow constituency within the working class. Union leaders ensured their hold on power through enforcement of strict work rules and by opposing further mechanization in order to protect the jobs of their members in a labor market weighed down by unemployment and underemployment. Despite the creation of a state-managed labor relations system, much of the workforce received little in the way of material benefits from the new order. Sugar-cane workers, who composed 25 percent of the national labor force, worked fewer than one hundred days per year. As for the Cuban middle class, a high per capita income relative to other Latin American countries hardly compensated for prices which rivaled those in the United States and continuing problems of declining real incomes. And no amount of nationalist rhetoric could obscure Cuba's very real political and economic dependence on the United States.

Conditions of economic stagnation, political deadlock and frustrated nationalism propelled the revolution which toppled Fulgencio Batista. However, given the fragmentation and dislocation of popular forces under the old regime, it was a small group of revolutionaries rather than a mass movement which initiated change. Nevertheless, their programs addressed much of the 1933 radical agenda of anti-imperialism, nationalism and social justice. In the nationalization of the sugar industry and General Electric, the Fidelista regime seized the leading symbols of revolutionary triumph and defeat for the generation of 1933. The Fidelistas' improvement of living standards for rural workers and promotion of worker participation targeted two of the ideals of the earlier revolutionary movement.[11]

By contrast, in Mexico the work of an earlier revolutionary elite ensured that the nation would not veer into such radical social and economic

---

11 For a comparison of the 1933 and 1959 revolutions, see Farber, *Revolution and Reaction,* passim.

experiments. The popular nationalism of Mexico's 1910 revolution and the Cardenist regime allowed the country's leaders to create a remarkably stable example of Third World development. The regulation of foreign investment and the nationalization of the oil industry enabled Mexico's rulers to play a direct role in national development. State regulation or control of public utilities, promotion of education in the professions and nationalistic hiring policies appeased the petite bourgeoisie and promoted the growth of a professional middle class. At the same time widespread land reform and gradual enactment of national labor regulations and state-supported primary education addressed some of the pressing needs for social justice. These conditions set the stage for Mexico's economic miracle between 1940 and 1960. With the state promoting the mechanization of agriculture and domestic manufacturing, agricultural production increased 100 percent, and industrial output jumped by 120 percent. Yet these achievements masked a set of intensifying problems.

The state directed most of its investment in agriculture into large commercial properties at the expense of peasant holdings, and it forced economic sacrifices on industrial workers to maintain the cheap labor force that fueled the process of national development. Those policies contributed to a widening gap between rich and poor. When peasants and workers engaged in militant protest actions in the 1950s and 60s, the state responded with a mix of cooptation and repression. At the same time, American corporate giants like Anaconda and ASARCO still played leading roles in the economy. While domestic interests controlled the majority of manufacturing enterprises, U.S. corporations achieved commanding positions in such important product areas as automobiles, chemicals and pharmaceuticals.

The Mexican development model, which excluded an ever larger number of its citizens, encountered serious problems as the rate of national economic growth dropped dramatically in the early 1970s. The government stimulated new growth with spending, but only by creating an unmanageable foreign debt, which plunged the country into a long-term economic crisis in the 1980s. The erratic performance of the economy prompted disaffected members of the middle class to join in protests with peasants and workers. The state has responded with ever more overt manipulation of the political process and an expanded version of its cooptation–repression policy. Yet even this very conservative economic and social strategy has not met with the approval of the United States.

The U.S. government responded aggressively to Latin American social and political militancy after World War II. In Cuba, Chile and Nicaragua, the United States imposed economic and diplomatic sanctions and finally resorted to covert intervention by the CIA in an effort to subdue these movements. The relatively conservative economic nationalism of the Peruvian military still prompted the U.S. to slash loan and aid programs. Despite the fact that Mexico has pursued a capitalist development model closely akin to that of the United States and given American corporations a large if restricted role in its economy, the U.S. government has consistently pressed for an end to Mexican protectionism.

The popular nationalists of the 1930s and the social reformers and revolutionaries of the 1960s are not linked by some simple line of historical causation.[12] As much as Fidelistas and Sandinistas proudly claimed the revolutionaries of the 1930s as their forebears, much had changed in three decades. Latin American workers had grown considerably in numbers and experience as they adapted themselves to the contours of capitalism. Both the middle and working classes had enjoyed the advantages of populism and learned its limitations. Furthermore, while rejecting the racism and exploitative aspects of American corporate culture, these groups had absorbed many American concepts of material betterment, individual uplift and democracy. The opportunities for new professional groups in a corporate society had increased the distance between much of the middle class and the working class, while peasants found themselves largely neglected by postwar political coalitions. Nevertheless, revolutionary symbolism and myth of the 1960s and 70s identified very real connections between the social protest, political activism and revolutionary zeal of two generations of Latin Americans. The most important of those links was the common experience of American corporate culture.

American multinational enterprise changed considerably from the early mercantile ventures of the fruteras in the last quarter of the nineteenth century to the sprawling telecommunications networks and industrial giants of the contemporary era. U.S. corporations gradually shifted their emphasis from export products to industrialization and their methods from simple forms of wage labor and early industrial technology to scientific management and the techniques of the second industrial revolution. They also began to shed some of their ethnocentric and nationalistic biases, incorporating Latin Americans into their management structures, instituting serious programs of industrial welfare and identifying their own corporate missions with the goals of national development in Latin America. Yet those modifications did not halt, and in some ways actually accelerated, the development of popular nationalism in Latin America.

Both before and after World War II the involvement of American enterprise in Latin America triggered both admiration and condemnation. American companies played a central role in promoting the growth of Latin American extractive industries, agriculture, electrical power and telecommunication systems as well as manufacturing. American corporate culture's promises of material wealth, individual achievement and freedom had compelling appeal for Latin Americans in both these periods.

12 Jorge G. Gastañeda, *Utopia Unarmed: The Latin American Left After the Cold War* (New York: Knopf, 1993).

Yet the presence of huge foreign corporations also meant national and, for many Latin Americans, personal dependence on foreign economic interests. Furthermore, while U.S. companies provided material benefits to a new professional class and to organized labor, they also accelerated social and economic differentiation in Latin American societies and did little to ameliorate the widening gap between rich and poor. For those most intensely exposed to American corporate culture, its benefits carried a substantial cost. American companies required discipline in the work place, the internalization of values such as individualism, competitiveness and sobriety, and most importantly a willingness to adapt to the ever changing needs of the corporation. Those requirements challenged many long-held beliefs about the importance of community, cooperation and social justice at the same time as they threatened values grounded in popular experience and history. In addition, Latin Americans discovered the limits of a consumer society which posits material goods as the palliative for every human need and woe.

Latin Americans, both before and after World War II, responded to American corporate culture by rejecting its dominance of their national economies and its challenges to long-cherished values and beliefs. At the same time the popular nationalists of the 1930s, and even many of the revolutionaries of the 60s and 70s, integrated American ideals of material prosperity and political democracy into the centuries-long struggle of Latin Americans to achieve national independence, social justice and economic democracy. Many also came to recognize the limits of protectionist policies which shielded local interests but often inhibited national development. This complex encounter of two cultures continues today, in the twilight of the American century.

Sources

Archival sources

Baker Library, Harvard Business School, Cambridge, Massachusetts
Thomas W. Lamont Papers
United Fruit Photograph Collection

Boise Cascade Corporation, Boise, Idaho
Electric Bond and Share Company Papers

Butler Library, Rare Book and Manuscript Library, Columbia University, New York
Grace Papers
Frank A. Vanderlip Papers

Chilean Nitrate Producers, Limited, London
Papers of the Chilean Nitrate Producers, Limited

Columbia University, Graduate School of Business, New York
Marvyn Scudder Financial Record Collection

Guildhall Library, London
Papers of Antony Gibbs and Sons

Library of Congress, Washington, D.C.
Philander C. Knox Papers
Elihu Root Papers
William Howard Taft Papers

New York Public Library
Moses Taylor Papers

Phelps Dodge Corporation, Phoenix, Arizona
Papers of the Phelps Dodge Corporation

Pierpont Morgan Library, New York
J. P. Morgan Papers

Public Record Office, Kew, Surrey
Foreign Office Files

Howard–Tilton Memorial Library, Tulane University, New Orleans, Louisiana
Ephraim George Squier Papers
Papers of the Standard Fruit and Steamship Company

Huntington Library, San Marino, California
Albert Bacon Fall Collection

United States National Archives, Washington, D.C.
Record Group 59: General Records of the Department of State (microfilm)
Record Group 84: Records of the Foreign Service Posts of the Department of State
Record Group 151: Records of the Bureau of Foreign and Domestic Commerce; Records Relating to Commercial Attachés' Reports

The Library, University College, London
Bank of London and South America Papers

University Press of America Microfilm Collection
U.S. Diplomatic Post Records, Honduras, 1930–45

Newspapers

The American, Bluefields, Nicaragua
El Chichicaste, Tela, Honduras
El Comercio, Lima, Peru
Excelsior, Mexico City
El Mercurio, Santiago, Chile
New York Times
El Universal, Mexico City
West Coast Leader, Lima, Peru

Government publications

Bain, H. Foster, and H. S. Muliken. *Nitrogen Survey, Part 1: The Cost of Chilean Nitrate.* Bureau of Foreign and Domestic Commerce, Trade Information Bulletin No. 170. Washington, D.C.: Government Printing Office, 1923.
Chile. Ministerio de Hacienda, Sección Salitre. *Antecedentes sobre la industria salitrera.* Santiago: Ministerio de Hacienda, 1925.
Great Britain. Department of Overseas Trade. *Survey of Economic and Financial Conditions in the Republics of Honduras, Nicaragua, El Salvador and Guatemala.* London, Department of Trade, 1923.
Peru. Ministerio de Fomento. *La labor constructiva del Perú en el gobierno del presidente Don Augusto B. Leguía.* Lima: Imprenta Torres Aguirre, 1930.
U.S. Department of Commerce, Bureau of Foreign and Domestic Commerce. *The Cane Sugar Industrial, Agricultural, Manufacturing and Marketing Costs in Hawaii, Porto Rico, Louisiana and Cuba.* Miscellaneous Series #53. Washington, D.C.: Government Printing Office, 1917.
U.S. Department of Commerce, Bureau of Mines. *Mining Methods and Costs at the Pilares Mine, Pilares de Nacozari, Sonora, Mexico.* Washington, D.C.: Government Printing Office, 1930.
Mining Methods, Practices and Costs of the Cananea Consolidated Copper Co., Sonora, Mexico. Washington, D.C.: Government Printing Office, 1930.
Recent Developments in the Mining Industry. Washington, D.C.: Government Printing Office, 1930.
U.S. Department of Commerce, Bureau of the Census. *The Statistical History of the United States: Colonial Times to 1957.* Stamford, Conn.: Fairfield Publishers, 1965.
U.S. House of Representatives. *Commercial Relations of the United States with Foreign Countries During the Year 1903.* House Doc. 722, 58th Cong., 2d sess., vol. 2. Washington, D.C.: Government Printing Office, 1904.
Commercial Relations of the United States with Foreign Countries During the Year 1912. House Doc. 1452, 62d Cong., 3d sess., vol. 1. Washington, D.C.: Government Printing Office, 1914.

Consular Reports, July 1903: Nicaragua. 57th Cong., 2d sess., House Doc. 438, pt. 3, vol. 72. Washington, D.C.: Government Printing Office, 1903.

U.S. Tariff Commission. *Sugar: Report to the President of the United States.* Washington, D.C.: Government Printing Office, 1934.

Industry publications

Anaconda Copper Company. *Annual Report for the Year 1924.* New York, 1925.

Braden Copper Mines Company. Annual reports. New York, 1917–25.

Facts About Sugar (1920–29).

UNIFRUTCO (1920–31).

United Fruit Company. Engineering Department. "Intensive Drainage Methods at Tela, Honduras." Boston: United Fruit Company, December 1930.

Books

Adams, Frederick Upham. *Conquest of the Tropics.* Garden City, N.Y.: Doubleday, 1914.

Aguirre, Manuel J. *Cananea: las garras del imperialismo en las entrañas de México.* Mexico City: Libro México, 1958.

Albert, Bill. *South America and the First World War: The Impact of the War on Brazil, Argentina, Peru and Chile.* Cambridge: Cambridge University Press, 1988.

Amaya Amador, Ramón. *Prisión verde* (1950). Tegucigalpa: Editorial Universitaria, 1987.

Anderson, Rodney D. *Outcasts in Their Own Land: Mexican Industrial Workers, 1906–1911.* De Kalb: Northern Illinois University Press, 1976.

Ashby, Joe C. *Organized Labor and the Mexican Revolution Under Lázaro Cárdenas.* Chapel Hill: University of North Carolina Press, 1963.

Asociación de Productores de Salitre de Chile. *Album editado en conmemoración del centenario de la industria del salitre de Chile, 1830–1930.* Valparaíso: Sociedad Imprenta y Litografía Universo, 1930.

Bain, Harry F., and Thomas T. Read. *Ores and Industry in South America* (1934). New York: Arno, 1976.

Bañados Espinosa, Julio. *Balmaceda: su gobierno y la revolución de 1891.* 2 vols. Paris: Garnier Hermanos, 1894.

Barger, Harold, and Sam H. Schurr. *The Mining Industries, 1899–1939: A Study of Output, Employment and Productivity* (1944). New York: National Bureau of Economic Research, 1975.

Bauer, Arnold J. *Chilean Rural Society from the Spanish Conquest to 1930.* Cambridge: Cambridge University Press, 1975.

Beals, Carleton. *Banana Gold.* Philadelphia: Lippincott, 1932.

  The Crime of Cuba. Philadelphia: Lippincott, 1933.

  The Long Land: Chile. New York: Coward-McCann, 1949.

Beautell, Cristóbal Lara. *La industria de energía eléctrica.* Mexico City: FCE, 1953.

Becker, William H. *The Dynamics of Business–Government Relations: Industry and Exports, 1893–1921.* Chicago: University of Chicago Press, 1982.

Benjamin, Jules Robert. *The United States and Cuba: Hegemony and Dependent Development, 1880–1934.* Pittsburgh: University of Pittsburgh Press, 1974.

Bergad, Laird W. *Cuban Rural Society in the Nineteenth Century: The Social and Economic History of Monoculture in Matanzas.* Princeton: Princeton University Press, 1990.

Bergquist, Charles. *Labor in Latin America: Comparative Essays on Chile, Argentina, Venezuela and Colombia.* Stanford: Stanford University Press, 1986.

Bermann, Karl. *Under the Big Stick: Nicaragua and the United States Since 1848.* Boston: South End Press, 1986.

Bermúdez Miral, Oscar. *Historia del salitre desde sus orígenes hasta la Guerra del Pacífico.* Santiago: Ediciones de la Universidad de Chile, 1963.

Bernstein, Marvin D. *The Mexican Mining Industry, 1890–1950: A Study of the Interaction of Politics, Economics and Technology.* Albany: State University of New York Press, 1965.

Berry, Charles. *The Reform in Oaxaca, 1856–1876.* Lincoln: University of Nebraska Press, 1981.

Bertrand, Alejandro. *The Chilean Nitrate Industry: Technology and Economics.* Paris: Imprimerie de Vaugirard, 1920.

Besserer, Federico. *El sindicalismo minero en México: 1900–1952.* Mexico City: Era, 1983.

Blanchard, Peter. *The Origins of the Peruvian Labor Movement, 1883–1919.* Pittsburgh: University of Pittsburgh Press, 1982.

Bledstein, Burton J. *The Culture of Professionalism: The Middle Class and the Development of Higher Education in America.* New York: Norton, 1976.

Bonilla, Heraclio. *El minero de los Andes.* Lima: Instituto de Estudios Peruanos, 1974.

Bourgois, Philippe I. *Ethnicity at Work: Divided Labor on a Central American Banana Plantation.* Baltimore: Johns Hopkins University Press, 1989.

Bowman, Isaiah. *Desert Trails of Atacama.* New York: American Geographical Society, 1924.

Branly, Roberto. *MINAZ-608: coloquios en el despegue.* Havana: Girón, 1973.

Braverman, Harry. *Labor and Monopoly Capital: The Degradation of Work in the Twentieth Century.* New York: Monthly Review Press, 1974.

Brown, Jonathan C. *Oil and Revolution in Mexico.* Berkeley and Los Angeles: University of California Press, 1993.

Browning, David G. *El Salvador: Landscape and Society.* Oxford: Oxford University Press, 1971.

Bruchey, Stuart. *Enterprise: The Dynamic Economy of a Free People.* Cambridge: Harvard University Press, 1990.

Buck-Morss, Susan. *The Dialectics of Seeing: Walter Benjamin and the Arcades Project.* Cambridge: MIT Press, 1989.

Bulmer-Thomas, Victor. *The Political Economy of Central America Since 1920.* Cambridge: Cambridge University Press, 1987.

Burns, Bradford. *The Poverty of Progress: Latin America in the Nineteenth Century.* Berkeley and Los Angeles: University of California Press, 1980.

Bushnell, David, and Neill Macaulay. *The Emergence of Latin America in the Nineteenth Century.* New York: Oxford University Press, 1988.

Cabrera, Olga. *El movimiento obrero cubano en 1920.* Havana: Instituto Cubano del Libro, 1970.

Calhoun, Craig. *The Question of Class Struggle: Social Foundations of Popular Radicalism During the Industrial Revolution.* Chicago: University of Chicago Press, 1982.

Caravedo Molinari, Baltazar. *Clases, lucha política y gobierno en el Perú (1919–1930).* Lima: Retama Editorial, 1977.

Carosso, Vincent P. *Investment Banking in America: A History.* Cambridge: Harvard University Press, 1970.

——— *The Morgans: Private International Bankers, 1854–1913.* Cambridge: Harvard University Press, 1987.

Carr, Barry. *El movimiento obrerero y la política en México, 1910–1929.* Mexico City: Sep-Setentas, 1976.

Ceceña, José Luis. *México en la órbita imperial: las empresas transnacionales.* Mexico City: Ediciones El Caballito, 1979.

Chandler, Alfred. *The Visible Hand: The Managerial Revolution in American Business.* Cambridge: Harvard University Press, 1974.

Chernow, Ron. *House of Morgan: An American Banking Dynasty and the Rise of Modern Finance.* New York: Atlantic Monthly Press, 1990.

Clark, Majorie Ruth. *Organized Labor in Mexico.* Chapel Hill: University of North Carolina Press, 1934.

Clawson, Dan. *Bureaucracy and the Work Process: The Transformation of U.S. Industry, 1860–1920.* New York: Monthly Review Press, 1980.

Clayton, Lawrence A. *Grace: W. R. Grace & Co.: The Formative Years, 1850–1930.* Ottawa, Ill.: Jameson, 1985.

Cleland, Robert G. *A History of Phelps Dodge, 1834–1950.* New York: Knopf, 1952.

Cockcroft, James D. *Neighbors in Turmoil: Latin America.* New York: Harper and Row, 1989.

Córdova, Arnaldo. *La clase obrera en la historia de México: en una época de crisis (1928–1934).* Mexico City: Siglo Veintiuno Editores, 1980.

Cross, Gary. *Time and Money: The Making of Consumer Culture.* London: Routledge, 1993.

Danhof, Clarence H. *Change in Agriculture: The Northern States, 1820–1870.* Cambridge: Harvard University Press, 1969.

Davies, J. G. *The Principles of Cane Sugar Manufacture.* London: Norman Rodger, 1938.

Dennis, W. H. *A Hundred Years of Metallurgy.* Chicago: Aldine, 1964.

DeShazo, Peter. *Urban Workers and Labor Unions in Chile, 1902–1927.* Madison: University of Wisconsin Press, 1983.

Dore, Elizabeth. *The Peruvian Mining Industry: Growth, Stagnation, and Crisis.* Boulder, Colo.: Westview Press, 1988.

Douglas, Paul H. *Real Wages in the United States, 1890–1926.* New York: A. M. Kelley, 1930.

Dozier, Craig L. *Nicaragua's Mosquito Shore: Years of British and American Presence.* Tuscaloosa: University of Alabama Press, 1985.

Drake, Paul W. *Socialism and Populism in Chile, 1932–52.* Urbana: University of Illinois Press, 1978.

Dubofsky, Melvyn. *Industrialism and the American Worker, 1865–1920.* New York: Crowell, 1975.

———. *We Shall Be All: A History of the Industrial Workers of the World* (1969). 2d ed. Urbana: University of Illinois Press, 1988.

Dumoulin, John. *Azúcar y lucha de clases, 1917.* Havana: Editorial de Ciencias Sociales, 1980.

Dunn, Robert W. *American Foreign Investments* (1926). New York: Arno, 1976.

Eichner, Alfred S. *The Emergence of Oligopoly: Sugar Refining as a Case Study.* Baltimore: Johns Hopkins University Press, 1969.

Elbaum, Bernard, and William Lanonick. *The Decline of the British Economy.* Oxford: Oxford University Press, 1986.

Ellis, Frank. *Los transnacionales del banano en centroamérica.* San José: EDUCA, 1983.

Encina, Francisco A. *Nuestra inferioridad económica: sus causas, sus consecuencias.* Santiago: Editorial Universitaria, 1912.

Eysenbach, Mary Locke. *American Manufactured Exports, 1879–1914: A Study of Growth and Comparative Advantage.* New York: Arno, 1976.

Farber, Samuel. *Revolution and Reaction in Cuba, 1933–1960: A Political Sociology from Machado to Castro.* Middletown, Conn.: Wesleyan University Press, 1976.

Feliú Cruz, Guillermo. *Santiago a comienzos del siglo xix.* Santiago: Editorial Andrés Bello, 1970.

Fergusson, Erna. *Chile.* New York: Knopf, 1943.

Fernández, Manuel A. *Proletariado y salitre en Chile, 1890–1910.* London: Monografía de Nueva Historia, 1988.

Figueroa, Virgilio. *Diccionario histórico y biográfico de Chile.* 5 vols. Santiago: Establecimientos Gráfico "Balcells & Co.," 1925–36.

Flores Galindo, Alberto. *Los mineros de la Cerro de Pasco, 1900–1930.* Lima: Pontífica Universidad Católica del Perú, 1974.

Foner, Philip S. *Business and Slavery: The New York Merchants and the Impossible Conflict.* Chapel Hill: University of North Carolina Press, 1941.

Foreign Policy Association. *Problems of the New Cuba: Report of the Commission on Cuban Affairs.* New York: Author, 1935.

Galarza, Ernesto. *La industria eléctrica en México.* Mexico City: FCE, 1941.

García, Alejandro, and Oscar Zanetti, eds. *United Fruit Company: un caso del dominio imperialista en Cuba.* Havana: Editorial de Ciencias Sociales, 1976.

García Suárez, Andrés. *Los fundidores relatan su historia.* Havana: Departamento de Orientación Revolucionaria del Comité Central del Partido Comunista de Cuba, 1975.

Gastañeda, Jorge G. *Utopia Unarmed: The Latin American Left After the Cold War.* New York: Knopf, 1993.

Gates, Paul W. *Landlords and Tenants on the Prairie Frontier: Studies in American Land Policy.* Ithaca: Cornell University Press, 1973.

Gilmore, A. B. *Manual de la industria azucarera cubana/The Cuban Sugar Manual.* Havana, 1928.

Gonzales, Michael J. *Plantation Agriculture and Social Control in Northern Peru, 1875–1933.* Austin: University of Texas Press, 1985.

Gootenberg, Paul. *Between Silver and Guano: Commercial Policy and the State in Postindependence Peru.* Princeton: Princeton University Press, 1989.

Gordon, David M., Richard Edwards and Michael Reich. *Segmented Work, Divided Workers: The Historical Transformation of Labor in the United States.* Cambridge: Cambridge University Press, 1982.

Gould, Jeffrey L. *To Lead as Equals: Rural Protest and Political Consciousness in Chinandega, Nicaragua, 1912–1979.* Chapel Hill: University of North Carolina Press, 1990.

Graebner, Norman A. *Foundations of American Foreign Policy: A Realist Appraisal from Franklin to McKinley.* Wilmington, Del.: Scholarly Resources, 1985.

Gutman, Herbert G. *Power and Culture: Essays on the American Working Class.* New York: Pantheon, 1987.

Hacker, Louis M. *The Triumph of American Capitalism: The Development of Forces in American History to the End of the Nineteenth Century.* New York: Simon and Schuster, 1940.
The World of Andrew Carnegie: 1865–1901. Philadelphia: Lippincott, 1968.

Haeger, John Dennis. *The Investment Frontier: New York Businessmen and the Economic Development of the Old Northwest.* Albany: State University of New York Press, 1981.

Hart, John Mason. *Anarchism and the Mexican Working Class, 1860–1931.* Austin: University of Texas Press, 1978.
Revolutionary Mexico: The Coming and Process of the Mexican Revolution. Berkeley and Los Angeles: University of California Press, 1987.

Healy, David. *The United States in Cuba, 1898–1902.* Madison: University of Wisconsin Press, 1963.

Hedges, James B. *The Browns of Providence Plantation: The Nineteenth Century.* 3 vols. Providence: Brown University Press, 1968.

Helms, Mary W. *Asang: Adaptations to Culture Contact in a Miskito Community.* Gainesville: University of Florida Press, 1971.

Herfindahl, Orris C. *Copper Costs and Prices: 1870–1957.* Baltimore: Johns Hopkins University Press, 1960.

Hindess, Barry, and Paul Q. Hirst. *Pre-Capitalist Modes of Production.* London: Routledge and Kegan Paul, 1975.

Hiriart, Louis. *Braden: historia de una mina.* Santiago: Editorial Andes, 1964.

Hitchman, James H. *Leonard Wood and Cuban Independence, 1898–1902.* The Hague: Nijhoff, 1971.

Hodas, Daniel. *The Business Career of Moses Taylor: Merchant, Finance Capitalist and Industrialist.* New York: New York University Press, 1976.

Hodges, Donald C. *Intellectual Foundations of the Nicaraguan Revolution.* Austin: University of Texas Press, 1986.

Horsman, Reginald. *Race and Manifest Destiny: The Origins of American Racial Anglo-Saxonism.* Cambridge: Harvard University Press, 1981.

Hoyt, Edwin Palmer Jr. *The Guggenheims and the American Dream.* New York: Funk and Wagnalls, 1967.

Ingersoll, Ralph M. *In and Under Mexico.* New York: Century, 1924.

Instituto de Historia del Movimiento Comunista y de la Revolución Socialista de Cuba. *El movimiento obrero cubano: documentos y artículos,* vol. 1: *1865–1925.* Havana: Editorial de Ciencias Sociales, 1975.
El movimiento obrero cubano: documentos y artículos, vol. 2: *1925–1935.* Havana: Editorial de Ciencias Sociales, 1977.

International Bank for Reconstruction and Development. *Report on Cuba*. Washington, D.C.: Author, 1951.

Jerome, Harry. *Mechanization in Industry*. New York: National Bureau of Economic Research, 1934.

Jobet, Julio César. *El partido socialista de Chile*. 2 vols. Santiago: Editorial Prensa Latinoamérica, 1971.

Johnson, Paul E. *A Shopkeeper's Millennium: Society and Revivals in Rochester, New York, 1815–1837*. New York: Hill and Wang, 1978.

Kaempffer Villagren, Guillermo. *Así sucedio, 1850–1925: sangrientos episodios de la lucha obrera en Chile*. Santiago: Imprenta Arncibia Hermanos, 1962.

Kapsoli, Wilfredo, and W. Reátagui. *El campesinado peruano: 1919–1930*. Lima: Universidad Nacional Mayor de San Marcos, 1972.

Karnes, Thomas L. *Tropical Enterprise: The Standard Fruit and Steamship Company in Latin America*. Baton Rouge: Louisiana State University Press, 1978.

Kaufman, Burton I. *Efficiency and Expansion: Foreign Trade Organization in the Wilson Administration, 1913–1921*. Westport, Conn.: Greenwood Press, 1974.

Kepner, Charles David Jr. *Social Aspects of the Banana Industry*. New York: Columbia University Press, 1936.

Kepner, Charles David Jr., and Jay Henry Soothill. *The Banana Empire: A Case Study in Economic Imperialism* (1935). New York: Russell and Russell, 1967.

Kirsch, Henry. *Industrial Development in a Traditional Society: The Conflict of Entrepreneurship and Modernization in Chile*. Gainesville: University Presses of Florida, 1977.

Klarén, Peter. *Modernization, Dislocation, and Aprismo: Origins of the Peruvian Aprista Party, 1870–1932*. Austin: University of Texas Press, 1973.

Kruijt, Dirk, and Menno Vellinga. *Labor Relations and Multinational Corporations: The Cerro de Pasco Corporation in Peru (1902–1974)*. Assen: Van Gorcum, 1979.

Laclau, Ernesto. *Politics and Ideology in Marxist Theory*. London: Verso, 1977.

LaFeber, Walter. *The New Empire: An Interpretation of American Expansion, 1860–1898*. Ithaca: Cornell University Press, 1963.

Lafertte, Elias. *Vida de un comunista*. Santiago: Empresa Editorial Austral, 1971.

Laite, Julian. *Industrial Development and Migration Labour in Latin America*. Austin: University of Texas Press, 1981.

Lamoreaux, Naomi R. *The Great Merger Movement in American Business, 1895–1904*. Cambridge: Cambridge University Press, 1985.

Latcham, Ricardo A. *Chuquicamata: Estado Yankee (visión de la montaña roja)*. Santiago: Editorial Nascimiento, 1926.

Laurie, Bruce. *Artisans into Workers: Labor in Nineteenth-Century America*. New York: Noonday Press, 1989.

Leach, William. *Land of Desire: Merchants, Power and the Rise of a New American Culture*. New York: Pantheon, 1993.

Leal, Juan Felipe, and José Woldenberg. *La clase obrera en la historia de México: del estado liberal a los inicios de la dictadura porfirista*. Mexico City: Siglo Veintiuno, 1980.

Lears, T. J. Jackson. *No Place of Grace: Antimodernism and the Transformation of American Culture, 1880–1920*. New York: Pantheon, 1981.

Lewis, Cleona. *America's Stake in International Investments*. Washington, D.C.: Brookings Institution, 1938.

Lingerfelter, Richard E. *The Hard Rock Miners: A History of the Mining Labor Movement in the American West, 1863–1893*. Berkeley and Los Angeles: University of California Press, 1974.

Lockmiller, David A. *Magoon in Cuba*. Westport, Conn.: Greenwood Press, 1969.

Long, Norman, and Bryan Roberts. *Miners, Peasants and Entrepreneurs: Regional Development in the Central Highlands of Peru*. Cambridge: Cambridge University Press, 1984.

Lorey, David E. *The Rise of the Professions in Twentieth Century Mexico: University Graduates and Occupational Change Since 1929*. Los Angeles: UCLA Latin American Center Publications, 1992.

Loveman, Brian. *Struggle in the Countryside: Politics and Rural Labor in Chile, 1919–1973.* Bloomington: Indiana University Press, 1976.

Lowenthal, Abraham F., ed. *The Peruvian Experiment: Continuity and Change Under Military Rule.* Princeton: Princeton University Press, 1975.

Lowitt, Richard. *A Merchant Prince of the Nineteenth Century, William E. Dodge.* New York: Columbia University Press, 1954.

Lynch, John. *The Spanish American Revolutions, 1808–26.* New York: Norton, 1973.

Macaulay, Neill. *The Sandino Affair.* Chicago: Quadrangle Books, 1967.

MacCameron, Robert. *Bananas, Labor, and Politics in Honduras: 1954–1963.* Syracuse, N.Y.: Maxwell School of Citizenship and Public Affairs, Syracuse University, 1983.

McCloskey, Donald N. *Economic Maturity and Entrepreneurial Decline.* Cambridge: Harvard University Press, 1973.

Mallon, Florencia. *The Defense of Community in Peru's Central Highlands: Peasant Struggle and Capitalist Transition, 1860–1940.* Princeton: Princeton University Press, 1983.

Mamalakis, Markos J. *The Growth and Structure of the Chilean Economy: From Independence to Allende.* New Haven: Yale University Press, 1976.

Mann, Wilhelm. *Chile luchando por nuevas formas de vida.* 2 vols. Santiago: Editorial Ercilla, 1935–36.

Manning, William R. *Diplomatic Correspondence of the United States Concerning the Independence of the Latin American Nations.* 3 vols. New York: Carnegie Endowment for International Peace, 1925.

Marcosson, Isaac F. *Anaconda.* New York: Dodd, Mead, 1957.

Colonel Deeds: Industrial Builder. New York: Dodd, Mead, 1948.

Martin, Percy F. *Mexico's Treasure-House (Guanajuato): An Illustrated and Descriptive Account of the Mines and Their Operations in 1906.* New York: Cheltenham Press, 1906.

Martínez de la Torre, Ricardo. *Apuntes para una interpretación marxista de la historia social del Perú.* 4 vols. Lima: Confederación General de Trabajadores Peruanos, 1947.

May, Earl Chapin. *2000 Miles Through Chile, the Land of More or Less.* New York: Century, 1924.

May, Lary. *Screening Out the Past: The Birth of Mass Culture and the Motion Picture Industry.* New York: Oxford University Press, 1980.

May, Robert E. *The Southern Dream of Empire, 1854–1861.* Baton Rouge: Louisiana State University Press, 1973.

Meyer, Lorenzo. *Los grupos de presión extranjeros en el México revolucionario, 1910–1940.* Tlateloco: Secretaría de Relaciones Exteriores, 1973.

Mexico and the United States in the Oil Controversy, 1917–1942, trans. Muriel Vasconcellos. Austin: University of Texas Press, 1977.

Miers, John. *Travels in Chile and La Plata* (1826). 2 vols. New York: AMS Press, 1970.

Millett, Allan Reed. *The Politics of Intervention: The Military Occupation of Cuba, 1906–1909.* Columbus: Ohio State University Press, 1968.

Mitchell, Sidney Alexander. *S. Z. Mitchell and the Electrical Industry.* New York: Farrar, Straus and Cudahy, 1960.

Monteón, Michael. *Chile in the Nitrate Era: The Evolution of Economic Dependence, 1880–1930.* Madison: University of Wisconsin Press, 1982.

Montgomery, David. *Workers' Control in America: Studies in the History of Work, Technology, and Labor Struggles.* Cambridge: Cambridge University Press, 1979.

Moore, Barrington Jr. *Social Origins of Dictatorship and Democracy: Lord and Peasant in the Making of the Modern World.* Boston: Beacon, 1967.

Morales, Salvador, Gloria García and María Sánchez. *Matahambre: empresa y movimiento obrero.* Havana: Instituto de Libros, 1971.

Moran, Theodore H. *Multinational Corporations and the Politics of Dependence: Copper in Chile.* Princeton: Princeton University Press, 1974.

Muñiz, José Rivero. *El movimiento obrero durante la primera intervención (1899–1902).* Havana: Universidad Central de Las Villas, 1961.

National City Company. *Sugar.* New York: Author, 1922.

Navin, Thomas R. *Copper Mining and Management*. Tucson: University of Arizona Press, 1978.

Neu, Irene D. *Erastus Corning: Merchant and Financier, 1794–1872*. Ithaca: Cornell University Press, 1960.

Noble, David F. *America by Design: Science, Technology and the Rise of Capitalism*. New York: Knopf, 1977.

Nogales y Mendez, Rafael de. *The Looting of Nicaragua*. New York: R. M. McBride, 1928.

North, Douglass C. *The Economic Growth of the United States, 1790–1860*. New York: Norton, 1961.

———. *Growth and Welfare in the American Past: A New Economic History*. New York: Norton, 1966.

Núñez Machín, Ana. *Memoria amagra del azúcar*. Havana: Editorial de Ciencias Sociales, 1981.

Nunn, Frederick M. *Chilean Politics, 1920–1931*. Albuquerque: University of New Mexico Press, 1970.

O'Brien, Thomas F. *The Nitrate Industry and Chile's Crucial Transition: 1870–1891*. New York: New York University Press, 1982.

O'Connor, Harvey. *The Guggenheims: The Making of an American Dynasty* (1937). New York: Arno, 1976.

Palacios, Marco. *Coffee in Colombia, 1850–1970: An Economic, Social, and Political History*. Cambridge: Cambridge University Press, 1980.

Palma, Milagros. *Por los senderos míticos de Nicaragua*. Bogotá: Editorial Nueva América, 1987.

Paula Taforó, Francisco de. *El libro de las carceles: rehabilitación del presidario*. Santiago: Imprenta i Litografía de B. Moran, 1876.

Pederson, Leland R. *The Mining Industry of the Norte Chico, Chile*. Evanston: University of Illinois Press, 1966.

Pérez, Louis A. Jr. *Cuba: Between Reform and Revolution*. New York: Oxford University Press, 1988.

———. *Cuba Under the Platt Amendment, 1902–1934*. Pittsburgh: University of Pittsburgh Press, 1986.

———. *Lords of the Mountain: Social Banditry and Peasant Protest in Cuba, 1878–1918*. Pittsburgh: University of Pittsburgh Press, 1989.

Perkins, Edwin. *The Economy of Colonial America*. New York: Columbia University Press, 1988.

Philip, George. *Oil and Politics in Latin America: Nationalist Movements and State Companies*. Cambridge: Cambridge University Press, 1982.

Pino Santos, Oscar. *El asalto a Cuba por la oligarquía financiera yanqui* (1973). Mexico City: Editorial Nuestro Tiempo, 1975.

Platt, D. C. M. *Latin America and British Trade, 1806–1914*. London: Adam and Charles Black, 1972.

Portell Vilá, Herminio. *Nueva historia de la República de Cuba (1898–1979)*. Miami: Moderna Press, 1986.

Porter, Kenneth W. *John Jacob Astor: Business Man*. 2 vols. Cambridge: Harvard University Press, 1931.

Posas, Mario. *Luchas del movimiento obrero hondureño*. Ciudad Universitaria Rodrigo Facio, Costa Rica: Editorial Universitaria Centroaméricana, 1981.

Posas, Mario, and Rafael del Cid. *La construcción del sector público y del estado nacional de Honduras, 1876–1979*. Ciudad Universitaria Rodrigo Facio, Costa Rica: Editorial Universitaria Centroaméricana, 1981.

Potter, Neal, and Francis T. Christy Jr. *Trends in Natural Resource Commodities: Statistics of Prices, Output, Consumption, Foreign Trade and Employment in the United States, 1870–1957*. Baltimore: Johns Hopkins University Press, 1962.

Prude, Jonathan. *The Coming of the Industrial Order: Town and Factory Life in Rural Massachusetts, 1810–1860*. Cambridge: Cambridge University Press, 1983.

Radell, David. *Historical Geography of Western Nicaragua: The Spheres of Influence of León, Granada and Managua, 1519–1965.* Berkeley and Los Angeles: University of California Press, 1969.

Rangel Contla, José Calixto. *La pequeña burgesía en la sociedad mexicana, 1895–1960.* Mexico City: Universidad Nacional Autónoma de México, 1972.

Reed, Merl. *New Orleans and the Railroads: The Struggle for Commercial Empire, 1830–1860.* Baton Rouge: Louisiana State University Press, 1966.

Reichstein, Andreas V. *Rise of the Lone Star: The Making of Texas,* trans. Jeanne R. Willson. College Station: Texas A&M University Press, 1989.

Rickard, T. A. *Journeys of Observation.* San Francisco: Dewey, 1907.

Rippy, J. Fred. *Globe and Hemisphere: Latin America's Place in the Postwar Foreign Relations of the United States* (1958). Westport, Conn.: Greenwood Press, 1972.

Rivera, Antonio. *La revolución en Sonora.* Mexico City, 1969.

Roeder, Ralph. *Juarez and His Mexico.* 2 vols. New York: Viking, 1947.

Rojas, Ursinio. *Las luchas obreras en el central Tacajo.* Havana: Ciencias Sociales, 1979.

Roseberry, William. *Anthropologies and Histories: Essays in Culture, History and Political Economy.* New Brunswick, N.J.: Rutgers University Press, 1989.

Rosell, Mirta, ed., *Luchas obreras contra Machado.* Havana: Instituto Cubano del Libro, 1973.

Rosenberg, Emily. *Spreading the American Dream: American Economic and Cultural Expansion, 1890–1945.* New York: Hill and Wang, 1982.

Rugman, Alan M., ed. *New Theories of the Multinational Enterprise.* New York: St. Martin's, 1982.

Ruiz, Ramón Eduardo. *Labor and the Ambivalent Revolutionaries: Mexico, 1911–1923.* Baltimore: Johns Hopkins University Press, 1976.

The People of Sonora and Yankee Capitalists. Tucson: University of Arizona Press, 1988.

Rumbarger, John J. *Power, Profits, and Prohibition: Alcohol Reform and the Industrializing of America, 1800–1930.* Albany: State University of New York Press, 1989.

Sáez Morales, Carlos. *Recuerdos de un soldado: el ejercito y la política.* 3 vols. Santiago: Ercilla, 1933.

Salas Lavaqui, Manuel. *Trabajos y antecedentes presentados al Supremo Gobierno de Chile por la Comisión Consultiva del Norte.* Santiago: Imprenta Cervantes, 1908.

Salazar Vergara, Gabriel. *Labradores, peones y proletarios: formación y crisis de la sociedad popular chilena del siglo xix.* Santiago: Ediciones Sur, 1985.

Sánchez, Luis Alberto. *Haya de la Torre y el Apra.* Santiago: Pacífico, 1955.

Sandberg, Lars G. *Lancashire in Decline.* Columbus: Ohio University Press, 1974.

Schmitz, Christopher J. *World Non-Ferrous Metal Production and Prices, 1700–1976.* London: Cass, 1979.

Scott, Rebecca. *Slave Emancipation in Cuba: The Transition to Free Labor, 1860–1899.* Princeton: Princeton University Press, 1985.

Scroggs, William O. *Filibusters and Financiers: The Story of William Walker and His Associates.* New York: Macmillan, 1916.

Seligson, Mitchell. *Peasants of Costa Rica and the Development of Agrarian Capitalism.* Madison: University of Wisconsin Press, 1980.

Selser, Gregorio. *Sandino,* trans. Cedric Belfrage. New York: Monthly Review Press, 1981.

Semper, E. and E. Michels. *La industria del salitre en Chile,* trans. and agumented Javier Gandarillas and Orland Ghigliotto Salas. Santiago: Imprenta, Litografía i Encuadernación Barcelona, 1908.

Silva Herzog, Jesús. *Petroleo mexicano.* Mexico City: Fondo de Cultura Económica, 1941.

Smith, Robert Freeman. *The United States and Cuba: Business and Diplomacy, 1917–1960.* New York: Bookman Associates, 1960.

The United States and Revolutionary Nationalism in Mexico, 1916–1932. Chicago: University of Chicago Press, 1972.

What Happened in Cuba? A Documentary History. New York: Twayne, 1963.

Stallings, Barbara. *Banker to the Third World: U.S. Portfolio Investment in Latin America, 1900–1986.* Berkeley and Los Angeles: University of California Press, 1987.

Stein, Steve. *Populism in Peru: The Emergence of the Masses and the Politics of Social Control.* Madison: University of Wisconsin Press, 1980.

Stern, Steve J. *Resistance, Rebellion, and Consciousness in the Andean Peasant World, 18th to 20th Centuries.* Madison: University of Wisconsin Press, 1987.

Stocking, George W., and Myron W. Watkins. *Cartels in Action: Case Studies in International Business Diplomacy.* New York: Twentieth Century Fund, 1946.

Suárez, Andrés García. *Los fundidores relatan su historia.* Havana: Departamento de Orientación Revolucionaria del Comité Central del Partido Comunista de Cuba, 1975.

Subercaseaux, Guillermo. *Monetary and Banking Policy of Chile.* Oxford: Clarendon Press, 1922.

Thomas, Hugh. *Cuba: The Pursuit of Freedom, 1762–1969.* New York: Harper and Row, 1971.

Thorp, Rosemary, and Geoffrey Bertram. *Peru, 1890–1977: Growth and Policy in an Open Economy.* London: Macmillan, 1978.

Trachtenberg, Alan. *The Incorporation of America: Culture and Society in the Gilded Age.* New York: Hill and Wang, 1982.

Tromp, L. A. *Machinery and Equipment of the Sugar Cane Factory.* London: Norman Rodger, 1936.

Trueba Lara, José Luis. *Cananea: 1906.* Hermosillo: Gobierno del Estado de Sonora, 1989.

Valcarcel, Luis. *Memorias.* Lima: Instituto de Estudios Peruanos, 1981.

van B. Cleveland, Harold, and Thomas F. Huertas. *Citibank, 1812–1970.* Cambridge: Harvard University Press, 1985.

Vicuña Mackenna, Benjamín. *El libro del cobre i del carbón de piedra en Chile.* Santiago: Imprenta Cervantes, 1883.

Vilas, Carlos M. *The Sandinista Revolution: National Liberation and Social Transformation in Central America.* New York: Monthly Review Press, 1986.

Villanueva, Víctor. *Ejercito peruano del caudillismo anárquico al reformismo militar.* Lima: Editorial Juan Mejía Baca, 1973.

Vitale, Luis. *Interpretación marxista de la historia de Chile.* 3 vols. Santiago: Prensa Latinoaméricana, 1971.

Walton, Gary M., and Robertson, Ross M. *History of the American Economy.* 5th ed. New York: Harcourt Brace Jovanovich, 1983.

Wasserman, Mark. *Capitalists, Caciques, and Revolution: The Native Elites and Foreign Enterprise in Chihuahua, Mexico, 1854–1911.* Chapel Hill: University of North Carolina Press, 1984.

Watts, Sarah Lyons. *Order Against Chaos: Business Culture and Labor Ideology in America, 1880–1915.* Westport, Conn.: Greenwood Press, 1991.

Wheelock, Jaime. *Nicaragua: imperialismo y dictadura: crisis de una formación social.* Havana: La Habana Editorial de Ciencias Sociales, 1980.

Whitaker, Arthur P. *The United States and the Independence of Latin America, 1800–1830.* Baltimore: Johns Hopkins University Press, 1941.

Wilkins, Mira. *The Emergence of Multinational Enterprise: American Business Abroad from the Colonial Era to 1914.* Cambridge: Harvard University Press, 1970.

The Maturing of Multinational Enterprise: American Business Abroad from 1914 to 1970. Cambridge: Harvard University Press, 1974.

Williams, William Appleman. *The Roots of the Modern American Empire: A Study of the Growth and Shaping of a Social Consciousness in a Marketplace Society.* New York: Random House, 1969.

Wilson, Charles Morrow. *Empire in Green and Gold: The Story of the American Banana Trade* (1947). Westport, Conn.: Greenwood Press, 1968.

Winkler, Max. *Investments of United States Capital in Latin America* (1928). Port Washington, N.Y.: Kennikat Press, 1971.

Winter, Nevin O. *Chile and Her People of To-Day.* Boston: L. C. Page, 1912.

Wright, Gavin. *The Political Economy of the Cotton South: Households, Markets, and Wealth in the Nineteenth Century.* New York: Norton, 1978.

Wright, Thomas C. *Landowners and Reform in Chile: The Sociedad Nacional de Agricultura, 1919–1940.* Urbana: University of Illinois Press, 1982.

Wyman, Mark. *Hard Rock Epic: Western Miners and the Industrial Revolution, 1860–1910.* Berkeley and Los Angeles: University of California Press, 1979.

Yepes del Castillo, Ernesto. *Perú, 1820–1920: un siglo de desarrollo capitalista.* Lima: Campodónico Ediciones, 1972.

Young, Mary Elizabeth. *Redskins, Ruffleshirts and Rednecks: Indian Allotments in Alabama and Mississippi.* Norman: University of Oklahoma Press, 1961.

Articles

Adleson, S. Lief. "Casualidad y conciencia: factores convergentes en la fundación de los sindicatos petroleros de Tampico durante la decada de los veinte." In Reunión de Historiadores Mexicanos y Norteamericanos, *Labor and Laborers Through Mexican History,* pp. 632–61. Tucson: University of Arizona Press, 1979.

Bazant, Jan. "Landlord, Labourer and Tenant in San Luis Potosí, Northern Mexico, 1822–1910." In Kenneth Duncan and Ian Rutledge, eds., *Land and Labour in Latin America: Essays on the Development of Agrarian Capitalism in the Nineteenth and Twentieth Centuries,* pp. 59–82. Cambridge: Cambridge University Press, 1977.

Becerra, Longino. "The Early History of the Labor Movement." In Nancy Peckenham and Annie Street, eds., *Honduras: Portrait of a Captive Nation,* pp. 95–101. New York: Praeger, 1985.

Besserer, Federico, José Díaz and Raul Santana. "Formación y consolidación del sindicato minero en Cananea." *Revista Mexicana de Sociología* 42 (October–December 1980), pp. 1321–53.

Bethell, Leslie, and Ian Roxborough. "Latin America Between the Second World War and the Cold War: Some Reflections on the 1945–8 Conjuncture." *JLAS* 20, pt. 1 (1988), pp. 167–89.

Blanchard, Peter. "The Recruitment of Workers in the Peruvian Sierra at the Turn of the Century: The Enganche System." *Inter-American Economic Affairs* 33 (1980), pp. 63–83.

Bonilla, Heraclio. "The War of the Pacific and the National and Colonial Problem in Peru." *Past and Present* 81 (1978), pp. 92–118.

Brading, David. "Hacienda Profits and Tenant Farming in the Mexican Bajio, 1700–1860." In Kenneth Duncan and Ian Rutledge, eds., *Land and Labour in Latin America: Essays on the Development of Agrarian Capitalism in the Nineteenth and Twentieth Centuries,* pp. 23–58. Cambridge: Cambridge University Press, 1977.

Brauer, Kinley J. "1821–1860: Economics and the Diplomacy of American Expansionism." In William H. Becker and Samuel F. Wells Jr., eds., *Economics and World Power: An Assessment of American Diplomacy Since 1789,* pp. 55–118. New York: Columbia University Press, 1984.

Campaña, Pilar, and Rigoberto Rivera. "Highland *Puna* Communities and the Impact of the Mining Economy." In Norman Long and Bryan Roberts, eds., *Miners, Peasants and Entrepreneurs: Regional Development in the Central Highlands of Peru,* pp. 88–106. Cambridge: Cambridge University Press, 1984.

Cardoso, Ciro F. "The Formation of the Coffee Estate in Nineteenth-Century Costa Rica." In Kenneth Duncan and Ian Rutledge, eds., *Land and Labour in Latin America: Essays on the Development of Agrarian Capitalism in the Nineteenth and Twentieth Centuries,* pp. 165–202. Cambridge: Cambridge University Press, 1977.

Cariola, Carmen, and Osvaldo Sunkel. "The Growth of the Nitrate Industry and Socioeconomic Change in Chile, 1880–1930." In Roberto Cortés Conde and Shane J. Hunt, eds., *The Latin American Economies: Growth and the Export Sector, 1880–1930,* pp. 137–254. New York: Holmes and Meier, 1985.

Carmagnani, Marcello. "Banques étrangères et banques nationales au Chili (1900–1920)." *Caravelle* 20 (1973), pp. 31–51.

Casson, Mark. "Transaction Costs and the Theory of the Multinational Enterprise." In Alan M. Rugman, ed., *New Theories of the Multinational Enterprise,* pp. 24–43. New York: St. Martin's, 1982.

Coatsworth, John H. "American Trade with European Colonies in the Caribbean and South America, 1790–1812." *William and Mary Quarterly* 3d ser., 24 (1969), pp. 243–66.

Cuenca Esteban, Javier. "The United States Balance of Payments with Spanish America and the Philippine Islands, 1790–1819: Estimates and Analysis of Principal Components." In Jacques A. Barbier and Allan J. Kuethe, eds., *The North American Role in the Spanish Imperial Economy, 1760–1819,* pp. 28–70. Manchester: Manchester University Press, 1984.

Cumbler, John T. "Labor, Capital, and Community: The Struggle for Power." In Milton Cantor, ed., *American Workingclass Culture: Explorations in American Labor and Social History,* pp. 149–66. Westport, Conn.: Greenwood Press, 1979.

Davies, Thomas M. "The Indigenismo of the Peruvian Aprista Party: A Reinterpretation." *HAHR* 51 (November 1971), pp. 626–45.

Dinwoudie, D. H. "Dollar Diplomacy in the Light of the Guatemalan Loan Project, 1909–1913." *The Americas* 26 (January 1970), pp. 237–53.

Dunning, John H. "Changes in the Level and Structure of International Production: The Last One Hundred Years." In Mark Casson, ed., *The Growth of International Business,* pp. 84–139. London: Allen and Unwin, 1983.

Echevarría y Uriarte, Juan Uribe, and Juan Guillermo Prado Ocaranza. "La Virgen de Andacollo en Chile y en la Argentina." *Folklore Americano* 32 (July–December 1983), pp. 5–52.

Ehrenreich, Barbara, and John Ehrenreich. "The Professional Managerial Class." In Pat Walker, ed., *Between Labor and Capital,* pp. 5–45. Boston: South End Press, 1979.

Ferguson, Thomas. "From Normalcy to New Deal: Industrial Structure, Party Competition, and American Public Policy in the Great Depression." *International Organization* 38 (Winter 1984), pp. 41–94.

Fernández, Manuel A. "El enclave salitrero y la economía chilena, 1880–1914." *NH* 3 (1981), pp. 1–44.

García, Fe Iglesias. "The Development of Capitalism in Cuban Sugar Production, 1860–1900." In Manuel Moreno Fraginals, Frank Moya Pons and Stanley L. Engerman, eds., *Between Slavery and Free Labor: The Spanish-Speaking Caribbean in the Nineteenth Century,* pp. 54–74. Baltimore: Johns Hopkins University Press, 1985.

Gootenburg, Paul. "Caneros y Chuno: Price Levels in Nineteenth-Century Peru." *HAHR* 70 (1990), pp. 1–56.

Gutman, Herbert G. "The Workers' Search for Power: Labor in the Gilded Age." In H. Wayne Morgan, ed., *The Gilded Age,* pp. 38–68. Syracuse, N.Y.: Syracuse University Press, 1963.

Henretta, James. "Families and Farms: Mentalité in Pre-Industrial America." *William and Mary Quarterly* 3d ser., 35 (1978), pp. 3–32.

Hoernel, Robert B. "Sugar and Social Change in Oriente, Cuba, 1898–1946." *JLAS* 8 (1976), pp. 215–49.

Holton, Robert J. "Revolutionary Syndicalism and the British Labour Movement." In Wolfgang J. Mommsen and Hans-Gerhard Husung, eds., *The Development of Trade Unionism in Great Britain and Germany, 1880–1914,* pp. 266–82. London: Allen and Unwin, 1985.

Hunt, Shane J. "Growth and Guano in Nineteenth-Century Peru." In Roberto Cortés Conde and Shane J. Hunt, eds., *The Latin American Economies: Growth and the Export Sector, 1880–1930,* pp. 255–381. New York: Holmes and Meier, 1985.

Illanes, María Angélica. "Disciplinamiento de la mano de obra minera en una formación social en transición." *NH* 11 (1984), pp. 195–224.

Kay, Cristobal. "The Development of the Chilean Hacienda System, 1850–1973." In Kenneth Duncan and Ian Rutledge, eds., *Land and Labour in Latin America: Essays on the*

Development of Agrarian Capitalism in the Nineteenth and Twentieth Centuries, pp. 103–39. Cambridge: Cambridge University Press, 1977.

Laite, Julian. "Processes of Industrial and Social Change in Highland Peru." In Norman Long and Bryan R. Roberts, eds., *Peasant Cooperation and Capitalist Expansion in Central Peru*, pp. 72–97. Austin: University of Texas Press, 1978.

McCreery, David J. "Coffee and Class: The Structure of Development in Liberal Guatemala." *HAHR* 53 (1976), pp. 438–60.

"Debt Servitude in Rural Guatemala, 1876–1936." *HAHR* 63 (November 1983), pp. 735–59.

Meza, Víctor. "Historia del movimiento obrero en Honduras." In Pablo González Casanova, ed., *Historia del movimiento obrero en América Latina*, pp. 128–95. Mexico City: Siglo Veintiuno, 1985.

Miller, Rory. "The Making of the Grace Contract: British Bondholders and the Peruvian Government." *JLAS* 8 (May 1976), pp. 73–100.

Monteón, Michael. "The Enganche in the Chilean Nitrate Sector, 1880–1930." *Latin American Perspectives* 6 (Summer 1979), pp. 66–79.

Moreno Fraginals, Manuel. "Plantations in the Caribbean: Cuba, Puerto Rico and the Dominican Republic in the late Nineteenth Century." In Moreno Fraginals, Frank Moya Pons and Stanley L. Engerman, eds., *Between Slavery and Free Labor: The Spanish-Speaking Caribbean in the Nineteenth Century*, pp. 3–21. Baltimore: Johns Hopkins University Press, 1985.

Novelo, Victoria. "De huelgas, movilizaciones y otras acciones de los mineros del carbón de Coahuila." *Revista Mexicana de Sociología* 42 (October–December 1980), pp. 1355–77.

O'Brien, Thomas F. " 'Rich Beyond the Dreams of Avarice': The Guggenheims in Chile." *Business History Review* 63 (Spring 1989), pp. 122–59.

Palma, Gabriel. "From an Export-Led to an Import-Substituting Economy: Chile 1914–39." In Rosemary Thorp, ed., *Latin America in the 1930s: The Role of the Periphery in World Crisis*, pp. 50–80. New York: St. Martin's, 1984.

Parker, David S. "White-Collar Lima, 1910–1929: Commercial Employees and the Rise of the Peruvian Middle Class." *HAHR* 72 (February 1992), pp. 47–72.

Peloso, Vincent. "Succulence and Sustenance: Region, Class and Diet in Nineteenth Century Peru." In John C. Super and Thomas C. Wright, eds., *Food, Politics and Society in Latin America*, pp. 45–64. Lincoln: University of Nebraska Press, 1985.

Pérez, Lisandro. "Iron Mining and Socio-Demographic Change in Eastern Cuba, 1884–1940." *JLAS* 14 (November 1982), pp. 381–405.

Pérez, Louis A. Jr. "The Imperial Design: Politics and Pedagogy in Occupied Cuba, 1899–1902." *Cuban Studies/Estudios Cubanos* 12 (Summer 1982), pp. 1–19.

Pickering, J. C. "The Mining Districts of Central Peru." *EMJ* 85 (May 16, 1908).

"Recent Developments at Cerro de Pasco, Peru," *EMJ* 85 (April 11, 1908).

"Transportation Costs and Labor in Central Peru," *EMJ* 85 (March 1908).

Pollitt, Brian. "The Cuban Sugar Economy in the 1930s." In Bill Albert and Adrian Graves, eds., *The World Sugar Economy in War and Depression*, pp. 97–108. London: Routledge, 1988.

Price, Richard. "The New Unionism and the Labour Process." In Wolfgang J. Mommsen and Hans-Gerhard Husung, eds., *The Development of Trade Unionism in Great Britain and Germany, 1880–1914*, pp. 133–49. London: Allen and Unwin, 1985.

Przeworski, Joanne Fox. "The Entrance of North American Capital in the Chilean Copper Industry and the Role of Government, 1904–1916." *Atti del XL Congresso Internazionale degli Americanisti (Rome–Genoa, September 3–10, 1972)*, pp. 391–415. Genoa: Tilgher, 1973.

Read, Robert. "The Growth and Structure of Multinationals in the Banana Export Trade." In Mark Casson, ed., *The Growth of International Business*, pp. 180–213. London: Allen and Unwin, 1983.

Reynolds, Clark Winston. "The Development Problems of an Export Economy: The Case of Chile and Copper." In Markos Mamalakis and Clark Winston Reynolds, *Essays on the Chilean Economy,* pp. 203–357. Homewood, Ill.: Irwin, 1965.

Rovira, José Ignacio, and Rodolfo Fraginals. "Historia de un centro de trabajo: la antigua Compañía Cubana de Electricidad, hoy Empresa Consolidada de la Electricidad Antonio Guiteras." In Comisión Nacional de Activista de Historia, Departamento de Orientación Revolucionaria del Comité Central del Partido Comunista de Cuba, *Los obreros hacen y escriben su historia,* pp. 276–325. Havana: Departamento de Orientación Revolucionaria del Comité Central del Partido Comunista de Cuba, 1975.

Salinas, Maximiliano. "Cristianismo popular en Chile, 1880–1920: un esquema sobre el factor religiosa en las clases subaltenas durante el capitalismo oligárquico." *NH* 12 (October–December 1984), pp. 275–302.

Sollis, Peter. "The Atlantic Coast of Nicaragua: Development and Autonomy." *JLAS* 21 (October 1989), pp. 481–520.

Spalding, Hobart Jr. "The Workers' Struggle: 1850–1961." *Cuba Review* 4 (July 1974), pp. 3–10.

Stansifer, Charles. "José Santos Zelaya: A New Look at Nicaragua's Liberal Dictator." *Revista Interamericana* 7 (Fall 1977), pp. 468–85.

Stone, Irving. "British Direct and Portfolio Investment in Latin America Before 1914." *Journal of Economic History* 37 (1977), pp. 690–722.

Thomas, Jack Ray. "The Socialist Republic of Chile." *Journal of Inter-American Studies* 6 (April 1964), pp. 203–20.

Thomson, Charles A. "Chile Struggles for National Recovery." *Foreign Policy Reports* 9 (February 14, 1934), pp. 282–92.

Thorp, Rosemary, and Carlos Londoño. "The Effect of the Great Depression on the Economies of Peru and Colombia." In Rosemary Thorp, ed., *Latin America in the 1930s: The Role of the Periphery in World Crisis,* pp. 81–116. New York: St. Martin's 1984.

Wionczek, Miguel S. "Electric Power: The Uneasy Partnership." In Raymond Vernon, ed., *Public Policy and Private Enterprise in Mexico,* pp. 21–110. Cambridge: Harvard University Press, 1964.

Wood, Leonard. "The Military Government of Cuba." *Annals of the American Academy of Political and Social Science* 21 (March 1903), pp. 153–82.

Wright, Thomas C. "Agriculture and Protectionism in Chile." *JLAS* 7 (May 1975), pp. 45–58.

Zeitlin, Jonathan. "Industrial Structure, Employer Strategy and the Diffusion of Job Control in Britain, 1880–1920." In Wolfgang J. Mommsen and Hans-Gerhard Husung, eds., *The Development of Trade Unionism in Great Britain and Germany, 1880–1914,* pp. 325–37. London: Allen and Unwin, 1985.

Unpublished works

Brand, Charles A. "The Background of Capitalistic Underdevelopment: Honduras to 1913." Ph.D. dissertation, University of Pittsburgh, 1972.

Caulfield, Norman. "Mexican Labor and the State in the Twentieth Century: Conflict and Accommodation." Ph.D. dissertation, University of Houston, 1990.

De Wind, Adrian Jr. "Peasants Become Miners: The Evolution of Industrial Mining Systems in Peru." Ph.D. dissertation, Columbia University, 1977.

Finney, Kenneth. "Precious Metal Mining and the Modernization of Honduras: In Quest of El Dorado (1880–1900)." Ph.D. dissertation, Tulane University, 1973.

Garrett, Gary Richard. "The Oncenio of Augusto B. Leguía: Middle Sector Government and Leadership in Peru, 1919–1930." Ph.D. dissertation, University of New Mexico, 1973.

Guevara-Escudero, José. "Nineteenth-Century Honduras: A Regional Approach to the Economic History of Central America, 1839–1914." Ph.D. dissertation, New York University, 1983.

Herbold, Carl F. Jr. "Developments in the Peruvian Administrative System, 1919–1930: Modern and Traditional Qualities of Government Under Authoritarian Regimes." Ph.D. dissertation, Yale University, 1973.

Houseman, Philip Joseph. "Chilean Nationalism, 1920–1952." Ph.D. dissertation, Stanford University, 1961.

Post, Charles. "Primitive Accumulation, Class Struggle and the Capitalist State: Political Crisis and the Origins of the U.S. Civil War, 1844–1861." Ph.D. dissertation, SUNY Binghamton, 1983.

Robinson, Henry Leslie. "American and Foreign Power Company in Latin America: A Case Study." Ph.D. dissertation, Stanford University, 1967.

Rugeley, Terry. "Orgins of the Caste War: A Social History of Rural Yucatan, 1800–1847." Ph.D. dissertation, University of Houston, 1992.

"Texas, Yucatan and the United States: Patterns of Intervention and Underdevelopment." Manuscript, University of Houston, May 5, 1989.

Stickell, Arthur Lawrence. "Migration and Mining: Labor in Northern Chile in the Nitrate Era, 1880–1930." Ph.D. dissertation, Indiana University, 1979.

Teplitz, Benjamin I. "The Political and Economic Foundations of Modernization in Nicaragua: The Administration of José Santos Zelaya, 1893–1909." Ph.D. dissertation, Howard University, 1973.

Thompson, Mark Elliot. "The Development of Unionism Among Mexican Electrical Workers." Ph.D. dissertation, Cornell University, 1966.

Yeager, Gene Sheldon. "Honduras, Transportation and Communication Development: The Rise of Tegucigalpa, 1876–1900." Master's thesis, Tulane University, 1972.

Index